'Carlo Bonomi is a master detective. In the two volumes of *The Cut* he attempts to decipher Freud's emotional world and its impact on his theories. Uncovering many new facts, and boldly connecting and re-interpreting known facts, he outlines the place of male and female circumcision, seen at that time as a measure preventing dangerous masturbation, in Freud's life and work. In the second volume he suggests that Freud's close disciple and friend Ferenczi absorbed Freud's preoccupation with symbolic castration, but transformed it into his innovative theory of trauma, which aroused Freud's ambivalence.'

– **Emanuel Berman, Ph.D.**, *Training and Supervising Analyst, Israel Psychoanalytic Society, Tel Aviv, Israel*

'With a deep knowledge of Freud's life and work, particularly as it is revealed through autobiographical notes and correspondences, Bonomi attempts to formulate a new narrative of Master Sigmund's evolution. The proposed hypothesis is fascinating, well documented and very innovative and enlightening. This second volume completes the oeuvre convincingly. A pleasure to read.'

– **André E. Haynal M.D.**, *Psychoanalyst (IPA) and Professor, University of Geneva, Geneva, Switzerland*

'By shedding a new light into the traumatic origins of psychoanalysis, Carlo Bonomi provides a meaningful and extremely rich context for the Freud-Ferenczi conflict. In his articulated narrative the author leans on the most founding dreams of the two men, their personal story, their deafnesses (in particular on Freud's neglect of the feminine), their most impressing cases as well as on mythologies and religions. Using all these elements, he shows how the theories of Freud and Ferenczi took their origin in all these sources, developed, intertwining, confronting or completing each other and finally resulting in a cut between their two conceptions of psychoanalysis which had lasting consequences on the evolution of the psychoanalytic community, its ways of thinking and practising.'

– **Dr Judith Dupont**, *Psychoanalyst, Member of Association Psychanalytique de France, Paris, France*

'Carlo Bonomi is indeed an original interpreter of the complex and complicated various steps of Freud in founding psychoanalysis. In the pages of the second volume of *The Cut and the Building of Psychoanalysis* he continues his journey into the origins of psychoanalysis, extending his exploration from Freud's mind to the minds of other classic authors, principally Sándor Ferenczi, who, though not in open opposition with the Master, created a new language for trauma, offering many elements of a metapsychology much more respectful of patients and closer to their suffering. I can only recommend this alternative narrative of the building of psychoanalysis to all the people interested and curious in the still partially secret history of psychoanalysis, because I am sure that any reader will gain a lot independently from agreeing or not with its principal theses.'

– **Franco Borgogno**, *Training and Supervising Psychoanalyst of the Italian Psychoanalytical Society (IPA), Professor of Clinical Psychology at Turin University, Turin, Italy*

The Cut and the Building of Psychoanalysis: Volume II

The Cut and the Building of Psychoanalysis: Volume II explores how the unformulated trauma associated with surgery performed on Emma Eckstein's genitalia, and the hallucinations that Eckstein experienced, influenced Freud's self-analysis, oriented his biological speculations, and significantly influenced one of his closest followers, Sándor Ferenczi. This thought-provoking and incisive work shows how Ferenczi filled the gaps left open in Freud's system and proved to be a useful example for examining how such gaps are transmitted from one mind to another.

The first of three parts explores how the mind of the child was viewed prior to Freud, what events led Freud to formulate and later abandon his theory of actual trauma, and why Freud turned to the phylogenetic past. Bonomi delves deeper into Freud's self-analysis in Part II and reexamines the possible reasons that led Freud to discard the impact and effects of trauma. The final part explores the interpersonal effects of Freud's self-dissection dream, arguing that Ferenczi managed to dream aspects of Freud's self-dissection dream on various occasions, which helped him to incorporate a part of Freud's psyche that Freud had himself failed to integrate.

This book questions the subject of a woman's body, using discourse between Freud and Ferenczi to build a more integrated and accurate narrative of the origins and theories of psychoanalysis. It will therefore be of interest to psychoanalysts, psychotherapists, psychologists and social scientists, as well as historians of medicine, science and human rights. Bonomi's work introduces new arguments to the contemporary debate surrounding Female Genital Mutilation.

Carlo Bonomi is President of the International Sándor Ferenczi Network and Chair of the 13th International Sándor Ferenczi Conference (Florence, 2018), a training and supervising analyst at the Società Italiana di Psicoanalisi e Psicoterapia Sándor Ferenczi (SIPeP-SF), Associate Editor of the *International Forum of Psychoanalysis* and on the editorial board of several psychoanalytic journals. He has taught History of Psychology and Dynamic Psychology at the State University of Florence and is a former President of the Centre for Historical Studies of Psychoanalysis and Psychiatry.

The Relational Perspectives Book Series (RPBS) publishes books that grow out of or contribute to the relational tradition in contemporary psychoanalysis. The term *relational psychoanalysis* was first used by Greenberg and Mitchell[1] to bridge the traditions of interpersonal relations, as developed within interpersonal psychoanalysis and object relations, as developed within contemporary British theory. But, under the seminal work of the late Stephen A. Mitchell, the term *relational psychoanalysis* grew and began to accrue to itself many other influences and developments. Various tributaries – interpersonal psychoanalysis, object relations theory, self psychology, empirical infancy research, and elements of contemporary Freudian and Kleinian thought – flow into this tradition, which understands relational configurations between self and others, both real and fantasied, as the primary subject of psychoanalytic investigation.

We refer to the relational tradition, rather than to a relational school, to highlight that we are identifying a trend, a tendency within contemporary psychoanalysis, not a more formally organized or coherent school or system of beliefs. Our use of the term *relational* signifies a dimension of theory and practice that has become salient across the wide spectrum of contemporary psychoanalysis. Now under the editorial supervision of Lewis Aron and Adrienne Harris, with the assistance of associate editors Steven Kuchuck and Eyal Rozmarin, the Relational Perspectives Book Series originated in 1990 under the editorial eye of the late Stephen A. Mitchell. Mitchell was the most prolific and influential of the originators of the relational tradition. Committed to dialogue among psychoanalysts, he abhorred the authoritarianism that dictated adherence to a rigid set of beliefs or technical restrictions. He championed open discussion, comparative and integrative approaches, and promoted new voices across the generations.

Included in the Relational Perspectives Book Series are authors and works that come from within the relational tradition, extend and develop that tradition, as well as works that critique relational approaches or compare and contrast it with alternative points of view. The series includes our most distinguished senior psychoanalysts, along with younger contributors who bring fresh vision. A full list of titles in this series is available at www.routledge.com/series/LEARPBS.

Note

1 Greenberg, J. & Mitchell, S. (1983). *Object relations in psychoanalytic theory*. Cambridge, MA: Harvard University Press.

The Cut and the Building of Psychoanalysis: Volume II

Sigmund Freud and Sándor Ferenczi

Carlo Bonomi

LONDON AND NEW YORK

First published 2018
by Routledge
2 Park Square, Milton Park, Abingdon, Oxon OX14 4RN

and by Routledge
711 Third Avenue, New York, NY 10017

Routledge is an imprint of the Taylor & Francis Group, an informa business

© 2018 Carlo Bonomi

The right of Carlo Bonomi to be identified as author of this work has been asserted by him in accordance with sections 77 and 78 of the Copyright, Designs and Patents Act 1988.

All rights reserved. No part of this book may be reprinted or reproduced or utilised in any form or by any electronic, mechanical, or other means, now known or hereafter invented, including photocopying and recording, or in any information storage or retrieval system, without permission in writing from the publishers.

Trademark notice: Product or corporate names may be trademarks or registered trademarks, and are used only for identification and explanation without intent to infringe.

British Library Cataloguing-in-Publication Data
A catalogue record for this book is available from the British Library

Library of Congress Cataloging-in-Publication Data
A catalog record for this book has been requested

ISBN: 978-1-138-82350-1 (hbk)
ISBN: 978-1-315-74203-8 (ebk)

Typeset in Baskerville
by Apex CoVantage, LLC

Contents

List of figures ix

Gaps, miracles, and ghosts: Introduction to *Volume II* 1

PART I
Theory in context 21

1 Infantile amnesia 23
2 Rise and fall of the seduction theory 37
3 Primal fantasies, biotrauma, and shock 55

PART II
The abyss 71

4 The fatal needle 73
5 The blood covenant 86
6 The timeless unconscious: Part I 99
7 The timeless unconscious: Part II 112
8 Necropolis 125

PART III
Transmission 139

9 Mute correspondence: I Catabasis 141
10 Mute correspondence: II Epopteia 150

11	Thalassa: A reparative fantasy	166
12	A blind spot	177
13	Nightmares are real	195
14	Freud and Ferenczi on the Acropolis	212
15	Flight into sanity	231
	Bibliographic references	245
	Index	267

Figures

6.1	Luca Signorelli (1441–1523): *The Triumph of Pan*. Berlin, Gemaeldegalerie, Staatliche Museen zu Berlin (destroyed during World War II). (Courtesy of Foto Scala, Firenze)	108
6.2	Sandro Botticelli (1445–1510): *The Birth of Venus*. Firenze, Galleria degli Uffizi. (Courtesy of Foto Scala, Firenze)	108
7.1	Luca Signorelli (1441–1523): *The Resurrection of the Flesh*. Duomo, Orvieto. (Courtesy of Foto Scala, Firenze/Opera del Duomo di Orvieto)	113
7.2	Luca Signorelli (1441–1523): *The Preaching and Deeds of the Antichrist*. Duomo, Orvieto. (Courtesy of Foto Scala, Firenze/Opera del Duomo di Orvieto)	115
7.3	Freud's original schema of his analysis of the Signorelli slip.	120
8.1	The Etruscan necropolis at the foot of Orvieto, photo circa 1890. (Courtesy of Fratelli Alinari, Firenze)	127
10.1	Ferenczi's three drawings in his letter to Freud of December 26, 1912.	161

Gaps, miracles, and ghosts
Introduction to *Volume II*

> ... Imagine, I obtained a scene about the circumcision of a girl. The cutting off of a piece of the labium minor (which is even shorter today), sucking up the blood, after which the child was given a piece of the skin to eat . . .
>
> [Denk dir, dass ich eine Szene von Mädchenbescheidung bekommen habe. Abschneiden eines Stückes von einem Kleinem Labium (das heute noch kürzer ist), Aufsaugen des Blutes, wonach das Kind das Stückchen Hut zu essen bekommen . . .]
>
> Sigmund Freud to Wilhelm Fliess, January 24, 1897

Gaps

In the chronicles of psychoanalysis – its historical emergence, its taking root in social discourse, and its transmission – 1910 was a glorious year, the year when the International Psychoanalytic Association was established. In this alternative narrative of the foundation of psychoanalysis, 1910 was a crucial year because Freud's second analysis of Emma Eckstein was shipwrecked and, shortly after, Sándor Ferenczi became the "uncanny double" of Freud, the heir of what Freud was unable to integrate in his mind.

Emma Eckstein, born in 1865, was the most important female patient Freud treated between 1894 and 1897. In Volume I we learned that she underwent circumcision in a period when female genital mutilations were not categorized as a trauma. This event, unformulated as trauma, became inscribed in the founding dream of psychoanalysis, the dream of Irma's injection, Freud's dream on the night of July 23–24 of 1895. In this second volume we excavate further how this unformulated trauma determined essential aspects of Freud's self-analysis, oriented his biological speculations, and was transmitted to his closest followers, Ferenczi in particular.

Sándor Ferenczi was born in Miskolcz, Hungary, in 1873.[1] He studied medicine and neurology, and both a liberal social orientation and a progressive outlook came to deeply influence his medical views. Ferenczi first met Freud in 1908 and immediately became his friend, confidant, and collaborator. This privileged position was lost only when, shortly before his premature death in 1933, Ferenczi's psychoanalytic thinking and practice began to develop along lines which diverged from those in current acceptance.

Numerous books have been written and published on Ferenczi's last contributions and most original works during the past few years.[2] The Ferenczi that I have chosen as my privileged interlocutor is however someone who has not yet found his own voice, someone who, being deeply identified with Freud, adopted his language, dreamed his dreams, entered into his nightmares as well. Exploring this communion, we will focus on the continuity between Freud and Ferenczi, linking Ferenczi's technical and theoretical reorganization of psychoanalysis with his incorporation and working through of Freud's split. Ferenczi was not just Freud's "uncanny double" (Aron & Starr, 2015, p. 160), but also a *wise baby* who "worked through for Freud what Freud could not consider in his own mind" (Bollas, 2011, p. xvi), all in an effort to fill the gap in the psyche from which the psychoanalytic cosmos had sprung.

This gap is inscribed in the founding dream of psychoanalysis, Freud's dream of Irma's injection. More precisely, it found a representation in the horrendous hole glimpsed in Irma's oral cavity. Besides pointing to Freud's own irretrievable trauma, this representation contained material which derived from the treatment and analysis of Emma Eckstein, the operation on her nose by Fliess, for instance. In my reconstruction and reading, Irma's oral cavity managed to also condense Emma's circumcision trauma, something which tapped into too many disagreeable and painful memories for Freud. Thanks to the extraordinary capacity for synthesis of the unconscious psyche, these many layers were condensed in the element that triggered and unleashed the founding dream of psychoanalysis, the disgusting odor of "amyl." Many scholars found that this word evokes the name of Freud's mother (Amalia). In the opening volume I also proposed that we read this element as a signifier, a transcript for "*milah*," the Hebrew word for "cut."

The same "cut" also came both to encode and to inform the final dream of Freud's self-analysis, his dream of self-dissection of the pelvis. In that dream, sometime in May of 1899, Freud, the father of psychoanalysis, is split in two: the emotional component in Freud is brutally injured and insensitive, indeed dead, with the intellectual part of his psyche allowing him to observe himself coldly from the outside as both spectator and scientist. Freud's closest pupils were deeply affected by this representation of a trauma encysted in the very foundation of our discipline. Indeed, the cut and split featured in the closing dream of Freud's self-analysis is the central element of this book, which would have fateful and wide-ranging consequences.

Freud's self-dissection dream brought into representation a split that transcended his biography and would have a profound impact on the vocation and meaning of psychoanalysis itself. Freud's greatness unquestionably rests with having given birth to a public space where unresolved traumas could be deposited for future exploration. By making large pieces of his self-analysis public through *The Interpretation of Dreams* and other works, Freud did transform this space into a place of possible transmission, affirming the idea that "children may perhaps achieve" what their fathers failed to do (Freud, 1900, p. 455).

Emma Eckstein's attempt at filling her gap

Freud defined trauma from the very beginning as a psychic reaction that failed to take place.[3] He then introduced the idea of a "gap in the psyche" in a draft written during the 1895 Christmas season, subtitled this "A Christmas Fairy Tale," and sent it to Fliess on the first day of January of 1896 (the day when Christians observed the feast of the circumcision of Christ). Describing the psychic effect of an early sexual shock, Freud wrote:

> The raising of tension at the primary experience of unpleasure is so great that the ego does not resist it and forms no psychical symptom . . . This first stage of hysteria may be described as 'fright hysteria'; its primary symptom is the *manifestation of fright* accompanied by a *gap* in the psyche [*psychischer Lücke*].
> (*SE I*, p. 228; see also Masson, 1985, p. 169)

It was just shortly after, in March 1896, that Freud coined the term "psychoanalysis" (Freud, 1896b, p. 162). Then, in April, Freud explained the purpose of the psychoanalytic method as aiming to fill the gaps in a person's psyche. In "The etiology of hysteria," after describing how traumatic memories of sexual experiences in childhood resurfaced during the course of the treatment, he wrote:

> It is exactly like putting together a child's picture-puzzle: after many attempts, we become absolutely certain in the end which piece belongs in the empty gap [*freigelassene Lücke*]; for only that one piece fills out the picture and at the same time allows its irregular edges to be fitted into the edges of the other pieces in such a manner as to leave no free space and to entail no overlapping.
> (Freud, 1896c, p. 204)

The elements in question were "scenes" accompanied by powerful emotional reactions, scenes entailing "violent sensations" and shame. Freud initially traced these dramatic scenes to actual traumatic memories, but after Emma Eckstein reproduced in analysis a scene featuring her circumcision, in January 1897, he changed his mind.

In the second half of the 19th century doctors had led a vigorous campaign against women and children who masturbated. As I reconstructed it, Emma Eckstein had been circumcised as a child in an attempt to cure her of the habit of masturbation. That she was born in Vienna in 1865 suggests her likely treatment by Ludwig Fleischmann, the director of the first pediatrics department established at the Vienna General Hospital and a frontman in the crusade against masturbation in babies.

In 1904, seven years after that analytic moment, Emma Eckstein published a 38-page booklet entitled "*Die Sexualfrage in der Erziehung des Kindes*" ["The Question of Sexuality in the Rearing of Children"].[1] She was apparently still struggling to make sense of her circumcision trauma. During the course of her research she turned to Freud for help, asking him to help her find material on the topic of her essay. In a letter dated October 11, 1902, Freud wrote her to say:

> Here is one of the books you asked for. Hirschprung is cited incorrectly, i.e.: in *Berl. Klin. Woch*[*enschrift*] 1866, volume 38. The article is not found there or in any other volume [*Band*] [of that journal]. I was also unable to find Behrend in the *Jahrbuch f. Kinder-heilkunde* (*für Kinderkrankheiten* does not exist, as far as I know) [*für Kinderkrankheiten giebt es meines Wissens nicht*]). Salzmann will require a more precise indication to help him find it. Revise and do not be discouraged.[5]

Behrend's article was published in the *Journal für Kinderkrankheiten*, the first German journal devoted to pediatrics. Behrend, who served as co-editor of the journal, was one of the pediatricians who had introduced the practice of medical circumcision (of foreskin in boys and labia in girls), excision (of the clitoris) and the cauterization (of the vagina) to treat masturbation in children in German-speaking countries.[6]

Emma Eckstein did not find Berhrend's article, but she did find one by Ludwig Fleischmann (1878), which she quoted repeatedly, together with Rohlender's monumental monograph on masturbation, published in 1899, and other articles by important pediatricians, Jacobi and Henoch among them. At the outset of her text she appears completely aligned with the views of these authorities in emphasizing the damages of masturbation to both body and mind. Quoting two clinical observations by Fleischmann, she strongly opposed the "wrong idea" that masturbation was not a great danger to children. The best proof in this regards was the scarcely known fact "that masturbation is found already in babies [Säuglingsalter], that children with less than one year can endure violent fits of masturbation and their dangerous consequences" (Eckstein, 1904, p. 9). She cited Fleischman (1878), who claimed that in such cases the bad habit could be treated by a "cauterization of the labia or of the entrance of the vagina" (p. 49) or with mechanical devices aimed at preventing self-stimulation (see *Volume I*, p. 29). She herself emphasized the fact that the methods of struggling against this evil depended first of all upon the age of the child. With children under two years, she recommended mechanical devices (bandages, light ties, and similar) to prevent exciting movements of the body (p. 15). After conceding that these methods were no longer effective with grown-up children, her discourse then turns into an awkward attempt at reconciling the urge to contrast the bad habit with a need not to hurt the sensitivity of the child with frightening punishments. "Psychical influence and physical hindrance," she wrote, "have to go hand in hand" (p. 16), since "the punished child feels alone and easily driven to search for oblivion and compensation for the withdrawn love in masturbation" (p. 17). "If you want to liberate the child from this dangerous habit," she concluded, "you have to make an effort to reward the child with love" (p. 18). One year later, in 1905, Freud published his *Three Essays on the Theory of Sexuality*, the second essay bearing the title "Infantile sexuality."

Emma Eckstein's second analysis

In 1909 Emma Eckstein started a second analysis with Freud. In an unpublished manuscript, Albert Hirst (her nephew and Freud's analysand as well) indicates that her second analysis had already started when Hirst began his treatment with Freud in the fall of 1909. Hirst's own analysis ended a year later, in the summer of 1910.[7]

Hirst informs us that his aunt enjoyed a more or less normal life as a result of her initial analysis with Freud. She, he reports, enjoyed bicycling, a popular sport at the time, and successfully ran her mother's house after her two sisters married. Sometime in 1909, however, she relapsed. Hirst suggests that the relapse occurred after the man she loved decided to marry another woman.[8] Emma Eckstein soon grew worse, her old difficulties and problems with walking returned and she "spent all her days on her couch, never left her room, not even for meals." Hirst reports that Freud began to visit her at her home to treat her *pro bono* – neither she nor her mother "could at that time afford his fee." At this time she informed her nephew that she and Freud, his analyst then, were in disagreement on a number of things:

> [Freud] considered her case a recurrence of her old neurosis, while she insisted that it was nothing of the kind, not a mental but a physical condition.
>
> Once she told me that Freud was simply vain and opinionated. That was a remarkable statement to take to me, a current patient of Freud . . . I answered her:
>
> "He may be well as vain and conceited as you say he is, but still I do not understand his position. If he is so vain he could readily say: 'You once had a neurosis. I cured you of that. That you now have a physical sickness is outside my field.'"
>
> I told this conversation to Emma's sister Therese and to Freud. Both thought that my answer was keen. But Emma brushed it aside with a brief: "You do not understand him."
>
> (p. 7)

Two important events took place during this period. Emma Eckstein appears to have attempted to commit suicide by overdosing with her sleeping pills. It was Hirst who informed Freud of the suicide attempt. The second featured an intervention by Dora Telecky, a physician personally known to Freud, to visit her friend Emma:

> She [Dr. Telecky] claimed suddenly to have discovered an abscess near to Emma's navel, and drained it. Dora claimed that she had found the source of Emma's illness and had cured it. She thus confirmed Emma in her rejection of Freud's diagnosis as recurrence of her old neurosis.
>
> When I told Freud the next day he was furious. He took Dora's diagnosis as a fake. That to him was a matter of course. He called it a highly unprofessional interference with a patient under another doctor's care. He immediately withdrew from the case, saying:

"That is Emma's end. Now she will never get well."

He was right. Emma was up and about for a short time, but soon returned to her couch on which she had lived so long. She survived as a hopeless invalid for another ten years.

(p. 8)

Referring anonymously to Emma Eckstein's case history in "Analysis terminable and interminable," Freud (1937a) noted that her hope for happiness in love and marriage had vanished. He then traced her relapse back to an outburst of masochistic fantasies and impulses, which her first analysis "had only incompletely resolved" (p. 222). According to Freud, the return of Emma Eckstein's illness and symptoms had "sprung from the same source as her first one." She experienced profuse bleedings which forced her to undergo a gynecological examination; a myoma was then found which made it necessary for her to undergo "a complete hysterectomy." Apparently she was operated on by an outstanding Viennese gynecologist for abscesses in her uterus and reached out to Freud for help when stomach pains following her surgery grew worse.

Putting together the accounts offered by Hirst, Telecky, and Freud, the chronology of Emma Eckstein's relapse would be as follows: 1) heartbreak; 2) enactment of masochistic impulses (hysterectomy); 3) second analysis with Freud; 4) incision and drainage of a fresh abscess on the site of her operation by Dr. Telecky; 5) takes to her couch and becomes an invalid.

We do not know whether Emma Eckstein had undergone a similar surgical procedure before she first came to Freud for treatment, sometime around the end of 1894 by my estimation. In Volume I, I presented the suspicion that this was indeed the case. Freud himself reported in 1937 that Emma Eckstein's hysteria "had defied many kinds of treatment" (p. 222). We know that she developed a traumatophilia, engaging in self-mutilating behavior (cutting) as a girl. It therefore seems possible that she had experienced other kinds of treatments as a young woman, before landing on Freud's couch. Her resistance to these treatments might perhaps explain why, in February of 1895, Freud allowed her to endure a new kind of treatment invented by Fliess: an operation on the nose.

Emma Eckstein's second analysis with Freud features a compelling incident which repeated the event of the psychosurgery she experienced at the hand of Fliess, except that it was now Dora Telecky who performed the surgery, a new incision which helped to temporarily free her from her pain. Telecky indicated that Freud then became furious about her surgical intervention, screaming at her: "Do you believe that hysterical pain can be cured by the knife?" (see Ludwig, 1957, p. 115).

The similarities between these two situations in Emma Eckstein's life are so uncanny that we can well imagine Freud hurling those same words at Fliess after he botched the nasal surgery by leaving a large piece of gauze in her nasal cavity. The words Freud yelled at Telecky may thus be easily interpreted as an emergence of those he failed to express to Fliess in 1895 after the surgical debacle, an event which not only featured a repetition of her childhood surgery (her circumcision), but also informed the founding dream of psychoanalysis, Freud's dream of Irma's injection.

The background of the Palermo incident

Freud appears to have been profoundly committed to Emma Eckstein's second analysis, and reacted to her return to treatment in dreams of Wilhelm Fliess, his former friend from Berlin. Freud also would be deeply disturbed by the abrupt end of Emma's second analysis. It was at this point that he stumbled upon President Schreber's *Memoires*. Analyzing Schreber's delusional system may have served a dual intent: to master his feelings about Emma Eckstein and to dissolve his old transference to Fliess. Ferenczi was a personal witness to this process, and was directly involved when he and Freud tried to work together to interpret President Schreber's delusional system. As we know, their "collaboration" abruptly failed, in the infamous "Palermo incident."

Freud was undoubtedly familiar with information which Niederland would eventually bring forward (1951, 1959a, 1959b, 1984) that Schreber's father, a medical doctor whom his son later in his delusion transformed into God, was an important protagonist in the active crusade against masturbation of the 19th century. Schreber's father believed that the "evil" of masturbation made boys not only "stupid and dumb" but "*lebensmüde*" (suicidal), rendering them "overly disposed to sickness, vulnerable to countless diseases of the lower abdomen" as well as "diseases of the nervous system [*Nervenkrankheiten*]." He also believed that it rendered boys "impotent" and "sterile" (Niederland, 1959b, p. 390). To save the children of the world, including his own son, he devised methods and instruments to keep them from masturbating.

Thus Schreber's father was a doctor who vigorously struggled against the "insidious plague" using practices similar to those in common use at the time of Freud's pediatric training. This phenomenon reached its apex during the middle of the 19th century. Daniel Paul Schreber (born in 1842) and Emma Eckstein (born in 1865) were each subject to the "great fear" of masturbation. As Freud wrote Ferenczi on October 6 of 1910: "What would you think if old Dr. Schreber had worked 'miracles' as a physician? But was otherwise a tyrant at home who 'shouted' at his son and understood him as little as the 'lower God' understood our paranoiac?" To Jung, Freud wrote on October 31, 1910: "The castration complex is only too evident. Don't forget that Schreber's father was – a doctor. As such, he performed miracles . . . the absurd miracles that are performed on him [Schreber] are a bitter satire on his father's medical art."

There is another element which sheds light onto Freud's replacement of Emma Eckstein with Schreber in the summer of 1910. Let us recall that the destruction of the internal organs and putrefaction of the abdomen (Freud, 1911, p. 17) which Schreber described became the starting point of his peculiar symptoms, his transformation into a sexually abused female and a figure who, like Christ, willingly accepted his martyrdom in order to save mankind. Emma Eckstein, in her turn, carried a surname, (Eckstein: cornerstone), which was symbolic of Jesus Christ as the "head of the corner" or "chief corner" of the Judeo/Christian building. In "Analysis terminable and interminable," Freud (1937a) moreover neatly summarized her state of mind during the final phase of her last analysis:

> She fell in love with her surgeon, wallowed in masochistic phantasies about the fearful changes in her inside – phantasies with which she concealed her romance – and proved inaccessible to a further attempt at analysis.
>
> (p. 222)

Although Freud's description might seem over the top, my sense is that the "masochistic phantasies about the fearful changes in her inside" were the same that had surfaced in Freud's founding dream when, looking down to examine Irma's throat, he was unable to tolerate what he saw, and recoiled. Freud's words illustrate the depth of Emma Eckstein's trauma.

As children, both Eckstein and Schreber had been victims of a treatment now recognizable as tactless and cruel. But at the time, it was considered the expression of a responsible attitude towards children, in contrast to a regrettable tendency to ignore the damages of masturbation. For his part, Freud did abhor these methods, and his attitude towards masturbation was liberal. For instance, Albert Hirst was very grateful to Freud for helping to calm his anguish and accept his autoerotic practices. Yet Freud did not take a clear public position on this issue, and, in Schreber's case, he failed to discuss the possible social and traumatic sources of his symptoms and illness. Just why Freud behaved in this way is not easy to answer, but this was a key point of friction with Ferenczi.

As Aron and Starr (2015) noted, Ferenczi encouraged Freud in March of 1910 to consider the possible role of social factors in the formation and appearance of psychological symptoms.[9] Freud's response, emphasizing the need at all costs of avoiding a hostile attack on society,[10] suggests that he never fully recovered from the icy reception he received in Vienna in 1896 when he decided to criticize society aggressively by highlighting the high frequency of child abuse and its malignant effects on children (Pines, 1989).

Ferenczi: Freud's "uncanny double"?

This is the background of the famous Palermo incident. Freud and Ferenczi decided to vacation in Italy together in September of 1910 with Freud proposing that they join forces to work on an interpretation of President Schreber's *memoirs*. Freud, however, proceeded with dictation rather than engaging Ferenczi in dialogue during their working vacation. When Ferenczi suddenly "rebelled" by objecting, Freud accused him of neurotic behavior, then proceeded to work on Schreber on his own. Recalling the episode in a letter to Groddeck years later, on Christmas of 1921, Ferenczi wrote: "I was left out in the cold [by Freud] – bitter feelings constricted my throat." Ferenczi's words remind us of the central scene in Freud's Irma dream, of Irma blaming Freud for the pains in her throat, stomach, and abdomen. This, it seems to me, was the precise moment when Ferenczi transformed into "Irma," taking into himself the material that Freud had failed to integrate.

Ferenczi referred to the Palermo incident on several more occasions when assessing his relationship to Freud. This episode remained particularly painful to him given that his "ideal of truth" had been an early product of Freud's own influence and teaching. As Ferenczi noted in a communication to Freud on October 3 of 1910, a month after Palermo, he deeply wished for "absolute mutual openness" between them, expecting "to see thoughts and speech liberated from the compulsion of unnecessary inhibitions in the relations of psychoanalytic-minded men," only to then be "forced back into the infantile role" as a result of Freud's response.

Freud tried to explain himself to Ferenczi in an often cited but scarcely understood letter which I quoted in Volume I. Circling back to it again, we can see that the present context renders the logic of Freud's communication much more transparent. Freud's letter to Ferenczi on October 6, 1910, said in part:

> Not only have you noticed that I no longer have any need for that full opening of my personality, but you have also understood it and correctly returned to its traumatic cause. Why did you thus make a point of it? This need has been extinguished in me since Fliess's case, with the overcoming of which you just saw me occupied. A piece of homosexual investment has been withdrawn and utilized for the enlargement of my own ego. I have succeeded where the paranoiac fails. . . . My dreams at the time were, as I indicated to you, entirely concerned with the Fliess matter, with which, owing to the nature of the thing, it was difficult to get you to sympathize.

The Palermo incident featured a primal fight scene and a disagreement between Ferenczi and Freud which both "foreshadowed and shaped Ferenczi's [future] personal analysis with Freud as well as their theoretical and technical divergences" (Aron & Starr, 2015, p. 153). Commenting on the clash of polarities at the heart of the Palermo incident, Aron and Starr (2015) proposed that it be viewed as a re-enactment of Freud's relation to Fliess, except in reverse. It was Freud who this time responded in paranoid fashion by placing Ferenczi in the position of a hysteric, a maneuver which then transformed Ferenczi into Freud's "uncanny double" (p. 160).

With Freud's preoccupation with Fliess precipitated by the dramatic termination of Emma Eckstein's second analysis, this also was the moment when unconscious aspects of Freud's unresolved relation to her were absorbed by Ferenczi. The same constellation resurfaced 25 years later in "Analysis terminable and interminable," as Freud (1937a) discussed cases which threw light on what analysis was and was not able to achieve. The two cases Freud selected were precisely those of Ferenczi and Emma Eckstein, each his former patient. In Freud's manuscript we also find Emma Eckstein's unformulated genital trauma returning in the idea of the "repudiation of femininity" as the proposed "bedrock" upon which psychoanalysis rested, an ultimate biological factor that Freud thought analysis was simply unable to penetrate and resolve (p. 252).

Miracles

Niederland recognized that the physical manipulations Schreber experienced at the hands of his father early on reappeared in his delusions as "divine miracles" God performed on his body. Niederland based his conclusion on Freud's statements regarding the kernel of truth in the mental productions of psychotic patients and Waelder's (1951) understanding of paranoia as involving a "return" of that which is "denied." It could simply be said that "miracles" are "gaps" in reverse.

Such a reversal squares with Emma Eckstein's own case history. The "divine miracle" in her case was the replacement of her genital cut with the somatic hallucination of a penis. The same reversal informs Freud's dream of Irma's injection, with the horrible gap magically filled by the vision of the trimethylamin formula, announcing the birth of psychoanalysis, Freud's new "solution." In *Volume I* we deduced this visual hallucination to be an acoustic conflation of the words *brith milah* (Hebrew for circumcision) and *three-amen*, with Freud's plan to replace religion with science. Psychoanalysis, like Schreber's delusional system, was his attempt to expose the logic behind "miracles." My years of research and immersion have brought me to believe that this is what stood behind and informed Freud's triumphal pronouncement to Ferenczi that he had succeeded where paranoiacs failed: he had fathered psychoanalysis instead of falling into madness.

Of undoubted further significance is the striking parallel between psychoanalysis and a delusional system. Using Freud's own formulation (1924c) it could be said that Emma Eckstein's genital mutilation became a lost piece of reality replaced by a psychotic delusion. Freud (1937b) himself once compared psychoanalytic constructions to psychotic delusions, and on one occasion even defined psychoanalysis as "a product of delusion" which had succeeded in becoming "a valuable part of reality" (1925a, p. 52). Thus the system Freud developed involves the re-creation of a piece of reality that had been disavowed. Emma Eckstein's trauma reverberates throughout the entirety of Freud's work and, in particular, through the significance of the Phallus within the conceptual system he created. In the perspective that I am now advocating, the (transcendental) Phallus is the product of a hallucinatory replacement of a traumatic piece of reality which has been denied.

The first reference to the Phallus in Freud's work appeared in the same letter Freud wrote to Fliess to report Emma Eckstein's circumcision scene. In that communication Freud first introduced the image of "the great Lord Penis [*der große Herr Penis*]" (Masson, 1985, p. 227). The sharp contrast and deep continuity between these two elements inspired me to develop a re-construction of the Freudian system titled: "From genital mutilation to the phallus cult" (Bonomi, 2006) proposing that Emma Eckstein's trauma was not only disavowed but remodeled, and fashioned by Freud into an object of secret veneration by analyst and analysand alike.

It could also be argued that Emma Eckstein's hallucination of a penis was incorporated into the Freudian system as a relic, that is to say, as an object of worship reminiscent of the devotion to anatomical body parts in ancient healing cults or even to the veneration of saints who were horribly mutilated during the Middle Ages. In all these cases, a violent amputation and dismemberment usually stood at the origin of the cult (Morehouse, 2012). A relic thereby becomes a shared or collective fetish and the Phallus, as central pillar of the Freudian system, thus affirms what Freud himself (1927a) observed about fetishes, namely, that they are erected as a memorial and a substitute for the concrete "horror of castration" (p. 154).

Ghosts

If Emma Eckstein's trauma, relived repeatedly over her lifetime through cutting and compliance, were accorded its proper place in the development of Freud's thought, our understanding of the origins of psychoanalysis would be vastly different. The reality of the genital mutilation she experienced during her childhood, however, has been neither acknowledged nor consensually validated. On the contrary, it has been suppressed, denied, and written out of history by psychoanalytic scholars, including the present and past directors of the Freud Archives.

Left out of the first edition of Freud's letters to Fliess (Bonaparte, Freud, & Kris, 1950), the scene describing Emma's circumcision and vaginal mutilation was first published by Max Schur (1966) in an important article commenting on Freud's dream of Irma's injection. Yet even Schur (1966) explained the genital cut as a product of Emma's "fantasy" life (p. 114). This expunged, from his mind and ours, what Freud reported to Fliess regarding Emma's circumcision scene. The emotional drama of her circumcision event was again displaced upward in the direction of Fliess's nasal operation on Emma Eckstein in February of 1895.

The cut Emma Eckstein suffered as a child was "disappeared" by the psychoanalytic community for the next three decades. I am not aware of anyone who has reflected on her trauma and its conscious and unconscious impact on Freud. Academic historians of psychoanalysis have not fared any better. When the complete edition of Freud's letters to Fliess was finally published in 1985, Freud's passage describing the cut on Emma Eckstein's genitals was available for the first time, yet even then it was overlooked and remained disappeared.

This scotomization is impressive precisely because this collective response has meant that the subject of actual trauma has remained taboo within our field. When Ferenczi attempted to bring trauma back into the center of discussion his work was resoundingly rejected collectively by the psychoanalytic community, and he was ostracized. The barbaric practice of castration procedures performed on women and girls to prevent masturbation and to punish sexual enjoyment, routine during the years when Freud worked as a young physician in Vienna, long remained unremarked upon, with the notable exception of Marie Bonaparte in 1948, followed by Renè Spitz.

Spitz (1952), responding to Bonaparte, initiated a vast research project resulting in a comprehensive bibliography on the topic.[11] Spitz's survey of this literature is what spurred Niederland (1959a, 1959b) to discover that Schreber's father, an important and respected physician, had actively crusaded against masturbation in children. Niederland (1968) then also found that Dr. Flechsig, Rector Magnificus of Leipzig University and a person whom Schreber felt had been persecuting him, had engaged in the practice of castrating women as a therapeutic procedure against nervous and psychological ailments.

These findings notwithstanding, the brutal realities of castration as a treatment of choice for hysteric women during the 19th century has remained invisible, utterly absent from psychoanalytic discourse.

Dismayingly, the Freud revisionists fared no better. Frank Sulloway (1979) demonstrated that Freud's ideas replicated those already aired within new evolutionary paradigms. However, he missed the connection of an abstract, scientific interest in childhood sexuality to the increasingly sadistic dimension of repression against the practice of masturbation. Masson (1986), two years after publishing his sensationalistic account of Freud's abandonment of the seduction theory, took steps to collect, translate, and publish a series of original psychiatric works on the surgical repression of sexuality in women and children, but without exploring any connection between this "Dark Science" and the birth of psychoanalysis.

This was the situation during the 1980s at the dawn of my interest in the birth and origins of psychoanalysis just as the role of actual trauma was beginning to re-enter social awareness and psychoanalytic discourse. The idea that "castration" involved a real event was still unthinkable. At a time when "symbolic castration" was a key concept in psychoanalysis, my interest in the theme of real castration is worth explaining.

The first volume of the Freud-Ferenczi correspondence was published in French in 1992. I was at once puzzled by the "antimetaphoric" character of Ferenczi's dream on Christmas, 1912. Ferenczi's dream featured the image of a terribly mutilated small penis being served on a saucer, a sort of totemic meal. Reflecting on Ferenczi's "holy communion" and sensing that this was a meta-dream about the very "language" of psychoanalysis, I began to entertain the fantasy that Freud's entire psychoanalytic project could have been built upon a single catastrophic event related to a real, actual event of castration. This fantasy was so at odds with everything consensually accepted at the time about the origins of psychoanalysis that it seemed bizarre, if not actually crazy. I soon grasped, however, that this possibly catastrophic event had been creatively transformed by Ferenczi in his *Thalassa* into a new founding myth. Ferenczi's Christmas dream was a confirmation, a sign of that transformation as the recipient of what Freud had failed to integrate in his own psyche. At that moment, I began my search for the seminal catastrophic event.

I decided to pay a visit to Professor Gerhard Fichtner, director of the Institute of History of Medicine at the University of Tübingen at the time, to discuss my "fantasy" and ideas. He listened and presented me with articles and books on the castration of women and the circumcision of children which had been published during the second half of the 19th century. Not familiar with this literature, I was greatly surprised by its contents. How was it possible, I thought to myself, that this cruel medical scenario had been so completely ignored by historians of psychoanalysis? Did not this shed new light on Freud's "discovery" of childhood sexuality as an attempt to overturn the cruelty toward the sexual behavior of children?

Reflecting on psychoanalysis as part of a wider social process to address the mitigation of "punishments," I then pursued archival research in Berlin. This was 1992.

First off, I found that Freud's pediatric studies in the city in 1886 had been misrepresented in the literature in various ways.[12] I presented my findings before a sophisticated audience a year later, in 1993, in a paper titled "Why have we ignored Freud the pediatrician?" (Bonomi, 1994a), with the thesis that Freud must have been deeply affected by medical attempts to cure masturbation in children and hysteria in women by performing surgical castration on their sexual organs, a common practice at the time. My purpose was not to challenge the psychoanalytic system *per se* but simply to invite scholars into reconsidering a chapter within the history of medicine which had been overlooked and which remained disconnected from the origins of psychoanalysis. Beyond this, it also felt vital to raise awareness of the gap in our collective memory as psychoanalysts.[13]

During the next two decades I gave lectures and published papers on the connection between actual castration and the birth of psychoanalysis. Despite the welcoming and positive responses elicited by my presentations, the contents of my arguments have seemingly not been absorbed. What makes it so difficult to acknowledge that Emma Eckstein was circumcised during her childhood? What keeps her "cut" disappeared?

I must confess that on occasion I have strongly questioned the validity of my position. Further, I have entertained doubts about my construction and interpretation of both Emma Eckstein's case history and Freud's treatment. Was Schur correct to claim that the circumcision scene Freud described to Fliess had never actually taken place? Was Schur correct that the entire event was merely a product of her fantasy? Was my knowledge of German so insufficient that I misunderstood, misread the original contents of Freud's communication and description to Fliess? Indeed, was it possible that the patient whose scene Freud described in his letter might perhaps be someone other than Emma Eckstein?

Such recurrent doubts were so powerful that I postponed writing this study for 20 years, and experienced a panic attack when the first volume was ready to be sent to the publisher. A vague memory crept into my mind that Professor Fichtner had once written or told me that the patient whom Freud described was not Emma Eckstein. I decided to write Albrecht Hirschmüller to ask him if he could recall whether Fichtner had ever made such a statement. Hirschmüller assured me that the female patient whose circumcision scene Freud described in his letter to Fliess was indeed Emma Eckstein. My doubts faded again.

Knowledge is undoubtedly a social phenomenon. It is difficult for any of us to believe in something that is not somehow shared and "consensually validated," to recall an observation Harry S. Sullivan once made. My own research received reinforcement and validation from several quarters. In 1994 I was approached by an elderly, world-renowned psychoanalyst who told me that my research had enabled him to better grasp the meaning of a memory which had remained fresh in his mind for years. When he was three years old, he was caught engaging in a sexual game with a girl the same age. The children were separated, and he was then taken to a doctor and circumcised. He never saw his female playmate again and did not know whether she too had been similarly punished. He suspected, though, that she had. He failed to tell me how this memory was treated or addressed, if at all, in his analysis. When he shared this story I thought: so, it is true! My research had not only affected him but made us witnesses for each other.

Extending this incident to my dialogue with Ferenczi, I can say that I became a witness for him too. Once inseminated by Ferenczi's Christmas dream, I could see that Ferenczi in his work had directly and indirectly spoken of a split in Freud's mind. There are numerous entries in Ferenczi's *Clinical Diary* of reflections on his relationship to Freud. In an entry on May 1, 1932 titled "Who is crazy, we or the patients? (the children or the adults?)" (Dupont, 1985, pp. 92–94), Ferenczi described Freud as an individual who was psychologically split, as a person who "only analyzes others but not himself," a mad doctor who projected his own "neurosis or psychosis" and fashioned his "delusions" into theories which "may not be challenged."

Ferenczi wanted to cure psychoanalysis of its "scientific delusion" (p. 94). Tellingly, the last of Freud's theories that Ferenczi did manage to challenge was Freud's "castration theory of femininity." On May 22, 1932, Ferenczi wrote to Freud:

> It will interest you to know that in our group lively debates are going on about the female castration complex and penis envy. I must admit that in my practice these don't play the great role that one had expected theoretically. *What has been your experience?*
>
> (emphasis added)

Freud was then actively working on his *New Introductory Lectures on Psycho-Analysis*. To reinforce his thesis that castration was the severest of all traumas, Freud (1933a) cited cases of circumcision performed on "boys" as "a cure or punishment" for masturbation (p. 87). *This was the only explicit reference Freud ever made to a practice he had undoubtedly encountered during his pediatric training in Berlin in 1886.* It required the passage of nearly half a century for Freud to refer to the horrific psychic impact of medically imposed castration. Now, in the *New Introductory Lectures on Psycho-Analysis*, Freud made the bold claim that an "analysis of cases in which circumcision, though not, it is true, castration, has been carried out on boys as a cure or punishment for masturbation" provided his theoretical "conviction" with its "last degree of certainty" (p. 87).

Yet at the same time, we encounter Freud repeating his old argument that women were incapable of experiencing the "fear of being castrated" if only because they had already experienced biological castration. Freud's insistence served to erase, from his mind and ours, the sadistic procedures (cutting of the labia, extirpation of the clitoris, cauterization and infibulation) commonly performed during his medical training. In particular, Freud overlooked the fact that Emma Eckstein, his principal patient during the foundational years of psychoanalysis, was herself the victim of such a procedure. Rather than acknowledge her genital trauma, Freud instead produced the substitute theory of a "biotrauma" – the theory that women had lost their penis in the course of biological evolution.

Ferenczi, for his part, felt he could not any longer accept the ease with which Freud had managed to sacrifice the "interests of women in favor of male patients," as he wrote in an entry in his *Clinical Diary* recorded on August 4, 1932 (Dupont, 1985, p. 187). This was a specific reference to Freud's assertion that girls had to accept "castration" as an accomplished fact in order to mature into proper females. But, according to Ferenczi, Freud was failing to consider the possibility that masculinity itself might also take hold "for traumatic reasons (primal scene), as a hysteric symptom" (p. 188). Ferenczi saw this failure as part of Freud's split attitude towards women. He linked Freud's "castration theory of femininity" to feelings of impotence and humiliation Freud must have experienced as a result of an incestuous ("passionate") relation he experienced early on with a "sexually demanding" mother. Instead of recalling the traumatic moment of his "castration," Freud created "*a theory in which the father castrates the son* and, moreover, is then revered by the son as a god." Over time Ferenczi grew convinced that Freud maintained the traumatic dissociation by adopting "the role of a castrating god" and not allowing himself to be analyzed.

Ferenczi formulated this unique interpretation of Freud's desire in an entry on August 4, 1932. A month later, on September 2 of 1932 and while on his way to the forthcoming psychoanalytic conference in Wiesbaden, Ferenczi went first to Vienna read to Freud in person the paper he would deliver at the conference. This, of course, was "Confusion of tongues between the adults and the child. The language of tenderness and of passion" (Ferenczi, 1933), which met an icy reception from Freud (Rachman, 1989), and caused "a conflicted response." This is the paper, Ferenczi's reformulation of Freud's theory of trauma, that today is recognized as a milestone in the psychoanalytic understanding and treatment of trauma.

The consequences of this final encounter with Freud were dramatic: Ferenczi lost Freud's confidence and personal protection and died just eight months later at the age of 59. Freud's response itself unleashed a collective reaction from members of the analytic community, resulting in Ferenczi's banishment from the psychoanalytic canon, his work marginalized for more than half a century, until the publication of the *Clinical Diary* in 1985.

This publication, persistently pursued by Judith Dupont despite all obstacles, at last allowed the psychoanalytic community to rediscover and reassess Ferenczi's work. This seemingly new chapter in the history of psychoanalysis is actually a very old one that had been traumatically foreclosed and now is open. The accumulations of the reassessment process are pressing the psychoanalytic community to consider afresh the contradictions and splits embedded and unquestioned within our discipline. Much work remains to be done. Central to this undertaking is Ferenczi's effort to reestablish traumatic memories as the building blocks on which the entire structure of psychoanalysis rests, making audible at last the reverberating echoes of Emma Eckstein's circumcision trauma.

Outline of *Volume II*

This book is the sediment of an exploration of a *terra incognita*, a journey in which the traveler doesn't know in advance what will be found. It is also a long Odyssey at the end of which we will be back home.

Volume II is divided into three parts: 1. Theory in context, 2. The abyss, 3. Transmission.

Part I reviews a series of key questions. The first chapter ("Infantile amnesia") examines how the mind of the child was viewed prior to Freud based on my original research nearly three decades ago. At the moment of psychiatry's emergence as a separate discipline, scientific consensus held that the mind of the child lacked the inborn disposition for "passions and vices," and that, consequently, "bad impressions" simply failed to register.

This changed radically circa 1860 with the conceptualization of the human body as a place capable of storing memories of experiences and events. A new image of the child took shape within the new general theories on biological evolution, degeneration, and atavism. It was during this period that the struggle against masturbation turned increasingly violent. Freud managed to challenge the idea that sexual assaults on small children were "without effect" with his presentation on the etiology of hysteria in Vienna in 1896 (1896b, p. 164), proposing "sexual shock" as the specific causal factor of hysteria.

The focus of Chapter 2 ("Rise and fall of the seduction theory") is on material related to Emma Eckstein's case history, material which led Freud first to formulate, and only a year later to abandon, his theory of seduction. Chapter 3 ("Primal fantasies, biotrauma, and shock") presents an explanation and interpretation of Freud's turn to the "archaic." Ferenczi was the only member of Freud's early inner circle to fully embrace Freud's speculations on the accumulated phylogenic inheritance that informs instinctual life. He not only shared Freud's understanding of heredity as involving the transmission of archaic happenings but also imagined the phallus, in *Thalassa* (1924), as the living memorial of a primordial catastrophe transmitted without interruption from one generation to the next. Ferenczi's scientific fairy tale thus became the starting point of his progressive deconstruction of Freud's phallocentric system. In the end, Ferenczi would create a new language for the fragmenting consequences of trauma on psychic life.

Contemplating possible reasons for Freud's decision to discard the impact of trauma, Ferenczi suggested that Freud was "first shaken and then disenchanted" when "the problem of counter-transference opened [up] before him like an abyss" (Dupont, 1985, p. 93). This *Abyss* is explored in Part II in four chapters which take up the question of Freud's self-analysis, the very theme that has disappeared from many of the studies appearing in the last three decades concerning the origins of psychoanalysis.

The central theme of Part II is Freud's incorporation of Emma Eckstein's genital trauma. Chapters 4 ("The fatal needle") and 5 ("The blood covenant") explore connections between the scenes Emma Eckstein presented to Freud during analysis with the fantasies and dreams these sparked for Freud during his self-analysis. Chapters 6 and 7 ("The timeless unconscious I and II") revolve around a key element of Freud's reductionism, the identification of the total ego with the penis. How but in response to Emma Eckstein's genital mutilation could Freud have arrived at envisaging Adonis, the Lord, as a personification of the penis? Soon to follow was his development of interest in a system of thought which informs and stands behind dreams, religious ritual, and myths. This allows us to better understand the impact of Luca Signorelli's cycle of frescoes on the end of the world when Freud encountered them in the summer of 1897. Freud's notorious Signorelli slip met his revival of incestuous fantasies in the summer of 1898. Emma Eckstein's castration, I contend, in Freud's mind was transformed into the paradigmatic punishment meted out against those who dared to violate the incest taboo.

Finally, bringing Part II to a close, there is in Chapter 8 ("Necropolis"), Freud's identification of the wish to return to the mother's womb, alongside the terrifying fantasy of being buried alive. This is Freud's final dream during his self-analysis, the dream of self-dissection of the pelvis. The spectacular castration event in that dream, besides pointing to the traumatic event of Freud's "castration" by his "sexually demanding mother" (Ferenczi), featured a mimetic reproduction on Freud's own body of Emma Eckstein's childhood castration event. Freud's early followers were all deeply impressed by the self-dissection dream, soon to be elevated as a symbol of the self-analysis.

The third and final part, *Transmission* explores the interpersonal effects of the self-dissection dream. My claim is that Ferenczi dreamed aspects of this on various occasions, starting with his Christmas dream of a small penis served on a saucer and tray as a totemic meal. This final section asserts that Ferenczi's dream of a severed penis, as 1912 drew to a close, represented his incorporation of the split off part of Freud's psyche that Freud himself was too frightened to integrate.

I first presented this idea at the 1993 International Sándor Ferenczi Conference in Budapest (Bonomi, 1994a). It was then reformulated in a long article titled "Mute correspondence" and published in 1996 in a special issue of the *International Forum of Psychoanalysis*. Later it reappeared in *Behind the Scene: Freud in Correspondence*, edited with Patrick Mahony and Jan Stensson in 1997. The original text (Bonomi, 1996) forms the basis of three chapters: 9 ("Mute correspondence I. Catabasis"), 10 ("Mute correspondence II. Epopteia"), and 11 ("Thalassa"). Chapter 12 ("A blind spot") examines Freud's thesis that excision (or amputation) of the clitoris served to further "feminize" women by removing this cardinal vestige of masculinity, and considers Freud's relationship with Marie Bonaparte.

Chapter 13 ("Nightmares are real") explains how Ferenczi was able to transform the conceptual system of Freud, focusing on three points: his reorganization of the fulcrum of psychotherapy, his creation of a new language for trauma, and his mutual analysis with Elisabeth Severn.

Like Marie Bonaparte, Severn was seen as royalty (Marie was of course an actual princess, Severn merely an imaginary one) but it turns out that she, also like Marie, underwent surgical castration. Bonaparte, as we know, submitted herself voluntarily to surgical interventions on her sexual organs while Elisabeth Severn had her ovaries removed against her will. Both women thus were uncanny reincarnations of Emma Eckstein, the keystone patient during Freud's self-analysis preceding the founding of psychoanalysis.

Chapter 14 ("Acropolis") describes an imaginary meeting between Freud and Ferenczi on the Acropolis, based on Freud's last piece of self-analysis ("A disturbance of memory on the Acropolis"), produced three years after the shock of

Ferenczi's death in 1933. The chapter brings to an end a reconstruction of the gap Freud filled with the theory of the transcendental Phallus. Thus Emma Eckstein endured not only a circumcision but an excision (amputation of the clitoris). Psychoanalysis was suddenly born from Freud's automatic reaction to and mimetic reproduction of her traumatic shock. How memory and fantasy are used to fill gaps is also considered. The 15th and final chapter ("Flight into sanity") reflects on Ferenczi's expulsion from the psychoanalytic establishment. Material in the chapter was previously published in the *International Forum of Psychoanalysis* (Bonomi, 1998), and a longer, more detailed version in the *International Journal of Psychoanalysis* (Bonomi, 1999).

Acknowledgments

I would like first of all to thank the friends of the Italian Ferenczi group, especially Franco Borgogno, Clara Mucci, and Gianni Guasto, for the important ideas and feedback they offered during our many years of vital discussion. I would also like to recall a dear friend, Risto Fried, and his *Freud on the Acropolis – A Detective Story*, which was published in 2003, shortly before his death. My thoughts here are to acknowledge how very significant his research and his musings were to the extended development of my own interpretations.

Adrienne Harris patiently followed the construction of this book, giving me again precious advice and support. As with the first volume of *The Cut and the Building of Psychoanalysis*, most of the preparatory work for this second volume was done with the assistance of Mario Beira, who again acted as English editor and valuable interlocutor. My greatest gratitude is for Judith E. Vida, an outstanding Ferenczi scholar and a dear friend. She and I first met in 1993 in Geneva, where we had both been invited to present at the conference *100 Years of Psychoanalysis: Contributions to the History of Psychoanalysis*. On that occasion we discussed passionately the germinal ideas now developed in the two volumes of this book. As a felicitous coincidence, at the precise moment when the final version of this manuscript was about to be delivered, Judith called me with congratulations for the first volume. She was really enthusiastic but expressed some reservations about the copyediting. I immediately sent her the Introduction, and thus began a wonderful collaboration, resulting in the final version of this volume. Judith's way with words and profound knowledge of the contents infused the right speed and rhythm into this long, unwieldy text.

Appreciation is expressed for permission to reprint in whole or in part the following works:

Chapters 10, 11, and 12: Bonomi, C. (1996). Mute correspondence. *International Forum of Psychoanalysis*, 5: 165–189.

Chapter 15: Bonomi, C. (1998). Jones's allegation of Ferenczi's mental deterioration: a reassessment. *International Forum of Psychoanalysis*, 7: 201–206.

A special thanks goes to Rainer Funk, the Literary Executor of Erich Fromm, for the permission to quote documents of the Erich Fromm Archives.

Notes

1 He was the eighth of 12 children born to Baruk and Rosa, who were both Jewish. The families of both parents originally hailed from Poland. His father, who was born Baruk Fränkel, decided to resettle in Hungary during his teen years. Baruk owned and operated a bookstore and was a committed supporter of the nationalist and liberal cause. As such, he decided to magyarize his family name from Fränkel to Ferenczi in 1879. Ferenczi's father died nine years later, in 1888, the year Sándor turned 15. After graduating from medical school in Vienna, Ferenczi moved to Budapest where he began to work as a general practitioner and neurologist at the hospice for the poor, a place where prostitutes and society's outcasts were treated.

2 Among these we can cite Borgogno (1999, 2011), Dupont (2015), Falzeder (2015), Guasto (2015), Harris and Kuchuck (2015), Haynal (1988, 2002), Jimenez Avello (2013), Lugrin (2012), Mészáros (2008), Muccci (2013), Rachman (1997, 2003), Rachman and Kett (2015), Rudnytsky (2002, 2011), Sabourin (2011), Sklar (2011), and Szekacs-Weisz and Keve (2012a, 2012b).

3 Freud initially assumed that distressing events aroused affects which required discharging if the internal organization of the psyche was to be preserved. Should this self-preserving reaction fail to occur, however, Freud then felt that the psyche experienced a trauma (Breuer & Freud, 1893, p. 11; Freud, 1893a, pp. 36–37). Freud's initial hypothesis was that the emotional reaction produced by the distressing experience remained "encapsulated" within the individual's psyche. Freud's interventions, which aimed at both investigation and cure, thus sought to facilitate its "abreaction," thereby "causing an unaccomplished reaction to be completed" (Freud, 1893a, p. 39).

4 I thank Aleksandar Dimitrijevic for having provided me with a copy of Emma Eckstein's (1904) book. Emma Eckstein had already published in 1900 a short article, titled *"Eine wichtige Erziehungsfrage* [An important child-raising question]."

5 My translation. This was one of 14 communications Freud wrote to Emma Eckstein between 1895 and 1906 which were donated by Albert Hirst (Emma's nephew) to the Library of Congress in Washington, DC (Sigmund Freud's papers, Supplemental File, 1765–1998, Box 61. Library of Congress, Manuscript division). I thank Mario Beria for having provided me with copies of this material. These 14 communications by Freud were mentioned by Masson (1984). Now they are readable online at www.freud-edition.net/briefe/freud-sigmund/eckstein-emma.

6 Emma Eckstein had apparently asked Freud for a copy or information on Friedrich Jacob Behrend's article from 1860, *"Über die Reizung der Geschlechtstheile, besonders über Onanie bei ganz kleinen Kindern, und die dagegen anzuwendenden Mittel"* [On the stimulation of the sexual parts, particularly concerning onanism in small children and the means of battling against it]. I quoted extensively from Behrend's article in Volume I of this study (p. 28). Freud apparently searched for Berhrend's article in the wrong place, in the *Jahrbuch für Kinderheilkunde*, a journal initially published in Vienna by local pediatricians; the journal appeared in print from 1857 to 1931. Freud's reply to her that the *Journal für Kinderkrankheiten* did not exist is rather astonishing given the fact that Freud had worked within pediatric circles for years.

7 Albert Hirst was born in 1887 and wrote his account of his experience of analysis ("Analysed and Reeducated by Freud Himself," undated manuscript) when he was more than 80 years old. Hirst's manuscript, 38 pages long, was donated by him to the Library of Congress in Washington along with the letters and postcards Freud wrote to Emma Eckstein. I thank Mario Beira for having provided me with copies of this material. Hirst's manuscript contains a chapter entitled "Aunt Emma."." His text reveals him committing a few mistakes; he states, for instance, that he began analysis with Freud sometime during the fall of 1910, confusing the beginning of his treatment with its end. Hirst, who lived in Prague with his family, desired to return to Vienna to resume his analysis with Freud in the fall of 1910. His father, however, vetoed his plans. Hirst

decided to move to the United States a year later, arriving in New York on November of 1911, where he became a successful lawyer.
8 Hirst wrote: "I have the notion that she was all her life in love with a certain Vienna architect, and that her relapse came after he got married, or after she became convinced in some other way that her love was hopeless" (p. 7).
9 Freud was working on "The future prospects of psycho-analytic therapy" at the time, a paper he planned to present at the Nuremberg congress scheduled to take place during the last two days of that month. It was during the Nuremberg congress that the IPA, as a result of Ferenczi's own urgings, was established (Mészáros, 2015, p. 27). In a letter dated March 22 (1910), a week before the congress, Ferenczi wrote the following to Freud: "in our analyses we investigate the real conditions in the various levels of society, cleansed of all hypocrisy and conventionalism, just as they are mirrored in the individual."."
10 "Society," said Freud, "is bound to offer us resistance, for we adopt a critical attitude towards it; we point out to it that it itself plays a great part in causing neuroses. Just as we make an individual our enemy by uncovering what is repressed in him, so society cannot respond with sympathy to a relentless exposure of its injurious effects and deficiencies" (1910b, p. 147).
11 Significantly, Spitz (1952) decided to make his bibliographic research public because, as he explained, knowledge of the sadistic methods which were being used to repress masturbation had failed to enter the psychoanalytic world.
12 For instance, no references to Freud's pediatric training can be found in the "Finding Aid" that staff members at the Sigmund Freud's Archives at the Library of Congress in Washington have assembled.
13 An important supportive exchange took place following my 1993 presentation at the conference "One hundred years of psychoanalysis."." On this occasion Albrecht Hirschmüller confided that in his Ph.D. dissertation on Freud's medical education, he had failed to investigate what Freud had learned from his study with Baginsky in Berlin. Although this had been commented upon during his defense of the dissertation, he further confided that he had never gone back to pursue the matter.

Part I
Theory in context

1 Infantile amnesia

> We forget how high are the intellectual achievements and how complicated the emotional impulses of which a child of some four years is capable, and we ought to be positively astonished that the memory of later years has as a rule preserved so little of these mental processes, especially as we have every reason to suppose that these same forgotten childhood achievements have not, as might be thought, slipped away without leaving their mark on the subject's development, but have exercised a determining influence for the whole of his later life. And in spite of this unique efficacy they have been forgotten!
>
> Sigmund Freud, *The Psychopathology of Everyday Life*, 1901, p. 46

> In most cases of infantile trauma, the parents have no interest in impressing the events on the mind of the child, on the contrary, the usual care is repression: "it's nothing at all"; "nothing has happened"...
>
> Sándor Ferenczi, *The Clinical Diary*, 31 January 1932

An age without memory

Psychiatry began to emerge as a distinct medical discipline at the end of the 18th century. During the early stages of its history, when insanity was seen as a product of sins, debauchery, and moral excesses, madness was imagined as not existing prior to the onset of puberty. At that time childhood was still viewed as an "age of innocence," as Hermann Emminghaus explained in 1887 when introducing the first monograph ever published in the field child psychiatry. Emminghaus's observation takes us to the heart of this chapter, namely, the relationship between innocence, memory and passions in psychiatric discourse on the child before Freud.

"Aren't all forms of madness [*aliénations*] merely passions pushed beyond limits?" asked the young J.E.D. Esquirol in his 1805 doctoral dissertation. Along with Pinel, Esquirol was one of the founding fathers of French psychiatry. Since childhood remained free of passion, to Esquirol it was obvious that madness was itself absent from this early period of life. Similarly Friedrich August Carus, a professor of psychology in Leipzig and director of the local asylum, maintained in 1808 that a child "can obviously be an idiot [*blödsinnig*] but never mad [*wahnsinnig*]" (p. 332).

This view was not based on clinical observation and experience; it was rather part of a larger system of thought at the time. For instance, according to Benjamin Rush, the father of American psychiatry, madness was a consequence of civilization and, therefore, was not to be found either among children nor "savages."[1] It was precisely around this time that the philosopher Arthur Schopenhauer (1816) proposed madness as an illness of memory. In the third book (§ 36) of *The World as Will and Representation* he wrote:

> The fact that violent mental suffering or unexpected and terrible calamities should often produce madness, I explain in the following manner. All such suffering is as an actual event confined to the present. It is thus merely transitory, and is consequently never excessively heavy; it only becomes unendurably great when it is lasting pain; but as such it exists only in thought, and therefore lies in the *memory*. If now such a sorrow, such painful knowledge or reflection, is so bitter that it becomes altogether unbearable, and the individual is prostrated under it, then, terrified Nature seizes upon *madness* as the last resource of life; the mind so fearfully tortured at once destroys the thread of its memory, fills up the gaps with fictions, and thus seeks refuge in madness from the mental suffering that exceeds its strength, just as we cut off a mortified limb and replace it with a wooden one.

Freud would later say that Schopenhauer's description of "the struggle against accepting a distressing piece of reality" stood in line with his own views on repression (Freud, 1914a, p. 15). Freud, moreover, would extend to all humankind and to its history the idea that gaps in memory were filled with fictions.

Though not with the singular clarity of this passage from Schopenhauer, the idea of madness as an illness involving gaps in memory seems to have been implicitly shared by many psychiatrists of the era. This is why childhood was felt to be free from mental illness: a child did not have memory. Unlike adults burdened by their memories, children seemed only to exist in an uncontaminated present. Not only was the child lacking an historical dimension but, as the French physician and phrenologist François-Joseph-Victor Broussais (1828, p. 335) argued, "bad" and painful "impressions" simply failed to take hold in the mind of a child. This belief, in various forms, deeply affected the way children were seen, represented, and treated at the time, and was closely related to the assumption that children were free from passions.

According to the psychology of the time, passions, while essential in a harmonic, healthy life, still needed to be guided by reason. If passion was the wind, reason was the compass. Without reason, passions would turn individuals into slaves of vice and sin. Thus, the lingering of bad impressions in the mind, secretly feeding the passions, only meant that vice and sin were more powerful than reason. *But this did not apply to children.* Children lacked both the autonomy and the mental strength to engage successfully in the struggle between good and evil, and were wholly dependent on the will of the parent. The struggle between passion and reason was thought to begin after puberty, with the necessity to confront choices (in matters of love, in particular) and to take up a new position within the circle of life.

During the first half of the 19th century, psychiatry did view sexuality as important, as the element called upon to assess a link between madness and sin. This link was identified in the work of such authors as Johann Christian Reil, Karl Wilhelm Ideler, Johann Christian Heinroth, and Heinrich Neumann, all known as *Psychikers* – a term from which the word "psychiatry" itself derived. *Psychikers* were typically contrasted with the *Somatikers*, who endorsed the theological belief that the human soul was incorruptible and immortal, and thus incapable of becoming sick.

The key clinical question these two opposing sides debated was whether "the closest condition of the psychic malady" was based "on the psychic itself or on the material, somatic organization of man" (Friedreich, 1839, p. 1). For the *Somatikers*, delusions failed to reflect the deepest wishes of the sick individual and only entered the human soul as a consequence of a sick body. As phrased by Friedreich: "The immoral man remains psychically sound as long as he remains somatically healthy."

The central argument of the *Psychikers* emphasized a structural distinction between febrile delirium and psychic delusions (*Wahnsinn*). Whereas a febrile delirium lacked meaning, the delusions of the madman were perceived by the *Psychikers* as harboring *meaning*, that is to say, as being informed by a *historical continuity* between the motives of the subject's behavior *before and after* the onset of the delusions. This historical continuity was viewed as proof of the soul's participation in insanity; indeed "historical continuity" functioned as the hermeneutic premise on which this entire interpretative system and therapeutic practice was based. Hence individual madness could be reformulated in terms of the history of the subject's passions, and was often seen as the final outcome of the subject giving in to vice and sin. This framework allowed for the development of a treatment approach that was personal: the "moral treatment," as psychotherapy was referred to at the time.

The collapse of the idea that childhood was free of madness and insanity

The unchallenged idea that childhood remained free and untouched by madness and insanity suddenly collapsed between 1850 and 1860.[2] The speed and homogeneity of this suggests that the belief system of the time was changing as well.

The reasons for the paradigm shift are displayed in the first article ever published in the psychiatric literature on the topic of insanity in children. The author was one of the most renowned *Psychikers*, Karl Wilhem Ideler, director of the Charité Hospital in Berlin. *Über den Wahnsinn der Kinder* (*On the insanity of the child*) appeared in 1852, just prior to the paradigm shift. Ideler presented the case history of Marie Schmidt, an 11-year-old girl admitted for treatment at his institution. Despite suffering from intermittent periods of erotic delusion (*Wahnsinn*), she was discharged completely recovered a year and half later, having experienced her first menstruation during the period of hospital confinement and treatment.

Marie's delusional ideation had set in shortly after going alone to a butcher shop near her home. She then developed an unshakeable belief that the butcher wanted to marry her, and began to ruminate that he might show up at her home to take her away. Scared and excited by the possibility, Marie remained fixated on her fantasies and thoughts. Ideler did not explicitly state that the girl had been sexually molested; he may likely have suspected this to have been the case. The key point is that her symptoms began when she had not yet entered puberty, too young for passion to generate delusional thinking. Thus there was no available theoretical model to permit a connection between an event of sexual molestation and symptoms of delusion before puberty.

Although at that time sexual assaults were included among the moral causes of insanity, the effects of assault on the victim were thought to be mediated by an internal factor, a factor required to "overturn the natural order of the soul, to divert it from all sane concepts and ideas, and to transform its active tension into a vain rummage and the haze of fantasy" (Ideler, 1852, p. 317). This internal factor was passion. If childhood was "exempted from all those passions that so often, at a later age, wield their despotic command on the soul" (p. 314) physicians, Ideler among them, could not fathom how a sexual assault occurring prior to puberty could possibly produce a delusion with an erotic dimension.[3]

Ideler did not underestimate children's experiences of suffering. He well knew that given their weakness and vulnerability children were more likely than an adult to be seriously distressed by their own fits of "anger, envy, rage, fright, anxiety and sadness." This held particularly true for abused children living within the framework of a disturbed family, the child being totally dependent on caretakers. Yet, experiences of suffering were not viewed as contributing to the true source of insanity, the perversion and corruption of the soul. The rather curious explanation between the lines of Ideler, as well as of the other authors of that period is this: if the suffering experienced by the child was beyond his or her capacity to deal with it, the child would perish from physical depletion. If, however, the child's physical constitution was sufficiently sturdy to endure the effects of mistreatment, all psychical traces of it disappeared, as though the soul of the child was left untouched by the experience. More precisely, the implicit assumption was that psyche of children did not react with splitting. Splitting meant a part of the psyche becoming perverted and turning against the healthy part, which related to a current idea influenced by Hegel that madness was always "partial" and never absolute (as in idiocy and senile dementia).

Evidence for this claim was drawn from the observed phenomenon of children quickly switching from painful crying to joyful smiling and laughing. This apparent light-heartedness was seized upon to support the notion that in children mistreatments and pain failed to be interiorized. But in 1852, Ideler's case history of Marie Schmidt laid bare the explanatory inadequacy of the existing paradigm. Thus began a paradigm shift.

During the awkward transition between old and new, doors were opened and then suddenly shut again. Here are two examples. In an article on the topic of suicide in children, during the midst of the crisis, Durand-Fardell (1855) introduced a new perception of the mind of the child, suggesting that fear, dread, and repulsion could all remain hidden under the surface, despite the characteristic light-heartedness. At the same time, the author drifted away from his insight into an invisible inward zone where painful experiences could be preserved by embracing in his conclusion the newest ideas of degeneration just appearing in those years.

The second example concerns Auguste Tardieu's *Étude medico-légale sur les attentats aux moeurs* (*A medico-legal study of assaults on decency*), first published in 1857 and reissued through a series of new editions until 1878. According to Tardieu, 79 percent of all reported rape or attempted rapes in France between 1858 and 1869 were of children who were under 16 years of age, mostly girls between the ages of 4 and 12. Of the 616 cases of alleged assaults which he had examined "339 were of rape or attempted rape of children under the age of eleven" (Masson, 1984, p. 23). Sexual abuse and molestation were identified as crimes by the law, and when these crimes were committed on children they were viewed as especially hateful. Tardieu provided detailed descriptions of their effects on the bodies of children, but was simply unable to see to describe their psychological effect. In the existing mental space, the latter remained unthought-of.

The emergence of the "drive-passion" model

The field of psychiatry underwent a profound reorganization between 1850 and 1860 as "*Naturphilosophie*" was replaced by "*Naturwissenschaft*," and the "soul" began to take a back seat to the brain. The nervous system was now seen as the mediator of the relationship of the individual with the environment. The body, its uncontrolled reactions, and inborn "passions" now provided a framework for the precocious onset of insanity. Here is a passage from Crichton Browne (1860), taken from a lecture on "Psychical diseases of early life," which he delivered at the Royal Medical Society of Edinburgh while he was still a student:

> The mind of childhood, which we are accustomed to look upon as emblematic of all that is simple, pure and innocent, may be assailed by the most loathsome of psychical disorders, viz, satyriasis, or nymphomania; the monomania of the sexual instinct. Sexual precocity has been frequently observed at an early age.
>
> (p. 308)

Browne illustrated this "disgusting anticipation" of the sexual instinct by discussing several cases of nymphomania and satyriasis in both male and female children. We encounter a similar turn, in less grotesque and dramatic tones, in authors from very different traditions as well. I am thinking of Charles West (1854, the 3° enlarged edition of his *Lectures on the diseases of infancy and childhood*), and of Oswald Berkhan (1863–1864), Brierre de Boismont (1858), John Connolly (1862), Emminghaus (1887), Wilhelm Griesinger (1861, the 2° edition of his 1845 famous work), Henry Maudsley (1867), Paul Moreau de Tours (1882, 1888), August Benedict Morel (1857, 1860), and Heinrich Neumann (1859) in particular.

All these authors now proposed that the view of a child as an innocent creature was "completely false." That a child was spared from experiencing and falling into madness was based on the assumption that passions were an artifact of civilization, but now the entire perspective on the question turned around. The child's lack of intellectual mastery, it was now thought, rendered any sensation, stimulus, or experience all the more potent. This argument, first advanced by Charles West (1854, 1860), was further developed by Henry Maudsley (1867). In time, it became the pillar for an altogether new paradigm. As Kindt (1971) underscored, the work of Maudsley offered the first attempt to anchor the psychopathology of the child on a specific structure, based on un-mastered forces of instincts.

This was when the idea of "masturbatory insanity" began to spread. A new psychiatric discourse emerged during the period when the methods used to treat masturbation in children suddenly grew more sadistic, featuring bodily restraints and "surgical treatments" (Spitz, 1952, p. 499). This topic is extensively discussed in *Volume I* and there is nothing further to add here, apart from the new meaning acquired by the human body: "the physician took direct action on the child's body in order to directly reach the mind and create a lasting memory. In spite of all physical justifications, the 'operation' had from the very beginning a psychic goal, since the body was viewed as a supplement to the mind" (*Volume I*, p. 28). Also in psychiatric discourse, the body was now associated with memory, and perceived as the place where sediments of the subject's prior history, going back to the very beginning of human evolution, were recorded and stored. The idea that sins committed by a child's ancestors were somehow capable of being transmitted to future generations was initially articulated by Benedicte August Morel. In his 1857 treatise, where the concept of *"degenerescence"* first appeared, Morel described how an external harmful agent, alcohol for example, might exercise a deleterious impact on an individual's future offspring, including the appearance of homicidal tendencies, progressive mental deterioration, and sterility in future generations.

Initially, the theory of degeneration led social scientists to formulate a powerful critique of society, focused on the degraded, harmful conditions of large cities and suburban areas. Moreover, the idea that the "sins of the fathers" could be transmitted to their descendants led psychiatrists to view children as capable of understanding and responding to sexual stimuli and impressions: "bad" impressions could be absorbed and magnified by the child's own imagination as a result of "bad dispositions." In this way children began to be seen as vulnerable to external impressions. However, the theory of degeneration contained many contradictions. Born as a revolutionary movement aimed at rescuing humanity by changing the world, the theory of degeneration soon became too easy a mode of explaining psychical illness in early life. Revolutionary momentum would be revived by Freud when he envisioned the "sins of the fathers" as actual incestuous events not only in slums but in the comfortable homes of the average bourgeois family.

"Born without humanity, the child carries all the vices of mankind"

Morel was a member of a Christian fundamentalist movement, and his idea of *"degenerescence"* featured a new myth of the Fall from the Paradise. The link between childhood and the notion of original sin traces back as far as St. Augustine. This link was severed at the start of the modern age, however, when secularization began to take hold and the world of the child was disconnected from the world of adults. Descartes transformed "sin" into "error," amenable to correction through insight and education. Another new framework took shape with Locke's view of the child as a "*tabula rasa*," that is to say, as a pure and uncorrupted blank slate. During the course of the 18th century, moreover, children would be seen in a new light with the emergence of the nuclear or "sentimental" family. The next view of childhood emphasized such qualities as grace, delicateness, and harmony, and presented the child as a "*mignon*," to cite Philippe Ariés (1960). Romanticism heralded yet another new period, presenting marriage as a product of individual choice rather than a relationship arranged by parents. Writers of the period soon began crafting novels around the conflicts between the individual and the family, often dramatizing the tragic consequence of allowing an individual's passion to determine their choice of a life partner. It was at the apex of this period, characterized by a growing separation between "public" and "private" life, that childhood was characterized as an age of "innocence."

This view would change course drastically in the second half of the 19th century. During the last decade of the century Jules-Gabriel Compayré (1893) asked whether the soul of the child could be affected by "evil." With regret he was forced to admit that a child's beginning was neither pure nor "absolute" and that children were not a "*tabula rasa*" as had been thought. Instead, Compayré argued children came into the world like a new medal "formed in an old mold," in other words, with a brain in which the history of his or her ancestors was "inscribed and engraved" (p. 188). As a consequence of this new view, several instincts found in the child were seen as "positively vicious" (p. 189). Not only was the child "perverted in certain cases by social surroundings" but the child was [now] also seen as "naturally perverse" (p. 205).

In a concluding chapter discussing the child's morbid dispositions, Compayré, a French psychologist and pedagogue, presented the law of heredity (according to which "the bad is transmitted much more easily than the good") as a "scientific formula" which was anticipated by "the dogma of original sin" (p. 259). This is how the idea of "original sin" regained a privileged and fundamental position, except that it was theorized by psychiatrists and doctors of the soul rather than priests.

The treatment of "hysteric, vicious, and degenerate" children was one of the main points of departure of the method of hypnotic suggestion which the members of the Nancy school had introduced in 1880. This led to the rediscovery of the "moral treatment" approach, newly packaged under the label of "psychotherapy."[4] Edgard Bérillon, general school inspector in France and the editor of the *Revue de l'hypnotisme et de la psychologie physiologique*, introduced the term "*orthopedie mental*" (mental orthopedic) during this period to better define the application of hypnotic suggestion to treat the vices, mental disorders, and perverse instincts in children.[5] Masturbation was particularly targeted by this form of treatment. "There is no vice as desperate as onanism whose consequences are so serious in children and adolescents," pronounced Auguste Voisin (1887) in his article,

"*Observations d'onanisme guéries par la suggestion hypnotique*" ("Observations on onanism healed by hypnotic suggestion"). The author commented on the successful treatment of two girls, ages nine and eleven, and of a nine-year-old boy. Comparing this new form of treatment with the prevailing corporal devices and tactics of humiliation and terror which the medical community still employed to treat onanism and endorsed at the time, Rose (2011) observed that "moral orthopedics was a revolutionary technology for treating obsessive self-stimulation while conserving the child's sense of autonomy" (p. 36).

Rose's observation is correct, but explains only one side of the proverbial coin. The other side reveals that this same shift from body to mind soon developed into a new narrative in which girls' and boys' complaints of sexual abuse were more and more presented as the product of their imagination. In 1882 the psychiatrist Paul Moreau de Tours (1882) published a book entitled *De l'homicide commis par les enfants* (*Murders perpetuated by children*). The text raised the following questions: "What motives do these young beings, some of whom are not yet beyond the first phase of childhood, follow? How exactly is it that a perverse idea first takes root? What is its original cause?" (p. 2). According to De Tours these "abominable" and "copious" crimes had to be understood from "the psychic and physiologic character of the typical child which we will call normal, free from all heredity . . ." (p. 3). The solution he proposed was that, not "knowing how to bind the ideas," these young creatures were dominated by the "most demanding instincts," including egoism, jealousy, vanity, and cruelty, and concluded: "*Né sans humanité, l'enfant a tous les vices de l'homme*" ("Born without humanity, the child carries all the vices of mankind") (p. 8).

These thoughts paved the way for the 1888 monograph *La folie chez les enfants* (*Madness in children*). In it, de Tours envisioned childhood as the place where an explosion of passions "*que l'on peu réellement qualifier de morbides*" (which really ought to be qualified as pathological) took place and unfolded (p. 20). Jealousy stood at the heart of outbursts of hatred, evil wishes, and desires for revenge operating within the mind of the child. This "egoistic jealousy," the French psychiatrist wrote, could be found among primitive people and among those who had not yet been civilized (p. 20).

Just a year earlier, in 1887, in the first ever monograph devoted entirely to *Die Psychischen Störungen des Kindesalters* (*The mental disturbances of the child*) Hermann Emminghaus advanced a new founding principle. Since psychic functions came to be balanced only in adulthood, the normal psychic state of a child, he suggested, was one and the same with what was pathological in adults (p. 7). In the case of children, wrote Emminghaus, there "are only wishes and appetites." With the absence of reason and free will in children, he saw the mental life of children as more likely to be affected "by passions" than was the case with adults (p. 8). Emminghaus's work was regarded by Kindt (1971) as foundational with respect to the emerging knowledge of psychopathology of the child. It nevertheless rested entirely on a questionable likening of a normal child to a mentally deranged adult.

For a long time, at least until the third decade of the 20th century, children were conceived mostly in terms of what they were *not yet*, in other words, by subtracting a set of qualities from principles and concepts which were typically attributed to a normal adult. This methodological approach had a deep impact upon early childhood psychiatry. Only when the child was no longer seen as an incomplete adult did the field of psychiatry begin to be truly established on a more methodologically solid foundation. Psychoanalysis was itself affected by the same methodological problem.[6]

The high level of suggestibility in children would play an important role in the medical-legal debate of the time. In 1882 Claude Etienne Bourdin, founder and president of the Paris Medical-Psychological Association, delivered a paper on "*Les enfants menteur*" ("Children who lie") to the association, claiming that children were "susceptible . . . to almost all the passions that trouble the heart of the adult" (Bourdin, 1883, p. 378; Masson, 1984, p. 48). In 1885 Alfred Binet and Charles Féré argued that children were particularly vulnerable to being manipulated and to be used as "instruments of crime." Two years later Pierre Ladame (1887) indicated that suggestion could be either inadvertently or intentionally utilized to influence a child's capacity to provide reliable and truthful testimony about their experiences.

Debate on this topic was lively in 1887, when August Motet published *Les faux témoignages des enfants devant la justice* (*False testimony given by children before courts of justice*). The nature of the debate was summarized by Edgard Bérillon in his 1892 article, "*Les faux témoignages suggérée chez les enfants*" ("False testimony suggested in children." Appealing to Bernheim's notion of "retroactive hallucination," and to Forel's ideas on "retroactive illusionary memory" as well, the author concluded that in children "*l'hallucinabilité*" [the disposition to hallucinate] went "well beyond anything we can imagine" (p. 209). Finally, in the first book ever published which featured the term "childhood psychiatry" in its title, Manheimer (1899) argued that a female child's active capacity to imagine "will suggest to her many things that one would not expect; in most cases it is a question of attempts at rape in which little girls claim to be the victims" (p. 137). The work of Freud was, in a way, an interminable and oscillating meditation on this disposition to hallucinate found especially in children.

Two opposing paradigms

The paradigm change during the last two decades of the 19th century was neatly summarized in "*Über Suggestion bei Kindern*" ("On suggestion in children"), which the German pediatrician Adolf Baginsky presented in 1900 to the members of the Berlin Society for Child Psychology. This presentation remains vitally important for several reasons. Baginsky was one of Freud's early mentors. Freud studied and trained with him in 1886 to improve his knowledge of children and their diseases. The modern psychological view of the child was only slowly beginning to take root in pediatric circles at the time. Pediatric discourse had long been fixated on the idea of children as "innocent" beings. While working as a forensic psychologist, Baginsky embraced the "modern" views about children and their psyche, and in his lecture summarized the shift from the old to the new paradigm as follows:

> ... previously the psyche [*Seele*] of the child was seen as clear and as transparent [*durchsichtig*] as a mirror, so that one had only to read the ways in which the impressions of the external world were reflected in it. Such a view has been essentially changed by modern pedagogical and psychological researches. What exists in the psyche [*Seele*] of adults must already be present in the psyche of the child in order for it to develop. The psyche of the child is therefore no longer seen as a clear lake in which the external world is reproduced unchanged ... The same drives and passions, conscious and unconscious deviations from the correct moral way, which we strikingly meet in the adult, are found already shaped in the child.
> (Baginsky, 1901, pp. 97–98)

Baginsky's description reveals the same clinical phenomena (hallucinations, fantasies, and enactments) in children being interpreted in radically different ways. Previously, they were seen as instigated by another person whose behavior was then reproduced by the child. That is, within the older physiologically-based paradigm, masturbation in children was the result of a sexual stimulation, which immediately suggested abuse by an older person. With the arrival of the new psychologically-centered paradigm, the same phenomena were increasingly viewed as a manifestation of an inborn sexual drive. While helping society to accept infantile sexuality, a paradoxical result of the paradigm change was a propensity to brush aside and deny the possibility of an actual sexual abuse. For instance, Baginsky (1909) concluded that "to the really experienced connoisseur of the child the testimonies of the child before the court are nothing [*null und nichtig*], completely worthless and without meaning" (p. 20). Especially telling is "*Die Kinderaussage vor Gericht*" ("The testimony of the child before the court"), which Baginsky delivered to the Berlin association of judges in 1910. Baginsky's further conclusion was that, because of his/her physical and psychical constitution – his/her inclination to illusions, fantasies, and lies – the child's testimony was impaired, uncertain, and unreliable, and a child shouldn't be allowed to testify in courts before the age of 16.

Freud founded psychoanalysis during a period in which these two opposing paradigms were clashing; the tension and differences between the two camps deeply affected his theorizing activities as well as his entire approach to symptoms and their treatment.

Freud in context

During his studies in Paris between 1885 and 1886, Freud would have been exposed to the brutality of sexual crimes on children.[7] Freud left Paris for Berlin in March of 1886 to train in pediatrics with Adolf Baginsky, and would have come into contact with specific material regarding the effects of seduction in children. In a letter to Martha Bernays from Berlin on March 10, Freud expressed his desire to devote his entire professional life to treating sick children, adding that he was unable to reveal to her the true "secrets of children's diseases," apparently referring to the reason children became sick was connected to sexual matters, likely abuse.

Freud began to work as a neurologist and a child therapist soon after, when he joined the staff of the *Öffentliches Kinder-Kranken-Institut* (Public Institute for Children's Diseases), a children's polyclinic in Vienna.[8] These experiences of treating children allow a better appreciation of the ways in which Freud, during his formative years, gained firsthand knowledge of the different competing paradigms for mental illness and the formation of psychological symptoms.

The field of pediatrics was established as a separate medical specialty during the second half of the 19th century. The Vienna General Hospital, one of the first in the world, first opened its doors during the final two decades of 18th century, with the first pediatric department being established a century later, in 1872, headed by one of Baginsky's colleagues, Ludwig Fleischmann. They both viewed onanism (uncontrolled masturbatory movements of the body) and active masturbation as the consequence of a premature stimulation of the child's genital organs, typically a seduction by an older girl or boy or caretaker, servant or nanny. At the same time, they recommended that masturbation must be battled against and treated through active measures, including mechanical restraints or surgery (circumcision, cauterization at the entrance of the vagina, cutting of the labia or of the clitoris). An article by Ludwig Fleischmann, posthumously published in 1878 in the *Wiener medizinische Presse*, provided a clear example.

As established in the opening volume, Emma Eckstein, the main female patient under Freud's care between 1894 and 1897, was likely circumcised as a child in an effort to cure her habit of masturbation. Emma, who entered the world in Vienna in 1865, and was raised in a well-established Jewish family, would very likely have been taken by her parents to see this reputable doctor for treatment and cure.

Freud never mentioned childhood sexual abuse in children directly while working as a child therapist. Only after he stopped his work with children, in 1896, did he address the theme by endorsing the theory that "seduction" in early age was as the "specific cause" of hysteria in his adult patients. In "The aetiology of hysteria," Freud (1896c) advanced the view that "our children are far more often exposed to sexual assaults than the few precautions taken by parents in this connection would lead us to expect." To support his position, Freud noted "several publications by pediatricians which stigmatize the frequency of sexual practices by nurses and nursery maids, carried out even on infants in arms" (p. 206). Since he failed to identify or quote from any of these publications, Freud most likely did not agree with their messages or methods.[9]

Freud's views were at odds not only with the members of the pediatric community at the time but also with the psychiatric establishment. His so-called "seduction theory," as we recall, had not been well received in Vienna. A deep rift between him and the members of the psychiatric community opened after he first proposed his ideas on the role of seduction in hysteria. Conrad Rieger (1896, p. 196) wrote:

> I cannot imagine that an experienced psychiatrist could read this essay [Freud, 1896b] without being truly horrified; and the reason for this feeling of horror is to be found in the fact that the author attaches great importance to paranoid blather of sexual content about purely haphazard events which, even when not based on inventions, are actually completely insignificant.
> (translation by Masson, 1983, p. 742)

This expression of "total indignation" is especially revealing because Conrad Rieger was considered one of the best minds of a new generation of physicians working to distance themselves from the contradictions of 19th-century psychiatry, in particular the idea that insanity was caused by "sins." Rieger (1900) was in fact laboring to emancipate psychiatry "from the superstitions of medicine" (p. 1).

According to the official history of psychoanalysis, Freud's proposal of his seduction theory was merely embracing ideas which "had been instilled into him" (Jones, 1953, p. 315). Jones's position is not only erroneous and unjust but profoundly misleading as well. The theory Freud proposed in 1896, a full decade after having learned the "secrets of children's diseases" during his training in paediatrics, featured a well-articulated psychological model of how the forgotten (repressed) memories of early sexual abuse managed to be preserved within the network of the adult's psyche.

Freud's theory of seduction challenged the prevailing psychiatric theory that "disposition" was a product of hereditary transmission, an expression of "degeneration." More precisely, at a philosophical level, he deconstructed the idea of degeneration to propose a different utopian model of "original sin," featuring an unbroken traumatic transmission from a generation to another. At the same time, at a clinical level, Freud proposed that a disposition for hysteria was acquired as a result of early sexual trauma. Freud developed this theory while working clinically with adults, as he worked to make sense of what he heard directly from patients during the course of a long-term emotionally rich treatment relationship with them. Freud's decision not to discard as irrelevant and meaningless the "paranoid blather with sexual content" of his patients was a deeply revolutionary action with many social implications. It was only as a result of this unique situation that *the voice of the traumatized child in the adult came to be listened to and heard for the first time* – hence the truly epochal significance of Freud's seduction theory, despite errors which his views on this topic might have contained.

Notes

1 In his *Medical Inquiries and Observations upon the Diseases of the Mind* Rush (1812) wrote: "The reason why children and persons under puberty are so rarely affected with madness must be ascribed to mental impressions which are its most frequent cause, being too transient in their effects, from the instability of their minds, to excite their brains into permanently diseased actions. It is true, children are often affected with delirium, but this is a

symptom of general fever, which is always induced, like the few cases of madness in children that I have mentioned, only by corporal causes" (p. 57). Rush, who was also a trained anthropologist, was profoundly admired by many European thinkers at the time for arguing that insanity and madness were not to be found among American "savages" (as Native Americans were called then). Both savages and children were seen by him as so closely related to a pristine "origin" (Nature) that they were immune from madness.

2 An increasing number of cases were reported in the psychiatric literature during the first half of the 19th century with Esquirol himself providing several of these in his treatise of 1838. These cases were however usually presented as being "exceptions." The only authors to challenge the general "rule," and only partly so, were Broussais (1928), who indicated that despite impressions failing to take hold within the mind of a child, the "intensity of these impressions" was itself capable of replacing "their duration" (p. 335), and Prichard (1835), who introduced the idea of "moral insanity" and used it in examining the psychical life and symptoms of boys and girls (see Bonomi, 2009).

3 In search of an alternative and different explanation, Ideler (1852) asked himself whether the natural instinct of "imitation," by which the well-known epidemics of insanity among children were most often explained, might [help to] clarify the question of how insanity could set in during this period of life. Imitation, he admitted, was indeed a powerful factor [as it served] to plant the seeds of good and evil in the soul. [The point, however, was that] During epidemics of madness, however, the phenomenon remained transitory and faded away after the external trigger was no longer present. Ideler thought this showed that children lacked the internal disposition for madness without the trigger of the temporary situation. Unlike epidemics of insanity, "true insanity" was always rooted in a diathesis which issued "from the most intimate part of the soul, the passions." Accordingly, sexual abuse could result in a lasting psychic perversion only by inflaming an internal passion. This model utterly failed to account for madness in children who were assumed to be free of passions.

4 Ambroise-August Liébeault (1883) conducted magnetic experiments with 45 children in 1882. At the beginning of 1883, however, he and Hippolyte Bernheim, and others, began using hypnotic suggestion on children for the purposes of education. The question of suggestion as a moralizing agent for children was debated in Nancy in 1886, during a meeting and conference of the French Association for the Advancement of Sciences. Summing up the advancements which the Nancy school had achieved over the work of James Braid, Charles Lloyd Tuckey wrote in his 1890 work *Psycho-therapeutics; or treatment by hypnotism and suggestion* that suggestion found "its best subjects in children between the age of three and fourteen" (p. 164).

5 Cf. Bérillon, 1898. Edgard Bérillon organized the first international congress on experimental and therapeutic hypnotism, held in Paris in 1889. During the congress, he offered a presentation on *"Les applications de la suggestion à la pédiatrie et à l'éducation mentale des enfants vicieux ou dégénérés"* ("The applications of suggestion to pediatrics and to the mental education of vicious or degenerate children"). Freud, fresh from his visit to Bernheim in Nancy, attended his talk.

6 In his article "Some critical comments on psychoanalytic conceptualizations of infancy," Emanuel Peterfreund (1978) argued that many typical psychoanalytic characterizations of early infancy, which lacked logical foundation and were not based on direct observation, were not useful for theorizing the infant's world. This issued directly from "two fallacies characteristic of psychoanalytic theories of infancy: the tendency to adultomorphize infancy and the tendency to label and characterize normal infant states with terms that apply to later psychopathological states" (p. 440). My view is that each of these two fallacies had been imported into psychoanalytic metapsychology directly as a consequence of the image of the child that had informed the field of psychiatry during the second half of the 19th century.

7 Freud wrote to his fiancée Martha Bernays on January 20 of 1886 to say that he had received permission to attend Professor Brouardel's course at the Morgue, while adding:

"The lecture was fascinating, the subject matter not very suitable for delicate nerves." As stressed by Jeffrey Masson (1984), Freud would later recall that Brouardel "used to show us from post-mortem material at the morgue how much there was which deserved to be known by doctors but of which science preferred to take no notice" (Freud, 1913d, p. 335).

8 The rich history of this institute was described in a book published to celebrate the 150th anniversary of its founding (Hochsinger, 1938). The institute stood as the oldest hospital for children in the world before it was forced to close its doors during the *Anschluss*. The records and files of the institution were unfortunately misplaced or destroyed as a result of World War II; an important historical source of the clinical work which Freud had carried out – work which had helped paved the way towards his founding of psychoanalysis – was thereby lost.

9 Since Freud never spoke of his "pediatric" life, there are only hypotheses. That Freud was so secretive in this important matter is puzzling and scarcely understandable.

2 Rise and fall of the seduction theory

> Hysterical phantasies do not lie when they tell us that parents and other adults do indeed go monstrous lengths in the passionate eroticism of their relations with children, while, on the other hand, when a quite innocent child responds to this half-unconscious play on the part of its elders the latter are inclined to think out severe punishments and threats which are altogether incomprehensible to him and have the shattering effects of a shock.
>
> S. Ferenczi, 1929, p. 121

Recovering memories

Freud first proposed the now well-known thesis that hysterics suffered "*mainly from reminiscences*" in his Preliminary Communication to the *Studies on Hysteria* (Breuer & Freud, 1895). Written in 1893, the text offered general recommendations for the treatment of psychological symptoms, specifically to help patients recover memories of traumatic events which had been dissociated. Initially Freud thought that traumatic memories would be easily accessible by patients during treatment, but things turned out not to be so simple. Before discovering the phenomenon of resistance, Freud in 1894 had become skeptical about the possibilities of psychological treatment for certain forms of anxiety (Volume I, p. 71), and in February of 1895 encouraged Emma to have her nose operated on by Wilhelm Fliess.

A riddle

Emma's nasal surgery was extensively discussed in Volume I and need not be recapitulated here, but it is crucial to recall that the treatment of Emma, and the complications which surfaced after her surgery, contained material which was encoded in Freud's dream of Irma's injection on July of 1895, as inferred by Anzieu (1986) and Schur (1966), and many other authors, on the basis of Freud's letters to Fliess about Emma's surgery. This material, though omitted from the first publication of the letters, was anticipated by Schur (1966), and only became fully accessible in the unabridged edition of the letters (Masson, 1985).

Before publication of this material, Erikson (1954) and Lacan (1954–1955), analysts from markedly different traditions, each proposed that the Irma dream marked the precise moment when psychoanalysis was born. In Volume I their views on Freud's founding dream were not only endorsed but expanded. In the dream itself Freud petitions Irma to open her mouth properly to localize the source of the pains in her body. Freud, however, was so shocked when he peered into Emma's oral cavity that he quickly stepped back to distance himself. The sight of Irma's damaged and rotting mouth tapped into Freud's observation of Emma's own mutilated vulva; this and the persistence of other images associated with her disfigured nose after surgery is persuasive that Fliess's surgical malpractice functioned as a repetition of Emma's genital trauma.

In the dream, as Irma is re-examined by a group of doctors, Freud suddenly began to feel Irma's physical pains within his own body. A solution to the riddle of the dream appeared to Freud in the bold image of the trimethylamin chemical formula. Five years later, Freud would describe this Irma dream as the singular event which had presented him with "the secret" to dreams (Masson, 1985, p. 417), and both Erikson (1954) and Lacan (1954–1955) credited Freud for associating the birth of psychoanalysis with the mystery of the trimethylamin formula.

Freud's initial attempt to penetrate the meaning of his Irma dream can be found in the opening chapter of his unfinished "Project for a scientific psychology," which Freud sent to Fliess in manuscript at the end of September of 1895, two months after the Irma dream. Then, a month later, there was a new insight and a new theory. On October 15 of 1895, while in the midst of feverish work, Freud wrote Fliess announcing a breakthrough, the discovery of a "great clinical secret." One day later, on October 16, invoking words strikingly similar to the words of his Irma dream, Freud wrote Fliess to say that he had secured the "formulas" (*Formeln*) and the "solution" (*Lösung*) to the "riddles" (*Rätsels*) of hysteria and obsessional neurosis. Freud was now "certain that both neuroses were, in general, curable." He was not referring to individual symptoms per se but to the general disposition for neuroses. This left him, he went on to say, with a "kind of faint joy – for having lived some forty years not quite in vain . . . ." These words allow a better appreciation of the depth and intensity of the rescue fantasies at work to father psychoanalysis.

These new etiological formulas centered on the role of childhood "sexual shock" in determining hysteria. What was now in question was the ultimate cause of the abnormal excitability of the nervous system, something he had previously envisioned as a somatic phenomenon and, as such, unresponsive to psychotherapy.

Freud's new ideas all connected to his treatment of Emma Eckstein. In October of 1895 Freud traced her fears of entering shops alone to an event at the age of 12 and, from there, back further still to an incident at the age of eight. As Freud (1895) explained:

> On two occasions she had gone into a small shop to buy some *sweets*, and the shopkeeper had grabbed at her genitals through her clothes. In spite of the first experience she had gone there a second time; after the second time she

stopped away. She now reproached herself for having gone there the second time, *as though she had wanted in that way to provoke the assault*. In fact a state of 'oppressive bad conscience' is to be traced back to this experience.

(pp. 353–354; emphasis added).

Emma's memory of the first of these two events, Freud reconstructed, had been reawakened after she had entered a shop alone shortly after the onset of puberty. Doing so triggered a "sexual release" for Emma which then "transformed into anxiety." Emma responded by running away from the shop. Freud explained her behavior and subsequent feelings of anxiety by postulating that they had issued from Emma's sexual maturation. Freud also argued that in hysteria "We invariably find that a memory is repressed which has only become a trauma by deferred action" (p. 356) – the German text reads: *"die nur nachträglich zum Trauma geworden ist,"* more properly rendered by "which becomes a trauma only after the event."

As noted in Chapter 1, the prevailing idea in the field of psychiatry at that time was that sexual seduction and the abuse which children experienced before puberty had little or no impact on their psyche. Although Freud was obviously caught up within this system of thinking, he adroitly bypassed this intellectual obstacle with a hypothesis that the apparently vanished memory instead had acquired a new strength as a result of her coming into puberty and a new meaning after the second event. Early traumatic memories did not vanish but were re-arranged in accordance with fresh circumstances. They underwent a "re-transcription" or recategorization. More in general, and using a neoestamentary language, a "second coming" (*parousia*) was necessary for an early trauma to achieve representability. The Greek word *"parousia,"* which means "official visit," is used in Christian theology to refer to the second coming of Christ. Here it fits not only with Faimberg's (2007) understanding of *Nachträglichkeit*, but also with the idea that Freud viewed "Eckstein" as the "chief corner" of the psychoanalytic building.

Freud gained further new insight into Emma's sexual trauma by partially identifying with a second patient, a young man under his analytic care at the time, who often experienced "homicidal tendencies" (Masson, 1985, p. 148) and who played an equally important role in helping to pinpoint and resolve "the riddle," leading to a new theory of self-reproaches presented at the conference on hysteria held in Vienna on October of 1895. This young man's feelings of depression and guilt, Freud reported, were rooted in actual and "real guilt." Since the painful memory of his guilt was repressed, however, his feelings grew out of proportion, thereby affecting any new action which could substitute for actual guilt he had experienced.

The idea that early sexual experience played a role in every case of a "defense neurosis" was developed by Freud at the end of December 1895, in a draft manuscript described as "a Christmas fairy tale" (*Weihnachtsmärchen*). In it, Freud proposed that a passive, dreadful, and unpleasant sexual experience provided the condition for later hysteria, while an active sexual aggression performed with pleasure served as the foundation for an obsessive neurosis. In the manuscript, "*all*" (Freud's word and emphasis) cases of obsessional neurosis he had treated "at a very early age, years before the experience of pleasure, there had been *a purely passive* experience" (Freud, 1895b p. 223; see also Masson, 1985, p. 165). In cases of hysteria, "the primary experience of unpleasure is so great that the ego does not resist it and forms no psychic symptom." Its primary symptom was "the *manifestation of fright* accompanied by a *gap* in the psyche" (p. 169). Freud was likely thinking of Emma, the cornerstone of his building, here.

Freud first presented this theory of seduction to the public in 1896 in three separate articles. In the first he justified his replacement of nervous heredity (Charcot's preferred predisposing factor) by precocious sexual experience. It was in this context that he first coined the term "psychoanalysis" (Freud, 1896a, p. 151). In the second, Freud introduced the idea that the "specific" etiology of hysteria was bound to unconscious memories of sexual traumas which the patient had suffered during early childhood.

Freud observed that the objection to his idea was that "sexual assaults on small children happened too often for them to have any aetiological importance." Relying on shared wisdom, Freud (1896b) explained: "these sorts of experiences are bound to be without effect precisely because they happen to a person who is sexually undeveloped" (p. 164). This view, baffling and indefensible today, merely affirmed the wisdom of the period, which viewed the psyche of children as too undeveloped and weak to retain any memory of painful experiences. Eventually Freud would challenge this assumption and radically alter it by postulating the *indestructibility of unconscious memory traces*. It was a bold and decisive step in this direction in 1896, when Freud realized that premature sexual experiences during the early years of life were capable of being "reproduced through the work of psycho-analysis in spite of the intervening decades" (1896c, p. 203).

Not to be overlooked is that it would have felt "mad" to entertain thoughts and views at such odds with the shared wisdom. In fact Freud did have recurrent doubts and was never completely convinced that sexual abuse was in itself traumatic (Freud, 1896a, p. 154, 1896b, pp. 164, 166 footnote 2, 1898a, p. 281). Thus prevented from better access to the child's subjective experience, Freud was left a prisoner of a number of false theoretical dilemmas – the question of why the memory of a pleasurable experience would later be repressed, for instance.

Despite Freud's successful isolation of the essential premises for a new theory, one which could lead to social and medical progress, the deeper analytical understanding of the effects of sexual abuse on children was only truly achieved in the analytic field decades later, and it was Sándor Ferenczi, rather than Freud, who accomplished this momentous achievement. In his 1932 paper on the "Confusion of Tongues," Ferenczi would explain the impact of sexual abuse on children by highlighting the process of psychological splitting (of the self), often leading the victim to identify with the abuser and aggressor. Both notions were indeed present in Freud's early meditation, but then they were lost.

Identification with the aggressor

In the second article devoted to the etiology of the neuroses, Freud (1896b) based his position and theory on the mechanisms responsible for severe neuroses on 13 individual cases:

> [In all of these] the illness was of many years' duration, and a few came to me after lengthy and unsuccessful institutional treatment. The childhood traumas which analysis uncovered in these severe cases *had all to be classed* as *grave sexual injuries; some of them were positively revolting.* Foremost among those guilty of abuses like these, with their momentous consequences, are nursemaids, governesses and domestic servants, to whose care children are only too thoughtlessly entrusted; teachers, moreover, figure with regrettable frequency. In seven out of these thirteen cases, however, it turned out that *blameless children were the assailants; these were mostly brothers who for years on end had carried on sexual relations with sisters a little younger than themselves.* No doubt the course of events was in every instance similar to what it was possible to trace with certainty in a few individual cases: *the boy, that is to say, had been abused by someone of the female sex, so that his libido was prematurely aroused, and then, a few years later, he had committed an act of sexual aggression against his sister, in which he repeated precisely the same procedures to which he himself had been subjected.*
>
> (pp. 164–165; emphasis added)

This important passage anticipates the importance that the theme of brother-sister incest would occupy within Freud's self-analysis. Freud's description of the boy who had aggressively repeated upon a younger sister an act of sexual abuse which he himself had experienced strikes a deeply autobiographical note.[1] This description also suggests that the phenomenon of "identifying with the aggressor," which Ferenczi would come to later identify and describe, had played an important and central role within this meditation. Freud's conception and understanding of this phenomenon differed considerably from Ferenczi, however. Even though this concept was never discussed by Freud, central ideas related to it were informally incorporated into the theoretical system as the masculine reaction to feminization, finally reaching the status of a theoretical notion in Anna Freud's (1936) book. Ferenczi, on his part, emphasized the helplessness and vulnerability of victims of childhood sexual abuse. Ferenczi's views on this topic eventually came to shed new light on the harmful impact of sexual abuse on its victims, leading typically to a collapse and fragmentation of the self. Moreover, the weak and not yet fully developed personality of the child, Ferenczi would argue, reacts to the sudden unpleasure by producing an "*anxiety-ridden identification and by introjection of the menacing person or aggressor*" (Ferenczi, 1933, p. 163). One of the impacts of trauma, Ferenczi would explain was the installation within a dissociated part of the victim's self of the feelings and thoughts of the adult perpetrator.

Despite limitations, Freud's theoretical work was unquestionably a momentous achievement in the history of human thought. Freud's groundbreaking work carried him well beyond his contemporaries. Indeed, that "invisible bond" which so often can be seen between aggressor and victim, the phenomenon powerfully emphasized by Ferenczi, was initially recognized and described by Freud himself.

The invisible bond

On April 2, 1896, Freud wrote Fliess to say:

> As a young man I knew no longing other than for philosophical knowledge, and now I am about to fulfill it as I move from medicine to psychology. *I became a therapist against my will*; I am convinced that, given certain conditions in regard to the person and the case, I can definitively cure hysteria and obsessional neurosis.
>
> (emphasis added)

Freud entered private practice on April 25 of 1886, immediately after his pediatric training with Baginsky, when sexual abuse on little children was categorized as a merely physical event, a hyper-stimulation of the genital "nerves" which could result into a reflex neurosis. A decade later, on Tuesday April 21 of 1896, Freud took a momentous step forward with a new approach to symptoms unveiled in his lecture on the "aetiology of hysteria" at the *Verein für Psychiatrie und Neurologie* in Vienna.

Freud based his presentation on 18 cases and had finally freed himself from the constraints of the reflex theory of the neurosis. This he achieved by emphasizing the helplessness shown by children who had been sexually abused and aroused prematurely. In his lecture, Freud also took steps to highlight the brutality which adult perpetrators often manifested toward their victims. Here is Freud (1896c) at some length:

> People who have no hesitation in satisfying their sexual desires upon children cannot be expected to jib at finer shades in the methods of obtaining that satisfaction; and the sexual impotence which is inherent in children inevitably forces them into the same substitutive actions as those to which adults descend if they become impotent. All the singular conditions under which the ill-matched pair conduct their love-relations – on the one hand the adult, who cannot escape his share in the mutual dependence necessarily entailed by a sexual relationship, and who is yet armed with complete authority and the right to punish, and can exchange the one role for the other to the uninhibited satisfaction of his moods, and on the other hand the child, who in his helplessness is at the mercy of this arbitrary will, who is prematurely aroused to every kind of sensibility and exposed to every sort of disappointment, and whose performance of the sexual activities assigned to him is often interrupted by his imperfect control of his natural needs – all these grotesque and yet tragic incongruities reveal themselves as stamped upon the later development of the individual and of his neurosis, in countless permanent effects which deserve

to be traced in the greatest detail. Where the relation is between two children, the character of the sexual scenes is none the less of the same repulsive sort, since every such relationship between children postulates a previous seduction of one of them by an adult. The psychical consequences of these child-relations are quite extraordinarily far-reaching; the two individuals remain linked by an *invisible bond* throughout the whole of their lives.

(pp. 214–215; emphasis added)

In this well-known, often cited passage by Freud, the crucial psychical consequence of childhood seduction is seen as producing an "invisible bond" between the aggressor and the victim. This bond, Freud insisted, endured and persisted through time. As Freud was to later explain, it also fed and informed repetition, that is to say, the mechanism associated with the compulsion to repeat. The idea of a silent and secret bond between the abused and his or her abuser might well be seen as the zenith point of Freud's seduction theory.

They can go to hell!

As Freud informed Fliess on April 26, 1896, this lecture on the etiology of hysteria received an "icy reception." To quote Freud:

A lecture on the etiology of hysteria at the psychiatric society was given an icy reception by the asses and a strange evaluation by Krafft-Ebing: 'It sounds like a scientific fairy tale.' And this, after one has demonstrated to them the solution of a more-than-thousand-year-old problem, a *caput Nili*! They can go to hell, euphemistically expressed.

(Masson, 1985, p. 184)

Richard von Krafft-Ebing, the chair of the meeting, was the author of *Psychopathia Sexualis*, the most important clinical-forensic study of perversions in those years. This famed study was first published in 1886 and in the ensuing 23 years had 12 new editions. From its first edition, it had contained a chapter on "Immorality with person under the age of fourteen." Beginning with the 1896 edition Krafft-Ebing introduced a newly coined category, "paedophilia erotica," to designate a morbid disposition in which the subject is drawn to children not in consequence of "degenerated morality" or "physical impotence," but rather by a specific psychosexual perversion.[2] Thus, he certainly was the right person to chair the meeting, and yet the distance between his views and those of Freud was so great that the text of Freud's lecture was not even printed in the proceedings of the *Vienna Society for Psychiatry and Neurology* and his colleagues soon began shunning him. Referrals from other physicians began to dry up as well; as Freud wrote to Fliess on May 4 of 1896: "Word was given out to abandon me, for a void is [now] forming all around me." Later he wrote:

the silence which my communication met with, the void which formed itself about me, the hints that were conveyed to me, gradually made me realize that assertions on the part played by sexuality in the etiology of the neuroses cannot count upon meeting with the same kind of treatment as other communications. I understood that from now onwards I was one of those who had 'disturbed the sleep of the world,' as Hebbel says.

(Freud, 1914a, p. 21)[3]

The text written by Freud is lucid and elegant, a splendid text in which the psychological reaction of the victim is described with care, sensitivity, and precision. Why such a visceral rejection in the audience? With the focus on the emotional experience of the victims, Freud was making an appeal on their behalf instead of punishing, blaming, or stigmatizing them. *This was unprecedented.*

There are other reasons as well. It is always a challenge for clinicians to endure their own feelings of impotence, vulnerability, and even violation that the traumatic memories of patients unleash. Instead of slowing down the process and of sustaining the emotional turmoil required to help Emma work through her trauma, Freud *overreacted* with tremendous intellectual speed. There is a similar overreaction in the dream of Irma's injection: unpleasant and unbearable sensations are transformed into a sudden "revelation," which then yields to a novel doctrine and a new *belief system*. Under the pressure of what Freud would in time describe as his "wish to catch a Pater as the originator of neurosis," all of his patients were suddenly now victims of early sexual abuse. In October of 1895 the number of patients Freud cited in support of the theory amounted to only two or three. By February of 1896, however, it had increased to 13, and two months later to 18. In short, in his presentation, Freud claimed that sexual trauma in childhood was *the sole and specific cause* of hysteria. Freud thought of this finding as akin to discovering "a *caput Nili* in neuropathology" (Freud, 1896c, p. 203). Freud's conviction that this was the solution to "a more-than-thousand-year-old problem" was the trigger for Krafft-Ebing's disparaging comment.

Freud's claim also betrayed a utopian desire to rescue humanity. He never recognized this as a rescue fantasy, despite its fundamental role in the establishment of psychoanalysis. Freud's grandiose aspirations and high claims had a seductive effect on his early followers. As Emanuel Berman (2003) had perceptively noted, none of the early pioneers of psychoanalysis, except Ferenczi, ever came to realize that rescue fantasies may be important and indeed relevant to this profession. Freud's "seduction theory" was discarded as an "error" instead of being perceived, accepted, and worked with in an attempt to raise the unheard voice of the victim, thereby breaking a structural aspect of trauma: active erasure and silence.

Yet, the negative reception of Freud's presentation by his Viennese audience was all too predictable: any group of medical professionals at the time would have reacted similarly. Commenting on Freud's presentation in Vienna, Mary Marcel (2005, p. 42) observed that for Freud to have presented "his findings on the basis of the unprovable, the unfalsifiable, was to invite attack, even ruin."[4] Marcel's observation introduces yet another consideration, namely, the negative consequences of Freud's own overreaction. Freud appears to have forced some of his patients into admitting that they had been the victims of sexual abuse and to have done so with "the strongest compulsion."[5] Freud seems to have been so intent on substantiating his claims that it led him at times to pressure his patients into recalling events that had never occurred. This further justified the hostility of Freud's academic and medical peers.

Particularly significant, in this regard, was the criticism Leopold Löwenfeld voiced in his 1899 book *Sexualleben und Nervenleiden (Sexual life and nervous disturbances)*. According to Löwenfeld, Freud's patients were not only "subjected to suggestive influence coming from the person who analyzed them," but the very fantasies which surfaced during treatment were "denied recognition as memoires of a real event."[6]

Even worse, Felix Gattel, an early pupil who had traveled from America to study with Freud, decided to gather material on the sexual causes of neurasthenia and anxiety neurosis at the psychiatric clinic of the General Hospital in Vienna. Gattel (1898) carried out this research between May and October of 1897 in an effort to scientifically validate Freud's theories, and a year later published his findings in a monograph. The monograph was unfavorably received by a number of medical specialists. As Schröter and Hermanns (1992) observed, the highly critical review published by P. Karplus, an assistant to Richard von Krafft-Ebing, was "indicative of Freud's standing in Vienna's academic circles at the time" (p. 101). It also helped to support the claim that Freud had induced his patients into inventing stories, a criticism which, as Schröter and Hermanns noted,

> did not pass Freud by without leaving any traces. He too later came to see the majority of the seduction scenes described to him by his male and female patients as 'invented' – however, he ascribed the weight of 'psychical reality' to such fantasies.
>
> (pp. 102–103)

The seduction theory would be abandoned just 16 months following this presentation in Vienna. Stepping back from his earlier views, Freud now proposed that hysterics in treatment with him had all fantasized the scenes of seduction they had recounted to him in analysis.

The recovery and working through of traumatic experiences is nowadays recognized as a difficult task that requires patience and time. Freud instead behaved impulsively with patients, at times even planting traumatic memories in their minds which they had neither lived nor experienced.

Emma's bleedings

Another striking event marked the period of preparation for the April 1896 presentation on the etiology of hysteria. Freud was suddenly seized by a strange dread of dying, in the aftermath of the death of the Viennese sculptor Victor Tilgner just prior to the public unveiling of his masterpiece, the famous Mozart statue found today outside the Vienna Opera House.

The talented sculptor had been beset by a number of premonitions prior to the unveiling and on April 15 of 1896, decided to engrave a few bars from Mozart's *Don Giovanni* at the base of the monument, upon which his sculpture would stand. The bars selected were from the scene of the ghost of the Commendatore arriving to take revenge upon Don Giovanni, the guilty scoundrel who had seduced his daughter and then murdered him. Tilgner, however, had a heart attack and died that same day. Upon reading Tilgner's obituary in the newspaper, Freud suddenly experienced symptoms similar to those afflicting the sculptor as he was struck down, though he quickly realized that his fear of dying was likely related to an unconscious identification with Tilgner.[7]

The "Tilgner incident" is significant because Freud's hysteric symptom had struck him precisely as he prepared his lecture on "The aetiology of hysteria" in Vienna. Modeled as it was on a unique and passionate denunciation of the crime of seduction, Freud's powerful *j'accuse* suddenly turned against him, as though he himself was a perpetrator and abuser (or a victim of an abuse). The observation circles back to the central question at the very heart of the Irma dream, except that it was now being posed much more dramatically: Was Freud innocent or guilty? And of what?

In the same letter to Fliess of April 16, Freud not only mentioned the Tilgner incident but also presented his friend in Berlin with "a completely surprising explanation of Eckstein's hemorrhages." Freud was at that time helping Emma to analyze and explore her erotic feelings and troubling fantasies, and would expand on his explanation in a number of letters to Fliess.

Ten days later, on April 26, 1896, Freud wrote to Fliess:

> First of all, Eckstein. I shall be able to prove to you that you were right, that her episodes of bleeding were hysterical, were occasioned by longing [*Sensucht*], and probably occurred at the sexually relevant times [*Sexualterminen*] (the woman, out of resistance, has not yet supplied me with the dates).

A week later, on May 4, Freud wrote the following:

> As for Eckstein – I am taking notes on her history so that I can send it to you – so far I know only that she bled out of longing [*aus Sensucht geblutet hat*]. She has always been a bleeder, when cutting herself in similar circumstances [*Wenn sie sich schnitt und dergleichen*: when she cut herself and did similar things], as a child she suffered from severe nosebleeds; during the years when she was not yet menstruating, she had headaches which were interpreted to her as malingering and which in truth had been generated by suggestion; for this reason she joyously welcomed her severe menstrual bleeding as proof that her illness was genuine, a proof that was also recognized as such by others. She described a scene from the age of fifteen, in which she suddenly began to bleed from the nose when she had the wish to be treated by a certain young doctor who was present (and who also appeared in the dream). When she saw how affected I was by her first hemorrhage while she was in the hands of Rosanes, she

experienced this as the realization of an old wish to be loved in her illness, and in spite of the danger during the succeeding hours she felt happy as never before. Then, in the sanatorium, she became restless during the night because of an unconscious wish [*Sensuchtabsischt*] to entice me to go there; since I did not come during the night, she renewed the bleedings, as an unfailing means of re-arousing my affection. She bled spontaneously three times and each bleeding lasted for four days, which must have some significance. She still owes me details and specific dates.

This appears to be Freud's first description of the severity of Emma's traumatophilia. Since the very beginning Emma's transference to Freud featured an erotic component, as attested by frightening fantasy that her analyst "might boldly take the initiative and give her a kiss."[8] Yet, the clinical picture now brings to light a masochistic side of her longing. Freud's remark that Emma frequently cut herself during her early years anticipates the final scene of her analysis. Indeed, it even sheds light on the dynamics and nature of Emma's relapse in 1910, at the time of her second analysis with Freud, as well as on what Freud wrote in "Analysis terminable and interminable": "She fell in love with her surgeon, wallowed in masochistic phantasies about the fearful changes in her inside" (1937a, p. 222). Freud's words support the depth and seriousness of Emma's traumatophilia. The most striking feature of Freud's letter to Fliess of May 4, 1896, is his recounting that Emma suffered from *a past history of bleedings and self-mutilating behaviors* (Freud doesn't say what else Emma might have done, besides cutting, to make herself bleed. Did she prick herself with needles?). In his letter Freud, however, avoided the possible traumatic origins of Emma's self-injuring behavior, instead focusing only on the erotic transference and wish-fulfilling function of her hysterical reproductions.

The so-called "seduction theory" of 1896 is often referred to as a theory of "real trauma," but this is not completely correct, since it didn't include *punishments and threats* as pathogenic factors. Oddly enough, this is something which psychoanalytic scholars have failed to notice. Had Freud categorized punishments and threats as potentially traumatic, Emma Eckstein's childhood circumcision could have been recognized as a trauma which was repeated again and again, deeply marking her entire life.

The main paradox embedded in reconstructing the origins of psychoanalysis is that while Freud was deeply emotionally affected by the event of Emma's circumcision, he failed to categorize it intellectually as trauma. In that spring of 1896 Freud came very close to identifying the traumatic origins of Emma's bleedings, self-mutilating, and cutting behaviors. The next chapters will show the profound effect of Emma's trauma on Freud, unleashing powerful fantasies and a stream of religious images, fantasies, and thoughts around which his personal self-analysis would revolve. Tellingly, however, Freud would defend powerfully against admitting this knowledge and in this instance would be merely repeating the primary scene of the founding dream of psychoanalysis, namely, his recoiling from the sight of Irma's damaged mouth (vulva).

Freud did come close in May of 1896 to recognizing Emma's self-cutting behavior as something which lay at the heart and center of her treatment. If he had, he could have moved forward by recognizing and acknowledging the severity of Emma's traumatophilia. Freud's theoretical understanding of Emma's malaise took on a tortuous and neurotic flavour, however. He – who viewed himself as belonging to the "obsessional type" (McGuire, 1974, p. 82) – took active steps to consult medical records in order to check on the dates of Emma's bleedings, but was "unfortunately" unable to obtain her "significant dates," as they had not been "recorded at the sanatorium" (see Freud to Fliess on June 4, 1896).

Emma Eckstein's case history was also affected by Freud's attempts at numerical and calendar calculations, a practice influenced by Fliess's own numerical theories on the male and female cycles. Freud's frantic efforts to isolate special dates (*Terminen*) and to pinpoint critical periods, Schur (1972) argued, functioned as a sort of obsessive defense which kept Freud from being able to identify Fliess as the agent responsible for Emma nearly hemorrhaging to death because of mistakes during surgery. This only touches the surface of the question, however. Freud's calculations of "critical dates," to say nothing of his less than analytically sound approach to Emma's symptoms, are best interpreted as his attempt to defend against his own countertransference. Freud's behavior not only reveals an effort to distance himself from having become an object of Emma's desire but shows him blinding himself to having become a traumatizing object for her as well. This was something Freud was not prepared to face.

The compulsion to repeat

At the onset of her treatment Emma Eckstein's sensation that her analyst "might boldly take the initiative and give her a kiss" helped Freud to develop his theory of wish fulfillment. A more comprehensive picture emerged by April of 1896. At its center stood Emma's episodes of bleeding, now seen by Freud as an expression of hysteria, the product of Emma's longing. The deeper meaning at work in the German term Freud employed then, "*Sensucht*" (nostalgia), was lost in translation. It tapped into an entire network of sensations, feelings, and strivings which Freud would come to later clarify in a letter to Fliess on December 6, 1896. Freud asserted that bouts of hysteria were typically "aimed at another person – but mostly at the prehistoric, unforgettable other person [*Anderen*] who is never equaled by anyone later." The "unforgettable other" Freud had in mind was in most instances an abusive adult, typically a dominant male figure, even a perverse father. Hysteria was thus seen as an unconscious attempt to keep alive the invisible bond to a worshipped abuser.

Freud's formula was deeply committed to the idea that victims of sexual abuse felt an unconscious attraction toward their abusers. Freud imagined the attraction, although he did not use the exact term, as a *libidinal fixation to a traumatizing object*. Modern object-relations analysts, in a simplification they find useful, that refer today as a "bad object." Freud's own description of the attraction of the victim for "the prehistoric, unforgettable Other" seems much more compelling.

The notion of a "compulsion to repeat" surfaced for the first time in this context. Freud employed the term "*Repetitionszwang*," for instance, in a letter to Fliess on December 17, 1896.[9] In the December 6 letter, Freud had remarked: "It seems to me more and more that the essential point of hysteria is that it results from *perversion* on the part of the seducer, and *more and more* that heredity is seduction by the father" (Masson, 1985, p. 212). Freud's theory of seduction was now being transformed into a theory featuring a traumatic transmission of perversion from one generation to the next with different possible outcomes: it led the victim of abuse either to repeat the perverse act, or to repress the perverse impulse that sexual abuse implanted in its victims. The second of these two possible outcomes, Freud argued, led the victim of abuse to succumb to neurosis. Neurosis was thus the result of an attempt to resist against repeating (on a younger person) the very abuse that a person had once suffered. Freud surmised that the effort at repression, that is, holding back and not acting out the perverse fantasy, served to squelch the sexual life of the subject, and noted the following:

1st generation – perversion
2nd generation – hysteria, and consequent sterility (p. 212)

In this instance Freud was using Morel's scheme of progressive degeneration, a notorious version of the Christian conception of original sin, though he replaced the hereditary factor with "seduction by the father." Freud illustrated this in the following clinical vignette:

A woman patient reported during analysis that her brother had just told her that when he was 12 years old, his sexual activity consisted in kissing (licking) the feet of his sisters when they were undressing at night. In association, she recovered from her unconscious the memory of a scene in which (at the age of four) she watched her papa, in the throes of sexual excitement, licking the feet of a wet nurse. In this way she surmised that the son's sexual preferences stemmed from the father, and the latter also was the seducer of the former (Masson, 1985, p. 213).

The brother then presented himself to Freud in his office to "declare, with tears in his eyes, that he is not a scoundrel but is ill, with abnormal impulses and inhibition of will." Freud noted that the brother "abhors all perversity, whereas he suffers from compulsive impulses." Freud's conclusion was: "If he could be perverse, he would be healthy, like the father" (Masson, 1985, p. 213). Freud's words were loaded with implications and show how the typical way of looking at the world had now been turned upside down (the real degenerates are the "healthy ones"!). This also attests to Freud's high level of sympathy for, and silent alliance with, "neurotic" subjects. Freud's position would be shaken in the next few months, however, when his belief in his theory began to vacillate.

The material Freud presented in this vignette featured a female patient who had likely abandoned treatment soon after it began. The family picture which emerged and its complex plot (a hysterical female patient, her obsessive brother and, behind them, a father who Freud described as a pervert) was nevertheless exemplary of the cases which Freud handled during those years. This same complex plot, which is strikingly similar to the material discussed in contemporary models of intergenerational transmission of trauma, likely applied to Emma Eckstein as well, who was the only woman in analysis with Freud at the time.[10]

Some scholars consider the "theory of the perverse father," which was never made public by Freud, a new and distinct theory. While certainly representing a new phase in Freud's theorization, Freud was also unfolding a dimension already present in "The aetiology of hysteria." In the lecture Freud (1896c) had presented his new theory as involving the discovery of "a *caput Nili* in neuropathology," the solution to "a more-than-thousand-year-old problem." This utopian dimension contained the implicit thought that a child who was abused in one generation became in his turn a father who then abused his own children. It also featured an unformulated hope to break the compulsion to repeat which crossed generations.

These ideas surfaced for Freud in December of 1896. It was shortly thereafter, in January of 1897, that Emma produced the two scenes which marked the apex of this process, the first of demonic possession. Later, in his 1923 essay, "A Seventeenth-Century Demonological Neurosis," Freud would remark that "in our analyses we so seldom succeed in finding the Devil as a father-substitute" (Freud, 1923c, p. 23, footnote 1). Emma's analysis seems to have been the only instance in which Freud encountered this lively fantasy. He was so frightened by this expression of Emma's erotic transference that repetition compulsion would remain closely associated with demonic possession for him (Freud, 1920, p. 35). Significantly enough, Freud reacted by identifying himself with a medieval inquisitor.

The second scene was of female circumcision. The effect of these scenes on Freud will be taken up in the second part of this book. At the moment it is sufficient to note that they marked a turning point. Max Schur (1966), for his part, concluded that these two "scenes" which Emma presented during the final phase of treatment were the main factor which led to the collapse of Freud's seduction theory (p. 114). I agree, yet the reasons why are not clear. Apparently, the appearance in analysis of Emma's circumcision would gradually determine a new agenda for Freud, marked by his own plunging into the "archaic," the deep time.

Vacillations

Freud's decision to abandon the theory of seduction seems to have concerned his suspicions of his father as a sexual pervert. Likely, this idea stirred a dream on the night before Jacob's funeral on October 25, 1896, of a printed notice on which appeared the sentence "You are requested to close the eyes" (Freud, 1900, pp. 317–318; Masson, 1985, p. 202). Later, on February 11, 1897, he wrote Fliess: "Unfortunately, my own father was one of these perverts and is responsible for the hysteria of my brother [Alexander] (all of whose symptoms are identifications) and those of several younger sisters" (Masson, 1985, pp. 230–231). The view of Jacob as a sexual pervert would be dismissed by Freud seven months later.

As Freud eventually realized, *The Interpretation of Dreams* was in part written in a reaction to his father's death on October 23, 1896. Shortly thereafter, between December 1896 and January 1897, Freud dreamt serially about Rome, marking the start of his self-analysis. In Volume I, Emma's circumcision scene was proposed as the precise moment of intersection of her analysis with Freud's own (Volume I, p. 197). In particular Freud became aware that Emma's circumcision trauma had evoked his own memories of the orthodox circumcision ceremony of his brother Alexander, triggering a sexual fantasy of fellatio, since at that time it was still common practice for the *mohel* to suck the penis after circumcision. Freud's fantasy that his father Jacob was a "pervert" may have been bound to this situation.[11]

It is unclear when and why Emma's analysis with Freud came to an end, possibly in the spring of 1897, just prior to Easter, when Freud met with Fliess in Nuremberg for one of their congresses. After producing her two important scenes, Emma's capacity to remember would have been greatly increased, including perhaps more realistic memories of her circumcision and of the circumstances that motivated such a harsh treatment (her masturbation). There doesn't seem to have been enough time to also fully recover memories of the events that awakened her libido. Of course, Freud and Emma had become convinced that her father Albert had sexually seduced her as a child, but probably there were vacillations in this regard, and likely they considered that the one who awakened her libido could have been one of her brothers. In fact, many years later Freud (1925a) would explain that the seducers "turned out as a rule to have been older children" (pp. 34–35).

The question of why Emma's treatment was terminated is made even more difficult to address because of Freud's complaints during this period of being unable to bring a single analysis to a successful conclusion.[12] It seems that in the final phase of her long treatment Emma began to recover her traumatic memories but that she did not have the time for a "working through" process. Could she have felt so much relieved after having recovered the memories of her circumcision that she decided to prematurely terminate her analysis? Emma appeared to be fully recovered and the family considered the treatment a great success. Perhaps, Freud too was relieved to conclude this uneasy and stormy treatment.

The *coup de grâce* arrived at the Easter meeting when Fliess suggested a new interpretation of Emma's recurrent dreams of gigantic snakes. In Nuremberg, Fliess had suggested that the gigantic snakes stood for the masculine impulses which in a woman are usually repressed (Masson, 1985, p. 465). Freud was stunned by Fliess's unexpected reading and this new view about inborn bisexuality and repression (Volume I, pp. 177–179). Did Freud, until then, consider Emma's recurrent dream of the gigantic penis-snake a sign of the sexual abuse by her father? A concrete token of the "prehistoric, unforgettable Other"?

Freud's dissatisfaction transpires from a letter he penned soon after their Easter meeting. In it, Freud recounted to Fliess his first session with a new patient, a "lucky chance" which brought him "a fresh confirmation of paternal etiology." Since the young woman was hesitant to speak about the events which Freud felt were behind her symptoms, he adopted a more direct approach with her:

"Then let us speak plainly. In my analyses I find it's the closest relatives, fathers or brothers, who are the guilty men." "It has nothing to do with my brother." "So it was your father, then."

Then it came out that when she was between the ages of eight and twelve here allegedly otherwise admirable and high-principled father used regularly to take her into his bed and practice external ejaculation (making wet) with her. Even at the time she felt anxiety. A six-year-older sister to whom she talked about it later admitted that she had had the same experiences with her father. A cousin told her that at the age of fifteen she had had to resist the advances of her grandfather. Naturally she did not find it incredible when I told her that similar and worse things must have happened to her in infancy. In other respects hers is a quite ordinary hysteria with usual symptoms.

(Bonaparte, Freud, & Kris, 1954, pp. 195–196; see also Masson, 1985, p. 238)

Freud's account of his "lucky chance" with this patient is particularly disturbing insofar as it reveals his lack of empathy and concern for her. Freud's intervention with this patient reveals him as rather distant and removed from her, a woman whom he suspected had been sexually molested. Freud not only appears to have been annoyed with his patient for her reticence and guardedness but responded by being tactless, dismissive, and even brutal when addressing her by saying, "Well then, let us speak plainly. In my analyses the guilty people are close relatives, father or brother." Freud's bitterness here carries a ripple of the disappointment experienced when his long and demanding analysis of Emma failed to confirm that "the guilty one" was the father.

By now Freud was becoming painfully aware that his seduction theory was also an expression of his "wish to catch a Pater as the originator of neurosis," to quote his words to Fliess while commenting on a dream in May 1897, the "Hella" dream (Masson, 1985, p. 249). A few months later, in the famous recantation letter of September 21, 1897, Freud reasoned that the notion that "in all cases, the father, not excluding my own, had to be accused of being perverse" had indeed been a surprising, even absurd position to maintain. The alternative solution then devised was that "the sexual fantasy invariably seizes upon the theme of the parents" (Masson, 1985, pp. 264–265). It was two days after, on September 23, 1897, that Freud joined the B'nai B'rith Society in Vienna, which literally means "Sons of the Covenant." Apparently, Freud was greatly relieved, in the course of his self-analysis, that his sexual initiator had not been his Hebrew father but his Catholic nanny, as he wrote to Fliess on October 3, 1897.[13]

Freud's change in position, as we know, paved the way to finding that a son's hostility towards his father to be motivated by rivalry for possession of the mother. Suddenly shifting from a Hebrew to a Greek-Roman scenario, Freud announced this new theory on the "universal" application of the Oedipus legend only three weeks later, in his letter to Fliess of October 15, 1897.

Freud's vacillations and wavering would continue. After her treatment with Freud came to an end, Emma had begun to work as an analyst, and in her new role she herself extracted "the identical scenes with the father" with one of her own patients around December of 1897. Freud found Emma's report on her patient so credible that he then briefly circled back to embrace the very theory he had just abandoned. Freud reported to Fliess on December 12, 1897, his "confidence in paternal etiology" had "risen greatly" afresh as a result of Emma's report. A few days later Freud encountered material which offered even more evidence of "the intrinsic authenticity of infantile trauma," as he treated yet another of his female patients. Reporting to Fliess, Freud wrote on December 22, 1897, to say: "A new motto: 'What has been done to you, you poor child?'"

Notes

1 Freud's words seem to signal back to his own experiences with his childhood nanny, his claim that she had been his "initiator" and "teacher in sexual matters" (Freud to Fliess, letter of October 3–4, 1897). At the same time, the passage also seems to point to personal memories related to a sexually aggressive act which he himself had enacted against younger "sister" figures (Pauline and Anna).
2 Krafft-Ebing's introduction of the term "paedophilia erotica" in the 1896 edition should be explored further. Was he influenced by Freud's presentation? In later editions Krafft-Ebing (1900) added that this perversion was "by no means rare" (p. 557). In his view, "a strongly marked degenerative predisposition [could] always be found in these individuals" (p. 559). Krafft-Ebing came to the conclusion that "all these cases might be reduced to fetichism" (p. 559).
3 At the same time, Freud described his "etiology" as a "mistaken idea." It had collapsed, he claimed, under "the weight of its own improbability and contradiction" (1914a, p. 17). This is one of the many instances when, listening to Freud, one has the baffling feeling of dealing not with single person but rather two distinct persons with opposed views. And since the burden of mastering the contradiction was and is entirely on the shoulders of his audience, the latter tends in turn to be split.
4 As Marcel (2005) noted, Freud inexplicably felt "impelled to make his case public" at a time when his data remained "at a rather premature state": "At the minimum, those data can be not unreasonably viewed as insufficient to support the sweeping conclusions he draws from them at that early time" (pp. 71–72).
5 See Freud (1896c, p. 204). Glossing this point, Marcel (2005) noted that Freud had overlooked "the distress that such opening to the light of day would cause to [his patients]" (p. 82), indeed the "devastating emotional impact" which such revelations might have led these patients to experience (p. 83).
6 As Löwenfeld (1899, pp. 195–196) added: "I also have a direct experience to support this second conclusion. By chance, one of the patients on whom Freud used the analytic method came under my observation. The patient told me with certainty that the infantile sexual scene which analysis had apparently uncovered was pure fantasy and had never really happened to him" (as quoted in Borch-Jacobsen & Shamsadani, 2012, pp. 149–150).
7 See Anzieu (1986, p. 165) and Schur (1972, pp. 100–104). Since Tilgner died on April 15, the same date as Freud's brother Julius, Blum (1977, p. 773) suggested that his dread of dying may be understood as an anniversary reaction, just as Freud's *non vixit* dream.
8 See Volume I, pp. 80–82. The "kiss" episode was related by Freud in the *Studies on Hysteria* (Breuer & Freud, 1895, pp. 202–203). Appignanesi and Forrester (1992) keenly reconstruct that the patient featured by Freud was likely Emma Eckstein.
9 Freud employed the term "*Repetitionszwang*" in [the context of] the following sentence (December 17 of 1896): "The explanation of the 'clownism' phrase in Charcot's formula of [hysterical] attacks lies in the perversion of the seducers who, under a compulsion to repeat dating from their youth, obviously seek their satisfaction to the accompaniment of the craziest capers, somersaults, and grimaces. Hence the 'clownism' in boys' hysteria, the imitation of animals and circus scenes, which are to be understood

by the connection between nursery games and sexual scenes . . ." (Bonaparte, Freud, & Kris, 1954, p. 182; see also Masson, 1985, p. 218). The same association with children's games resurfaced as Freud later attempted to conceptualize the phenomenon of the "compulsion to repeat," a fact which attests to the continuity found at work between his earlier and later understanding of this concept. In his essay on the uncanny, for instance, Freud (1919b) proposed that the compulsion to repeat was "very clearly expressed in the impulses of small children" (p. 238). In *Beyond the Pleasure Principle* he again related it to "the impulse which leads children to play" (Freud, 1920, p. 23).

10 Freud's practice was "not yet lively at all" during this period (se Freud's letter to Fliess of October 9, 1896) as he had only three patients under regular analysis at the time, Emma and two long-term male patients (Mr. E. and a young man who suffered from homicidal tendencies). It should also be noted that since Emma's father had contracted syphilis and died from the disease in 1881, Freud must have entertained the possibility of a degenerative process in the family. Material found in Kurt Eissler's interview with Albert Hirst (Emma's nephew) suggests as much. As Lynn (1997) indicated: "Freud told Hirst that his maternal grandfather's syphilis was important as a cause of Hirst's [own] neurosis. He told him not to blame the grandfather or to be ashamed of him, but to see this illness as a tragic accident that could happen to anyone. Freud believed that all of this man's children (including Emma Eckstein, of course) had inherited neurotic traits as a result of this syphilis, even though he saw their mother as unaffected. Freud maintained that the grandchildren, including Albert Hirst, had then inherited neurotic traits, on the same basis, from their grandfather. Hirst found it remarkable that Freud did not express these ideas as possibilities or theories but put them very positively, much more positively than most of his other conclusions" (p. 82).

11 The possible impact of Alexander's *brith milah* on the 10-year-old Freud is extensively discussed in Volume I (especially pp. 202–205), identifying an uncanny "fellatio fantasy" which surfaced, for instance, in Freud's work on Leonardo. Could this ceremony have stirred up other deep-seated memories such as his "sexual initiation" at the hands of his Catholic nanny, as suggested by the conflation of *brith milah* and *three-amen* in the trimethylamin formula of his Irma dream?

12 On March 7, 1897, Freud writes to Fliess: "I have not yet finished a single case; am still struggling with the difficulties of treatment and of understanding . . . ." On April 28 Freud describes himself as "still in doubt about matters concerning fathers"; on May 16, after a patient "took off at a critical point, just before he was to bring me the last scenes," Freud says: "so I shall wait still longer for a treatment to be completed. It must be possible and must be done." Finally, on September 21, the first argument advanced in his famous recantation letter is the following: "The continual disappointment in my efforts to bring a single analysis to a real conclusion; the running away of people who for a period of time had been most gripped [by analysis]; the absence of the complete successes on which I had counted."

13 As noted by Risto Fried (2003): "It had been bad enough for Freud to learn that his father might have been involved in counterfeiting. But at least fitted in with traditional Jewish non-violent, money-related crime. Incest was incomparably harder to reconcile with the image of the Jewish father who comes home to his family every Friday evening with a loaf of bread carefully wrapped for the Sabbath" (p. 286).

3 Primal fantasies, biotrauma, and shock

> Dreams and neuroses seem to have preserved more mental antiquities than we could have imagined possible; so that psycho-analysis may claim a high place among the sciences which are concerned with the reconstruction of the earliest and most obscure periods of the beginnings of the human race.
>
> Sigmund Freud, *The Interpretation of Dreams*, 1900, pp. 548–549 (paragraph added in 1919)

This chapter considers why Freud shifted his focus from actual trauma to biology and heredity, and why Ferenczi, having shared with Freud a profound passion for the "archaic," shifted the focus back to actual trauma and shock.

Freud on Freud

Freud's decision to abandon his initial theory of hysteria and to adopt a drive based model of the human psyche remains one of the most debated and controversial topics in the history of psychoanalysis. It gave rise to powerful polarizations within the field and has been interpreted in dramatically different ways by members of the analytic community. Freud's various accounts of his shift and change on position with regards to trauma is, moreover, inconsistent and troubling for a number of reasons (Ahbel-Rappe, 2006; Roazen, 2002; Zepf & Zepf, 2011).

Freud first made his theoretical change public in 1906.[1] Freud (1914a) then described his change in position as involving the dramatic and sudden collapse of his belief that hysteria was a product of early sexual trauma and seduction. Apparently Freud had realized that the scenes of seduction his patients reported in analysis were mostly imaginary, in the context, he said, of "definitely ascertainable circumstances" (p. 17).

Rachel Blass and Bennett Simon (1994) analyzed Freud's abandonment of his seduction theory in detail and concluded that the "circumstances" which had supposedly enabled him to distinguish fantasy from reality had simply never existed. Freud, they argue, never managed to come up with a method which would distinguish between fact and fantasy, indeed, "even today we do not have such a reliable method" (p. 670). What Blass and Simon found instead was that Freud had traveled a "serpentine path" and did so "only with great difficulty over a period of close to

20 years" (p. 689). Freud experienced significant doubt about his decision to adopt a new theoretical paradigm. On numerous occasions he complained about the difficulty of producing a completely analyzed case in his practice, and this pressed him to retain in his new fantasy-based oedipal paradigm many of the central concepts that informed the earlier trauma-based theory.

Freud's most balanced account of his theoretical shift is found in a footnote that he added in 1924 to the second of the three papers of 1896. In that paper Freud noted that he had "attributed to the aetiological factor of seduction a significance and universality" it did not possess and, further, that "seduction" still managed to retain "a certain aetiological importance" for him. More importantly, Freud (1896b) added: "even to-day I think some of these psychological comments are to the point" (p. 168). As Roazen (2002) perceptively argued, however, Freud's subsequent accounts of his decision to abandon his seduction theory were "troubling in their inconsistencies" (p. 12). Roazen was particularly puzzled that Freud repeatedly reassessed the validity of what he had retracted, thus "taking away with one hand what the other hand had just given" away (p. 9). In his "Autobiographical Study," for instance, Freud (1925a) indicated that he felt "completely at a loss" to realize that the scenes of seduction his patients reported had in fact "never taken place" (p. 34). At the same time, he also claimed that the seducers "*turned out as a rule to have been older children*" (pp. 34–35; emphasis added), thereby suggesting that the "stories" told to him by patients were displacement products of an actual event. Finally, Freud belittled the potential traumatic significance of sexual seduction between siblings, as though disappointed that the "guilty one" was a brother rather than a "*pater*."

Freud's final account of the decision to discard his seduction theory thus signaled back to the disappointment he presumably experienced during the last phase of Emma's analysis in 1897. Glossing his final position, Freud (1933a) explained that during the period in which he had directed his interests towards discovering infantile sexual traumas he discovered that "almost all" of his female patients were lying to him (p. 120). A number of scholars have examined Freud's position and argument closely and found his claim highly problematic.[2]

Primal fantasies

Freud, however, also turned "hysterical lies" in a new kind of "truth."[3] As he wrote in his text on "On the history of the psycho-analytic movement" (1914a),

> If hysterical subjects trace back their symptoms to traumas that are fictitious, then the new fact which emerges is precisely that they create such scenes in phantasy, and this psychical reality requires to be taken into account alongside practical reality.
>
> (pp. 17–18)

According to Ferenczi (1929), it was this paradox which helped to guarantee the survival of psychoanalysis when Freud was forced to "wrestle with the temptation to pronounce all the material" that his patients shared with him as "untrustworthy"

(p. 110). By virtue of pronouncing the "deceptive unveracity of his patients" as worthy of further investigation, as a "psychic reality" which deserved being taken into account, Freud, said Ferenczi, managed to save psychoanalysis "from the imminent danger of being . . . lost in oblivion" (Ferenczi, 1929).

What ultimately saved psychoanalysis from bankruptcy was Freud's decision to explain the same phenomena and "scenes" which surfaced in analysis by assuming the existence of genetically programmed innate ideas in the human psyche. Freud thus became a rationalist in the manner of a Descartes, declaring that certain ideas and concepts (the idea of God, for instance) were acquired by humans independently of sense experience. As opposed to Descartes, however, Freud interpreted this inborn intuitional knowledge within a materialistic framework. After arguing that the sexual traumas his patients were telling him were "fantasies" and not grounded in memories of actual lived events, Freud concluded that they were the expression of inborn "primal fantasies." "It seems to me quite possible," Freud (1916–1917) insisted

> that all the things that are told to us to-day in analysis as phantasy – the seduction of children, the inflaming of sexual excitement by observing parental intercourse, the threat of castration (or rather castration itself) – were once real occurrences in the primaeval times of the human family.
>
> (p. 371)

According to Laplanche (1992), fantasies for Freud found their "full justification only in the existence of phylogenetic schemata, tantamount to categories which *a priori* inform every individual experience" (p. 430). Evolutionary biology and, in particular, the idea of phylogenetic schemata, presented the possibility of a "synthetic a priori" dimension of the human mind, a concept introduced by Kant but then developed along materialistic lines. Freud was deeply influenced by the claim that innate ideas could be biologically transmitted from one generation to another. This claim, which became increasingly popular among scientists during the 19th century, was proposed by Herbert Spencer in his *Principle of Psychology*, which first appeared in 1855, prior to Darwin publishing *On the Origins of Species* (1859). Spencer's work was committed to the adaptationism of Jean Baptist Lamarck, that is, that learned associations in the brain of one generation would be transmitted to subsequent generations.

Freud's assumption that "primal fantasies" could be ultimately traced back to an actual event in human history became an essential part of his system. It provided him with a sort of alternative space that kept his original interest in trauma alive following his bitter disappointment.

The human beast (Born perverse)

The sexual life of the child became a social problem and a medical concern around the middle of the 19th century. This underwent further specific development in the writings of *fin de siècle* sexologists, such as Havelock Ellis and Albert Moll. The main goal of these scientific investigators was the liberation of human sexuality from religious and social prejudices. As George Makari (2008) put it: "Sexologists were encouraged to study varieties of human sexual experience not as vices, sins, or crimes, but as an integral part of the natural world" (p. 93).

Toward this end, the sexologists proposed to the public that human sexuality could be understood as involving the transitory resurfacing of archaic factors and that "perverse" infantile behavior remained the rule rather than the exception in the human animal. These ideas were endorsed and taken further by Freud, who saw the unrepressed "polymorphously perverse" child as "a vestige of our primitive forebears" (p. 117). As Makari underscored in his perceptive interpretation of the creation of psychoanalysis:

> In 1914, when Freud wrote a preface to the third edition of the *Three Essays*, he baldy stated that human "disposition is ultimately the precipitated of earlier experience of the species." Carrying inside them the cumulative weight of evolution, a child was driven by archaic, perverse impulses.
>
> (p. 118)

In the final quarter of the 19th century evolutionism and degenerationism often intermingled and informed each other. Perversion and criminal behaviors were reinterpreted as an "atavism," that is to say, as the re-emergence of archaic factors which had supposedly been conquered during the course of phylogenetic evolution. Lombroso's (1876) popular theory of the "inborn criminal" was classic in this regard: man remained at the mercy of his accumulated genetic heritage, a biological force capable of pulling him back to earlier states which featured aggressive and violent behaviors. Lombroso interpreted such episodes and instances of regression as the reappearance of an ancestral animal violence which led humans to behave in criminal and anti-social ways.

Traces of this archaic and pre-human past, Lombroso noted, could be seen in the behaviors of children, savages, and insane individuals, who were "born criminal." Freud simply extended Lombroso's formula to the normal child, with the claim that children were "born perverse." This was not devaluing but, on the contrary, full of admiration and envy, because the child was being perceived as free from both the burdens of civilization and the constraints of morality. Prior to their socialization, children were seen as still endowed by undiminished orgiastic vitality. Successful socialization would require them to abandon their unlimited desire and to renounce their animal instinctual life. Moreover, by proposing that perversion was an "original and universal disposition of the human sexual instinct" itself, Freud (1905, p. 231; also p. 165 and p. 191) managed to challenge the traditional religious and moral views held of humans; this further blurred the differences between "pure" and "impure" which still persisted in psychiatric discourse at the time, particularly through the idea of "degeneration."

Freud's position was connected to a larger ideological context that viewed childhood as a stage of transition between primitivism and civilization. In fact, this was how children were seen at the time. Once theorized within the framework of new evolutionistic theories and Ernst Haeckel's (1866) biogenetic law, including the idea that "ontogeny is the short and rapid recapitulation of phylogeny," however, the child was perceived as a living remnant of the descent of man. By offering scientists a direct path into the deepest regions of man's evolution, children thus became the object of systematic observation in an effort to trace and better define the stages figuring in the transition from an instinctual and animalistic phase of life towards civilized human behavior and the building of culture.

Describing the mind of the child as a continuum from animal instincts up to the capacity for acquiring moral values was the central task of such works as Wilhem Preyer's *Die Seele des Kindes* (*The soul of the child*, published in 1882), and George John Romanes's *Mental Evolution in Man* (1888). The first of these signaled the advent of the scientific psychological study of children. The second became a milestone in the field of comparative psychology by suggesting that the similarities in the emotional life of children and non-human animals presented proof of the genetic continuity between beasts and man. The idea that animals displayed "the same phenomena" as humans during the "early stages" of childhood (Baldwin, 1899, p. 35) became the point of departure of James Mark Baldwin's *The Story of the Mind*. In it, the talented American developmental psychologist suggested that child psychology was a field "more valuable than the study of the mind of animals. The latter never become men," he argued, "while children do" (p. 68).

When and how this transition occurred remained a crucial problem which Freud attempted to address in his work. Such questioning issued from the eclipse of the idea of a supernatural soul and involved an attempt to explain the transition from animal to human behavior and civilization. If God failed to exist, whence did the idea of God and morality spring? The God-idea in medieval philosophy and the ideals of Beauty, Goodness, and Truth were seen as constitutive elements of the supernatural soul. On the other hand, Freud saw them as sublimations and reactive formations, with shame and morality acting as a barrier against the undiminished orgiastic potentiality of the untamed child, which in turn manifested itself in a natural inclination for incest and all sorts of perversions. According to Freud "Mother Nature" was unable to successfully transmit to humans an innate abhorrence against incest, the considered hallmark of bestiality. On the contrary, the barrier against incest was a fragile construction achieved only slowly during the course of humanization, which each generation was required to renew. This was one of the meanings Freud gave to the "Oedipus complex": an "innate program" bound to pass away, nearly automatically, as Freud (1924a) would explain in "The dissolution of the Oedipus Complex" (p. 174).

The trigger Freud isolated was the "more or less plain" "more or less brutal" threat of castration, which was voiced, and sometimes actually carried out, as a punishment against masturbation. This typically led to the "destruction" of the boy's phallic aspirations and the introjection of the figure and authority of the father which then took hold in the child's psyche as the father's "prohibition against incest" (pp. 174–177). The innate dimension of this program, Freud argued, was amply attested to by the recurrence of certain themes in mythology – in the myth of Kronos who "emasculated his father Uranus, and was afterwards himself emasculated in revenge by his son Zeus" (Freud, 1926b, p. 211).

The same fertile imagination which produced myths could also be found at work in the mental life of children. Therein one could "detect the same archaic factors which were once dominant generally in the primeval days of human civilization." In his mental development, Freud (1926b) noted, the child "would be repeating the history of his race in an abbreviated form, just as embryology long since recognized was the case with somatic development" (p. 212). Stephen Jay Gould (1977) correctly considered Freud "a devout recapitulationist" (p. 156). Now the point is that "instincts," in the recapitulation perspective, functioned as the "unconscious remembrance of things learned so strongly, impressed so indelibly into memory that the germ cells themselves are affected and pass the trait [on] to future generations" (p. 96). In other words, in the recapitulation perspective embraced by Freud, *it was impossible to distinguish the compulsion to repeat, a passively endured trauma, from a positive drive or "instinct."*

The compulsion to repeat

Freud encountered the clinical phenomenon of the compulsion to repeat (*Wiederholungszwang*) in a particularly violent form in his patient Emma. As noted, the idea and concept of repetition had surfaced briefly in December 1896 (*Repetitionszwang*) only to disappear from Freud's vocabulary for an extended period of time. Freud returned to the concept in his essay, "Remembering, repeating and working-through" (1914c), describing it as a force to establish a "transference neurosis" for clinicians: to use to cure neurotics in therapy (p. 154). Freud (1912a) now envisioned the work of analytic therapy as a battle "between the doctor and the patient, between intellect and instinctual life, between understanding and seeking to act" (p. 108).

But he became increasingly pessimistic about mastering the compulsion to repeat (see Falzeder, 1994). When he again broached the topic six years later in *Beyond the Pleasure Principle* (1920), he presented it as "a universal attribute of instincts and perhaps of organic life in general" (p. 36), a fact which was now to be explained along recapitulationist lines. The "germ of a living animal," Freud suggested when introducing the idea of a death instinct, is thus "obliged in the course of its development to recapitulate (even if only in a transient and abbreviated fashion) the structures of all the forms from which it is sprung" (p. 37).

It is important to note that Freud's recapitulationist arguments lent credence to his position from the beginning. In a letter to Fliess on December 6, 1896, after concluding that hysteria was "repudiated perversion," Freud introduced the following: "Furthermore, *behind this lies the idea of abandoned erotogenic zones* [abandoned during the course of animal evolution]." The idea of a *biologically* based compulsion to repeat, explored in *Beyond the Pleasure Principle*, had been at work in Freud's theoretical system since 1896–97. It was active in the form of a second line of thought which took command as soon as Freud's "theory of the perverse father" was no longer retained to explain "perversion" (or its "negative," hysteria). The image of the little skull which appeared in the dream Freud experienced between October 3 and 4 of 1897 offers evidence of this new line of thinking. Freud associated the skull in his dream to Goethe's vertebral theory of the skull, an essential step in the theory of animal evolution.[1] A few weeks later, on November 14 of 1897, he wrote Fliess to say:

> I have often had a suspicion that something organic plays a part in repression; I was able once before to tell you that it was a question of the abandonment of former sexual zones . . . . In animals these sexual zones continue in force in both respects; if this persists in human beings too, perversion results.
>
> (p. 279)

Sulloway (1979) has suggested it was Fliess who influenced Freud's biological shift and reorganization of his clinical material, particularly emphasizing the influence of Fliess's idea of universal bisexuality as the primal motive force of repression (see Volume I, pp. 178–180, 219–220). Here the essential point is that the clinical element inspiring Fliess to develop his theory was tied to an important symbolic expression of Emma Eckstein's genital trauma, namely, her recurrent dreams of "gigantic snakes."

It is not known whether Emma's clitoris had been destroyed at the time of her "circumcision." Yet Fliess's reading of Emma's dreams and his new theory must have led Freud to be curious about the origin and significance of the clitoris, for it was not long before he formulated his extinction theory of the "male genital zone" in girls (Masson, 1985, p. 280). Freud, in other words, theorized the clitoris as a "vestige" of a phylogenetic past (an abandoned sexual zone), and the related psychic function (the masculine fantasy of having a penis) as a throwback or an "atavism." Later he would formulate the theory that a girl has to give up her clitoris-based eroticism, with its fantasy of having a penis, to become a woman (Freud, 1905, pp. 220–221).

The clitoris has always represented a riddle. An association of an abnormally large clitoris to a penis could be found as early as the first and second centuries AD in the gynecological treatise of the Greek physician Soranus of Ephesus. Soranus proposed to cure the deformity by cutting the tip of the clitoris with a scalpel, which would be later embraced and reiterated by numerous writers. During the 16th and 17th centuries, missionaries and explorers reported the existence of abnormally large labia minora and of a long clitoris in African women. A view then emerged that the disgust elicited by these deformities was why the cutting of the labia and clitoris spread so rapidly and widely in Africa (Johnsdotter, 2012; Knight, 2001). Measuring the size of the clitoris became an integral part of anthropology during the 19th century. Researchers, for instance, decided to measure the length of the clitoris in prostitutes. Other investigations were also undertaken to highlight racial differences. The idea spread that in northern and cold countries, the clitoris remained small; in southern and warmer countries women developed a larger clitoris. A review of the various studies undertaken to investigate this topic can be found in the 1897 edition of *Das Weib in der Natur- und*

Völkerkunde (*Woman: An Historical Gynaecological Compendium*) by Heinrich Ploss and Max Bartel. The long chapter on the external sexual organs of the woman (pp. 137–202) also contains a section on "The inborn enlargement of the clitoris" (pp. 173–174). Even though the authors remarked upon great variations in clitoral size even among European women, the general idea was that a large clitoris was a sign of *primitivism*. Even today, some surgeons regard the clitoris as an unnecessary organ; an inclination toward removing it or reducing its size may even persist in contemporary society in service of maintaining gender division. The clitoris represents indeed not only a riddle but a challenge to a clear separation of the genders (see Fausto-Sterling, 2000).

A further idea circulating at the end of the 19th century was that nature was trying to abolish the clitoris as civilization advanced. The idea is found, for example, in Robert Morris (1892) article, "Is evolution trying to do away with the clitoris?" Freud may have embraced this idea, which would resurface in Helene Deutsch's evolutionary-adaptational theory of female sexuality. A psychoanalyst quite close to Freud, Deutsch developed Freud's view of the clitoris into an overtly teleological theory: the resignation of the clitoris in favor of the vagina and reproduction is proposed as part of a biological plan which is provisionally resisted by the preservation of the clitoris' excitability during the latency period (Deutsch, 1944–1945, II, p. 80). This "useless" organ neither releases the active-aggressive drives of a real penis nor facilitates the turn toward passivity. The girl's lack of both a purely active (real penis) and a purely passive organ (vagina), she reasoned, constitutes her "genital trauma" (see also Wimpfheimer & Schafer, 1977).

The essential ambiguity of the clitoris played a crucial role in Freud's theories as well, as he theorized the psychological consequences of this ambiguity. Starting with the assumption that girls were born with the feeling of having a penis, Freud concluded that only when a girl compared her tiny clitoris with an actual penis did she perceive herself as inferior and lacking. She then had to console herself with the idea that her clitoris would in time grow to become as "gigantic" as a boy's penis. Even when she appeared to give up her hope, said Freud, she would still fantasize that "at some earlier date she had possessed an equally large organ and had then lost it by castration" (Freud, 1924a, p. 178).

The essential point here is that Freud began to elaborate this theory while under the impact of Emma's dreams of gigantic snakes and Fliess's interpretation of it. The solution he fashioned to answer the great riddle of sex was a biologically based theory erasing the concrete historical dimension of Emma's trauma on the one hand and, on the other, dramatized it as a universal biotrauma. Women were not castrated by men but by "Nature," an impersonal biological force which was progressively working to do away with all vestiges of the male organ, but burdened by traumatic fixations; this archaic relic (the woman's penis) was ready to resurface in female hysterics. Freud, fascinated by Emma's hallucinatory sensation of having a penis, interpreted this as "atavism" and failed to trace the matter back to the event of her genital mutilation.

Freud's stroke of genius was to understand that the fantasies of his severely traumatized patients were akin to basic elements of mythology and religion.

However, in turning away from the experience of actual trauma, Freud deprived himself of the opportunity to define a clear connection between trauma, shock, hallucinations, and religious fantasies. Since then a polarization between traumatic memories and inborn fantasies has plagued psychoanalysis. To overcome this polarization, the reality of traumatic events must be acknowledged, on the one side, and the reactions of our psyche according to innate and universal patterns must be recognized on the other.

Trauma: Shock or precipitating factor?

Fixation upon a shocking event, often reproduced in dreams or repeated in a dissociated mental state, was the most remarkable clinical feature when the notion of psychic trauma was introduced between 1883 and 1893. Extending this stoppage of time to normal (i.e. non-traumatic) hysteria, Freud in 1893 claimed, with Breuer, that hysterics suffered mainly from reminiscences. In Freud's etiologic theory of hysteria, early sexual shocks were assumed to be both predisposing causes and fixation points. When the concept of "constitution" returned to central consideration, trauma lost the characteristic of being a "shock" and was downgraded to the role of a precipitating factor. Freud then adopted a more traditional etiological schema, now based on a "complemental series" of endogenous and exogenous, predisposing and precipitating factors, which apparently allowed him to fashion the theory in a more balanced manner. In truth, Freud imported to psychoanalysis a *psychiatric* way of reasoning which nullified the notion of trauma as a breaking point.

Reviewing the theory and function of the precipitating factor (as trauma is codified within the complemental series approach), James *Strachey (1931)* concluded that a precipitating factor was an event which "fitted in some sense with the predisposing factors," making it "possible . . . to draw conclusions as to the nature of the personality affected by it" (p. 330). In other words, this psychiatric way of reasoning shifted the focus from the disruptive event to the "personality" of the victim, reintroducing the idea of the victim as an "abnormal" person. This is in sharp contrast with the feeling of a loss of innocence commonly found in those with a history of trauma or abuse.[5]

It was not only the traumatic moment to be now downplayed. In Freud's new perspective traumatic experiences were viewed as incapable of damaging the true or core self of the individual.[6] It was only the defensive superstructures that were affected, as this passage from *Three Essays on the Theory of Sexuality* (1905), the very essay introducing Freud's ideas on the inborn disposition to perversion:

> It is an instructive fact that under the influence of seduction children can become polymorphously perverse, and can be led into all possible kinds of sexual irregularities. This shows that an aptitude for them is innately present in their disposition. There is consequently little resistance towards carrying them out, since the mental dams against sexual excesses – shame, disgust and morality – have either not yet been constructed at all or are only in course of construction, according to the age of the child. In this respect children behave

> in the same kind of way as an average uncultivated woman in whom the same polymorphously perverse disposition persists. Under ordinary conditions she may remain normal sexually, but if she is led on by a clever seducer she will find every sort of perversion to her taste, and will retain them as part of her own sexual activities. Prostitutes exploit the same polymorphous, that is, infantile, disposition for the purposes of their profession; and, considering the immense number of women who are prostitutes or who must be supposed to have an aptitude for prostitution without becoming engaged in it, it becomes impossible not to recognize that this same disposition to perversions of every kind is a general and fundamental human characteristic.
>
> (Freud, 1905, p. 191)

This passage is cited in its entirety precisely because it neatly captures one of the most questionable aspects of his theoretical change, namely, his apparently "objective" conclusion that sexual abuse only served to bring about an inborn disposition to perversion, thus representing the denouement of a *natural state* otherwise screened by reactive formations. This questionable dimension of Freud's position on the "instructive" aspects involved in "seduction" is further underscored by Freud's hostile attack on women and their sexuality.

Freud's idea of the full action of biological sexual drives as only disclosed through trauma need not to be completely discarded. If applied to clinical practice, however, the logic of Freud's argument can lead to unwise conclusions about the victims of sexual and other kind of abuses. Tellingly enough, while attempting to remain faithful to Freud's teaching, Karl Abraham (1907a, 1907b) coined the notion of "traumatophilia" to explain a fixation towards trauma as a product of the child's own *perverse disposition*. In "On the history of the psychoanalytic movement," Freud (1914a) not only endorsed this view but explained that Abraham had "pointed out that the sexual constitution which is peculiar to children is precisely calculated to provoke sexual experiences of a particular kind – namely traumas" (pp. 17–18). And yet, as Michael Good (1995) indicated, Abraham's

> adultomorphic view of some children unconsciously seeking trauma would, by contemporary standards, not only be unfortunate medicolegally but also tragically harmful in social terms. (Compare the current issue of patient vulnerability to violations of treatment boundaries.) Abraham's traumatophilic hypothesis may be seen as implicitly blaming the victim and ignoring children's vulnerability.
>
> (p. 1140)

Freud seems to have indirectly discouraged the possibility of exploring the subject of traumatophilia further. After Abraham's two contributions, no efforts were undertaken psychoanalytically to investigate the phenomenon of child sexual abuse until 1929, when Ferenczi revived the theme through a series of articles (1929, 1931, 1933).

Ferenczi on trauma

Ferenczi was the only one among Freud's early followers to fully embrace Freud's speculations on the accumulated phylogenic inheritance that informs instinctual life. In *Thalassa* (1924) Ferenczi took active steps to further develop the recapitulationist position. In particular, Ferenczi envisioned the erect penis as the living remnant of a primordial catastrophe of cosmic proportions which behaved similarly to unresolved trauma in the case of the traumatic neurosis, that is, by compelling "a perpetual repetition of the painful situation," which is then uninterruptedly transmitted from one generation to the other (p. 66). A later chapter will detail Ferenczi's scientific fairy tale, becoming the starting point of a progressive deconstruction of Freud's phallocentric system from within. Thus Ferenczi did bring trauma back from the phylogenetic scenario to real life and rediscovered it as a shock.

Ferenczi embraced Freud's views and systematically focused on their yet unthought aspects. For instance, in his 1927 article, "The adaptation of the family to the child," Ferenczi reversed the usual perspective of "adaptation" to reflect upon the intergenerational implications of infantile amnesia. After his biological turn, Freud came to view infantile amnesia as an automatic (inherited) repression of sexual impulses necessary for the normal development of a civilized individual. Ferenczi, however, saw that children's inability to recall events experienced during their initial years served as the very cause of the adult's failure to understand their world; the "blindness which clouds our vision on nearly all matters connected with the sexual activity of children" (p. 71).

In "The principle of relaxation and neocatharsis" (1929) Ferenczi indicated that, after having given "due consideration to fantasy as a pathogenic factor," he became increasingly forced to acknowledge that pathogenic trauma was far more rarely the result of constitution than of "improper, unintelligent, capricious, tactless, or actually cruel treatment" (p. 121). Indeed, Ferenczi now began to see hysterical fantasies as the products of severe punishments and threats which remained "incomprehensible" to the child and, moreover, had "the shattering effect of a shock" (p. 121), that is, of a transitory psychosis.

Ferenczi's views during the last years of his life have often been interpreted as a return to Freud's "seduction theory." But, clearly, "punishments" (such as the one which Emma endured) were not a feature of Freud's seduction theory in 1896. Finally, in his 1931 article on "Child-analysis in the analysis of adults" Ferenczi introduced a new language to explain the effects of trauma upon the human psyche, replacing Freud's assumption that "castration" was the key trauma with a new metapsychology of the fragmentation of mental life.

According to Ferenczi, trauma derived from an experience of misrecognition of the true self by the other, leading as a consequence to the destruction, and really, the murder of the victim's psyche, for which terms such as splitting, fragmentation, and sequestration would apply. The most vulnerable part of the human psyche, he recognized, was the emotional component. The human psyche required a receptive, welcoming human environment to develop successfully. Without positive intersubjective interactions with fellow human beings, the psyche was simply unable to achieve integration.

The experience of trauma, Ferenczi noticed, only served to disconnect and sever links, producing psychical deadness, numbness, and insensitivity while destroying the subject's developmental capacity for interactions and emotions. Ferenczi also introduced the idea of a "traumatic progression" leading toward a form of super-intelligence which could operate while disconnected from the emotional life of a subject crushed by trauma. The split between intellect and affect was Ferenczi's hallmark of trauma. True "perversion" could not in his view be reduced to an "abnormal" sexual practice but should instead be understood as pure intellect stripped of emotions.

Ferenczi's reformulation of the gap in the psyche

Freud initially based his definition of psychic trauma on the subject's inability to react either with pain, hatred, or defenses to a distressing event. To preserve the internal organization of the psyche, the subject must successfully discharge the affects aroused by the distressing event. When this self-preserving psychic reaction failed to occur (Breuer & Freud, 1893, p. 11; Freud, 1893a, pp. 36–37), the result was traumatic: trauma defined in terms of the psychic reaction failed to take place.

By defining psychical trauma thus, Freud assumed that it was, in principle, possible to react to a distressing experience in another more "appropriate" way. This is difficult to articulate phenomenologically, so Freud instead developed an economic definition: a reaction is appropriate if it lowers the tension in the psychical apparatus preserving its dynamic stability (homoeostasis).

It soon occurred to Freud, however, that this same goal might be attained some other way, via hallucination for instance. A baby can, after all, temporarily cope with a distressful state of hunger by hallucinating the mother's breast (Freud, 1895, p. 319, 1900, p. 565, p. 1911, p. 219 footnote 4). More generally, Freud found that wish fulfillment could preserve the equilibrium of the psychic system (1900, p. 565), but failed to link this line of thought with his previous preoccupation with shock. A new perspective would later be disclosed when he introduced a distinction between two opposite ways of reacting to distressing events: one based on the pleasure principle, the other on the reality principle. In the first situation, the ego was able to cope with a distressful state by means of hallucination; in the second it was able to tolerate displeasure and to produce a real alteration of the real circumstances in the external world instead of turning away from reality (Freud, 1911).

Within this new perspective, the fundamental function of maternal care and interpersonal interactions in maintaining the equilibrium of the psychic organization of the child was for the first time understood. This was Ferenczi's important article, "Stages in the development of the sense of reality" (1913d). Ferenczi was concerned with organization, adaptation, and the process of internal structure, which would, in time, inform the object of ego-psychology. Ferenczi would increasingly emphasize the role of the caring adult in making displeasure tolerable for the child, in fostering the capacity to react to distressing events in a more realistic, less hallucinatory fashion.

Freud and Ferenczi began in 1916 to speak of autoplastic (modifying oneself instead of the outside world) and alloplastic adaptation (Ferenczi, 1924, pp. 91–92 footnote; Freud, 1924c, p. 185). In particular, Ferenczi suggested that only alloplastic reactions enable the ego to maintain its existing equilibrium or organization unchanged. He noted, however, that this required a highly developed sense of reality and a high capacity to tolerate displeasure. In contrast with this, psychic trauma essentially involved a failure to maintain the ego's equilibrium by changing the external world, hence an autoplastic rather than an alloplastic reaction (1930–1932, pp. 220–221, 1933, p. 163).

In his paper on the "confusion of tongues," Ferenczi (1933) proposed that the reason why his patients were "unable to react to unjust or unkind treatment with pain or with hatred and defence" was because the nucleus of their personality "got stuck in its development at a level where it was unable to use the *alloplastic* way of reaction but could only react in an *autoplastic* way by a kind of mimicry." Ferenczi thus concluded that such patients simply lacked "the ability to maintain" themselves stable "in face of unpleasure – in the same way as the immature find it unbearable to be left alone, without maternal care and without a considerable amount of tenderness" (p. 163).

According to Freud's structural theory of the 1920s, the ego experienced an external trauma as both abandonment and attack by the super-ego. Not only does a psychic trauma awaken the unbearable experience of being abandoned, argued Ferenczi, but also leads to the fragmentation of the ego in an attempt to maintain instances of tenderness in a hallucinatory fashion. In cases involving a hostile attack by an aggressor, this meant that the latter might disappear "as part of the external reality," becoming "intra- instead of extra-psychic" and being subject to primary process (p. 162). Ferenczi, in other words, managed to pick up on and to extend Freud's initial definition of psychic trauma in terms of psychic reactions and responses which had failed to occur and take hold, successfully describing these phenomenologically.

Ferenczi grounded his descriptions in the organization and structure of the ego, presenting clinical examples which described in detail how the traumatized individual directed reactions inward and transformed these into self-harming behaviors, which at times even led to the complete fragmentation and disintegration of the psyche. Ferenczi appealed to Freud's own theory of wish fulfillment to explain how it was that the person's psyche under attack was nevertheless still able to be preserved and protected during the process. Thus Ferenczi successfully bridged the gap between Freud's theoretical positions of before and after the summer of 1897.

Ferenczi on Freud

Ferenczi expressed his personal dissatisfaction with the direction in which the field of psychoanalysis had been developing. During the final years of his life, he attempted to reorganize it on the basis of a less defensive, more open attitude of analysts towards their patients. He was profoundly troubled that Freud abandoned his early views on trauma. Ferenczi's position on this issue was intimately connected with his own views on the history and development of psychoanalysis: a single problem stood at the heart of both – the emotional defense of the clinician before the traumatized patient.

Ferenczi's revision of Freud's psychoanalysis conceptualized the psychoanalytic situation as a relationship, an altogether different approach to regression, and a new understanding of a patient's compulsion to repeat. "Repetition compulsion in the traumatized," wrote Ferenczi in his *Clinical Diary*, involved a "renewed attempt" by the patient "at a *better solution*" (Dupont, 1985, p. 182), which only came to fruition if the work of therapy occurred within a receptive therapeutic environment.

The starting point of Ferenczi's revision of the compulsion to repeat can be found in his work with Otto Rank in 1924. Ferenczi and Rank thought of Freud's decision to abandon Breuer's cathartic method as merely the first step in a process which favored intellectualization and from which psychoanalysis had to necessarily recover. It could be able to accomplish this task if affects were once again placed at the center of the analytic process.

Ferenczi strongly advocated a return to the origins of psychoanalysis, something he saw as vitally important to the future of the entire field. In his reflections on the ultimate ground from which psychoanalysis had sprung, Ferenczi (1929) noted Breuer's remarkable contribution in having trusted Anna O – the founding patient of psychoanalysis – at a time when most doctors simply dismissed their patient's stories, reducing them to "the fantastic inventions of a mentally abnormal" individual (p. 109). Freud, while following Breuer at the time, did travel further than his friend and older colleague in considering the instinctual aspects of psychic life, a dimension the reality of which Freud was able to confirm with what his patients were saying in treatment.

In his *Clinical Diary* Ferenczi framed an interpretation of Freud's retreat from his patients. Ferenczi kept his views on the history of Freud's treatment approach private for years. Indeed, in 1932 he wrote his *Clinical Diary* as a memorandum on the evolution of his own theory and technique, and as a testimony of his conflicts and differences with Freud. This finally allowed Ferenczi to present his personal views on treatment and to elaborate on the faulty path he saw psychoanalysis to be traveling.

Ferenczi's *Clinical Diary* remained unpublished for more than half a century after his premature death in 1933. Its publication in 1985 finally allowed his vision and his voice, suppressed for years, to be heard by the psychoanalytic community. To Ferenczi's witness, Freud had originally "followed Breuer with enthusiasm and worked passionately, devotedly on the curing of neurotics," but was "first shaken and then disenchanted" when "the problem of countertransference opened [up] before him like an abyss." Ferenczi surmised that Freud, after this initial shock and disillusionment, simply turned away and emotionally abandoned his traumatized patient, allowing him safely to land in the materialism of natural science, adopting the position of a natural scientist. In Ferenczi's view, Freud remained committed and devoted to analysis "intellectually but not emotionally" (Dupont, 1985, p. 93).

As for the moment when "the problem of countertransference" had opened up to Freud "like an abyss," Ferenczi reflected:

> This may well correspond in Freud's case to the discovery that hysterics lie. Since making this discovery Freud no longer loves his patients. . . . Since this shock, this disillusionment, there is much less talk about trauma, the constitution now begins to play the principal role. Of course this involves a certain amount of fatalism. After the psychological wave, Freud has thus landed, first, in the materialism of the natural scientist again. He sees almost nothing in the subjective, except the superstructure of the physical; the physical itself is something much more real.
>
> (Dupont, 1985, p. 93)

Ferenczi's hypothesis challenges the still prevailing understanding of the origins of psychoanalysis. This official version has Freud's self-analysis as the axis on which he leaned to found a new science of the mind. The enduring canonical narration has conceived of Freud's self-analysis as evidence for supreme ego autonomy, which Freud had supposedly managed to achieve, the accomplishment that paved the way towards the momentous founding of psychoanalysis. Ferenczi for his part interpreted Freud's self-analysis as a retreat from relatedness, indeed as an event that involved a "narcissistic split of the self."[7]

Ferenczi's unique interpretation of this split in Freud – the split that determined the foundational, and consequently wrong, direction of psychoanalysis – remains a *novum*. Ferenczi's take on this issue secures an altogether new understanding of Emma's analysis, one which must now be brought into dialogue with the history of psychoanalysis and the thorny question of Freud's desire, a topic surfacing powerfully within our field during the past few decades. Ferenczi's interpretation of Freud's split thus allows the exploration of how Freud's self-analysis came to be affected and influenced by Emma's traumatophilia. The next section reviews a series of crucial moments of Freud's self-analysis in an effort to restore its intersubjective dimension, starting with one of the most famous symbols of the founding dream of psychoanalysis: the dirty needle.

Notes

1 As Freud noted at the time, in the new perspective it was "no longer a question of what sexual experiences a particular individual had had in his childhood, but rather of his reaction to those experiences – of whether he had reacted to them by 'repression' or not" (Freud, 1906, pp. 275–276).
2 The discrepancy between this passage and Freud's previous reports has been described as both "perplexing" (Kupfersmid, 1993, p. 277) and "bothersome" (Roazen, 2002, p. 11). Freud's statements regarding his female patients communicating to him that they were sexually seduced by their fathers has been closely examined by Schimek. Freud's initial conclusion, Schimek (1975, 1987) observed, was not directly based on his "patients' reports" but instead featured "a great deal of selective interpretation and reconstruction"

(1987, p. 938). Another reason for why Freud's assertion has been found bewildering, Good (1994) noted, is that no analyst has "apparently ever published a case in which a patient told of a parental seduction that turned out to be a verifiable fantasy" (p. 81).
3 On the paradoxical nature of the concept of "psychical reality," which like the hybrid idea of "imaginary memories" (Freud, 1906, p. 274) is the product of two competing lines of thought, see Rand and Torok (1995, pp. 35–60).
4 Masson (1985, p. 269). Goethe was not only a gifted poet but a talented scientist as well. In 1786 it was the famous botanical garden of the University of Padova that inspired him to theorize that all plants derived from a common type, or *Urpflanze*. A new field, "morphology," was born which was not limited to botany. Goethe took a second trip to Italy in the spring of 1790 and found the skull of a sheep at the Lido in Venice, which inspired him to develop his vertebral theory of the skull, an essential step in the theory of animal evolution. Freud identified powerfully with Goethe and, like Goethe he also mixed poetry and science while in his efforts to reveal and unearth patterns underlying laws of nature. His reference to the vertebral theory of the skull in his letter to Fliess of October 3–4 of 1897 clearly reveals Freud's interest in the archaic phylogenetic past, powerfully revived in his case during the summer of 1897. In particular, it signaled the direction of Freud's emerging interest in the biogenetic law which Haeckel proposed in his *General Morphology* (1866) and which combined Darwinism with Goethe's morphology.
5 As stressed by Grotstein (1997), the idea of "innocence" was "neglected as a developmental line in psychoanalytic theory, perhaps largely because of the traditional emphasis that psychoanalysts impute to the original sin motif associated with the instinctual drives" (p. 319). Grotstein also pointed out that the lost feeling of innocence is replaced by "cynical despair, followed often by militant martyrdom or perverseness" (p. 320).
6 Use is made here of a notion (true self) which was not in play at the time.
7 This is a notion Ferenczi introduced in 1931.

Part II
The abyss

4 The fatal needle

> I can push a pointed needle through a fold of the skin without the patient reacting against it.
>
> S. Freud, 1886, p. 28

Sticking needles

Freud, at times, pricked his hysteric patients with a needle to help him isolate and pinpoint the hysterogenic areas in their body, to better diagnose their illness and malaise. Apparently, he became familiar with this pricking procedure from Charcot, who viewed demonic possession as the first psychic theory of hysteria. As Freud noted in his essay on "Hysteria," the discovery of "anaesthetic and non-bleeding areas (*stigmata Diaboli*) was regarded as evidence of witchcraft" (1888, p. 45).

According to religious authorities during the Middle Ages, witches were women who had engaged in sexual intercourse with the devil. One of the methods of inquisitors to identify witches consisted in pricking them with needles to isolate the somatic zones in their bodies that were numb but, at times, hypersensitive as well. Charcot described such areas in the body as "hysterogenic zones."

Further developing this line of thought, in "The aetiology of hysteria" Freud (1896c) wrote: "If you touch a particular spot, you do something you did not intend: you awaken a memory which may start off a convulsive attack . . ." (p. 218). In an effort to explain the "abnormal, exaggerated, hysterical reaction to psychical stimuli" Freud introduced the notion that patients "establish 'false connections' between the most recent cause, which they are conscious of, and the effect, which depends on so many intermediate links" (p. 218; see also Breuer & Freud, 1895, pp. 67, 302–303).

Freud's idea of "transference" was an elaboration of this early notion. The "abnormal response" to a given stimulus, Freud thought, was ultimately coded by an unconscious memory which reached back into the patient's childhood, tapping into a traumatic experience the ego was unable to process and treated therefore as "*non arrivé.*" The split-off memory was nevertheless encoded still within the patient's psyche as a "foreign body," the material then typically finding expression through recurrent somatic sensations or hallucinations (Freud, 1894a, 1893a). The view of contemporary psychotraumatologists that "the body keeps the score" is already

74 *The abyss*

found in this early contribution by Freud, in his theory of the splitting of consciousness. Between 1894 and 1895, the term "splitting" disappeared from Freud's vocabulary, however, as the early theory was replaced by the new model of "repression." This chapter will bring back into the scene what was split off and erased from Freud's dynamic model of intrapsychic struggling, to remain encysted in his theoretical corpus as a veritable "foreign body."

The dirty needle

When Freud first examined Fräulein Elisabeth von R. in 1892 he proceeded to test the areas in her legs where pain reached its greatest intensity by making use of the technique which featured pricking her body with a needle. The prick was in her case "met with a certain amount of unconcern" (Breuer & Freud, 1895, pp. 135–136). Since Emma Eckstein complained about leg problems and suffered from ambulating symptoms similar to those which afflicted Fraülein Elisabeth, it may be assumed that Freud would have examined Emma's legs at the beginning of treatment by pricking the affected areas with a needle as well. How did Emma react to this? Did she respond coldly or with high affect? What is certain is that Emma's erotic transference took later the frightening appearance of a demonic possession and that, in this situation, Freud identified himself with a medieval inquisitor who pricks witches with needles.

During the early months of 1895, Freud revised his "foreign body" theory, feeling that the pathogenic material rather behaved like an "infiltrate" (Breuer & Freud, 1895, p. 290). It was only a few months later that the new metaphor surfaced for him through his dream of Irma's injection. In the Irma dream a numbed "piece of skin" on Irma's left shoulder had been "infiltrated" (p. 107), with Freud then feeling the infiltration "on his own body" (p. 113).

Analyzing this dream, Freud recalled that just the day before, he had run into the son of an elderly female patient whom he had regularly injected twice a day with morphine, and the son had complained that his mother was suffering from phlebitis. Freud then quickly tried to reassure himself that he had taken constant active measures to insure that the needle he used to inject his patient was always "clean" and, furthermore reminding himself that he had not caused "a single infiltration" (p. 118) during the two years he he had been treating her. Freud's high level of anxiety and worry was only relieved in his dream when Otto, the person who had supposedly injected Irma by using a *dirty needle*, was blamed by Freud as responsible for Irma's malaise.

The guilt dimension of Freud's dream surfaced indirectly through the many reproaches voiced throughout the dream. Particularly significant here was Freud's self-reproach for having hastened the death of his friend Ernst von Fleischl by prescribing cocaine. As Bernfeld (1953) noted, however, Freud denied that he advocated the use of a "harmful needle" in the administration of the drug. Despite his denial and attempt to defend himself, however, guilt broke through in the Irma dream in the summer of 1895 through the image of the dirty needle.[1] Instead of carefully analyzing and integrating the guilt in the dream, Freud instead responded with a grandiose phallic fantasy, envisioning the image of injecting women as a sign of sexual potency, intercourse being imagined as a possible "cure" (*Kur*) for abstinent widows (Freud, 1900, p. 116).

Despite Freud's defensive posture and denial, the fateful "needle" magically reappeared and broke through in January of 1897, in a scene which Emma presented him during the final phase of her analysis. This "needle scene" was described by Freud in a letter to Fliess on January 17, 1897, and soon followed by the "circumcision scene" which Freud reported a week later, on January 24. The two scenes were clearly related and interconnected; indeed they each seemed to point to an act of bodily violation and a compulsion to repeat a trauma which Emma had suffered as a child, and as such, they fill a gap in Freud's analysis of his Irma dream.

Freud's "Royal Road" to the unconscious, one psychoanalytic scholar has observed, turned out in the end to be a *via dolorosa* and a path through hell (Anspaugh, 1995, p. 438). In December of 1896 Freud associated the unconscious with the infernal regions, and soon he settled on a motto for a section on sexuality for a book in progress: "From heaven through the world to hell" (Masson, 1985, p. 220). Just shortly after, Emma presented Freud with a concrete, tangible instance of the motto with a hellish scene of the "diabolus." Here is a long passage from Freud's letter to Fliess on January 17, 1897:

> What would you say, by the way, if I told you that all of my brand-new prehistory of hysteria is already known and was published a hundred times over, though several centuries ago? Do you remember that I always said that the medieval theory of possession held by the ecclesiastical courts was identical with our theory of a foreign body and the splitting of consciousness? But why did the devil who took possession of the poor things invariably abuse them sexually and in a loathsome manner? Why are their confessions under torture so like the communications made by my patients in psychic treatment? Sometime soon I must delve into the literature on this subject. Incidentally, the cruelties make it possible to understand some symptoms of hysteria that until now have been obscure. The pins [*Stecknadeln*] which make their appearance in the oddest ways; the sewing needles [*Nähnadeln*] on account of which the poor things let their breasts be mutilated and which are not visible by X-ray, though they can no doubt be found in their seduction stories! Eckstein has a scene where the diabolus sticks needles [*Nadeln*] into her fingers and then places a candy on each drop of blood. As far as the blood is concerned, you are completely without blame! A counterpart to this: fear of needles [*Nadeln*] and pointed objects from the second psychic period. In regard to cruelty in general: fear of injuring someone with a knife or otherwise.
>
> Once more, the inquisitors prick with needles [*Nadeln*] to discover the devil's stigmata, and in a similar situation the victims [*Opfern*: the victims of a sacrifice] think of the same old cruel story in fictionalized form [*fällt in Dichtung ein*] (helped perhaps by disguises of the seducers). Thus, not only the victims but also the executioners recalled in this their earliest youth.

In this long passage, Freud referred to needles on five different occasions (*Stecknadeln*, *Nähnadeln* with *Nadeln* being repeated thrice). This instance of repetition can be interpreted as a direct consequence of the scene Emma had just presented him. In the passage cited, Freud suggests that cruel acts ("cruelties") made it possible for him "to understand" a number of "symptoms of hysteria" which had remained "obscure" to him until then. He then mentions the "pins" which "make their appearance in the oddest ways" in cases of breast mutilation, and to sewing needles, and needles which "are not visible by X-ray" but which nevertheless "can no doubt be found in the seduction stories" which hysterical women recount during analysis. Could this be a reference to Emma Eckstein in particular?

Freud had described Emma to Fliess as a "bleeder," as a woman who regularly and habitually cut herself during her early years. It is quite possible that she made herself bleed by pricking herself with needles and, further, that she experienced a recurring hallucinatory sensation of having needles lodged in her body as well. Was this sensation her "abnormal, exaggerated, hysterical reaction" to Freud having pricked her with a needle at beginning of treatment? Did Freud's diagnostic method reactivate bodily memories that were enacted, hallucinated, and finally dramatized in the scene which Emma reported to Freud in January of 1897?

The action of pricking a human finger with a needle brings together a host of scenes with sado-masochistic re-enactments of bodily violations that Emma suffered during childhood. The image of a needle is thus both a concrete signifier and a symbol of Emma's painful path, her *"via dolorosa."* Emma not only carried a surname, Eckstein, which matched the term that was used to present Christ as "chief cornerstone" of the Judeo/Christian building but, like Jesus, wore her own "crown of needles" as well.

In particular, Emma's needle scene evokes an act of punishment for masturbating (sticking needles into her *fingers*). Just as fingers are natural signifiers for masturbation, the image of a "needle" can be a signifier for Emma's circumcision/excision trauma. Freud appears to have grasped these connections at some level. Emma's needle scene triggered his thoughts related to the *"fear of injuring someone with a knife or otherwise"* (emphasis added). These thoughts in turn anticipated a second and more important scene that Emma presented to Freud during treatment. Freud reported this only a week later, in his letter to Fliess of January 24, 1897. This is the scene with the "cutting off of a piece" of Emma's "labium minor." Freud brought these two scenes together, suggesting to Fliess that he now understood "the harsh therapy of the witches' judges." This puzzling statement becomes understandable only in light of Emma's fantasy to have a penis and Freud's new idea that the broomstick of the flying witches was "the great Lord Penis". Apparently, the "harsh therapy" consisted in the excision of this source of magic—the clitoris.

The progressive unfolding of these two scenes confirms that the image of the "needle" had from the very beginning operated as a key signifier within Emma's analysis, organizing unconscious elements silently at work between her and Freud during treatment. Thus does the possible meaning of the "needle" that closes the dream of Irma's injection move beyond the phallic one preferred by Freud.

James Grotstein (1979, 2000) described dreams as dramatic constructions by an anonymous dreamer, employing both narrative and visualization to organize and rework the fragmented accretions of mental pain within a field shaped by inter-subjective forces. Seen from this angle, the "dirty needle" of Freud's Irma dream may function as a concrete symbol of Emma's masochistic enactments. Similarly the piece of skin in Irma's body which had been infiltrated and that Freud was able to feel in his own body offers a foundational paradigm that is, the unconscious incorporation of the patient's traumata by the analyst.

Freud seems to have been deeply shaken by Emma's needle scene in January of 1897, enough that he came close to recognizing needles as a signifier for the trau-matophilia embedded in Emma's erotic transference. Once again Freud became frightened, however, recoiling from this preconscious awareness, again repeating the central scene found in his Irma dream, distancing from the shocking image of Irma's mouth/vagina in the dream. Despite this, or even precisely because of it, the image of the "needle" arrived to haunt Freud in strange ways. In his inner world a needle became the signifier of aggressive fantasies toward women, which he then powerfully denied.

There is a further possible association of Emma's January 1897 scene with nee-dles to another detail of Freud's Irma dream, which was discussed in Volume I (pp. 130–131): the "pale and puffy" Irma as a representation of the dreamer's pregnant mother, so that Freud's anxiety was the same that broke through in the boyhood dream of his "dead mother."[2] At the age of nine and a half, when his mother Amalia was pregnant with Alexander, the only male child born to her after Julius's death, Freud dreamed that his beloved mother was carried by bird-beaked figures derived from an ancient Egyptian funerary relief (Freud, 1900, pp. 583–584). Anzieu (1986) considered the anxiety in that boyhood dream to be the result of a "sadistic representation of intercourse" (pp. 305, 584).

Thus the "dirty needle" of the founding dream of psychoanalysis pointed not only to a hallucinatory revival of the past in the here-and-now transference of the patient, but also to "the problem of countertransference" that had opened up to Freud "like an abyss" – too heavy a burden for Freud's "infiltrated" shoulders.

Paralysis

Freud (1900) came to associate the "dirty needle" which featured in his Irma dream to the injection of morphine that he gave his elderly patient twice a day. Therese Frankel was a 90-year-old lady who lived in an upper-floor apartment in Vienna and played an important role in Freud's fantasy life. Twice a day Freud traveled to her flat where he would wait to be let in to treat her with an injection.

On one occasion, as Freud walked up the building's stairs past her floor, he experienced an ambitious daydream of climbing "ever higher and higher" (Freud, 1901, p. 165). On another occasion, Freud found himself irritated by past reproaches for his always "going too far" in his speculations and writings (Freud, 1901, p. 165). The humiliation of having to travel to his patient's apart-ment and of being made to wait to see her, the reproaches which he at times received from his patient's household help, combined with his desire to "climb" ever higher, served to transform the staircase to his elderly into a stage where his frustrated ambition was played out. Instead of being revered as "Herr Professor" – he had by now abandoned any prospects of an academic career – he instead twice a day had to climb up a set of stairs to inject an elderly patient. Even worse, her hostile servants often made him sit in a waiting room before being allowed in to treat her.

On yet another occasion Freud dreamed that he was traveling up a flight of stairs "with very few clothes on, and taking three steps at a time, as if flying, to rush up the stairs. All of a sudden he noticed a woman, a "maidservant," coming after him, and suddenly felt both "excited" and "ashamed," indeed "paralyzed" and "glued to the spot" all at once. These feelings, he reported, were not anxiety but instead "erotic excitement." This exhibitionistic dream was first mentioned in a letter to Fliess on May 31, 1897, together with his Hella dream, and later reported in slightly different form, in his dream book (1900, p. 238).

Freud viewed going up a stair in dreams as a symbol of copulation (Freud, 1900, pp. 354, 355 footnote). Indeed, and as Risto Fried (2003) noted when commenting on Freud's dream of rushing up the stairs, if a house "represents the woman's body, and the staircase her vagina, then the entire body of the dreamer becomes a phallus" (p. 481). This dream of Freud's was thus an important expression of his identification with the phallus, indeed of a regressive fantasy to return to his mother's womb.

In Freud's dream, traveling up the stairs three at a time gave a feeling of elation, underpinning a "mood of powerful and even exaggerated self-assertiveness." Freud analyzed this feeling at length in his dream of the "Open air closet" (Freud, 1900, p. 470), washing away the excrement from a toilet with his super-powerful urinary stream while feeling no shame or disgust for doing so. Feelings of disgust, he said, were washed away by the thought of how much his patients respected and honored him: "the stream of urine which washed everything clean was an unmistakable sign of greatness. . . . I was the superman [*Übermensch*]" (p. 469).

This same feeling appears to be at the heart of Freud's grandiose fantasy of unimpaired health and sexual potency, dramatized by the exhibitionistic dream of rushing up the stairs. In dreams, and not only in dreams, a shameful mortification may be easily transformed into an act of exhibitionism, elation, and megalomania.[3]

The staircase of Freud's exhibitionistic dream was the same one he had to climb whenever he visited his elderly patient to inject her. Just the day before the staircase dream, however, Freud was reproached by his patient's concierge for spitting on the staircase as he made his way up to treat the old lady. His patient's maidservant, it turns out, was also angry with him for neglecting to properly wipe his shoes and for tracking mud inside onto the red carpet of the apartment.

The spitting (urination) and mud (defecation) brought the feeling of hostility and degradation into Freud's representation of the sexual act traveling up the stairs to "inject" his patient. This same feeling of degradation may also be found in Freud's representation of the female love object as nasty and old: women are seen as stern, unattractive, and disapproving, just like the nurse from his childhood days in Freiberg who made him feel clumsy and ashamed.

When Freud dreamt of stern, disapproving, and nasty women, he saw them as reincarnations of his prehistoric nanny. In his lively imagination, the elderly patient and her female servants were simply new versions of his "two mothers": the superior and unapproachable mother and the carnal and debased mother substitute. Fried (2003) ventured that the paralysis Freud experienced as he climbed up the stairs in his dream reflected a need to thwart his frightening sexual desire, including the "sexualized murder of his mother" (p. 487).

Freud's way to the Oedipus myth

This same pattern would play an important role in the development of a universal application of the Oedipus myth, which suddenly became meaningful and significant in torturous circumstances, as Freud described in *The Psychopathology of Everyday Life*. Freud's medical duties for his elderly patient were not limited to regular injections with morphine; he also applied lotion to her eye (1901, p. 178). Between October 4 and October 15 of 1897, he confused these two routines, and instead of eye lotion, mistakenly placed a few drops of morphine into his patient's eye.[1] Freud grew "greatly frightened" by his mistake but calmed himself by convincing himself that "of the two possible errors" he "had chosen by far the more harmless one." His sudden feelings of fear, he then concluded, must have derived "from another source."

Analyzing his mistake, Freud understood that he was under the influence of the dream of one of his male patients from the previous evening. The content of this patient's dream "could only point to sexual intercourse with his own mother," and this, in turn, led Freud to the Oedipus legend. It was precisely at that point that Freud committed the error when visiting his elderly patient. Exploring the double meaning of the German word "*vergreifen*" (which means not only "to make a blunder" but "to commit an assault") Freud then realized that he had done "violence to or committed a blunder on 'the old woman'" (p. 178). But instead of opening up this emotional reproduction and plunging himself into the abyss so clearly inscribed in it, Freud reacted intellectually, deducing that he must have been on his way towards "grasping the universal human application of the Oedipus myth as correlated with the Fate which is revealed in the oracles."

Commenting on this rather astonishing passage, Jennifer Eastman (2005) wondered how Freud was able to "convert such anger, here directed at the old woman, to the love for the mother he claimed as part of the Oedipus complex?" (p. 339). Blum (1996) for his part concluded that the meaning of Freud's mistake was important for interpreting his dream of Irma's injection, and noted that the connection between Freud's bungled action and the Irma dream "is almost transparent" (p. 529). In another passage, Blum suggested that the guilt memorialized by Freud's Irma dream traced back to a "sadistic assault on the mother figure" (p. 523).

Freud's feelings of aggression toward his mother were however systematically dissociated from the idea of incest and denied. As Eastman (2005) observed, Freud "did not feel his feelings" but "somaticized them," mainly as gastrointestinal symptoms which "endured every Sunday throughout his life while visiting his mother" (p. 342). Appignanesi and Forrester (1992, p. 133) thought that Freud displaced his aggression from the mother figure to Therese Frankel, the elderly patient that Freud would attend every Sunday after visiting his mother.

Freud never abandoned the idea that the bond between a mother and her son was, as he weirdly argued, the "most perfect, the most free from ambivalence of all human relationships" (Freud, 1933a, p. 133). Starting with Rank, many psychoanalytic scholars have found Freud's most powerful "blind spot" to be his unacknowledged impotence and murderous rage towards the pre-oedipal mother (Rank, 1926b, pp. 142–143; Slipp, 1993, p. 95; Stolorow & Atwood, 1978, p. 236). Following Ferenczi, however, feelings of impotence and murderous rage towards the *incestuous mother* speak more compellingly.

These observations serve an understanding of the repression of fantasies of aggression that then resurfaced through Freud's mistakes and bungled actions. Particularly significant is Freud's own observation that his mistake with the elderly patient had led him to identify with his young male patient, most likely a young man who obsessively accused himself of "homicidal tendencies." Freud (1900) identified powerfully with this patient, an individual whom he described as a "softhearted man" (pp. 457–458) during several crucial stages in his self-analysis (see Anzieu, 1986, p. 247; Rudnytsky, 1987, p. 63).

The young man, Freud (1900) reported, felt inhibited and "unable to go out into the street because he was tortured by the fear that he would kill everyone he met." He thus "spent his days in preparing his alibi in case he might be charged with one of the murders committed in the town" (p. 260). The patient was constantly vigilant, always trying to guard himself from harming anyone by accounting for and controlling every movement and moment of his day.

However "if anyone suddenly escaped his watchful eye, he was left with a distressing feeling and the idea that he might possibly have got rid of him." He therefore stopped going out on walks and spent his days "incarcerated" within his own four walls at home. Reports in local newspapers about murders began to elicit new doubts in him, till when one day "the possibility came into his head that he might have left his house *while he was in an unconscious state and have thus been able to commit the murder without knowing anything about it*" (p. 457; emphasis added). Freud (1900, p. 455) used similar wording when recounting one of his own dreams, his Hollthurn dream of July 1898. The depth of Freud's identification with his young male patient was demonstrated in the following:

> I knew that the root of his illness had been hostile impulses against his father, dating from his childhood and involving a sexual situation. In so far, therefore, as I was identifying myself with him, I was seeking to confess to something analogous.
>
> (1900, p. 458)

Freud could have found that hostile impulses against female figures were operating in his Irma dream as well as in the mistake he made when treating the elderly lady he visited twice a day. But instead he focused on the murderous rage of male children against their fathers. This particular angle of the Oedipus story was most attractive to Freud, which he seized upon most vigorously as the Oedipus complex.

The "needle" in the Oedipus legend

Anthropologist and psychoanalyst George Devereux has suggested that Freud's interpretation of the Oedipus legend was one-sided and half-blind, which was then maintained by his followers. Devereux (1953) noted, in his 1953 article, "Why Oedipus killed Laius":

> It must be assumed that this continued scotomization . . . is rooted in the adult's deep-seated need to place all responsibility for the Oedipus complex upon the child, and to ignore, whenever possible, certain parental attitudes which actually stimulate the infant's oedipal tendencies. . . . The trend away from the recognition of the seductive behaviour of adults, which was bolstered up not only by Freud's genius and prestige, but also by social pressure and by the analyst's own need to scotomize this anxiety-arousing idea, was too strong to be reversed even by the findings of Ferenczi and of certain of his students, who stressed that, presumably by means of the 'dialogue of the unconscious', children recognize the true instinctual roots of the tenderness which adults display towards them.
>
> (p. 132)

Sander Gilman (1993) also questioned – 40 years later! – why Freud had repressed one of the most salient features of the legend, namely, Oedipus's deformed feet, the visible marker of Oedipus's own early trauma. This is a truly curious oversight by Freud, and revealing, magnified by his repression of Oedipus piercing his own eyes with a needle as his story reached its tragic end. Ferenczi (1912b, 1913e) based his own reading of the Oedipus legend precisely on these two points: the image and the use of a needle. Here, to highlight its internal logic, is the Oedipus story, connecting the end of the tragedy with its beginning, and also to illustrate the power of "fate" (or, in psychoanalytic terms, the determining power carried by the compulsion to repeat).

According to the story, Laius, in response to an oracle predicting his death at the hands of any son born to him, ordered a spike to be driven through his son's feet soon after birth, and commanded one of his servants to leave the child to die on Mount Cithaeron. The infant was miraculously saved and named Oedipus (swollen foot) because of the injury to his ankles from the spike driven through them.

In his essay on "Symbolism" Ferenczi (1912b) looked upon Oedipus's swollen feet and act of self-blinding as the two "somatic symbol-phenomena" on which Sophocles's entire tragedy rested, proposing that Oedipus's swollen or injured feet symbolized the phallus (p. 263). The name Oedipus thus referred to an identification of the Greek hero with an erect, engorged, or swollen male organ. Here

Ferenczi suggested that the image of the phallus could represent a person's entire human body. This very equation, which explains the so-called "womb-fantasy," is one of Ferenczi's most important and generative contributions, indeed both a theoretical and a clinical element allowing him to question Freud's entire phallocentric system of thought. Although Ferenczi here failed to establish a link between trauma and erection, it was precisely this connection, however, that would inform his Thalassa myth. Though *Thalassa* would not be published until 1924, its essential traits had already been conceived in 1913. In other words, Ferenczi elaborated a new version of the Oedipus myth in which the active striving of the phallic hero issued, from the very beginning, from a passively endured trauma. Thus did Ferenczi integrate what Freud had left outside when theorizing Oedipus.

In the Greek legend, the sensitivity Oedipus developed in response to his early trauma unconsciously shaped his hostile actions against his father Laius. Raised as the son of the king and queen of Corinth, and wanting to avoid the oracle's prediction, Oedipus decided against returning home to Corinth and instead to travel to Thebes. At the intersection of three roads Oedipus encountered a chariot transporting his biological father. The two men quarreled over who had the right of way, and during a violent exchange between them, Oedipus fatally injured Laius.

In one version, Oedipus grew furious and, in a fit of rage, killed first the driver and then Laius when the wheel of the king's chariot ran over Oedipus's foot. De Klerk (2008, p. 293) noticed that it was being struck in the traumatized area of his body (his foot) that unleashed Oedipus's murderous rage. Oedipus's hostile action against Laius betrays an unconscious identification with the aggressor.[5]

Finally, it was the combination of his own peculiar injury with the resultant sensitivity that in the end enabled Oedipus to solve the riddle of the sphinx and thus fulfill the second prophecy. Continuing on towards Thebes after killing his father, Oedipus encountered a sphinx just outside the city who stopped all travelers to pose a riddle. A traveler who failed to solve the riddle would be killed by the sphinx; if solved, however, the sphinx would kill itself, and the traveler could continue.

The particular riddle that the sphinx posed to Oedipus, as is the case with all such riddles, was enigmatic: "What walks on four feet in the morning, two in the afternoon, and three in the evening?" Oedipus responded: "Man: as an infant, crawls on all fours; as an adult, he walks on two feet and, in old age, uses a cane or walking-stick to help him ambulate." Oedipus solved the riddle and defeated the sphinx precisely because his trauma with his father was registered in his feet; his lifelong concern with the challenge of ambulating smoothly thus rendered him uniquely sensitive to the riddle of the sphinx.

The entire scenario of Oedipus's story helps to illustrate perfectly Ferenczi's idea of "traumatic progression." Trauma not only contributes to a process of "fixation" but to a rapid and precocious maturation in the person who suffers the trauma: Oedipus's childhood trauma sensitized him to issues bearing on the challenges of walking. At the same time, it also led him to fulfill his fate. His reward for liberating Thebes from was succession to the throne along with the hand in marriage of the recently widowed Queen Jocasta, his mother. In the end, Oedipus indeed killed his father and married his mother, just as the oracle predicted.

The "needle" piercing Oedipus's foot at his father's command functioned within the story as a signifier of the trauma Oedipus endured, and of the sensitivity it engendered, determining not only his name but his phallic desire and tragic fate as well. In the end, Oedipus punished himself for his actions by piercing his own eyes with a needle.

The further function of that needle as a powerful signifier was in driving Oedipus to repeat compulsively the very trauma he had passively endured early on. The horror of his bleeding eyes, the image by which he is best known, presents the image of a wound which leads back to the original trauma of Oedipus's early life, the needle in both cases is what binds both injuries together.

This same image was at the center of Ferenczi's own interpretation of Oedipus's self-blinding, which introduced the following vignette as an illustration of the equation between self-blinding and self-castration: a young lady suffered from a phobia of sharp objects, "especially needles." Her obsessive fear was that needles might pierce her eyes. Ferenczi interpreted her symptoms by suggesting that she was engaging in an intimate relationship with a friend but that she anxiously guarded against penetration. This "would have impaired her anatomical integrity by rupturing the hymen" (Ferenczi, 1913b, p. 270). In yet another vignette, Ferenczi pointed to the displacement of sado-masochistic fantasies and impulses from the genital towards a different organ susceptible to injury (the eye). In thus reviewing the "somatic symbol-phenomena" at work in the Oedipus myth, Ferenczi managed to adroitly fill the gaps Freud left when shifting from Emma's genital trauma to the formulation of the Oedipus complex.

Freud avoided seeing Oedipus as repeating an earlier trauma. He never mentioned the role of a needle in Oedipus's legend, and never noted that the needle signifier had made its way back at the end to provide a perfect demonstration of "fate," that is to say, of the compulsion to repeat.

The needle in Freud's metapsychology

Freud's attempt to understand the repetition compulsion was notably tortuous, oscillating between traumatic memories and inborn drives. In the end, he would read this phenomenon in light of the death instinct (Thanatos). In *Beyond the Pleasure Principle* Freud (1920) associated the repetition compulsion with the "appearance of some 'daemonic' force at work" (p. 35), suggesting that his reasoning was still being guided by Emma's "needle scene."[6]

Spikes and needles remained linked to the repetition compulsion for Freud. This preoccupation with needles would resurface in a bizarre metaphor for the effects of early traumata proposed in his *Introductory Lectures on Psycho-Analysis* (1916–1917, p. 361) and, later, in *An Outline of Psycho-Analysis* (1938b):

> The damage inflicted on the ego by its first experiences gives us the appearance of being disproportionately great; but we have only to take as an analogy the differences in the results produced by the prick of a needle [*Nadelstich*] into a mass of cells in the act of cell-division (as in Roux's experiments) and into the

84 *The abyss*

fully grown animal which eventually develops out of them. *No human individual is spared such traumatic experiences; none escapes the repressions to which they give rise.*

(1938b, p. 185; emphasis added)

Commenting on this passage, Max Stern (1968) observed that trauma "could be defined as a transitory failure of adaptation which leaves a scar". In Freud's final theory, however, trauma is seen as "an inevitable biological event occurring in every infant's development. One may call it *biotrauma*" (p. 14). Yet, it is inescapably irrational if not frankly bizarre to consider the "prick of a needle" as Freud did, that is, as a *biological, universal*, and *inevitable* event, as something that "no human individual" was spared.

One might therefore wonder whether the unconscious model of the "inevitable biological event" signified by the "needle" ultimately was the unformulated trauma endured by Emma Eckstein—the loss of her "Phallus" (her "castration").

Freud had celebrated the injection given to Irma in his specimen dream as a grandiose phallic fantasy. What he dissociated, however, would reappear in his discussion of the repetition compulsion in *Beyond the Pleasure Principle*. Freud (1920) was further led to illustrate the phenomenon by referring to a piece of classic Italian epic literature, "the most moving poetic picture of a fate" (p. 22), the piercing of the beloved Clorinda in Torquato Tasso's *Gerusalemme Liberata (Jerusalem Delivered)*. After having unwittingly pierced and killed his beloved, Tancred makes his way into a strange magic forest. Here,

> He slashes with his sword at a tall tree; but blood streams from the cut and the voice of Clorinda, whose soul is imprisoned in the tree, is heard complaining that he has wounded his beloved once again.
>
> (p. 22)

Tancred's hallucination of blood gushing from a tree carried a very special meaning for Freud: he invoked it to explain how one of his patients, the Wolf-man, who as a boy experienced a similar hallucination, had connected his mother's hemorrhages with the castration of women – or their "wound," as Freud (1918a, pp. 84–85) referred to it then.

Of Tancred's hallucination of blood in *Beyond the Pleasure Principle*, Freud further wrote: "If we take into account observations such as these, we shall find courage to assume that there really does exist in the mind a compulsion to repeat which overrides the pleasure principle" (1920, p. 22). Apparently, in theory Freud used the death drive to fill a gap left empty by the erasure of Emma Eckstein's actual castration.

Notes

1 See Volume I, pp. 130–131. That Freud was reminded of his friend Fleischl when associating to his Irma dream grows more revealing: Fleischl experienced an endless series of surgical amputations, all the result of neuromata which developed on his right thumb. The cocaine was thus prescribed and administered by Freud in an attempt to alleviate his friend's great suffering. This is one of many elements which strongly suggests that one of

the central ideas of Freud's Irma dream issued from his unconscious reaction to the "cut" Emma endured when she was circumcised as a child.
2 Freud (1900) himself associated the infiltration caused by the dirty needle in his Irma dream to the thrombosis of his pregnant wife (p. 118).
3 Rudnytsky (2012) observed that Freud's use of the word *Übermensch*, with its inescapable Nietzschean connotations, betrays the fact that his urination fantasies were an attempt to compensate for the shame expected in a mortified and frightened child. Tellingly enough, Freud associated urinary incontinence with early sexual arousal and abuse. In "The aetiology of hysteria," it was listed among those hysterical symptoms which regularly traced back to infantile sexual scenes that were "very repellent" (Freud, 1896c, p. 214) and grotesque, feelings which, as Freud explained, issued from the prematurely aroused child not being in "control of his natural needs" (Freud, 1896c, p. 214)
4 These dates were all carefully reconstructed by Rudnytsky (1987, p. 63).
5 The role of identification with the aggressor in Oedipus's killing of Laius was highlighted by George Devereux (1953): "Only rarely . . . is there any mention of Oedipus' own proneness to violence, which, it is specified, is similar to that of Laius. In other words, even where impulsiveness is attributed also to Oedipus, this character-trait of the son is derived from, or correlated with, the father's character structure" (p. 135 footnote 11). Deveraux also noted that the Oedipus myth "did not derive Oedipus' hostility to Laius from heterosexual, but from homosexual sources." As he noted: "What we do find in Greek accounts is an explanation of Oedipus' aggression against Laius in terms of Laius' character-structure: his propensity for homosexual rape, and for unconsidered, injudicious violence and overbearingness ('hybris')" (p. 135). According to various Greek sources, Oedipus's murderous and incestuous wishes were "neither purely heterosexual nor truly spontaneous ones, but were induced by the behaviour of his father Laius. In fact, it may even be suggested that Oedipus' partly heterosexual attraction to Jocasta was to a certain extent motivated by his desire both to escape and to gratify indirectly his own sado-masochistic and homosexual wishes which had been stimulated by his father's behaviour" (p. 135). On this issue see Marcel (2005) and Percy (1996).
6 Freud was so profoundly impacted by the scene in which the diabolus stuck needles in Emma's fingers that he ordered a copy of the *Malleus Maleficarum* [literally: "*Hammer of evil-doing (women)*"] and studied the text "diligently," as he said to Fliess a week later, on January 24, 1897. Written in 1486, the *Malleus* was the most popular handbook of legal authorities during the long period of witch hunting which lasted from the 15th until the early 17th centuries. The central thesis of the *Malleus* was that "all witchcraft comes from carnal lust, which is in women insatiable" (Mackay, 2006). Though the misogynist arguments derived from previous authors, the systematic linkage of witchcraft, femininity, and sexuality was new. As Hans Peter Broedel (2003) noted, witchcraft now "expressed itself most typically in sexual, reproductive, or marital dysfunction" (p. 178). That witches had the power to render men impotent was part of an old traditional wisdom, yet in the *Malleus* the idea that witches removed and collected penises was particularly emphasized. The *Malleus* devoted an entire chapter to this topic (Chapter 7 of Part II of the text). Freud would have found the material featured in the chapter most interesting.

5 The blood covenant

> Eckstein has a scene where the *diabolus* sticks needles into her fingers and then places a candy on each drop of blood.
>
> Freud to Fliess, January 17, 1897

A stream of religious images and fantasies

Freud's mission in life was to father a science of the mind which would be as rigorous as any of the physical sciences. Concepts like "force" and "energy" were often invoked as a way to provide psychoanalysis with scientific rigor. Freud's materialistic discourse and naturalistic framework for psychoanalysis, however, was increasingly infiltrated by a stream of religious metaphors and images starting in 1895, though they remained mostly below the surface. There is a remarkable aspect of Erikson's (1954) effort to fill in the missing gaps in Freud's interpretation of the Irma dream, as described in Volume I. Erikson associated the dream of Freud with the dream of one of his female patients, with a visually shocking image from a painting she had seen at the Louvre Museum in Paris titled "The Circumcision of Christ" (p. 18).

Erikson was courageous enough not to censure his own free associations when reflecting on this dream, though he was ignorant of Emma Eckstein's circumcision and could not grasp that the founding dream of psychoanalysis had been encoded by Freud's unconscious reaction to Emma's genital trauma. Yet, Erikson's seemingly inappropriate, impertinent, and intrusive thought turned into a splendid illustration of how the unconscious works, when the description of Jesus as the "cornerstone" of the Judeo/Christian building ("*Eckstein*," in Luther's translation) is taken into account.

Freud identified a new formula for hysteria soon after his Irma dream. Gathering his many thoughts on trauma and its possible role in the formation of psychoneurotic symptoms, in December of 1895, he carefully worked his ideas into a manuscript that he named *Weihnachtsmärchen* (*A Christmas Fairy Tale*) and sent it to Wilhelm Fliess as a New Year's Day present on January 1, 1896.

According to the Catholic calendar prevalent in Europe at the time, the first day of the year celebrated Christ's circumcision, eight days after his birth. Christian theology has seen the circumcision, the first instance when Christ's blood was shed, as an anticipation of the crucifixion.

The first day of the year in the Christian calendar had originally been celebrated on December 25, the day Jesus had supposedly entered the world. Pope Gregory moved New Year's Day forward in 1582 to the day when Christ would have been circumcised to enter the covenant. Thus the Gregorian calendar replaced the Julian. Tractenberg (1989) noted the following:

> The extraordinary symbolic importance of the Jewish injunction to circumcise male children at the age of eight days is confirmed by the Gregorian calendar, invented by Pope Gregory XII and still in use today. This calendar has New Year's Day, 1 January, on the feast of the circumcision of Our Lord Jesus Christ, rather than on his birthday, 25 December. According to Nunberg (1947), the 'death of the year' and the 'rebirth of the New Year' coincide with the date of circumcision of the infant Jesus, these occasions thus being associated with the ancient rites of initiation which represent filicide and the resurrection of the son.
>
> (p. 462)[1]

By sending his text to Fliess on January the first, Freud shared his "fairy tale" manuscript with someone who had concocted his own theories out of a veritable worship for the calendar and the "miracle of the year" (see Fliess, 1906, 1925). As 1896 unfolded, Freud actively fantasized about meeting Fliess in Rome on Easter Sunday, and by year's end he was dreaming about the Italian capital city. In the second of his Rome dreams Freud made a revealing association to the "*via dolorosa*" (*Leidensstation*) (Freud, 1900, p. 195), the annual re-enactment of the crucifixion and passion of Christ.

There is a striking continuity and consistency in Freud's many religious reveries, made visible by his ongoing effort to decode them. Even more striking is the resurfacing of this very pattern during Freud's self-analysis, in particular his "bad treatment" dream (October 3, 1897), his Signorelli parapraxis (September 1898), and his dream of self-dissection (about May 1899).

Emma's bleeding episodes had a powerful effect on Freud's unconscious, deep enough to arouse religious reveries. Such a response in countertransference is not unusual when working with those with a history of abuse in childhood (Grotstein, 1997). These reveries came to influence Freud's self-analysis, continuing to affect him even after Emma's analysis had ended. Freud's self-analysis can thus be characterized as his effort to work with the memories and fantasies that Emma's childhood trauma had reawakened, even though Freud was partly unaware of this connection. Freud's own view of his self-analysis was as a mournful reaction to his father's death. Jacob's death on October 23 of 1896, Freud once said, had revolutionized his soul, as he wrote to Fliess only a week later: " . . . in [my] inner self the whole past has been reawakened by this event."

At this precise time Freud decided to place two plaster casts in his office purchased shortly before, in Florence, during his second trip to Italy.[2] Freud's desire to travel south began in August 1895, a month after the dream of Irma's injection, and accompanied his entire self-analysis. Indeed it became the main expression of what has been called Freud's "transference neurosis" (Buxbaum, 1951), an exacerbation of symptoms which in 1897 organized around the desire to meet Fliess in Rome. Freud himself later described this longing as "deeply neurotic" in nature (letter to Fliess of December 12, 1897). Jones (1955, p. 21), as well as other psychoanalytic scholars, proposed that Rome for Freud stood as a symbol for the oedipal mother, the neurotic component keeping Freud from entering Rome being thus the incest taboo. But Freud's "longing" and fantasies were also informed by his emotional response to the resurfacing in the analytic situation of Emma Eckstein's childhood trauma.

Rome from afar

In the letter of December 6, 1896, Freud also expressed his wish for a congress with Fliess "on Italian soil (Naples, Pompeii)." Fliess countered Freud's offer with a proposal to meet instead in Prague. Freud agreed. The fantasy of meeting Fliess in Rome on an Easter Sunday only increased, however, and soon began to affect his dreams. Freud's series of dreams on Rome took place between December 1896 and January 1897, that is to say, during the final period of Emma Eckstein's analysis.

The first of Freud's dreams on Rome was triggered by an engraving of the city seen in the sitting room of one of his patients – likely the 90-year-old Therese Frankel he injected twice a day. The engraving of this was a pictorial representation of the Tiber River passing under the Ponte Sant'Angelo, the famous bridge in front of Castel Sant'Angelo. The view of Rome from here is particularly beautiful and had already inspired countless artists; now it would likewise stir a longing in Freud that would slowly materialize and unfold in his dreams.

Before this, Freud, in "The aetiology of hysteria," had made use of the Latin expression "*caput Nili*" (the source of the Egyptian river Nile), as a way to designate the premature sexual experiences which at the time he thought lay behind cases of hysteria. Just a few months later, in December 1896, it was the Tiber that was transformed into Freud's private "Nile," the starting point of his quest to identify the source of his personal neurosis. Alongside Freud's own religious imagery, water and rivers had a notably important role in the practice of many religions. Robertson Smith (1889–1890), an author Freud greatly admired, called attention to streams and rivers as sacred emblems of the blood shed by victims of sacrifice during ritual slaughter. Freud, moreover, often characterized libido as a "stream."

The first of Freud's Rome dreams was a view of the Tiber River seen from a railway-carriage window as his train pulled out of the station, though Freud quickly realized that he himself had not yet "set foot in the city" (p. 194). The second Rome dream was a less complex view, as "someone" led Freud to "the top of a hill" to show him "Rome half-shrouded in mist":

> it was so far away that I was surprised at my view of it being so clear. There was more in the content of this dream than I feel prepared to detail; but the theme of 'the promised land seen from afar' was obvious in it.
>
> (p. 194)

Anzieu (1986) proposed that the central wish of Freud's initial two dreams about Rome was of "seeing the 'promised one' – fiancée, sisters, niece and other playmates from childhood, and lastly mother" (p. 186). Carl Schorske (1974) perceptively noted when glossing Freud's dreams on Rome:

> Freud conflates dream images of Catholic Rome with Jewish ideas and situations. In one dream Rome appears as "the promised land seen from afar," implying Freud to be in the same relation to Rome as Moses to Israel. The vision, though Freud does not say so, seems to express a forbidden wish: a longing for assimilation to the gentile world that his strong waking conscience – and even his dream censor – would deny him. He also identifies Rome with Carlsbad, Bohemia's equivalent of our Palm Springs, a city of pleasure, rest, and cure; in short, an earthly city of recreation (re-creation), of resurrection. Freud compares himself in the analysis of this dream to a poor, gentle Jewish character in one of the Yiddish stories he loved so well. Because the little Jew did not have the train fare to Carlsbad, the conductor beat him up at every station; but, undaunted, he continued on his *via dolorosa* (the expression is Freud's). Thus the lofty vision of Moses-Freud seeing Israel-Rome "from afar" had its lowly analogue in the picture of the little-Jew-Christ-Freud reaching Carlsbad-Rome on a *via dolorosa*. A third dream reinforces the Christian theme, but telescopes it into that of ancient, pagan Rome. From a train window Freud sees across the Tiber the Castel Sant'Angelo, at once papal castle and Roman imperial tomb. Tantalizingly, the train moves off before he can cross the Bridge of the Holy Angel to reach the castle – a house of both buried paganism and Christian salvation.
>
> (p. 48)

The via dolorosa

In the third dream Freud finally reached Rome. The scenery, however, was Freiberg, the little town where he was born, and its environs, the famed river in Rome, the Tiber, replaced by "a narrow stream of dark water":

> There was a narrow stream of dark water; on one side of it were black cliffs and on the other meadows with big white flowers. I noticed a Herr Zucker (whom I knew slightly) and determined to ask him the way to the city.
>
> (Freud, 1900, p. 194)

After a series of associations with themes of flowers, meadows, and dark cliffs Freud decided that the "instigation to this dream had been a proposal made by my friend in Berlin that we should meet in Prague at Easter. What we were going to discuss there would have included something with a further connection with 'sugar' and 'diabetes'" (p. 195).

Prague was undergoing a political crisis at the time, with nationalistic protests and revolts against the Austrian empire. Freud thought that the city might not be safe, particularly for those who spoke German. Prague, he concluded, might "not be an agreeable place for a German to walk about in" (p. 195). Prague merged with Rome in this dream. Freud always felt a deep, irresistible attraction to the Eternal City. The psychical overlapping of these two cities captured Freud's ardent desire for, as well as his irrational fear of, entering Rome, a complex symptom which became an important focal point of his self-analysis.

Freud's dream was clearly coded by past events and memories from his life, which he would in time be forced to work with in his self-analysis. Two seem particularly obvious. First, as Freud scholars have noted, the meadows with flowers featured a reference to the fields in Freiberg where Freud played with his niece and nephew (John and Pauline) as a child. Freud had carried out an aggressive act against his slightly younger niece Pauline back then which harboured sexual connotations: his forcefully snatching a bunch of yellow flowers from her as they played in a meadow. Freud's memory of the event was later screened through what Peter Swales (1987) described as Freud's "language of flowers" (Freud, 1899, p. 311).

Second is this third dream pointing back to Freiberg, the little Czech town where Freud was born and spent the first three years of his life. In "All Roads Lead to Rome: The role of the nursemaid in Freud's dreams," Grigg (1973) proposed that the Czech landscape in Freud's dream is a direct reference to his "prehistoric" Czechoslovakian and Roman Catholic nursemaid, the woman Freud described to Fliess as his "initiator" (*Urheberin*) in sexual matters.

The location of the meadows with flowers in Freud's third dream thus touched upon premature sexual experiences which Freud experienced during his early years in Freiberg, one passively, the other actively. The connections between the two scenes were likely viewed by Freud through the prism of an idea from "The aetiology of hysteria," namely, that a male child seduced by an adult of the female sex "under the pressure of his prematurely awakened libido and compelled by his memory," typically tried "to repeat with . . . [a] little girl exactly the same practices that he had learned from the adult woman, without making any modification of his own in the character of the sexual activity" (Freud, 1896c, p. 215). Freud's description hinted towards his own experience or fantasy of early sexual abuse at the hands of his nanny in Freiberg, was later referred to in his letter to Fliess of October 3 and 4 (1897) describing his childhood nanny as his initiator and "teacher on sexual matters."

Another possible reference by Freud to an experience or fantasy of sexual abuse as a child is present in his reference to Herr Zucker (Mr. Sugar) in the third dream of Rome. Anzieu (1986) describes Herr Zucker as "the Death figure of Germanic legend whom the lost traveler innocently and unwisely asks the way" (p. 194). Zucker could be an adult abuser or sexual perpetrator, a hint of Freud's "theory of the father," which he had been actively working on at the time of the dream. Important thoughts on this topic can be found in Freud's letter to Fliess, December 6, 1896, musing that bouts of hysteria aimed "at the prehistoric, unforgettable other person who is never equaled by anyone later." With this description Freud anticipated his ideas on *traumatophilia* and the phenomenon of the compulsion to repeat.

The natural human attraction to candy (sugar) speaks in support of the idea of the mechanisms involved in libidinal fixation.

Grinstein (1980, p. 74) commented on the figure of Herr "Zucker" and noted that "The diagnosis of diabetes is made by the examination of the urine for sugar." Since Freud and Fliess both saw trimethylamin as a chemical product associated with sperm and excreted in urine, Freud's reference to diabetes may well allude to themes associated with sexuality. Anzieu (1986, p. 193) addressed the issue more concisely: "Fliess is here Herr Zucker, just as in the dream of 'Irma's injection' he is to some extent Herr Trimethylamin." Anzieu and Grinstein's readings of Freud's dream are keen and on target, though providing no solid rationale for their conclusions.

A much clearer picture surfaces relating the content of Freud's dream to the treatment of Emma Eckstein. A scene which helped Freud to solve the riddle of hysteria in October 1895 serves to better isolate the logic behind his narrative. The scene was of eight-year-old Emma Eckstein, who had entered "a small shop to buy some *sweets*, when the shopkeeper had grabbed at her genitals through her clothes." Freud (1895) noted that Emma decided to return to the shop, as though "*she had wanted to provoke the assault*" (pp. 353–354; my emphasis). Emma would have explored the meaning of this scene in detail during her analysis, and as her treatment progressed, "sweets" and "sugar" would have become words for issues associated with Emma's libidinal fixation to a traumatizing object. This would include the active production of situations which might result in fresh assaults, self-cutting behaviors, and further episodes of bleeding. Freud, just eight months before, had interpreted such behaviors as a re-actualization of Emma's trauma (letter to Fliess of May 4, 1896).

Seen within this matrix, Freud's associations and allusions grow clearer. In Grigg's view (1973) "sweets represent sexual favors, and valleys and ravines symbolize the vagina, in the same way that cliffs do the labia" (p. 115). These equivalents become less vague as soon as connected to Emma's mutilated labia. Freud would link "sugar" (*Zucker*) to Karlsbad, where patients with diabetes ("*Zuckerkrankheiten*"; literally: sugar-illnesses) were often sent by their doctors for treatment. The journey to the spa itself, on the other hand, was likened by Freud (1900) to a *via dolorosa* (*Leidensstation*) (p. 195).

Freud's own associations reveal a widening of his "Easter fantasy," which in part explains how the cities of Jerusalem and Rome would overlap in his mind, in this particular situation. The *Via Dolorosa* (Via Crucis, Way of Sorrows, or Stations of the Cross) provides a perfect metaphor of re-enactment, as the painful path Jesus was forced to walk in Jerusalem on his way to crucifixion. The event observed throughout the Christian world, and, in particular, Rome during Easter week, is the flagellation of Christ on the *Via Dolorosa* carried out as a devotional practice.

Returning to Emma Eckstein, her bleedings strongly resemble a re-enactment of her sexual abuse, indeed an expression of devotion to her abuser ("the prehistoric, unforgettable other person"), "Herr Zucker," or her Candy Man. These images also suggest that Emma's treatment itself became her own *via dolorosa*, the re-enactment and psychical reliving of her trauma. But why should we associate all these images and situations with Emma Eckstein? Beyond Emma's passion for "sweets," are there other reasons for doing so?

A strong reason indeed can found in the first of the two scenes Emma produced during analysis. Freud described the scene in a letter he sent to Fliess on January 17, where he wrote:

> Eckstein has a scene where the *diabolus* sticks needles into her fingers and then places a candy [*Zuckerl*] on each drop of blood. As far as the blood is concerned, you are completely without blame!

Before now, the obvious connection between "*Zuckerl*" (candy) in Emma's scene and *Herr Zucker* in Freud's third dream on Rome has escaped the notice of scholars. It seems as though Freud and Emma had each been reading each other's unconscious, sharing the same fantasies, and dreaming the same dreams. It cannot be pinpointed with certainty whether Freud's dream or Emma's scene came first, but it is tempting to think of Emma's "*Zuckerkrankheit*,"[3] her libidinal fixation to trauma, as a trigger for Freud's third dream of Rome. If so, it would identify Freud's dream as a countertransference dream, highlighting his corresponding and complementary identification with Emma.

Freud's fourth dream of Rome followed soon after Emma's presentation of the circumcision scene, as examined in Volume I. In this dream, Freud finds himself feeling surprised to find a series of German posters on a street-corner in Prague. Previously, this element, the "street-*corner*" (*Strassen-ecke*), was regarded not only as the idea of a central point of intersection but was also a direct linguistic representation of Freud's most important patient: *Eck*-stein (corner-stone). Emma's circumcision scene itself marked a crucial "crossroad" in the history of psychoanalysis, functioning as "the corner [*Ecke*] where Emma's analysis and Freud's own self-analysis intersected and criss-crossed" each other (Volume I, p. 197).

Experimenta crucis

The two scenes Emma produced and Freud reported to Fliess on January of 1897 shared the form, and hinted at the idea, of a *blood covenant*, a subject Clay Trumbull (1885) investigated in depth. Trumbull thought of blood as the most important symbol of life, and the blood covenant was the most solemn and binding agreement possible in ancient times: "blood-transfer is soul-transfer" (1885, p. V). Expanding on this idea, Robertson Smith (1889–1890) saw that "the bond of religion was originally coextensive with the bond of blood" (p. 47). Blood sacrifices served to symbolically transform the physical body into a social body, extending social ties and creating new moral obligations symbolic participation in "one blood." Freud himself embraced this line of thought in *Totem and Taboo*. In psychoanalytic terms: transference is the transfer of mental pain from one person to another person (Grotstein, 1997).

Emma's analysis most likely ended near Easter of 1897. The blood covenant theme resurfaced a few months later, right in the midst of Freud's self-analysis. On

October 3, Freud wrote to Fliess that it was not his father but his nanny who had served as his "initiator." That very night Freud experienced his "bad treatment dream." "Today's dream," Freud added in a postscript to the letter written the day after, had "under the strangest disguises":

> she was my teacher in sexual matters and complained because I was clumsy and unable to do anything.
>
> (Neurotic impotence always comes about in this way. The fear of not being able to do anything at all in school thus obtains its sexual substratum.) At the same time I saw the skull of a small animal and in the dream I thought "pig," but in the analysis I associated it with your wish two years ago that I might find, as Goethe once did, a skull on the Lido to enlighten me. But I did not find it. So [I was] a "little blockhead [*Schafskopf*]" [literally, a sheep's head]. The whole dream was full of the most mortifying allusions to my present impotence as a therapist. Perhaps this is where the inclination to believe in the incurability of hysteria begins. Moreover, she washed me in reddish water in which she had previously washed herself. (The interpretation is not difficult; I find nothing like this in the chain of my memories; so I regard it as a genuine ancient discovery.) And she made me steal *zehners* (ten-kreuzer coins) to give them to her. There is a long chain from these first silver *zehners* to the heap of paper ten-florin notes which I saw in the dream as Martha's weekly housekeeping money. The dream could be summed up as "bad treatment." Just as the old woman got money from me for her bad treatment, so today I get money for the bad treatment of my patients. A special part was played by Mrs. Q., whose remark you reported to me: that I should not take anything from her, as she was the wife of a colleague (he of course made it a condition that I should).
>
> A harsh critic might say of all this that it was retrogressively fantasied instead of progressively determined. The *experimenta crucis* must decide against him. The reddish water would indeed seem to be of that kind. Where do all patients get the horrible perverse details which often are as remote from their experience as from their knowledge?

This bad treatment dream was the outcome of Freud's immense self-analytic effort between September and November of 1897, when he deciphered the meanings of memories and "scenes" from the first three years of his life in Freiberg. Freud quickly realized that the meaning of reddish water was crucial: could this be a genuine memory or was it something retrogressively fantasized?

Scholars have been deeply affected and intrigued by the contents of Freud's letter to Fliess reporting memories of his Catholic caretaker. Suzanne Cassirer Bernfeld (1951, pp. 122–123) associated Freud's reddish water with the blood of Christ, and to Freud's wish to meet Fliess in Rome on an Easter Sunday. Robert Holt proposed that the scene conflated two distinct sets of associations, each relating to blood: menstrual blood and baptism, the latter of being "washed in the blood of the Lamb" (Vitz, 1988, p. 21). Paul Vitz linked the "skull of a small animal,"

Freud's association to his dream of bad treatment at the hands of his Catholic nanny, with Christ's crucifixion on Golgotha or "place of the skull" (ibid).[1] Wendy Colman (1994) interpreted the reddish water in which Freud had been bathed by his nanny as a reference to the blood of a Jewish child's ritual circumcision (p. 613). Swan (1974) found in Freud's Irma dream a reversal of the "bad treatment" dream, as though Freud had assumed "the role of the nurse," while "making others the objects of his bad treatment" (p. 39). Grigg (1973, p. 115), was impressed that the reddish water depicted the narrow stream of dark water from the third of Freud's dreams on Rome. Since the latter was a reaction to Emma's bleeding, it can be safely suggested that the reddish water brought into relief the '*caput Nili*' of his neurosis, that is, a scene of "sexual initiation" which Freud retrieved through his mimetic identification with Emma.

Finally, Risto Fried (2003, p. 328) offered that the "sexual initiation" of little Sigismund at the hands of his nanny might have involved a rather common practice: she taught the young boy to masturbate her, at times chastising him for the clumsiness of his performance. Taking this further now, the reddish water could have been interpreted by Freud as repulsive menstrual blood responsible for his clumsy performance. The *experimenta crucis* entailed deciding whether the memory was genuine or something that he had retrogressively fantasized.

This is the first conflict between memory and fantasy that appears in the documentation of Freud's self-analysis. Freud was unable to secure a definitive answer to his dilemma, and his self-analysis remained inconclusive. Indeed, in his letter to Fliess on November 14, 1897 he regretted that he was only able to analyze himself while analyzing others, and that "true self-analysis" was in fact "impossible." *This was a truly dramatic moment in the life of Freud and in the history of psychoanalysis.*

For several months traumatic memories had pressed to break through, resulting in incomprehensible sensations and "twilight thoughts" (Masson, 1985, p. 254), but in the absence of a caring "other person" and a reassuring environment, it was impossible for Freud to enter into closer contact with his emotional recollections. He was only able to analyze himself intellectually, "like an outsider." Thus split in two, he postulated that only opposition between traumatic memory and retrogressive fantasy could be considered; there was no room to consider a possible complementarity. Freud ended up discarding his theory of actual trauma just when he needed to understand how Emma's *via dolorosa* had reawakened his own buried memories, oddly similar to the way shades awaken "to some sort of life" in the Odyssey, as "soon as they had tasted blood" – to recall a metaphor utilized by Freud himself (1900, p. 248).

Psycho-mythology

The reddish water in the bad treatment dream connected to a wide array of Freud's fantasies, a scar on his chin from an accident while living in Freiberg when he was two or three, involving the same cupboard at the heart of another memory about his longing for his beautiful mother, namely, his well-known "*Kasten* scene." Freud recalled attempting to climb on a stool to fetch an object he desired which was high up on the cupboard – perhaps a candy (*Zuckerl*) – but the stool tipped over, its corner striking him behind his lower jaw (Freud, 1900, pp. 17, 560; also 1916–1917, p. 201).

There was a considerable loss of blood, and a doctor had to be summoned to close the wound with some stitches. Although Freud only introduced this material in later editions of *The Interpretation of Dreams* (between 1909 and 1922), he noted the following in his disguised autobiographical paper on *Screen Memories* in 1899, published just before the first edition of his dream book appeared: "I can still feel the scar resulting from this accident, but I know of no recollection which points to it, either directly or indirectly" (Freud, 1899, p. 310).

The scar from the injury that Freud could not recall can be interpreted as the first inscription of symbolic castration within the Freudian "corpus." It may also be seen as a symbolic reminder of the first scar inscribed in his own body, the scar which issued from his circumcision eight days after he was born. Freud's fantasizing about his "scar," it turns out, synchronized with his notion of the universal application of the Oedipus legend in October of 1897 (see his letter to Fliess of October 15).

Anzieu (1986) wondered why such important information had been kept secret from Fliess and why Freud had kept it out of the first edition of *The Interpretation of Dreams* [cf. the editorial footnote in Freud, 1900, p. 17], and speculated that Freud's scar fantasy functioned as an essential complement to his own fantasies and conjectures about Oedipus. Anzieu glossed this important link as follows: "the scar [which Freud had received as a result of his fall and injury on his lower jaw and chin] has marked on his flesh the punishment for his incestuous wishes" (p. 242). Anzieu's is a sound conclusion; more important, however, is that Freud's fantasies about his scar tap directly into his identification with Emma. Could Freud have unearthed his memory of his accident and scar from his childhood accident had Emma not shared her circumcision scene with him during analysis? Could he have dramatized the childhood injury that he suffered as a result of his chin striking on the "corner" (*Ecke*) of a piece of furniture if Eckstein had not been his patient? Could Freud have identified with Emma as deeply as he did if her symptoms of bleeding had been more thoroughly analyzed? Turning the question around: could Emma's symptoms and bleedings have affected Freud as they did had he been more in touch with his unconscious before treating her?

Following Schur (1972), Maciejewski (2002) held that Freud's memory of being bathed in reddish water by his nanny, his feelings of resentment against his childhood schoolmaster, and the injury which resisted recollection, were part of a single psychic constellation: the one which the event of his own circumcision had left behind (pp. 47–49).

The event of Freud's circumcision, Maciejewski proposed, found an unconscious outlet in a unique form of representation, namely, via Zipporah, a woman in the Bible who circumcised a boy. To quote the Old Testament: "Then Zipporah took a flint, and cut off the foreskin of her son, and cast it at his feet; and she said, surely a bridegroom of blood art thou to me" (Ex 4:25). According to Maciejewski, the ultimate content of Freud's bad treatment dream was the fantasy of a boy circumcised as the "bridegroom of blood of his mother." This fantasy, Maciejewski argued, paved the way towards Freud's later thoughts about the Oedipus complex. Indeed, it was shortly thereafter that Freud announced his insight into the psychic meaning of the Oedipus myth to Fliess on October 15, 1897:

> A single idea of general value dawned on me. I have found, in my own case too, [the phenomenon of] being in love with my mother and jealous of my father, and I now consider it a universal event in early childhood, even if not so early as in children who have been made hysterical. (Similar to the invention of parentage [family romance] in paranoia – heroes, founders of religion).

By identifying with Oedipus and assuming that the feelings of love and hate of a boy towards his parents were the starting point of the entire drama, Maciejewski (2002) thought that Freud both displaced and replaced his own circumcision trauma with a new theory, this novel interpretation of the Oedipus myth. The image of castration played an essential role in Freud's new theory. Maciejewski (2002), however, argued for the castration complex as

> in reality a secondary trauma, a deferred [*nachträgliche*] trauma, the historic truth of which consists in the return of repressed prehistoric traumas [*Urtraumas*], namely, the partial castration suffered as a result of being circumcised. By overlooking the trauma of his circumcision Freud . . . passed over to the *Sorrows of young Oedipus*, to the trauma which featured an abandonment (exposition) and a pierced foot.
>
> (p. 60)

Maciejewski's is a powerful hypothesis concerning the specific meaning and origins of the castration complex, the key element of Freud's reading of the Oedipus legend, to see the castration complex as Freud's own circumcision trauma in disguise. This latter found representation through the "bridegroom of blood" fantasy, which drew upon circumcision as "the traumatic central event of Jewish socialization and ethnogenesis" (Maciejewski, 2002, p. 309). This expression of a Jewish ethnic unconscious, which surfaced in a number of Freud's dreams, was repressed, left unanalyzed by the founder of psychoanalysis,[5] and finally replaced by a Greek legend, the Oedipus myth.

The *Kasten* (box)

On October 3, 1897, Freud wrote Fliess to say that in his case the "prime originator" was not his father but, rather, his Catholic nanny. The same cupboard, case, casket, or box (*Kasten*) which featured in his fantasy a "punishment" for his desire of something to eat (a *candy*?) also featured in the event of the sudden disappearance of his nanny from his life.[6]

This nanny, Monika Zajic[7], was arrested for stealing from the Freud family and punished with a 10-month prison sentence circa January of 1859. Freud preserved a puzzling screen memory of her disappearance. As he explained to Fliess on October 15 of 1897, a scene kept emerging in his conscious memory without his being able to make sense of it:

> My mother was nowhere to be found; I was crying in despair. My brother Philipp (twenty years older than I) unlocked a wardrobe [*Kasten*] for me, and when I did not find my mother inside it either, I cried even more until, slender and beautiful, she came in through the door. What can this mean? Why did my brother unlock the wardrobe for me, knowing that my mother was not in it and that thereby he could not calm me down? Now I suddenly understand it. I had asked him to do it. When I missed my mother, I was afraid she had vanished from me, just as the old woman had a short time before. So I must have heard that the old woman had been locked up and therefore must have believed that my mother had been locked up too – or rather, had been "boxed up" [*eingekastelt*] – for my brother Philipp, who is now sixty-three years old, to this very day is still fond of using such puns.

Suzanne Cassirer Bernfeld (1951) thought that the sudden disappearance of the nanny was experienced by little Sigismund as a repetition of Julius's sudden disappearance a half-year earlier. Bernfeld was also deeply interested in Freud's desire to meet Fliess in Rome on an Easter Sunday. In her essay "Freud and archeology," she considered Freud's religious imagery as related to the consolations and emotional support which his Catholic nanny might have provided when his younger brother Julius suddenly died. It would have been natural for Freud's nanny to encourage young Sigismund to imagine that Julius, like Jesus, would magically return to life and the family.

Julius passed away on April 15, 1858, a week and a half after an April 4 Easter Sunday. His remains were laid in a simple wooden casket and buried in the Jewish cemetery at Weisskirchen (now Hranice, Moravia) 15 kilometers west of Freiberg (now Pribor). Information on the burial ceremony itself is lacking. Lawrence Ginsburg (1999) suggested that Freud not only was deeply marked by traditional Jewish ritualistic practices but that the death and burial of his younger brother, occurring as it did when Freud was two, explains why images featuring a "death watch" haunted Freud throughout his life. Freud's anxiety about the encasement of another significant family member in a '*Kasten*' was thus a product of Julius's tragic death in 1859.

Freud's 'beautiful' mother Amalia disappeared partially from Freud's life after she gave birth to Anna on the last day of December of 1858; her unavailability served to reawaken Freud's anxiety about losing a significant person in his life. To quote Suzanne Cassirer Bernfeld (1951): "Once when he couldn't find her he became desperate, because he was afraid that her absence meant he had killed her, as he had once killed Julius" (p. 117).

Freud mentioned the cupboard incident several times in his writings, interpreting it in various ways during his self-analysis. The incident no doubt reminded him of his experiences of early loss. In Freud's reconstruction, however, the *Kasten* (box) itself functioned as a symbol for "his mother's inside" (Freud, 1901, pp. 49–51, footnote). As Cassirer Bernfeld (1951) noted, the cupboard was in Freud's case "over-determined as box, coffin, and symbol of pregnancy" (p. 117). This conclusion was stimulated by a similar process of overdetermination that had come to inform the image of the Etruscan tomb which Freud recalled in the analysis of his dream of self-dissection. Cassirer Bernfeld's deeper idea, however, was that the image of the empty cupboard, through which the mother's inside merged with the idea of a coffin, determined Freud's later passion for archaeology. The "psychological value of archaeology to Freud," she wrote, "offers the notion of a status that is neither death nor life" (p. 119). This theme will be further explored in the last chapter of this section, "Necropolis."

Notes

1 The feast of Christ's circumcision was removed from the Catholic calendar during the 1960s, the first day of the year now being seen by the Catholic Church as the day when the "Solemnity of Mary, Mother of God" is observed.
2 Freud wrote to Fliess on December 6, 1896, that these two pieces served as "a source of extraordinary invigoration" for him. One of the plaster casts was of Michelangelo's *Dying slave*, a piece modeled on the famed piece of Laocoön and his sons found in the Vatican Museum today.
3 The notion of "*Zuckerkrankheiten*" (diabetes; literally: sugar-illnesses) seems to push two lines of thought together; one is centered on trauma, on which I am here focusing, the other on the toxicological theory of libido, adumbrated by the trimethylamin formula ("the immensely powerful factor of sexuality").
4 Holt's personal communication to Paul Vitz, quoted in Vitz (1988, p. 21). Vitz (1988) interpreted the metaphor of "baptism" quite literally, proposing that Freud might have been "secretly baptized" by his Catholic nanny. Vitz's hypothesis was built on rather flimsy evidence.
5 Despite criticisms in Volume I of Maciejewski's conclusions regarding the Oedipus complex as a byproduct of a Jewish ethnic unconscious, he advanced some solid points, heuristically useful and deserving of further exploration. The legend of Zipporah, for instance, allows a better grasp of the logic of yet another piece of the Freud puzzle, concerning Freud's powerful identification with the figure of Moses as well as his profound conflicts with his father, Jacob. Recalling the Zipporah incident in *Moses and Monotheism*, Freud (1939, pp. 26–27) underscored that God became "angry with Moses" precisely because he had "neglected" a custom which had become holy to the Jewish people. Moses was however saved "from God's wrath" by his wife when she stepped in to circumcise the boy. Since Freud saw God as a projection of the father-imago, his description of the scene can be interpreted in this way: Freud's father, Jacob, became angry with his son Sigmund/Schlomo for disobeying and failing to circumcise his male children. Moses himself had failed to fulfill and make good on the central ritual of the covenant between God and the Jewish people. As the Bible notes, Moses neglected to circumcise his firstborn child, the result being that "the Lord, met him, and sought to kill him" (Exodus 4:20–26).
6 I am here following Suzanne Cassirer Bernfeld's (1951) reading of young Freud's accident and injury.
7 Historical information about Freud's nursemaids can be found in Sajner, 1968; Gicklhorn, 1969; Buriánek, 2015.

6 The timeless unconscious
Part I

> In retrospect we can conjecture that the human ensemble of worship – religion, mystery, and spirituality – stand, alongside literature, myth, and aesthetics, as the lost family from which psychoanalysis was born.
>
> James Grotstein, Why Oedipus and not Christ? (1997, p. 201)

Grundsprache

The notion of "unconscious" surfaced long before Freud. Freud, however, did stumble on something new: that the unconscious had a deep structure not tied to chronological time or history. In *The Psychopathology of Everyday Life*, Freud (1901) would say that "a large part of the mythological view of the world, which extends a long way into the most modern religions, *is nothing but psychology projected into the external world*" (p. 258). Freud presented this "*supernatural reality*" as a construct

> destined to be changed back once more by science into the *psychology of the unconscious*. One could venture to explain in this way the myths of paradise and the fall of man, of God, of good and evil, of immortality, and so on, and to transform *metaphysics* into *metapsychology*.
>
> (p. 259)

Freud's claim that religious myths were "reflections [projections] of our psychic internal [world]" (Masson, 1985, p. 286), and that the same psychic elements were also found in the scenes of neurosis and perversion, remained an essential feature of psychoanalysis. It allowed Freud to see religion as a universal neurosis, and to propose neurosis as a private religion (Freud, 1907b, pp. 125–126). This is one of the most important of Freud's insights, which, being at the crossroad between the clinical and the philosophical, has the potential to disclose new perspectives. However, this didn't come to full fruition. Seeing religion as a socialization tool for the Human Beast and placing himself within the tradition of Enlightenment critics of religion, Freud found that the common ground of both religious practice and neurotic illness was *instinctual renunciation*. Focusing only on the ambivalent struggle enacted in obsessive-compulsive observances of formulaic ritual behavior, Freud narrowed his field of inquiry to obsessionality, failing to realize that the common ground of both religion and psychoanalysis consists of unbearable, traumatic psychic pain.[1] In short, remaining in the background and not directly addressed was the question of the hystero-traumatic origin of "supernatural reality."[2]

This latter was however already inscribed in Charcot's meditation, which inspired Freud's plan to translate "*metaphysics* into *metapsychology*."[3] Introducing *Les demoniaques dans l'art* (*The possessed in art*) (Charcot & Richer, 1887), Charcot noted that in ancient times the soul was portrayed in the moment of leaving the body as a winged creature replicating the material body. For him this Greek model of the soul was the inspiration for early Christian artists to represent a demon in exorcism. Indeed the idea of splitting is perfectly illustrated by the dark medieval imagery, and also by the simple idea of a soul as a second divided self. Since the same duplication typically represents the moment of shock, the ripping out of oneself, it seems natural to surmise that traumatic shock could be at the root of the religious phenomena and sacrifices that Freud wanted to transform into "metapsychology." Years later, this view would resurface in Ferenczi's new metapsychology of the fragmentation of mental life.

Freud was not interested in this traumatic dimension, focusing instead on the archaic thinking of myths, religion, and dreams. Yet, to give this archaic thinking a name, Freud borrowed the phrase *Grundsprache* (basic language), coined by "the paranoic Schreber" (1916–1917, p. 166, 1925c, p. 135). "*Grundsprache*," for Schreber, was the language spoken by God himself. Schreber was a scholarly man, familiar with the notion of God as "*der Grund allen Seins*" ('the ground of all being') (Niederland, 1951, p. 585, 1969).

Grotstein (1990) traced the idea of a "basic language" which schizophrenics speak as a reaction to the catastrophic experience of psychic extinction. Threatened by psychic death, such individuals experience the terror of falling into a cosmic abyss, or "black hole," and substitute "archaic, apocalyptic (meaningful) scenarios in order to prevent their minds from dissolving into the maelstrom of nothingness" (p. 265). These scenarios are a result of an inborn human capacity for stopping the process of dissolution with a hallucinatory, wish-fulfilling reaction to prevent a catastrophic implosion. In Grotstein's (1990) view, "nothingness" was the Chaos which existed before the "Big Bang" of Creation (p. 273).

Freud, of course, never referred to the notion of a "black hole"; but in his Irma dream, he did experience the prospect of dissolving into a maelstrom of nothingness as he peered into Irma's mouth. As put by Erikson (1954), he "might have awakened in terror over what he saw in the gaping cavity" (p. 35). Freud, in this founding dream, was also able to stop the process of dissolution, and to re-emerge with a discovery, a new system of thought. Ellenberger (1964) spoke in this regard of a "*maladie créatrice*" (creative illness). This chapter will review Freud's acquaintance with the language of God, and, in turn, shed some light on his perplexing yet crucial "Signorelli slip."

Creation myths

An attempt to explain the *Grundsprache* can be found in Herman Nunberg's (1947) article, "Circumcision and problems of bisexuality." Nunberg, in this important contribution, discussed the dreams and fantasies of a man who was circumcised at the age of five as an attempt to cure him of masturbation. This trauma led Nunberg's patient to fantasies strikingly similar to those found in the delusional systems of individuals with schizophrenia, and indeed to elements often found at the heart of creation myths (p. 150).

In each case, there is a fantasy that an original hermaphroditic or bisexual creature has been cut or split into two equal parts, creating two distinct beings who, as in the Platonic myth of Androgyny, seek the other half with the hope of becoming whole again. Just as the birth act features the presence of a primordial cut, the union between the two sexes is here seen as involving the nullification of that primordial cut. It does this through an attempt to achieve symbolically a prenatal state which, by virtue of reuniting male and female elements, repairs and make things whole.

To highlight the primordial cut of creation myths, Nunberg (1947) recalled both the creation story of the Bible and the myth of Kronos, with Aphrodite born out of the foam from Uranus's severed testicles when cast into the Aegean Sea. In the Jahwist/Elohist account (Genesis 2:4b-25), Adam is described as both male and female. Eve, on the other hand, owes her existence to being fashioned by God from Adam's body (his rib). In Nunberg's view: "God circumcised Adam and made a woman out of his prepuce" (Nunberg, 1947, p. 151). Nunberg observed that in many creation myths the two parts which are severed and split-off from each other are often imagined as siblings, typically as a brother and sister pair. This presents sexual relations between a brother and a sister as involving a process of reunification. In Nunberg's patient these themes came together when he fantasized that if he married his sister it would help him to "heal his wound" and to regain the foreskin he lost at the age of five from circumcision (p. 152).

This fantasy of reunion informs many collective myths and private fantasies and ought to be considered an automatic and universal reaction to trauma, a predisposition for fantasies of rescue and salvation independent of the actual content of traumatic experience. The essential feature of this inborn reaction and disposition is the undoing of the cut. The adaptive function of this magic thought preserves a hope of repairing what has been broken, of finding what has been lost, of resuscitating what is dead, and of reuniting what has been separated. A paradigmatic example is Plato's famed myth of a being who was both "man – woman," a being sliced in half by Zeus to separate male and female elements from each other. In *Beyond the Pleasure Principle* Freud (1920) appealed to Plato's myth of the Androgyne to introduce his theory of instinct as featuring a compulsion "to restore an earlier state of things" (p. 56; see also vol. I, pp. 166–170).

Genital worship

Did Emma Eckstein experience similar fantasies? Freud's letters to Fliess reveal that this kind of magical thinking was there in her analyst, and that it was instrumental in helping Freud to become acquainted with the "*Grundsprache*."

The most important of these fantasies was reported by Freud in his letter to Fliess on January 24 of 1897. After Emma produced a scene of demonic possession during analysis, Freud fantasized the broomstick upon which witches are often portrayed riding as "*der große Herr Penis*" or "the great Lord Penis." This is the initial appearance of the idea of the transcendental Phallus in Freud's work. Indeed, and remarkably enough, the link was first posited in the very letter to Fliess reporting Emma's description of her circumcision. The January 24, 1897 letter fails to pinpoint a connection between Emma's genital cut and the "convincing evidence" which Freud would invoke to argue that the human genitals were "originally" the "pride and hope of living beings," indeed "worshipped as gods" (Freud, 1910c, p. 97). The parallel construction in the text of Freud's letter to Fliess, however, is sufficient to locate a point of departure from his attempt to transform the mythological view of the world into a science of the unconscious.

Crucial in this regard is that Freud, when reporting to Fliess on Emma's fantasy about her genital cut, wrote of beginning to grasp a new idea, that at the root of both perversion and neurosis stood "a remnant of a primeval sexual cult, which once was – perhaps still is – a religion in the Semitic East (Moloch, Astarte)."

The word "remnant" and the present tense in this statement are to be understood in light of the recapitulationist thesis that psychic activity in children is informed by the same fantasies that were active in primitive people. Freud would later say that myths are the precipitate of the imaginative activity of primitive man, and that the latter is active in children as well (Freud, 1926b, p. 211). Moloch and Astarte, Lord and Lady, are therefore "father" and "mother" in the minds of both primitive people and children.[1] After this letter, Freud never more referred to Moloch and Astarte. Yet, these Semitic idols continued to inform his writings as their Greek equivalents: Kronos and Aphrodite.

Freud referred many times to the Greek creation myth. In light of a previous focus on the role of Moloch/Kronos in Freud's fantasies and slips, here now the emphasis is on the figure of Astarte, the Queen of Heaven in the Old Testament.

The name Astarte likely derived from the Phoenician word for "womb" or, perhaps, from that "which issues from the womb" (Patai, 1978, p. 57). In Syria, Astarte melded with similar deities and was thus associated with sacred prostitution and castration. Emma's circumcision scene reminded Freud of Astarte probably because "the myths and the cultic practices of the Great Mother Goddess explicitly stressed and actually demanded a perfectly real castration" (Brenner, 1950, p. 322). Indeed, a reference to the "castration by which the sacrifice of emasculation is offered to the obscure Goddess, who sends death and destruction" can be found under the entry for "Astarte" in Roscher's *Lexicon of Greek and Roman Mythology*, a text which Freud was fond of quoting (Roscher, 1884–1890, I, p. 654).

This ancient religion spread throughout the entire Mediterranean, entering the Hellenic world through Cyprus, where Astarte was worshipped as Aphrodite and partly transformed into the myth of the Hermaphrodite. In Cyprus, Aphrodite was originally worshipped as a goddess endowed with a penis (a bearded Aphrodite was called Aphroditus). In Athens, phallic statues with a female head were called *hermæ* of Aphroditus. Plato's (428–348 B.C. ca) myth of an androgynous creature was likely inspired by this cult, which had originated in the Semitic East.

Freud believed that the primeval worshipping of the genitals was first sublimated in innumerable divinities and then repressed during the course of cultural development. He was obviously aware that the most vigorous repression occurred in the religion of Israel, where the most popular names for the repressed idols were Astarte and Adonis, pronounced Adon, Adoni, and Adonai in Hebrew.[5] The fact that the repressed name of Adonis managed to return through the pronunciation of YHWH with the vowels of Adonai was, as Arthur Feldman (1944) observed, a "most remarkable example of the return of the repressed in the repressing force. Yahweh was to supplant all of the other gods and his name was pronounced Adonai" (p. 387).

Freud saw the Astarte-Adonis myth as paradigmatic of primeval genital-worship. In his letter to Jung on November 21, 1909, there is a remarkable revelation: "In private I have always thought of Adonis as the penis." Freud then went on to explain that the meaning of the "joy" which women experienced "when the god she had thought dead rises again" was "too transparent!" (McGuire, 1974, p. 265). This statement becomes particularly significant with the idea of Adonis as the penis already inscribed in the image of "the great Lord Penis," which Freud had provided in January of 1897.

Freud's desire for a universal application of the Oedipus legend some months later, in October 1897, was thus preceded, accompanied, and sustained by the thought of Adonis as a personification of the penis (Oedipus himself, we have seen, was a phallic hero, that is, an expression of the identification of the total body with the penis). This idea, which came to Freud through his analysis of Emma, was not allowed to enter the foreground. Only with a focus on the figure of Adonis, making explicit an identity among Adonis, Oedipus, and Christ, can the depth of field which Freud consulted to deconstruct mythology and religion be appreciated.[6]

Blood, moreover, plays an important role in the Adonis myth. According to legend, Adonis died in the arms of his lover, his blood coloring the waters of the Adonis River red after he was mortally wounded. The Adonis River, near Byblus, is also known as the Abraham River. Writing of the alternation of wailing and festivity, death and sexuality, Frazer (1890) described the dramatic cycle of dying and resurrection in the Adonis myth:

> At Byblus the death of Adonis was annually mourned with weeping, wailing, and beating of the breast; but next day he was believed to come to life again and ascend up to heaven in the presence of his worshippers. This celebration appears to have taken place in spring ... At that season the red earth washed down from the mountains by the rain tinges the water of the river and even the sea for a

great way with a blood – red hue, and the crimson stain was believed to be the blood of Adonis, annually wounded to death by the boar on Mount Lebanon. Again, the red anemone was said to have sprung from the blood of Adonis; and as the anemone blooms in Syria about Easter, this is a fresh proof that the festival of Adonis, or at least one of his festivals, was celebrated in spring. The name of the flower is probably derived from *Naaman* ("darling"), which seems to have been an epithet of Adonis. The Arabs still call the anemone "wounds of the *Naaman*."

(p. 280)[7]

The Adonis legend played a crucial role in James Frazer's famous work *The Golden Bough*, the first edition appearing in 1890. Frazer claimed that the central theme of all world mythologies featured the periodic sacrifice of a king who stood as the incarnation of a Lord who died but was resurrected before entering into a mystic marriage to an Earth goddess. In the Adonis myth the annual decay and revival of vegetation furnished the model for the cycle of dying and reviving. This cycle was later transferred to the Easter celebration, which featured the death and resurrection of Christ.

According to Frazer (1890), what best indicated that the figure of Adonis was originally a deity of vegetation were the well-known "gardens of Adonis," which were charms to promote the growth of vegetation. Practiced chiefly or exclusively by women, these "gardens" were baskets filled with earth in which various kinds of plants and flowers were sown and tended for eight days. As Frazer (1890) noted in his description of the gardens:

> Fostered by the sun's heat, the plants shot up rapidly, but having no root withered as rapidly away, and at the end of eight days were carried out with the images of the dead Adonis, and flung with them into the sea or into springs.
>
> (p. 284)

These gardens of Adonis were then ritually thrown into water in order "to effect the resurrection of the god" (p. 287). Such rituals, Frazer argued, derived from a single prototypical ritual aimed at preventing the process of enfeeblement and decay by celebrating the rejuvenation of a divine life incarnated in a material body.

By "seeing" the dying and resurgent god in the tumescent penis, Freud reframed the idea of a "divine life" in terms of libido. Freud's views might well have been facilitated by the fact that in Judaism "divine life" is not only celebrated through the ceremony of circumcision but incarnated in the male organ, the penis, in particular. That the standard blooming time of the gardens of Adonis (eight days) matches the period of time stipulated by Jewish law to pass before a newborn is circumcised (eight days) rendered the connection all the easier for Freud; it might even have provided him with additional evidence to support his decision to equate Adonis with the penis.

The Greek legend of Adonis also demonstrated a process of mitigation and sublimation as it substituted and replaced "blood" with "flowers." The most famous instance of the substitution in question is found in Ovid's *Metamorphoses* (Book X), where the pain and grief of Aphrodite before the dead Adonis is recalled with the following words:

> and the representation of thy death, repeated yearly, shall exhibit an imitation of my mourning. But thy blood shall be changed into a flower.

This same "language of flowers" came to encode dreams and screen memories which Freud himself encountered and analyzed during his self-analysis.[8] In particular, in Freud's self-analysis the "language of flowers" coded the theme of brother-sister incest, a theme first surfacing in the dream reported to Fliess on May 31 of 1897.[9] This was the "Hella" dream.

Beautiful or horrible?

In his dream Freud experienced "over-affectionate feelings" for his 10-year-old daughter Mathilde, who was then recovering from near death with diphtheria.[10] In Freud's dream Mathilde was called Hella, a name explained by her being "enthralled by the mythology of ancient Hellas" (Masson, 1985, p. 249). Freud also noted, however, that before the dream he had received a photo of Hella, his three-year-old niece, the daughter of his sister Anna living in New York at the time. As Barbara Mautner (1993) perceptively noticed, the "Hebrew name for both Hella and Anna is Hannah." In her interpretation of Freud's dream, Mautner proposed that Freud must have been deeply struck by the resemblance in the photograph between his three-year-old niece and her mother Anna at the same age. The incestuous ("over-affectionate") feelings in the dream thus featured the return of feelings he had once felt for his sister Anna, when she was three and he was five years old, as in the visual memory reported in the dream of the Botanical Monograph. Those feelings, Mautner believed, informed Freud's Hella dream, to the point of serving to "make up the latent skeleton" of his Irma dream (p. 275).

Freud's Hella dream also marked an important "aesthetic turn" for William McGrath (1986), supprting Freud's abandonment of the rigid medieval imagery associated with atrocities and witch-hunting – all elements connected with the reviving in analysis of Emma's circumcision trauma in January 1897 – in favor of the classical idea of beauty as the year progressed.

The Hella dream is usually viewed as the switch point from the seduction theory to the discovery of the Oedipus complex, namely, as Jones (1953) put it, the view "that irrespective of incest wishes of parents towards their children, and even of occasional acts of the kind, what he [Freud] had to concern himself with was the general occurrence of incest wishes of children towards their parents, characteristically towards the parent of the opposite sex" (p. 354). Yet most authors found this switch point confusing, at the least. Freud's dream inspired his first meditation on the "horror of incest" (Masson, 1985, p. 252). At the time Freud interpreted it as a "fulfillment" of his "wish to catch a *Pater* as the originator [*Urheber*] of neurosis" (p. 249). Commenting on this point, Jones wrote to Strachey on October 27, 1951:

"He [Freud] got at incest by the inverse way of his ascribing it to the father" (Steiner, 1994, p. 514). The question seems to be more complex, however.

Swan (1974) noticed that the word "*Urheber*" (originator), in Freud's attempt at rationalizing his sexual feelings toward his daughter, anticipated the word "*Urheberin*," which would refer, a few months later, to his nanny, the "sexual teacher" and "prime originator" who scolded, shamed, and humiliated him (p. 17). The reversal embedded in the Hella dream conflates therefore many things, among them the disconnection from a familiar Hebrew context and its displacement into an idealized Greek scenario, the replacement of shame with phallic exhibitionism, and the turning of something "horrible" into "beautiful." The key question here concerns Freud's desire. As again pointed out by Swan, Freud "says nothing . . . about his desire for his daughter which, because of this rationalizing evasion, takes on the appearance of a very severe taboo" (p. 13), one which would later resurface his 1913 essay, "The theme of the three caskets [*Kasten*]," a hymn to repetition compulsion, where the fixation to a incestuous mother figure returns as an incestuous desire for the daughter.

Behind Freud's intellectual detours and great defensiveness, we can sense here that something traumatic was pushing to emerge.

Signorelli's *The Triumph of Pan* and the reviving of Hellenic paganism in the Italian Renaissance

Short after the Hella dream, Freud underwent a strange "intellectual paralysis" as well as "curious states incomprehensible to Cs., twilight thoughts, veiled doubts" (letter to Fliess of June 22, 1897). The medicine Freud self-prescribed was to travel south in search of "a punch made of Lethe" (oblivion), as he wrote Fliess from Siena on September 6, 1897.[11] Three days later, Freud was standing in a side-chapel inside the famed Cathedral of Orvieto before a cycle of frescoes on the theme of *Last Things* (death, judgment, heaven, and hell) painted by Luca Signorelli (1445–1523). So impressive was this particular cycle of frescoes that Freud later described it as "the greatest" he had "seen so far."

The idea of "absolute beauty" had an important part to play in Freud's search for oblivion. He wrote to Fliess on August 18, a month before his visit to Orvieto:

> You promised me, by the way, a congress on Italian soil, of which I shall remind you in due time. . . . This time, it is my hope to penetrate somewhat more deeply into the art of Italy. I have some notion of your point of view, which seeks not that which is of cultural-historical interest, but absolute beauty in the harmony between ideas and the form in which they are presented, and in the elementary pleasing sensations of space and color. At Nuremberg I was still far from seeing it.

Fliess may not have explicitly mentioned Signorelli when they met in Nuremberg on Easter of 1897, but in any case Signorelli's great fame in German-speaking countries was closely associated with a painting that strongly supported Fliess's idea of "absolute beauty in the harmony between ideas and the form," so typical of Italian Renaissance art. It was *The Triumph of Pan* (1489–90) (also known as *Pan as god of natural life*, or *The education of Pan*), a work either destroyed or stolen during the bombing of the city in World War II. William Bode, the famed founder of the Royal Museum in Berlin, had purchased it in 1873, an acquisition widely advertised in German-speaking countries thanks to Robert Vischer's (1879) monograph *Luca Signorelli und die italienische Renaissance* (*Luca Signorelli and the Italian Renaissance*).[12]

Freud visited the Royal Museum for the first time on March 10, 1886, when he lived in Berlin to train in pediatrics with Adolf Baginsky. Since Signorelli's newly restored painting of Pan was one of the Museum's most prized possessions, it is likely that Freud did not pass up the opportunity of seeing it during his first visit to the Museum. He may have seen the famous painting later as well, when he traveled to Berlin to visit Wilhelm Fliess on several other occasions: in May of 1893, August of 1895, July of 1896, for instance. Freud could have visited the Royal Museum again during one of these visits, perhaps even accompanied by Fliess himself.

Signorelli's painting of Pan was a companion to another work associated with the idea of "absolute beauty" and "the harmony between ideas and form": Botticelli's famous painting of *The Birth of Venus* (1480 ca), depicting the Greek myth of Aphrodite, goddess of love and beauty. The two paintings were originally commissioned by Lorenzo the Magnificent; each was associated with the revival of Hellenic paganism during the Italian Renaissance. Botticelli (1445–1510) became a follower of the Italian Dominican Friar and moral preacher Girolamo Savonarola during the 1490s. Deeply disturbed by powerful feelings of guilt, Botticelli then destroyed many of his canvases with nude bodies. *The Birth of Venus* only survived by chance. Signorelli's painting of Pan survived as well, seen and described by Giorgio Vasari (1511–1574) but then was lost before being found again in Florence during the 19th century. When it reappeared, the naked figures in the painting had been covered from head to toe with drapes. Only this censorship had saved the painting.

These two works were a direct expression of the Neoplatonic intellectual circle "*Arcadia*," named after Virgil's "Tomb in Arcadia" (*Eclogues V*, 42ff). The Arcadia circle not only inspired Signorelli's painting of Pan but the poem *Arcadia* (1502) by Jacopo Sannazzaro as well. The poem effectively transformed Virgil's *Arcadia* into a utopian world of bliss and beauty, which was then celebrated though funeral hymns, yearning love songs, and melancholic memories.

In popular iconography, Pan was a forerunner of the medieval Christian devil: both were typically depicted with legs of a goat and with horns. In Sannazzaro's idyllic poem, however, Pan is portrayed as a holy being. Representing the natural cycles of birth and death, he is the master of "all demons" in the lost realm of natural life that preceded civilization. As "*Santo Pan*" (Holy Pan) he was a source of that harmony, bliss, and beauty. Vischer (1879) observed this saintly conception of Pan in Signorelli's painting of the Greek god of the wild. Indeed, as the god of natural life, Pan also was a forerunner of the Savior, the Good Shepherd.

Figure 6.1 Luca Signorelli (1441–1523): *The Triumph of Pan*. Berlin, Gemaeldegalerie, Staatliche Museen zu Berlin (destroyed during World War II). (Courtesy of Foto Scala, Firenze)

Figure 6.2 Sandro Botticelli (1445–1510): *The Birth of Venus*. Firenze, Galleria degli Uffizi. (Courtesy of Foto Scala, Firenze)

Though Signorelli's Pan had the legs of a goat he was not a devilish monster. Pan's bronzed body is not disfigured but beautiful, his posture balanced and reassuring. To emphasize a holiness derived from nature, Pan's horns were fashioned from light, with the light then a halo in a representation of the conjunction of the sun and moon. The Pan of Signorelli is thus Lord of All, and "*Pan*" in Greek means "All."

The association between Signorelli and Botticelli would materialize for Freud in the "Signorelli slip," the replacement of "Signorelli" with "Botticelli" in his analysis of forgetting the artist's name. Both Signorelli's Pan and Botticelli's Venus (Lord and Lady) present sophisticated sublimations of the primeval genital worship preserved in mythology and religion. The figure of Pan was often represented with an erect penis. Moreover the death of the Great Pan was closely related to the worship of Adonis (or Tammuz), namely of the god that Freud viewed as a personification of the penis.[13] Aphrodite was in turn supposedly born out of Uranus's severed penis, the male organ having been cut off and thrown in the Aegean Sea by his son Kronos.

In Signorelli's painting, the figure of Pan is a substitute for Christ. The pale figure of Nymph, on the other hand, stands in for a Magdalena, the repentant prostitute and holy witness of the crucifixion, burial, and resurrection of the Lord, often seen in medioeval Church iconography (Vischer, 1879, p. 241). Finally, in Botticelli's *Birth of Venus*, the shell in which the naked figure of Venus is riding upon as she reaches the seashore alludes to the female genitals. Freud's replacement of "Signorelli" with "Botticelli" as he struggled to recall Signorelli's name can be related to the shared genital theme of these paintings.

This image of "*Santo Pan*" thus supplies a link of "*der große Herr Penis*" (the great Lord Penis) with Signorelli, and indeed *Triumph of Pan* anticipates the triumph and resurrection of Christ as a theme. Let us now turn to Signorelli's apocalyptic cycle of frescos in the Cathedral of Orvieto.

Notes

1 As noted by Balint (1950), Freud's preference for obsessionality and situations characterized by withdrawal from the object, was not specific of his philosophy of religion, but shaped more in general his psychological theory and method.
2 The shift from a trauma passively endured to obsessionality is prominent in *Totem and Taboo*, where instead of stressing the victimization of sons by a brutal father, Freud (1913a) based his narrative on the guilt feelings of rebellious sons, and on the phenomenon of incorporation later named by Ferenczi "identification with the aggressor."
3 Freud wrote, in his obituary for Charcot, that the use of "splitting" instead of "demonic possession" was only "a matter of exchanging the religious terminology of that dark and superstitious age for the scientific language of to-day" (Freud, 1893b, p. 20).
4 Moloch and Astarte are also known as Baal and Baalat, names that refer to "Lord" and "Lady" in all Semitic languages. The name Moloch derived from a distorted pronunciation of *Melek* (King, Lord) and issued from "the scruples of the later Jews, who furnished the consonants of the word MLK with the vowels of *bosheth*, 'shameful thing,' whenever it was to be understood as the title of a false god" (Smith, 1889–1890, p. 67).A Great Mother goddess of fertility, love, and death, Astarte is called Ashtoreth (1st Kings 11:5, 11:33, and 2nd Kings 23:13) in the Hebrew Bible. The name appears to be a conflation

110   *The abyss*

of Astarte and *bosheth*, which hints that the Hebrews felt contempt for her cult. Freud considered both names to be expressions of a primeval sexual religion (genital worship).

5 According to Arthur Feldman's (1944) psycho-historical reconstruction, a systematic attempt to stamp out this original source of the religion of Israel was undertaken by Ezra the Scribe in 458 B.C. His efforts, which were successful, led to the emergence of Torah-Judaism. Ezra turned with the great passion against the beliefs associated with the mother-goddess cult, redirecting and refocusing the religion of ancient Israel upon a single God (Yahweh). As Feldman (1944) observed, Torah-Judaism "was uncompromisingly hostile to everything that had anything to do with the Astarte-Adonis belief and cult. All its sanctuaries and cult objects were commanded to be ruthlessly destroyed, root and branch (Num. XXIII, 52; Deut. VII, 25–26; XII, 2–3; Lev. XX, 24, etc.)" (p. 376). He also noted: " . . . the belief and cult of Astarte-Adonis was abandoned, sacred prostitution entirely ceased, idolatry disappeared, child-sacrifices were given up, and other immoral and condemned practices were relinquished by the Jews in the centuries after Ezra" (p. 383). Feldman maintained that in the third stage of the Israelitish religion, known as Pharisaic-Rabbinic Judaism, the Israelites managed to secure substitutes for the old cults.

6 An allusion to the identity which holds between Adonis, Oedipus, and Christ is contained in the central page of *Totem and Taboo* (Freud, 1913a, pp. 151–152).

7 It is quite plausible to think that this scenario came to color Freud's own recollections of the reddish water in which his nanny, his private Aphrodite, bathed him during childhood. Freud's "bad treatment" dream of October 3 and 4 of 1897 might well carry within it the inchoate stirrings of his fantasy that Adonis equals the penis.

8 In particular, analysing the dream of the Botanical Monograph, Freud (1900) recalled a visually rendered memory of himself at age five as he and his three-year-old sister Anna blissfully ripped a Persian travel book with colored plates (*Tafeln*) to "pieces (*leaf by leaf*, like an artichoke . . .)" (p. 172; emphasis added). Then, in his "Screen memories" paper, Freud reports on an important scene from his childhood in Freiberg, when Sigismund and John "as though by mutual agreement," fell on Pauline and snatched "away her *flowers*" (Freud, 1899, p. 311; emphasis added). Formally a "niece," Pauline, who was slightly younger than Freud, was more like a "sister" to Sigismund (John and Pauline were children of Freud's half-brother Emanuel, who was much older than Freud). Glossing the word '*Tafeln*' (plates) Lippman (2009, pp. 581–582) suggested that it pointed to the Decalogue or Ten Commandments (*Die mosaischen Gesetztafeln*). The act of destroying the biblical tablets itself obviously signaled in the direction of a violation of the Law.

9 For Freud, brother-sister incest fantasies were a displaced expression of the Oedipus complex. Yet, reviewing this theme in literature and myth, Pedro Luzes (1990) found that the sibling object often functions as a double of the pre-oedipal mother and, further, that the fantasy of brother-sister incest might be regarded as pre-oedipal, as a unique case with both a narcissistic aspiration and a search for reintegration and wholeness: "Man feels a profound dissatisfaction; he feels separated from something fundamental, of which he has no precise memory, but which he believes to have existed before Time and History" (p. 106).

10 This awful situation materialized the "act of retribution on the part of destiny," which in Freud's Irma dream was engraved in the words "this Mathilde for that Mathilde," expressing the fantasy that his lack of medical conscientiousness had to be repaid with the death of his daughter (Volume I, pp. 138–142).

11 Lethe and Acheron were rivers which both flow through the underworld. At the beginning of the year Freud was led to think of "Acheronta" (the infernal region bordered by the river Acheron) when seeking a motto for symptom formation. In Greek mythology Acheron was a river that the soul of dead had to cross. According to Plato (Phaedo), this stream of pain was so huge that it was surpassed in size only by the ocean. Freud found himself plunged in this "great stream" in the course of his analysis of Emma. Then, in

September 1897, he was invoking the water of the Lethe River, which led to forgetfulness before reincarnation. As noted by a psychoanalytic commentator: "The effects of the water are mysterious. They induce a forgetfulness . . . And yet all that is forgotten will be repeated again in the life that is to be. It is repeated as if in a dream, unconsciously, so that humans live their lives in this peculiar masque, as if they are about to remember but can only reenact, dreamily, what has happened before" (Purcell, 1999, p. 350).

12 Freud mentioned the work of Theodor Vischer, Robert's father, on various occasions but appears not to have referred to the Robert Vischer monograph. Given Freud's fascination with Signorelli's art, however, it seems unlikely that he never consulted it before, during, or following the visit to Orvieto in the summer of 1897.

13 Pan was the only god in the Greek Pantheon who was mortal and died, his death grounding the belief that gods of the ancient world had now come to their end and that a new order would now be instituted as a result of the birth, death, and resurrection of Christ. Widely debated among historians of religion, this peculiar story has usually been explained by tracing the death of Pan back to the annual celebrations of the death of Tammuz-Adonis in his native Syria (Reinach, 1912). In *The Dying God*, the fourth volume of the third edition (in 12 volumes) of *The Golden Bough*, Frazer (1911) wrote: "In modern times, also, the annunciation of the death of the Great Pan has been much discussed and various explanations of it have been suggested. On the whole the simplest and most natural would seem to be that the deity whose sad end was thus mysteriously proclaimed and lamented was the Syrian god Tammuz or Adonis, whose death is known to have been annually bewailed by his followers both in Greece and in his native Syria" (p. 7). Freud was well acquainted with the story of the death of Pan through Rabelais, who discussed it in book IV of his *Gargantua and Pantagruel* (1552).

7 The timeless unconscious
Part II

The resurrection of the flesh

The construction of the Cathedral in Orvieto, dedicated to the Assumption of Mary, began in 1290 and lasted three centuries. The gothic façade remains one of the great masterpieces of the Late Middle Ages. The bas-reliefs, found in the inferior piers of the building, depict the history of the destiny of man, from the beginning of time to the end of the world. This was precisely the theme of Signorelli's cycle of frescoes in the Cappella Nuova of the Church in Orvieto.

These frescoes were originally commissioned to Fra Beato Angelico. The blessed Friar, however, died after having painted only two sections of the ceiling. Half a century later, Signorelli was commissioned by church officials to complete the work begun by Fra Angelico. A belief that the world would soon be coming to an end had led to an upsurge in feelings of guilt among the European populace just before the year 1500, and artists of the time were commissioned to decorate churches with scenes depicting the end of the world (*finis mundi*). Engaged to create an apocalyptic cycle of frescoes, Signorelli successfully executed the commission in Orvieto between 1500 and 1503.

The central scene in Signorelli's cycle of frescoes is *The Resurrection of the Flesh* (or *of the Dead*), illustrating one of the central tenets of the Christian faith, the promise of Christ's resurrection to all individuals who believe in him as the son of God that they will be resurrected in the flesh on the Day of Judgment, and that the Kingdom of Heaven, the New Jerusalem, will then be established for the Elects.

The fresco is thus a cosmogony in reverse. As all creation myths rupture an original state of plenitude and wholeness, myths of world's end all fulfill a wish for happy reunion. In Signorelli's fresco, this final reunion with the Queen of Heaven offers a symbolic return to the womb, in which the human body is a phallus symbolically lifted into a celestial womb, embodying the fantasy of an earthly paradise. The scene of the *Resurrection of the Flesh* captures Freud's view that the religious idea of resurrection following death was modeled on the coming to life (erection) of the male organ, the concrete token of longing. Indeed, the scene also evokes the fantasy of a prenatal state of wholeness, to nullify the primordial cut that separates every newborn from the mother to enter the world.

Signorelli's visualization of a hallucinatory wish fulfilment and reintegration fantasy fails to erase the traces of disintegration and death. On the contrary, the

Figure 7.1 Luca Signorelli (1441–1523): *The Resurrection of the Flesh*. Duomo, Orvieto. (Courtesy of Foto Scala, Firenze/Opera del Duomo di Orvieto)

corruption and rotting of the flesh is powerfully in the fresco, in the skeletal figures seen struggling to emerge from the ground (grave). Margaret Owens (2004) observed that Signorelli's decision to introduce skeletal figures is suggestive of a *danse macabre* in reverse, to "undermine the impression of splendour and triumph" (p. 23). The consequence is that the imagery of wholeness and immortality promised by Christian doctrine is here "shadowed by an insistent strain of fragmentation" (p. 28), the same which would inform Freud's dream of his self-dissection.

Lucifer amor

Freud's conception of the devil changed drastically in September of 1897. At the beginning of the year, Freud imagined the devil as a "perverse father" in disguised form. Once back in Vienna from his trip to Orvieto in September of 1897, however, he changed his mind. Two elements appear to have played a pivotal role in Freud's new view.

The first was the death of his father Jacob 11 months earlier and the mourning process that followed. On September 21, after returning from his vacation in Italy, Freud wrote Fliess to announce his decision to abandon his so-called seduction theory, dropping his earlier charges against Jacob of having been a seducer and child molester.

The second element was quite possibly Luca Signorelli's contribution as the first to transform the medieval grotesque representation of the devil into a fully humanized form. According to Vasari, an important theoretician of the Italian Renaissance, this initiated a transformation of the visual representation of man, which he named *Terribilità*[1] – a blend of beauty, fear, and awe which would later be more fully developed by Michelangelo.

Vischer (1879) explained that within the mindset of the Medieval Ages, the god of hell was the destroyer of the good and the beautiful, and typically represented as a desecrator, a monster. By portraying the devil with a complete human figure, however, Signorelli now presented him as beautiful. For this reason, Signorelli is today regarded as "the founder of the beautiful *Terribilità* [*Schrecklichkeit*] in the representation of the hell" (p. 215).

As opposed to the image of Satan of the Old Testament, Christian demons not only wage war against the good but are instruments of morality, punishing sinners and operating as guardians of "the borders of moral consciousness" (p. 216). Indeed, they were defined by Tertullian at the end of the second century as *ministri poenarum* (ministers of justice and administrators of punishments). Signorelli's greatness, Vischer argued, rested in having transferred this ethical advancement from Satan to Lucifer at an aesthetic level. Like Lucifer, the devil is punished by God to serve as an admonition to all who might follow his ways. At the same time, by punishing the sinner who has wounded the good, the devil acts in favor of the good. Lucifer, the fallen god of hell, is thereby re-established as beautiful. Signorelli's positive representation of the devil as such was informed by acknowledging the devil as an "ethical necessity of fantasy" (p. 216). And yet, as Vischer also noted, the "contradiction, which is implied in the fact that the devil is at the same time seducer and punisher [*Verführer und Strafrichter*], is highly uncanny [*hat eine erhabene Unheimlichkeit*]" (p. 216). This dimension of the uncanny soon began to inform Freud's work.

The devil, a "perverse father" in disguised form, was described by Freud as monster and desecrator in January of 1897. After returning to Vienna from the September trip to Italy, Freud began to overcome the biblical idea of the devil as a pure principle of destruction, as his meditation was infiltrated by the double essence, criminal and moral, of the Christian demon. The theme of the repression of libido then became increasingly manifest and, like Signorelli, Freud transformed the figure of the devil/father into a source of morality. In particular, Freud focused on the role of memories of sexual punishments (castration) to turn the devil/father into a "guardian of the borders of the moral consciousness."[2] He thus came to see the devil as a representation of the "obscure forces from the depths of the mind" (Freud, 1900, p. 613), and a "personification of the repressed unconscious instinctual life" (1909, p. 174). Freud's ability to examine a hellish dimension within his own psyche took on a certain Luciferian quality. Writing to Fliess on July 10, 1900: "Everything is in flux and dawning, an intellectual hell, with layer upon layer; in the darkest core, glimpses of the contours of Lucifer-Amor."

The Antichrist

Early Christians expected Jesus to return to Earth from heaven in the near future, and were disillusioned when the end of the world failed to materialize. This led Paul to warn of a "final enemy" who would be slain when Jesus made his return. It also led John to introduce the term "Antichrist" in his letters and to describe in the Book of Revelations a great, bloody battle between the evil power that had reigned and the triumphant victory of Jesus over the forces of the Antichrist. Despite the fact that the word "Antichrist" does not appear in the Book of Revelation (Apocalypse), the image of the beast in that text was always interpreted as a symbol of the Antichrist in Christian tradition. This prophecy was represented by Luca Signorelli in a huge fresco which depicted the *Preaching and Deeds of the Antichrist*.

Deviating from the canonical sequence of scenes of the Last Judgment, Signorelli offered a most unusual scene: the figure of the false prophet standing on a throne and preaching his message of destruction. The mob around him have piled up gifts at the foot of his throne; in the foreground a brutal massacre is taking place, a young woman is selling her body to an old merchant, amidst aggressive and evil-looking men, as scenes of horrors and of miraculous events are taking

Figure 7.2 Luca Signorelli (1441–1523): *The Preaching and Deeds of the Antichrist*. Duomo, Orvieto. (Courtesy of Foto Scala, Firenze/Opera del Duomo di Orvieto)

place in the background. While the preacher appears to resemble Christ, closer inspection reveals him being fed his words by Satan, who is standing next to him and whispering into his ear. The figure of the Antichrist preaching, in the middle of the fresco, appears to be the devil taking possession of Christ, the world's redeemer and savior.

This fresco of the Antichrist is rendered even more enigmatic by Signorelli's decision to include his own image in the work, standing at the bottom left-hand corner. Fra Angelico, who started the frescoes but died before completing the task, is featured in the work as well, and can be seen standing just to the left of Signorelli. The two artists are standing side by side, dressed in black and observing the Antichrist while contemplating the action unfolding before them. Signorelli is looking towards the viewer, and the blessed Friar is pointing with his left index finger towards the center of the fresco and the Antichrist. Signorelli and Fra Angelico have thus become not only spectators but interpreters of an enigma in the design of world history. Vischer (1879, p. 183) described this fresco as a *Mysterienspiel*, a "holy play" or "representation of a secret."

Freud was deeply moved by this particular fresco in when he first saw it in September of 1897. It could have reminded him of his own dialogue and collaborative efforts with Fliess. Freud, of course, had good reasons to see himself as an Antichrist, a political term aimed at secessionists and later applied to any entity denying Christian beliefs. In fact, Freud was deconstructing the doctrine of the Resurrection of the Flesh, to trace it back to the erection of the male organ, as his theoretical fantasy about Adonis and his positing of the Lord as the penis suggests. As a double of Christ, the Antichrist was traditionally imagined as a Jew.[3] Ideas bearing on past instances of anti-Semitism likely rushed to Freud's mind as he looked at Signorelli's fresco to examine the scene before him. Freud did take a side-trip to Lake Trasimeno that same day, a further likely reminder of his admiration of the Semitic hero Hannibal, his symbol for "the conflict between the tenacity of Jewry and the organization of the Catholic church," as he (1900) observed when analyzing the fourth of his dreams on Rome (p. 197, see also Masson, 1985, p. 285).

Finally, it is noteworthy that Friedrich Nietzsche's *The Antichrist* was published in 1895, attacking Christian morality and its decadent conception of God. For Nietzsche, Christian morality stood as a "declaration of war against life, against nature, against the will to live!" (*The Antichrist*, § 18). If Christians were less decadent and sick, their God would instead be brave, virile, and destructive, rather than purely good.[4]

Travelling with Minna

A central symptom of Freud's neurosis was his anxiety and fear of traveling by train (Jones, 1953, p. 335). Freud was convinced that this travel-phobia traced back to the train trips moving with his family from Freiberg to Leipzig in 1859, when Freud had turned three. The family first moved to Leipzig before relocating, soon after, to Vienna. Freud preserved vivid memories of this journey and its train travels, recalling his sexual excitement upon seeing his mother naked on the overnight train. He also recalled feeling frightened in Breslau: when the train pulled into the station at night, the gaslights appeared as "spirits burning in hell" (Freud, 1985, pp. 268, 285). Freud's transference neurosis in the years of his creative illness thus featured the reliving of these exciting and anxiety-filled train trips of 1859.

Freud's urgent desire to travel south began in August 1895, shortly after the dream of Irma's injection. Freud's younger brother Alexander had regularly accompanied Freud on his trips. After Easter of 1898, however, Alexander would no longer tolerate Freud's hectic traveling pace – "moving too rapidly from place to place and seeing too many beautiful things in a single day" (Freud, 1900, p. 432), and decided not accompany Freud on his next vacation. But Freud found it difficult to travel alone and began to think of his sister-in-law as a possible travel companion. Freud liked Minna, an intelligent, open-minded individual. Besides Fliess, she was the only other person in Freud's life at that time with whom he actively discussed his work.[5]

Rumors concerning Minna having "replaced her sister" for Freud's affections have a long history in the analytic literature (Jones, 1955, p. 431; also 1953, p. 153), and picked up new energy after Peter Swales (1982) proposed that Freud's neurotic wish and anxiety to enter Rome functioned as a screen for his desire for Minna. Swales, however, took his hypothesis further, claiming that Freud had also engaged in a sexual affair with Minna, which led to her becoming pregnant and having an abortion.[6] Unlike Swales, Anzieu (1986) considered Freud's desire for Minna as an expression of a wider oedipal constellation informing his neurotic position on Rome – a 'promised land' which in Freud's case could "only be seen from afar" (p. 184). Freud came closer to his forbidden promised land when he and Minna began traveling and vacationing alone together in the summer of 1898. According to Anzieu, the trips which Freud and Minna took together then served to re-actualize Freud's personal incest taboo (p. 328; 542–543).

As a matter of fact, Freud became increasingly preoccupied with the theme of brother-sister incest during the summer of 1898, as he and Minna made plans for a trip to Italy together.[7] Freud's expectations, memories, and fantasies in this regard broke through in two important dreams of July 1898, his Hollthurn dream and his Count Thun dream, which is also known as a "revolutionary dream" because of the prominent role played by the themes of defiance and rebellion against a superior power.

Superman

On August 2 or 3 of 1898 Freud delivered a lecture on hysteria and perversion in Kraft-Ebing's large lecture room. Feeling dissatisfied and depleted, Freud decided to thumb through Jules Garnier's illustrations of Rabelais before going to sleep. He found the deeds of Gargantua, Rabelais's "superman," highly amusing, particularly Garnier's drawing of Gargantua taking revenge on the Parisians by "sitting astride on Notre Dame and turning his stream of urine upon the city" (1900, p. 469).

That night Freud dreamt himself micturating on a long seat at the end of an open-air closet. The seat was "covered with small heaps of feces of all sizes and degrees of freshness." In the dream, he felt no feelings of disgust as his long stream of urine "washed everything clean" (1900, p. 469), the stream itself being "an unmistakable sign" of Freud's own feelings of greatness, imagining himself as powerful, indeed as "superman" (Freud, 1900, p. 470), a term reflecting Nietzsche's own vision of the *Übermensch*.

Tellingly enough, in his first meditation on the horror of incest (Draft N, of May 1897) prompted by the Hella dream, Freud imagined that any individual who managed to liberate himself from the chains of civilized morality and thus broken the social prohibition of incest was a "superman" (Masson, 1985, p. 252). This idea surfaced in a meditation inspired by Nietzsche's critical vision of holiness and the ascetic ideal that informs the Judaic-Christian religion (Holmes, 1983, pp. 195–196). Freud never abandoned this idea and in fact made use of it, in 1912, when speculating on the primal father of the wild horde who, enjoying total freedom, power, and independence, needed no approval from others to make decisions to fulfill his every desire. Nine years later, in *Group Psychology and the Analysis of the Ego*, Freud described the savage father of the horde: "He, at the very beginning of the history of mankind, was the 'superman' [*Übermensch*] whom Nietzsche only expected from the future" (Freud, 1921, p. 123).

Freud's dream of an "open-air closet" thus anticipated his upcoming trip to the fair land of Italy (the closet in the dream resembling those found in small towns throughout the country). Only a day or two later, Freud and Minna vacationed alone together for the first time. Between August 4 and 15 of 1898, they made their way through the Austrian Tyrol, Italy, and Switzerland. They also slept in the same room for a few nights, registering at the Hotel *Schweizerhaus* in Maloja (not far from Trafoi) on August 13 as "*Dr. Sigm. Freud und Frau* [and wife]" (Maciejewski, 2006, 2008).

When the letters between Freud and Minna Bernays were published in 2005 they revealed a rich, dense family life scarcely compatible with the idea of a secret double life between them (Hirschmüller, 2005). Maciejewski's recent finding that Freud and Minna registered in a hotel in Maloja as a married couple who slept overnight in the same room, however, has naturally helped to revive the old "malicious and entirely untrue legend," to quote Jones (1953, p. 153), of a secret sexual liaison between them.[8] The chance of a possible affair between Freud and Minna, however, remains at odds with what is known of the sexual life of the founder of psychoanalysis, namely, that his *vita sexualis* was not exactly something he was proud of.

Elisabeth Roudinesco (2014, p. 68) calculated that Freud's sexual life during his marriage lasted roughly nine years; the rest of the time, she argued, Freud practiced abstinence. Roudinesco (2015) thought it was precisely Freud's sublimation of his sexual impulses that fueled his creative energies: "When Freud . . . refers to his 'subdued' or '*enberne* [half-mast]' libido, one mainly receives the impression that the abstinence to which he forces himself was not alien to his daring search for the sexual causes buried in the unconscious" (p. 18).

Truth be told, Freud was not proud of his abstinence either. Like Nietzsche, he saw it as a sign of enfeeblement and decay in men. It was in no way a virtue but, rather, a burden of "aging" which Freud lived out with resignation. Alongside his psychosomatic symptoms, it undergirded his pessimism and fostered an image of himself as an old and depleted man.[9] Sexual fantasies thus functioned as an antidote to Freud's foul mood and psychic constellation, and in general, appeared to exercise a re-vitalizing effect on his psyche, but not in this particular case. Judging it from its consequences, Freud's sleeping in the same hotel room together with Minna was a frightening nightmare to disremember.

Forgetting

Following his vacation alone with Minna, Freud spent two weeks in Aussee with his family, and soon began to have episodes of "forgetting." In August of 1898, he was suddenly unable to recall the name of the author of a poem on a rebel who became a popular hero after he was executed (Masson, 1985, p. 324), and just shortly after, he found himself unable to recall the name "Signorelli."

Riding to Herzegovina in a horse-drawn carriage in the first week of September, Freud found himself amiably conversing with a fellow German tourist about previous vacations in Europe. The two men soon began exchanging idea on beautiful experiences they had each enjoyed in past journeys. Freud wanted to communicate to his fellow traveller that the frescoes in the Cathedral in Orvieto were a must, not to be missed. He was however suddenly unable to recall the name of the Italian artist who painted the frescoes. Freud's frustration soon grew into inner torment as he was unable to recall the name of the artist for several more days.

A specific scene from one of the frescoes (*The Preaching and Deeds of the Antichrist*) appeared to Freud's mind in vivid fashion as he tried to recall the name of the Italian painter. The name, continued to escape him. Instead, the names Botticelli and Boltraffio rushed to mind as he tried to recall the forgotten name. It was not until a "cultivated Italian" finally provided him the lost name (Signorelli) that Freud was able to finally free himself "from his inner torment." As Freud noted in his letter to Fliess on September 22, 1898, soon after returning to Vienna and his vacation with Martha: "I was myself able to add the artist's *first* name, *Luca*." It was only after the missing name was fully restored that the ultra-lucid (*überdeutlich*) vision of the master's features, found in the bottom left-hand corner of the Antichrist fresco, faded away from the window of Freud's mind (Freud, 1898b, p. 291, 1901, p. 12).

Freud traced this act of forgetting back to a previous conversation while vacationing in Trafoi in which the themes of "death and sexuality" were discussed. Talk of these themes, Freud reckoned, touched on memories which led him to repress the name Signorelli. He had spoken the word "*Herr*" ("*Signor*" in Italian) twice during his effort to retrieve the lost name; first in relation to the peculiar resignation which Bosnians held towards death – "*Herr* [Sir], what is there to be said? If he could be saved, I know you would help him" – and, second, when reflecting on the importance which Bosnians supposedly attached to sexual pleasure ("*Herr*, you must know that if that comes to an end, then life is of no value.")

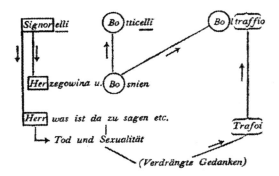

Figure 7.3 Freud's original schema of his analysis of the Signorelli slip.

Freud had stopped speaking Italian and switched to German during his trip precisely because the man sitting next to him was from Berlin and spoke German. Freud (1898b) argued that his forgetting of Signorelli had been facilitated by the translation of the word "*Signor*" into German: "*Herr*" (pp. 292–293). Hence, what was ultimately and truly lost during the process of translation was the word "*Signor*" (Lord, in Italian).

A number of scholars (Schimek, 1974, p. 222; Vitz, 1988, pp. 77, 158–159; Zilboorg, 1962, p. 167) have suggested that the word which disappeared during the process of translation (Signor) signalled back to God. The German "*Herr*," it turns out, not only translates Signor from Italian but also means Lord or God in German. Lacan (1973), as he pondered Freud's repression of Signorelli, could not help but to be reminded of Nietzsche's famous pronouncement "God is dead."[10]

The phenomenon of forgetting proper names is a common occurrence that typically does not involve repression, when the inability to recall is easily overcome with a roundabout. During his conversation with the tourist from Berlin, for instance, Freud could have easily resolved his problem through his fellow traveler in saying that the artist he was trying to recall was the author of the most prized possession of the Royal Museum in Berlin, *The Triumph of Pan*. As noted, it can be assumed that Freud was well acquainted with this particular canvas, and had several opportunities to talk about it with Fliess, either before or immediately after visiting Orvieto in September of 1897, when he traveled to Berlin to meet him. That Freud failed to employ this strategy confirms not only that an act of repression by Freud had indeed occurred but that Signorelli's painting of the Lord of the Wilderness must have played a role in Freud's inability to recall the name of the artist.

This particular painting, not mentioned by Freud during his analysis of Signorelli, offers an important missing link for better grasping the reason for this repression, rendering Freud's substitution of the name Signorelli with Botticelli, for instance, more understandable and logical. It also highlights the deep thematic connection between the *Triumph of Pan* and the *Birth of Venus*, paintings with a shared sexual/genital theme. The valuation of the genitals was hinted at by Freud by association in his effort to analyze his repression of Signorelli: "*Herr*, you must know that if that comes to an end then life is of no value." In short, the reintegration of this missing link (the *Triumph of Pan*) suggests that the repressed "Signor" was associated in Freud's mind with Adonis, the Lord he saw as a personification of the penis, and, ultimately, with the "great Lord Penis" he referred to in the letter to Fliess of January 24, 1897.

Another detail to consider is the fact that Signorelli's painting of Pan, at least according to the Berlin Museum guide for 1886 (Königliche Museen zu Berlin, 1886), hung in the *Gemälde-Galerie* along with three other canvases by Signorelli and a "rare" painting by Boltraffio.[11] Boltraffio was the second name which came to mind as Freud tried to retrieve the lost name. In his analysis Freud traced the first syllable (Bo) back to the "Bo" found at the beginning of Bosnia and Botticelli. He then linked the word "Traffio" to a village in the Tyrol where he had stayed just a few weeks earlier, on August 8 of 1898, but failed to specify that he had been vacationing at the Tyrol alone with Minna at the time.[12] The gap Freud left open obviously touched back to his own 'superman' fantasy.

It cannot be known what, if anything, occurred sexually between Freud and Minna in Maloja. The evidence suggests that it was not a pleasant experience and that what Freud most desired was to erase it from his mind. Freud's analysis of Signorelli allowed him finally to restore his own personal sense of self-worth. It was precisely at this point that Freud grasped the fear of castration as a barrier against incest, an idea he came to soon after, in analyzing his dream of The Three Fates at the end of September or the beginning of October of 1898.

When analyzing this dream, Freud (1900) recalled the first novel he ever read: the hero in it went "mad and kept calling out the names of the three women who had brought the greatest happiness and sorrow into his life" (p. 204). The novel in question was Charles Kingsley's *Hypatia*, a fictionalized account of the life of the pagan philosopher who headed the Neoplatonic school at Alexandria (Grinstein, 1980, pp. 189–192). In this popular work the monk Philammon was sent to convert Hypatia, who instead seduced Philammon and convinced him to abandon Christianity. The monk then fell in love with Pelagia – a Greek beauty who had been cast in the role of Aphrodite in sensual pagan ceremonies – before discovering, to his horror, that she was also his sister. Unable to contain himself before Pelagia's sensual erotic dance, Philammon suddenly cries out: "Pelagia! Sister! My sister! . . . ." According to Grinstein (1980, p. 191), it was Freud's memory of this particular scene that informed his associations and analysis of his dream of the Three Fates.

Freud (1900) commented that one of the thoughts standing behind this dream was that "one should never neglect an opportunity, since life is short and death inevitable" (p. 207). Freud, however, also noted that the idea of seizing the day (*carpe diem*) was contrasted by "restraining thoughts of every kind and even threats of the most revolting sexual punishments" (p. 208). While the *carpe diem* motto seems to signal toward a possible missed encounter and "opportunity" with Minna

122 The abyss

in Maloja, his allusion to "the most revolting sexual punishments" brings back to the center of action the genital mutilation which Emma suffered as a result of her being circumcised as a child. Indeed, it serves to reveal just how powerfully Emma's shocking punishment had transformed into an obsessive self-restraining thought for Freud: the naked, crude fact of Emma's genital mutilation had in Freud's mind morphed into a concrete token of castration, the paradigmatic punishment meted out against those who dared to violate the incest taboo.

Notes

1 Vischer (1879) described the *Terribilità* as a core feeling of every religion, the original dread unconsciously objectified in gods and demons, as in the thundering Zeus, the panic terror in Pan, or the Christian demon of possession. During the course of the Italian Renaissance, this feeling became progressively embodied in the concrete life of people living at the time. At the end of this process, which culminated with the appearance of Michelangelo's work, the *Terribile* [in Italian], the source of the terror was no longer localized in an external entity (a god or a demon) but was now instead portrayed through the human figure. It became "a second ego, alien and tyrannical," which was revealed by "the rage through the gaze, the threat through the visage and the action" (p. 228).
2 In Freud's dream book, the connection between libido and punishment is attested to by his interpretation of the "devil-dreams" which a 13-year-old boy experienced – a case of *pavor nocturnus* previously reported in the pediatric literature. The boy had masturbated years earlier and been threatened with severe punishment by his parents for it. With the onset of puberty, the temptation to masturbate returned, unleashing "a struggle for repression." Because of this struggle the libido was suppressed and transformed into anxiety." Freud (1900) concluded that the "anxiety had taken over the punishments" with which the boy "had been threatened earlier" (p. 586).
3 As Hippolytus saw it, the "circumcision of the Saviour came into the world, and he [Antichrist] in like manner shall come" (quoted in Bousset, 1896, p. 136).
4 Significantly enough, paraphrases of the expression "*Umwertung aller Werte*" (transmutation of all values), which Nietzsche used in several works, including *The Antichrist* (§ 62), can be found in the letter Freud wrote to Fliess on September 21 of 1897. In was in that letter, as we recall, that Freud abandoned his theory of trauma. The impact of Nietzsche's statement may also be found in *The Interpretation of Dreams*. Freud used the expression "*in dieser Sturz aller Werte*," translated by Strachey and later Masson as "in this collapse of everything valuable," in his letter to Fliess of September 21 of 1897. In his dream book, however, he used "*Umwertung aller psychischen Werte*," translated by Strachey as the "trans-valuation of all psychic values" (Freud, 1900, p. 330) (Steiner, 1994, p. 543, footnote 37; see also Mazlish, 1968).
5 Minna traveled to Vienna to assist the Freud family during Martha's final pregnancy in 1895. She decided to move in, joining the Freud household a year later, in the summer of 1896. Freud appears to have been attracted to Minna from the beginning. Minna became engaged to Ignaz Schönberg in 1882, but her fiancée contracted tuberculosis not long after and died four years later, in 1886. Minna remained "unmarried and unattached." Anzieu (1986) suggests that Freud must have seen her as "an available, desirable, and prohibited libidinal object" from the beginning (p. 542).
6 Minna was admitted into a treatment center in Merano after symptoms of her tuberculosis returned in 1900. Swales came to his controversial conclusion as a result of his interpretation of Freud's Aliquis slip (Freud, 1901, p. 11). See Swales (1992, 2003).
7 On June 10 of 1898, for instance, he frivolously wrote to Martha: "I announce to you that this evening I unfaithfully go to Salzburg where I will meet Minna in the morning . . . "

(Hirschmüller, 2005, p. 37, footnote 16). Freud began reading Conrad Ferdinand Meyer's *Die Richterin* [The woman judge] at this time and, a few days later, sent Fliess a brief essay on the Swiss writer. The opening sentence of Freud's manuscript reads: "there is no doubt that this [Meyer's essay] is a defense against the writer's memory of an affair with his sister" (Masson, 1985, p. 256). Peter Rudnytsky (2012) isolated a number of allusions to literary works Freud made between 1897 and 1901 which connected to this theme. Freud's references and allusions, Rudnytsky argued, should be seen as "an unconscious memoir" of his "deepening involvement with [his sister-in-law] Minna Bernays."

8 The reader is referred to Burston (2008), Hirschmüller (2007), and Lothane (2007a, 2007b). As Roudinesco noted in her preface to Freud's correspondence with Minna, published in France in 2015, "dozens of novels, articles, [and] essays" have been dedicated to Freud's possible "liaison" with his sister-in-law. Indeed, the rumor has become "one of the main traits of anti-Freudian historiography at the end of the XX and the beginning of the XXI century" (p. 18). On this point see also Roudinesco (2010, 2014, p. 297). While true, the idea of something being "anti-Freudian" only serves to polarize an already highly contentious field in which opinions differ widely. There are many scholars who are not "Freud bashers," who, after examining the evidence, remain convinced that Freud engaged in a sexual affair with Minna. Among them are Daniel Burston, Peter Gay, and Peter Rudnytsky.

9 Freud's fantasy of self-depletion was so intense that it affected a number of the individuals around him at the time. Jung's wife, for instance, once wrote to encourage Freud to adopt a less resigned view of life. Freud had supposedly confided to her that his marriage had long been "amortized" and that "there was nothing more to do" in his case "except – die" (McGuire, 1974, p. 456).

10 Nietzsche's famed pronouncement, said Lacan (1973), had perhaps functioned as "a shelter against the threat of castration" (p. 27). Lacan appears to have been particularly fascinated by the verbal ruins which Freud's attempt to isolate and pinpoint the reasons for his repression of Signorelli had left behind. Indeed, we can often find Lacan returning to the "hole" which surfaced in Freud's mind as a result of his inability to recall the name of the artist who painted the famed fresco of the Last Judgment in the Cathedral in Orvieto. Lacan discussed Freud's repression of Signorelli in his seminar on several occasions: Seminar 2 (lectures of February 3, February 10 and June 6, 1954), Seminar 5 (lectures of November 13 and November 20, 1957), Seminar 11 (lecture of January 22, 1964) and Seminar 12 (lecture of January 6, 1965).

11 Giovanni Boltraffio (1467–1516) was not a well-known painter. How, then, did Freud secure knowledge of his name and art? Philip Kuhn (2000) has proposed that the "cultivated Italian" who provided Freud with the forgotten name (Signorelli) was Giovanni Morelli, alias Ivan Lermolieff, an Italian physician and author in 1897 of *Della Pittura Italiana*. Freud purchased Morelli's book while visiting Milan on September 14 of 1898, a week after he was unable to recall "Signorelli." Morelli's book mentions the work of several Italian painters, among them Signorelli, Botticelli, and Boltraffio (Ginzburg, 1989, p. 101). Peter Swales (2003) has examined the relation between these three Italian artists and Morelli's art collection (viewable at the Galleria Morelli in Bergamo) by relying on Morelli's book as the source of Freud's knowledge of Boltraffio. However, Freud must have first become acquainted with Boltraffio's work when he visited the Berlin Museum 11 years earlier, in March of 1886 (Bonomi, 1994b). He may have visited the Berlin Museum again between 1886 and 1898.

12 Instead, he only mentioned that he had received the news of the suicide of one his patients while at the Tyrol. Freud presented three separate and different versions of his attempt to trace the source of his repression of Signorelli. It was only during his last account (Freud, 1901) that he was finally and publicly able to explain the role which the village of Trafoi played in his repression of Signorelli. It occurred, Freud explained, on account of thoughts concerning "death and sexuality" which had reached him while vacationing in Trafoi. Freud relates that he not only received news of the suicide of one

of patients while there but that the patient had decided to take his life "on account of an incurable sexual complaint" (p. 3). A careful survey of the material suggests that Freud's account of his repression of Signorelli featured a last minute attempt by him to bridge the gap left open during his attempt to analyze his repression of the name, most likely as a result of his wanting to hide the personal and private details that played a role in his repression of Signorelli (Billig, 2000; Swales, 2003).

8 Necropolis

> Dismembered limbs, a severed head, a hand cut off at the wrist, . . . feet which dance by themselves, . . . – all these have something peculiarly uncanny about them, especially when, as in the last instance, they prove capable of independent activity in addition. As we already know, this kind of uncanniness springs from its proximity to the castration complex. To some people the idea of being buried alive by mistake is the most uncanny thing of all. And yet psycho-analysis has taught us that this terrifying phantasy is only a transformation of another phantasy which had originally nothing terrifying about it at all, but was qualified by a certain lasciviousness – the phantasy, I mean, of intra-uterine existence.
>
> Sigmund Freud, The uncanny (1919b, p. 244)

Psychic tombs

Psychic tombs are disconnected localities, cut off from the flow of time, "inaccessible," yet "preserved," like the city of Pompeii (Freud, 1907a, p. 40). Freud's profound fascination with archeology informed his vision of the split-off regions in the psyche. Ever since *Studies on Hysteria*, Freud compared his treatment method to the process of an archeological excavation, and his passion for archeology was reflected in the word "propylaea," a keyword of the founding dream of psychoanalysis. Greek in origin, this words refers to the labial entry to the vagina and the ceremonial gateway of Greek Temples, providing a "switch point" between flesh and stones, and linking the human body with a house, building or architectural structure (Volume I, p. 8, 117–118). Apparently, during the period when he labored to found psychoanalysis, Freud entertained the fantasy of Emma as a precious "founding-" or "corner-stone," as suggested by her family name: "Eckstein" (Volume I, pp. 159–160).

This fantasy seems to inform the famous "archeological metaphor" in "The aetiology of hysteria" in April of 1896. Discarding the gynecological method, which consisted of directly inspecting the anatomy of the genitals, Freud now likened symptoms of hysteria to monuments, proposing a method to unearth the causes of symptoms buried in the psyche as akin to that of archaeologists. As Freud wrote:

> Imagine that an explorer arrives in a little-known region where his interest is aroused by an expanse of ruins, with remains of walls, fragments of columns,

and tablets with half-effaced and unreadable inscriptions. He may content himself with inspecting what lies exposed to view, . . . But he may . . . uncover what is buried. If his work is crowned with success, . . . the fragments of columns can be filled out into a temple; the numerous inscriptions, which, by good luck, may be bilingual, reveal an alphabet and a language, and, when they have been deciphered and translated, yield undreamed-of information about the events of the remote past, to commemorate which the monuments were built. *Saxa loquuntur*! [The stones speak!]

(Freud, 1896c, p. 191)

Comparing hysterical symptoms to "monuments" was a stroke of genius. This is far beyond a mechanic conception of causality. In no way is a monument "caused" by the event it commemorates; rather, it is inhabited by it, and in ways which correspond to Sartre's phenomenological description of the imaginary as a quasi-hallucinatory inscription of an absent object into the present). Freud's language in this passage moves well beyond the level of description, however. Read in the light of the naked, crude fact of Emma's genital cut, it is a clear and concrete example of how language can function as a natural habitat for dissociation. The meaning of the "little-known region" in the passage is transparent enough; the ruins and fragments are Emma's mutilated labia. The bilingual inscription encountered by the lucky explorer is an echo of the trimethylamin chemical formula in the Irma dream, as is the hidden language working below the surface of Hebrew. The key word unearth is "*brith milah*," the stone ("Stein" in German) which "speaks," in this case to the direction of Emma's family name: Eck-*stein* (Stein = saxa). The foundation stone of Freud's archeological metaphor was inhabited by a ghost.

It was only in the summer of 1897 that the ghost suddenly became real for Freud. On the way to Orvieto, Freud visited a museum, likely in Chiusi, with an important collection of Etruscan objects. Freud was attracted to a number of black pottery objects that were rectangular in shape, part of a bereavement toilet-set of an Etruscan Lady and had the form of a ship; they also greatly resembled, Freud noted, modern "breakfast-sets."

One of these objects resurfaced (in May 1898) in Freud's only dream of himself together with his brother Alexander. The object in the dream reminded Freud (1900) of "the funeral boats in which dead bodies were placed and committed to the sea for burial" (p. 466). Since the ship in his dream was broken in the middle and "cut off short," Freud saw it as "the return after a shipwreck ['*Schiffbruch*,' literally: 'ship-break']" (p. 466).

The fragmentation and incorporation of this dream suggest that Emma Eckstein's "cut" reawakened in Freud memories of the early catastrophe of his mother's grief over the death of her infant son Julius in April 1858 (see Volume I, pp. 214–216). Was this the moment when little Sigismund had to face "the task of having a sexually demanding mother, and having to satisfy her"? Ferenczi made the conjecture in his *Clinical Diary*, and added: "At some point, his mother's passionate nature may have presented him with such a task. (The primal scene may have rendered him relatively impotent.)" (Dupont, 1985, p. 188). What is certain is that the bodily sensation of breaking into pieces announced in Freud's "breakfast-ship" dream, and visualized in the verbal fragments of his Signorelli slip, was about to become actual in the dream of self-dissection.

An Etruscan grave

Under the fresh impression of the Etruscan black pottery, and after seeing Signorelli's Last Judgement, on September 9 of 1897 Freud visited the Etruscan necropolis at the foot of the rock on which the medieval city of Orvieto was constructed.

The necropolis was built like a town, a product of the Etruscans' belief that the dead were not really dead. The typical tombs of the necropolis were grouped into blocks, most of them consisting of single, rectangular chambered tombs aligned along burial roads. Funerary inscriptions, incised into the entrance lintels, featured the name of the tomb's owner. These inscriptions were often written in a possessive style, allowing the tomb to speak metaphorically: "I belong to . . . . ." These remains of an archaic age are found in a volcanic area bearing the name of Necropolis at "Crocefisso del tufo" (Tuff crucifix), as an old crucifix had once helped to mark the place.

Figure 8.1 The Etruscan necropolis at the foot of Orvieto, photo circa 1890. (Courtesy of Fratelli Alinari, Firenze)

Walking the stony roads of the Etruscan necropolis would likely have stirred Freud's associations to Rider Haggard's novel *She*. The starting point of the novel is the death of the hero's mother while giving birth to her son. In the narrative, the birth of the hero in the novel is pinpointed as May of 1856, the month and year of Freud's own birth.[1] The hero of the novel, Leo Vincey, receives instructions from his dead father to travel to a lost kingdom in the African interior. After a perilous journey he reaches the subterranean realm of Kôr, a series of catacombs built as tombs inside a dormant volcano by an ancient and mighty civilization of the Dark Continent. This kingdom was ruled with absolute power by Ayesha, an enchanting and bewitching phallic woman who is referred to as "She-who-must-be-obeyed," or simply "She" in the novel.

Ayesha had learned the secret of immortality and lived for more than two millennia while waiting for the return to life of Kallikrates, the man she loved but killed in a fit of jealous rage. With her magic powers, she preserved his body in a secret death chamber, a holy crypt she visited daily in hopes of his resurrection. Leo Vincey, himself a descendant of Kallikrates, is quickly recognized by Ayesha as the reincarnation of her lover. Now ardently desiring Leo, she discards Kallikrates's body while wishing that Leo remain with her forever.

Once the narrative sheds its Victorian garb, what remains is a version of the Adonis-Astarte legend. Leo is obviously an Adonis, Ayesha an Astarte. Indeed, Ayesha destroys her lover while mourning his corpse, finally rejoicing to recognize his reincarnation in Leo, his descendant. According to Grinstein (1980), Ayesha is a "magna mater of ancient times," a woman who treats her lovers as "a phallic possession" (p. 402).

In the novel, Ayesha is determined to make Leo immortal like her. In the final scene in the novel, they slowly descend into the heart of the volcano, the "womb of the earth," to reach the eternal flame of life. To cross a chasm, they carry a plank which, at a certain point in the story, is dropped and falls down to the depths below (this detail would later feature as an element in Freud's dream of self-dissection). In the novel, Ayesha loses her immortality and perishes in the fire of the eternal flame of life. Leo, the novel's hero, is then able to make his way up from the volcano to resume his life.

The same does not happen with Freud: a part of his mind never did rise back to the surface. It was precisely in the Etruscan necropolis near Orvieto that Freud purchased the first of what would grow to become his large collection of antiquities. His first purchase was an Etruscan cinerary urn.[2] Freud's consulting room would in time be cluttered with Etruscan, Egyptian, Greek, and Roman vases and statuettes, reproducing the interior of a grave, as he himself would say to one of his patients (Freud, 1909b, p. 176; Gamwell & Wells, 1989). Even more important, as he walked along the streets of the necropolis at the foot of the city of Orvieto, Freud decided to climb down one of the Etruscan graves.[3]

In the French edition of his study of the founder of psychoanalysis, Didier Anzieu claimed that Freud made his way down the tomb with his sister-in-law. Freud, proposed Anzieu, must have begun fantasizing about the fact that "married couples" were "buried in the same death chamber" (Anzieu, 1975, pp. 552–554).

This erroneous claim was removed when Anzieu realized that Freud had vacationed in Orvieto in 1897 with his brother Alexander rather than Minna.

While mistaken, Anzieu's interpretation of the scene was not altogether off target as it offers the Etruscan grave as the psychic place where Freud's incestuous desire lay buried, thus affirming what Freud himself indicated while commenting on his dream of self-dissection. In the analysis of that dream, Freud presented his entombment as a tabooed primal scene, quoting Mephistopheles's words from Goethe's *Faust* (Part I, Scene 4):

> After all, the best of what you know
> may not be told to boys.

These lines were also cited in a letter to Fliess, complaining that it was "a pity that one always keeps one's mouth shut about the most intimate thing." The "intimate things" were most likely his view of Minna as a "reincarnation" of a female figure from his childhood.[1] Now here is Freud's final dream.

The "eternal return of the same"

Freud (1900) brought *The Interpretation of Dreams* to an end with these words:

> By picturing our wishes as fulfilled, dreams are after all leading us into the future. But this future, which the dreamer pictures as the present, has been moulded by his indestructible wish into a perfect likeness of the past.
>
> (p. 621)

By May of 1899 Freud had virtually completed his dream book and was reviewing the final chapter, the chapter containing his "ultimate explanations" of the mental apparatus, when the dream appeared. While Freud was likely reflecting on the tendency of psychic life to endlessly repeat the past, a Lady, whom Anzieu (1986, p. 427) identified as Minna Bernays, asked him to lend her something to read.[5] Freud responded with a copy of Rider Haggard's novel *She*, "A *strange* book, but full of hidden meaning . . . the eternal feminine, the immortality of our emotions . . .," Freud had begun to say. Minna interrupted him, however, because she wanted to read his own work. Freud then admitted that his own "immortal works" had not yet been published. "So . . ." Minna went on to say, "when are we to expect these so-called ultimate explanations of yours which you've promised even *we* shall find readable?"

Freud did not respond to Minna's mocking remark. Instead, he silently reflected on the sacrifice entailed by the process of writing his dream book and making its contents public. That very night Freud (1900) dreamed:

> Old Brücke must have set me some task; *Strangely Enough*, it related to a dissection of the lower part of my own body, my pelvis and legs, which I saw before me as though in the dissecting-room, but without noticing their absence in

myself and also without a trace of any gruesome feeling. Louise N. was standing beside me and doing the work with me. The pelvis had been eviscerated, and it was visible now in its superior, now in its inferior, aspect, the two being mixed together. Thick flesh-coloured protuberances (which, in the dream itself, made me think of haemorrhoids) could be seen. Something which lay over it, and was like crumpled silver-paper, had also to be carefully fished out.

(p. 453)

In the second part of his dream Freud was initiating a long journey, first penetrating through a house on a cab before passing through a changing landscape. During the journey he was accompanied by an Alpine guide who physically carried him, out of consideration for his tired legs. Finally, after passing a slippery ground, Freud and his guide reached and entered a small wooden house, at the end of which Freud sees an open window. Once inside, the guide sets Freud down and lays two wooden boards, which were standing ready nearby, upon the windowsill, so as to help bridge a chasm which had to be crossed over from the window. The wooden house, Freud wrote, was "also, no doubt, a coffin, that is to say, the grave." Freud wrote that all the anxiety he did not feel in the dissection room was now displaced into his tired legs, with the expectation he would die. When he noticed that two grown-up men were lying on wooden benches inside the wooden house in his dream and, further, that two children were sleeping beside them, the thought suddenly occurred that what would make "the crossing possible was not the boards but the children." At that precise point Freud woke up from his dream in a state of "mental fright" (p. 453).

Freud did not offer a real analysis of this dream, reminiscent of a grand event of castration, but restricted himself to a few general observations. The condensation process at work in his self-dissection dream, he tried to explain, was simply too great to examine in detail. When glossing the dream, however, Freud noted that the "*Präparation*" (self-dissection) stood for his self-analysis.

Freud's peering down at his own eviscerated pelvis in the dream pulls forth the image at the starting point of his self-analysis, the horrible spectacle upon opening Irma's mouth/vagina in the dream of Irma's injection. Freud's long and difficult journey thus seems to end with this image circling back to the very beginning. The horrible spectacle was now no longer that of a rotting mouth/vagina but, rather, Freud's own eviscerated pelvis. The cut endured by Emma now lay buried within the personal wound of his dream.[6]

The evisceration scene found in Freud's final dream brought into representation not only the emotional component which had been brutally injured in Freud but also his capacity to observe himself coldly as a spectator from the outside, as a scientist.

In the second half of the dream, he has undertaken a perilous journey in the hope of reaching an "undiscovered region." The journey in Freud's dream strongly related to the contents of two novels by Rider Haggard, with perilous journeys to the "womb of the Earth." Freud thought that this dream work achieved a masterful production at representing "the most unwished-for of all thoughts," namely his own death, "by a wish-fulfillment." Freud was convinced at the time that all dreams, including anxiety dreams, involved the fulfillment of a wish:

> I had already been in a grave once, but it was an excavated Etruscan grave near Orvieto, a narrow chamber with two stone benches along its walls, on which the skeletons of two grown-up men were lying. The inside of the wooden house in the dream looked exactly like it, except that the stone was replaced by wood. The dream seems to have been saying: "If you must rest in a grave, let it be the Etruscan one." And, by making this replacement, it transformed the gloomiest of expectations into one that was highly desirable.
> (pp. 454–455)

This is a puzzling claim. Freud himself admitted a split between intellect and emotions in his dream, by noticing that that the dream work transformed the idea of dying but not the corresponding "affect":

> I woke up in a 'mental fright,' even after the successful emergence of the idea that children may perhaps achieve what their father has failed to – a fresh allusion to the strange novel in which a person's identity is retained through a series of generations for over two thousand years.
> (p. 455)[7]

Grinstein (1980) glossed on this point: "The connection between the theme of repetition-compulsion and death . . . and the wish to master a traumatic event, all seem to foreshadow Freud's concept of the death instinct in the years to come" (p. 402).

What follows expands on this association with the repetition-compulsion theme, selecting only a few points: the child-bridge, the penis-fish, and the womb-tomb.

The bridge

In Freud's dream the wish for immortality was expressed by the bridge, a penis symbol, as proposed by Ferenczi.[8] Citing Ferenczi's note, Freud (1933a) went on to suggest that bridges in dreams first of all mean "the male organ." It tallies with this, he added, that a "woman who has not overcome her wish to be a man has frequent dreams of bridges that are too short to reach the further shore" (p. 24). This remark suggests that Freud viewed the short bridge as a symbol of the clitoris as well.

In Freud's self-dissection dream the too short bridge was represented by the "two wooden boards . . . upon the window-sill," which Freud had to use to make his crossing possible. This element in the dream was taken straight from Rider Haggard's *She*, with the plank across a chasm. The dropping of the plank in the novel, falling down to the depths below, thus recalls Emma's trauma, the cut sustained when she was circumcised as a child – as though her short penis (clitoris) was destroyed in the process.

Freud awoke from this self-dissection dream in a state of mental fright at the thought that what would make his crossing possible were not two wooden boards but rather two children. The bridge theme in the dream referred to Professor Brücke (meaning "bridge" in German), a revered paternal figure after whom Freud had named the last of his three male children (Ernst). The two boards/children may thus represent the two sons Freud failed to circumcise (Jean Martin and Oliver). Jacob Freud in 1891 had reminded Freud of his failure to live up to his religious duties with his presentation of the gift of the old Freud family Bible bound in new leather as a 35th birthday present (Volume I, pp. 244–245).

In contrast with a penis, which merely strives to re-establish what has been lost, the figure of a child introduces a messianic dimension into the bridge symbolism of the dream. A child, after all, is the concrete embodiment of a man's hope to change the world. In contrast with the "eternal return of the same," Freud's dream mandates a new and better world: the hope that "children may perhaps achieve what their father has failed to [achieve]" (Freud, 1900, p. 452) and, further, that he should have to leave it to his children "to reach the goal of [his] difficult journey" (p. 477). Reflecting on Freud's dream, William McGrath (1986) perceptively noted that although

> Strachey's English translation somewhat obscures it, Freud's own analysis of the dream's conclusion recalls the image of Moses being denied entry into the promised land. Freud indicated that the idea being expressed at the end of the dream was that "perhaps the children will attain [*erreichen* – reach] what has been denied [*versagt*] to the father." At a later point in his discussion he repeated this idea in even more suggestive language: "I would have to leave it to the children to arrive at the goal [*ans Ziel*] of the hard journey [*in the schwierigen Wanderung*]." Here the children alluded to that part of the Moses story reported in Numbers 14 and 20.
>
> (p. 300)

Here the theme of the two wooden boards/children seems to involve a reference to the Bible, the story in which God spared two adults, Joshua and Caleb, so they could lead the children of Israel over into the Promised Land (Numbers 14). The Bible story recounts God's anger with the Israelites for their lack of faith, and condemned them, except for Joshua and Caleb, who remained true, to wander and perish in the desert.

Just a few chapters later, in chapter 20, a similar fate awaits, as God tells Moses in punishment: "you shall not pass over into it." In Freud's dream, wrote McGrath (1986), the children appear to represent Freud's

> followers, and the underlying wish pointed toward his founding the psychoanalytic movement. Freud hoped to secure intellectual followers to spread the understanding and practice of psychoanalysis, and the image of Moses was extremely appropriate to such an enterprise. Freud used it specifically with reference to himself and his movement ten years later in a letter to Jung. He

wrote, "If I am Moses, then you are Joshua and will take possession of the promised land of psychiatry, which I shall only be able to glimpse from afar."

(p. 302)

The bridge in Freud's self-dissection dream thus appears to designate a symbolic location, around which the entire psychoanalytic movement would gather years later, transmitting a not-abreacted trauma while also signaling towards a point of hope – which, in the next section of the book, will be revealed as also a stage for ghosts.

The fish

In this final dream Freud was surprised by the absence of gruesome feelings. Though Freud had previously been unable to withstand the gaping hole in Irma's mouth, so horrified by the dream image that he immediately recoiled, now the split-off intellectual part allowed Freud to coldly observe and examine himself from the outside. Freud neither recoils nor steps back in this dream. Instead he is able, even determined, to look down to examine his own eviscerated pelvis. What Freud saw in that part of his body was a piece of crumpled silver-paper. This drew Freud toward the name of the author of a dissertation on the nervous system of fish as well as his own first publication, an investigation of a fish assigned to him by Professor Brücke, his mentor at the University.[9]

An expansion of Freud's allusion to scientific treatise on a fish sheds light on Freud's idea of dreams as "a picture of a phylogenetic childhood – a picture of the development of the human race" (Freud, 1900, p. 548, added in 1919). The fish stood in fact as a powerful symbol for the archaic phylogenetic past. This was closely associated with Haeckel's theory that an individual organism's biological development recapitulates the story of the species, in other words, that the human embryo passed through a stage resembling a fish before proceeding to another stage to resemble a reptile, thus repeating the adult forms of the evolutionary history of the organism.

Freud was deeply impressed by Haeckel's theories while a student.[10] He later claimed that "the whole of embryology" stood as "an example of the compulsion to repeat" (Freud, 1933a, p. 106): the most impressive proof of an organic compulsion to repeat could be found in the spawning migration of fishes. Freud (1920) proposed in *Beyond the Pleasure Principle* that certain fishes "undertake laborious migrations at spawning-time in order to deposit their spawn" in "localities in which their species formerly resided but which in the course of time they have exchanged for others" (p. 37; see also 1933a, p. 106).

This example of the spawning migration of fishes seems particularly useful for understanding the dream of self-dissection precisely because Freud's excursion, in the second half of his dream, was linked to a journey to the "womb of the Earth," which also is a tomb. Grinstein (1980, p. 416) thought that Freud's desire to rest in an Etruscan grave harbored the wish to "return to the mother," to which it can be added that fishes are compulsively driven to return to their home streams, making their way through diverse habitats in an effort reach their beginning as their final destination.

Freud's home stream was evidently the "reddish water" of his "bad treatment" dream. The same theme was repeated and elaborated in the self-dissection dream. The reddish water connected to the flow of sacred streams. Similarly, the bloody evisceration of Freud's pelvis in the self-dissection dream recalls a sacrifice performed on an altar, thus iterating images at the heart of primeval sexual religions, with their acts of ritualistic sacrifice and dismemberment. Here is the same set of thoughts which surfaced in response to Emma's circumcision scene, in particular, the importance of the image of the fish in pagan rituals, especially in Syria where it was served as a ritualistic food, its consumption uniting the faithful with their goddess Atatargis, as Astarte was called in certain parts of Syria. The name of her son was Ichthys (fish).[11]

The fish as symbol of the mysterious life of Nature was something highlighted in the entry for "Astarte" found in Roscher's mythological *Lexicon*, consulted regularly by Freud.[12] The core element of the votive ceremonies of the sea-goddess of Ascalon required the ritual self-castration of its worshippers.[13] Nunberg had appealed directly to this ritual in his essay on circumcision and bisexuality. Addressing the Zipporah legend, Nunberg (1947) noted:

> in the religions of the ancient Middle East, the cradle of Western civilization, men castrated themselves in religious ecstasy and offered their genitals on the altar of the Great Mother, the goddess Astarte, also known under other names. *What men really did in ancient times, they dream and fancy in modern times.*
>
> (p. 175; emphasis added)

This last observation by Nunberg returns to Freud's dream of the self-dissection. In the passage cited above, Nunberg fails to mention the bloody self-castration performed by Freud in his dream (*"What men really did in ancient times, they dream and fancy in modern times."*) The reference here to Freud's self-dissection dream is however rather transparent. Wondering why the man of antiquity offered his genitals up to the Great Mother, and why modern man experienced this same wish through dream and fantasy, Nunberg found in this specific act of self-sacrifice an expression of guilt towards women which might be seen as follows: "*What I have taken away from you, i.e. the penis, I am restoring to you*" (p. 175, fn.107, emphasis added). These words capture Freud's emotional reaction to Emma's cut, and clarify Freud's concern with the idea that the woman had been deprived of her penis in the course of biological evolution.

This same unconscious fantasy undergirded the image of the "great Lord Penis" in Freud's letter of January 24, 1897. The "fish" as object of Freud's scientific interest emerges here as a powerful religious symbol, the mark of Jesus (Ichthys, ἰχθύς). Tertullian had referred to Christ as "our Ichthys" and baptized Christians as "little fishes," making use of symbols which took their meaning from Judaism (Goodenough, 1953–1968). As Friedman (1960) further noted:

> Jewish tradition, contrasts this 'little fish' with the 'great fish', Leviathan, symbolizing the glory of the Messianic age when it will be caught and its kosher

flesh given to the faithful. This saving power of the fish's pure flesh for those who eat it is a constant theme from paganism to Judaism and Christianity. Such continuity of the symbol and rite of the fish meal was made possible only by Jewish and, later, Christian reinterpretation. Thus to the Jews of that era eating the fish represented a mystic sharing in the divine power which would be fully manifest in the Messianic age, and in which each faithful Jew placed his hope for resurrection and future life.

(p. 257)

The theme of resurrection and future life is indeed central to Freud's self-dissection dream. The Big Fish can be "the Judeo-Christian Deity" (Leach, 1986, p. 132) that Geza Róheim (1940) traced to the "Great Serpent Mother" slain by Marduk who then created the world from the two halves of her body. In the Hebrew version of the story, the dragon that rises from the ocean is pierced, cut to pieces, and eaten by the hero God: Yahve. At the end of the world, the Messiah will supposedly catch the great Fish Leviathan who will then divide its flesh as food among the faithful.

The great Fish, Serpent, or Dragon thus reiterates the formula of the *trimethylamin* (itself a product of decomposition of fish), namely the messianic element of the founding dream of psychoanalysis, while announcing the transcendental function of the Phallus in Freud's final system of thought. This messianic element proclaimed a new intent: to replace religion with a science of the unconscious. At the same time it was precisely what made psychoanalysis akin to a religion. It stood for a Mystery and a Revelation. The third and final part of this book examines the unconscious transmission of this secret, which, after the death of Ferenczi, resurfaced in Freud's final self-analytic meditation, "A disturbance of memory on the Acropolis" (Freud, 1936). Only then will conclusions be drawn about the concrete meaning of the gigantic snake, a key element of Emma Eckstein's recurrent dream reported to Freud during her analysis. Was Emma clitoris destroyed? Did Freud understand her recurrent dream as a concrete token of "The Resurrection of the Flesh"?

The tomb

The brief conversation with Minna when Freud spoke of "the eternal feminine, the immortality of our emotions" (Freud, 1900, p. 453), suggests that Freud viewed his own entombment as being akin to Faust's in Goethe's play on the modern hero, who, having lost confidence in the Holy Scriptures, continues to strive to achieve immortality.

The idea of the "eternal feminine [*das ewig Weibliche*]" in Goethe's play is highly controversial, not only mitigating Faust's tragic character but introducing the idea of his salvation on the model of the Deposition and Resurrection of Christ. When Faust dies, he describes Hell as the wide-open jaws of an abyss (Faust, 11644), and his soul is lifted up to heaven thanks to the "Eternal Feminine," which "Draws us on high" (act 5, Heaven, final line of the play).[11] Unlike Faust, Freud was neither lifted up nor saved from the jaws of the abyss. On the contrary, in his dream, he remained trapped in a tomb.

Apparently Freud envisioned his own entombment as the expression of a mother-womb-fantasy, of the wish of returning into her womb, which is confirmed by Freud's letter to Ludwig Binswanger on May 17 of 1909, proposing the following to explain a coffin fantasy: "Now coffin = womb; being buried alive = life *in utero*. Thus the phantasies show that what is involved here is a return to the womb of the mother." Later, in "The uncanny," Freud (1919b) would trace back the "terrifying fantasy" of being buried alive to the fantasy of "intra-uterine existence" (p. 244).

These passages show Freud's failure to distinguish between a successful regression to the prenatal state, which is accompanied by agreeable sensations of floating and flying (Balint, 1955, p. 231, 1960, p. 41, 1968, p. 74), and the claustrophobic fantasy of being buried alive, which entails the repetition of a traumatic scene, as occurs, for instance, when incest proceeds beyond fantasy and is realized as an actual event. Freud seemed to have had no dreams of flying and floating, nor could he access the "oceanic feeling" within himself. This emotional numbness found representation in the Irma dream in the "dull area" (Freud, 1900, pp. 107, 112, 113), the locus of his identification with her.

It would be Ferenczi who managed to overcome this split, accomplishing the task by deeply reworking Freud's re-union fantasy and by restoring a welcoming environment for the child/penis/fish, through his text on Thalassa.

This "funeral fantasy" accompanied Freud throughout his life and found expression variously, in Freud's fainting spells and neurotic preoccupation with his possible or impending death, for instance. Freud often ruminated about the possible date of his death, and his frequent concerns with personal demise deeply affected many of the people around him. In particular, Freud was scared by the "terrifying thought" (Jones, 1955, p. 220) of dying before his mother did.[15] When Amalia passed away in 1930, at the age of 94, Freud decided to not attend her funeral. He wrote Ferenczi to say: "No pain, no grief . . . at the same time a feeling of liberation, of release . . ." (September 16, 1930).

Notes

1 This "striking coincidence," as Grinstein (1980) noted, could "hardly have escaped his [Freud's] notice" (p. 418) and obviously served to reinforce his identification with the novel's hero. Rider Haggard was himself born in June 1856.
2 See the postcard which Freud sent to Martha on September 9, 1897 (Freud, 2002). Freud purchased a bowl with an "occhiale" (two eyes with the form of spectacles) painted on it to avert the "evil eye." He later gave the object away as a gift to a friend, the one eye surgeon Leopold Königstein (Freud, 1901, p. 638). Freud regretted his decision so much that later on, when he went to bed one night feeling thirsty, dreamt that that his wife Martha offered him water to drink from the cinerary urn which he had given away to Königstein. Freud often experienced dreams of this sort and noticed that if he quenched his thirst in the dream, he no longer needed to drink water, thereby convincing him that dreams were wish fulfillments. In this specific case, however, the water tasted so salty that Freud (1900) woke up from his dream because of "the ashes in the urn" (p. 124).
3 Freud's visit to the Etruscan grave, near Orvieto, was so important to him that he recalled it some 30 years later, in the *Future of an Illusion*. Discussing the state of helplessness which children experience early on in life, Freud (1927b) wrote: "The sleeper may

be seized with a presentiment of death, which threatens to place him in the grave. But the dream-work knows how to select a condition that will turn even that dreaded event into a wish-fulfillment: the dreamer sees himself in an ancient Etruscan grave which he has climbed down into, happy to find his archaeological interests satisfied" (p. 17).

4 Freud (1900) quoted Goethe's lines on two occasions in *The Interpretation of Dreams*: first when he explained censorship in dreams (p. 142) and, secondly, when analyzing his dream of self-dissection (p. 453); see also Freud, 1930b. His letter to Fliess where he quoted the lines was written on December 3 of 1897. In it, Freud described his visit to Orvieto while relating and tying his feelings during his vacation to his "neurotic longing" for "Rome." The idea that Freud saw Minna as a "reincarnation" of his nanny, the woman who had once served as young Sigmund's "teacher" in sexual matters, was first suggested by Peter Swales (1982).

5 In Freud's account, this lady is referred to as "Louise N."

6 According to Anzieu (1986) the self-dissection in Freud's dream was informed by Freud's identification with a bleeding female figure, perhaps a "menstruating woman" (p. 427). Since the second part of the dream features an Alpine guide who carried Freud as a mother would her child, Anzieu reckons that Freud's identification with a bleeding female issued from an anxiety reaction which involved "the loss of the mother (the individual identifies with the beloved object in order not to lose it) – an anxiety that precedes, and is more intense than, castration anxiety." Freud's dream, Anzieu argues, therefore "wishes to deny that loss . . ." (p. 427). This is correct but seems insufficient to explain the conflations of different set of memories which characterize this dream.

7 Reflecting on Freud's words Immanuel Velikovsky (1941) wondered: "Is not the Jew also the one whose 'identity is preserved through a series of generations through two thousand years'?" (p. 507). Maciejewski (2002, p. 58) for his part observed that what maintains the process of identification and identity in Judaism alive and unbroken is circumcision.

8 In the "Bridge symbolism and the Don Juan Legend" Ferenczi (1922) was led to see bridges as symbols of birth (the transition from the maternal body to life) and death (the transition from life to the Mother-Earth-womb). He also suggested bridges as symbols of the male genital organ which, during coitus, is placed or buried in the same place which originally gave birth to the child. Because of the regressive identification of the whole person with the penis, Ferenczi proposed that the process of inserting the penis inside the vagina is experienced by Don Juans as claustrophobic anxiety. The wish of returning to the maternal body is transformed by such individuals into a fear of being buried alive. Such individuals thus equate coitus with castration and experience sexuality as both hellish and annihilating.

9 See Freud (1900, p. 413). Freud's first publication appeared in 1877, three months prior to the appearance of a text he wrote earlier, when the not yet 20-year-old Freud spent his Easter holiday in 1876 at the Marine Zoological Station in Trieste dissecting 400 eels in the hope of locating their testes.

10 The reader is referred to the letters Freud wrote to Silberstein on December 20, 1874 and March 7 of 1875 (Boehlich, 1990).

11 The fish also functions as a symbol for the penis. In artwork from the Middle East, the mother goddess of fertility is often portrayed being made pregnant by a fish. At the same time, the fish also operates as a symbol for the womb and has historically been associated with the cult of the Great Mother. Beira (private communication) reminds me that Lacan (1966) associated the fish with the Phallus in his *Ecrits* (pp. 626–627, 805).

12 There we come across a passage which helps to clarify a number of the thoughts at work in Freud's reaction to Emma circumcision scene: "According to the Syrian vision the mysterious life of Nature reveals itself first of all in fishes; therefore fishes are holy to Atargatis (also known as Derceto) in Hierapolis-Bambyce; and in Ascalon, where the same Goddess is also worshipped, she is represented with a fishy body . . . . The *prostitution* in the service of the Goddess, which we found in Babilonia, is also very spread

138   *The abyss*

   among the Semitic of the West and first of all in Cyprus . . . . The antithesis to this is the *castration* by which the sacrifice of emasculation is offered to the obscure Goddess, who sends death and destruction" (Roscher, 1884–1890, I, pp. 653–654).
13 This cult and the ritual self-castration of the priests of the Mother Goddess is described in some detail by Lucian of Samosata in *De Dea Syria*, a treatise from the second century AD.
14 Goethe was mainly inspired by the frescoes in the cloister of the cemetery of Pisa (the Campo Santo), especially the *Triumph of Death*, from which many details in his poem derived. The image of rose petals being showered on the elects as angels lift them up to heaven was taken from Signorelli's fresco on the *Last Judgment* in Orvieto. Goethe was not a devout Christian; his choice was a purely formal matter, as he explained in his conversation with Johann Peter Eckerman on June 6 of 1831: "You will understand that the conclusion, with the upward journey of the redeemed soul, was very difficult to write, and that in dealing with such supernatural, scarcely imaginable matters I might very well have lost my way in a nebulous void if I had not used the sharply defined figures and concepts of Christian and ecclesiastical tradition to impose on my poetic intentions the salutary limitation of a certain form and solidity" (as quoted in Luke, 1994, p. Lxxiii). Goethe's skepticism is however attested by the comical details, such as the scene where Faust's soul is lifted up to heaven (interpreted by many as a parody).
15 As Freud wrote to Karl Abraham in 1918: "My mother will be 83 this year . . . Sometimes I think I shall feel a little freer when she dies, because the idea of her having to be told of my death is something from which one shrinks back" (letter of May 29, 1918).

Part III
Transmission

9 Mute correspondence
I. Catabasis

> We may safely assume that no generation is able to conceal any of its more important mental processes from its successor. For psycho-analysis has shown us that everyone possesses in his unconscious mental activity an apparatus which enables him to interpret other people's reactions, that is, to undo the distortions which other people have imposed on the expression of their feelings. An unconscious understanding such as this of all the customs, ceremonies and dogmas left behind by the original relation to the father may have made it possible for later generations to take over their heritage of emotion.
>
> Sigmund Freud, *Totem and Taboo* (1913a, p. 159)

Introduction

Ferenczi first met Freud in 1908 and the two men quickly entered into a relationship which Freud would later describe as a "fellowship of life, thoughts, and interests" (January 11, 1933). The rare intensity of their relationship is amply attested to by their exchanges between 1908 and 1914, covered in the first volume of their correspondence. This was a period when Ferenczi was motivated by a "burning desire to win [Freud's] approval by showing that [he] had understood him completely, and by immediately going in the direction he recommended" (Dupont, 1985, p. 185). Ferenczi's deep desire to build an intimate relationship with Freud and to win his approval proved crucial in making him "the most perfect heir" of Freud's ideas (p. 184).

This early period of intellectual symbiosis between the two men reached its peak with the publication of Ferenczi's Thalassa myth, in 1924. Thereafter Ferenczi began drifting away from Freud. The personal and theoretical distance between the two men grew considerably in 1929 and there emerged an intense conflict which was only truncated by Ferenczi's illness and premature death in 1932.

Excluded from the mainstream of the psychoanalytic movement for decades, the value of Ferenczi's work was only rediscovered after his *Clinical Diary* was published in 1985. Ferenczi is today considered by many to be "the prescient innovator of all modern trends, champion of egalitarianism and mutuality, crusader for the recognition of child abuse and trauma . . . the precursor of relational developments in psychoanalysis," indeed as the analyst who sowed "the fascinating seeds that have flowered and evolved within the main body of psychoanalytic thought." (Aron & Harris, 1993, p. 1).

The Freud-Ferenczi controversy has as such become the fertile symbol of the multiple dichotomies and polarizations which characterize the debates of the contemporary psychoanalytic scene ("one-person psychology" vs. "two-person psychology," interpretation vs. participation, insight vs. regression, metapsychology vs. experience, the role of the "father" versus the figure of the "mother" in symptom formation and psychic development, and so on). Selectively based on Ferenczi's final contributions as it is, this newfound appreciation of the great Hungarian analyst has remained largely disconnected from an understanding of the actual continuity and deep connections between the work of Freud and Ferenczi. My intent to address this gap in the literature begins by highlighting the unconscious transmission of Freud's "heritage of emotion."

The title of this chapter ("Mute Correspondence") already hints at the echoing relationship between these two men, if only from the unconscious dimension of their communications. Indeed, the title suggests a further significance, for it also hints at a correlation between the process of burial and repression (= dumbness), that allowed Freud to equate language with the place of a "burial," and to dream the *talking-cure* as an ongoing "excavation" by which what is silent and buried may be brought back and restored to life via speech. I will build the interpersonal implications of this intrapsychic model around the armature of the idea that Freud's closest followers were unavoidably attracted by the verbal tombs of the master, indeed unconsciously driven to excavate their hidden and buried meaning. Freud himself fed this process by relentlessly enacting his own burial.

I begin with reviewing an important moment in the history of psychoanalysis: Freud's journey to America in 1909. As did other psychoanalysts from the first generation, Ferenczi entered into contact with Freud via Carl Jung.[1] In December 1908 Freud received an invitation from Stanley Hall, the president of the Clark University in Worcester (Massachusetts), to present on psychoanalysis during festivities to celebrate the 20-year anniversary of the University. Ferenczi accompanied Freud on this trip, while Jung was also invited to present. The trip to America allowed the three men in the traveling party to engage in informal discussions and interaction. The journey to America, which lasted from August 19 to September 29, 1909, set the stage for the break soon after between Freud and Jung. Their break in part traced back to an incident which touched on the issue of mutual analysis. Ferenczi was himself deeply marked by the experience as well.

Two skulls in the cellar

Jung's dream of the house with two skulls in the cellar, in August of 1909, struck Jung as tied to questions about the foundations upon which Freud proposed to establish his new psychological science. In the dream, Jung was in a rococo room on the second floor of a building. He felt a desire to explore the building further. The ground floor was dark and decorated with furniture from the medieval period, and the cellar dated from Roman antiquity. He then suddenly found, in the sub-basement of the building, pottery, bones, and two skulls, all dating from prehistoric times (Jung, 1961a, p. 161). The "Roman cellar" is evocative of Freud's "Rome neurosis" with elements (pottery, bones, and skulls) as described in the chapter "Necropolis," such as the Etruscan grave, the Etruscan pottery in his "break-fast-ship" dream, and the two boys/bridge in the dream of self-dissection. What follows will detail Jung's experience of his dream of the two skulls, suggesting how Jung himself came to interpret its contents. Jung's dream would have a lasting impact on his person.

On January 17 of 1909 Freud wrote Jung to say: "If I am Moses, then you are Joshua and will take possession of the promised land of psychiatry, which I shall only be able to glimpse from afar." Freud decided to adopt Jung symbolically as his "eldest son," appointing him as his "successor, " the future leader of the psychoanalytic movement. Jung visited Freud in Vienna on April of that year. A strange event occurred during the visit: a loud noise detonated in one of the bookcases in Freud's office, which Jung interpreted as a poltergeist phenomenon. When Freud protested Jung's interpretation of the event, accusing the Swiss of mysticism and irrationality, Jung predicted that another crash would soon follow, and it did.

This incident caused an intense emotional reaction in Freud who, on April 16, decided to send a long letter to Jung reflecting on what had happened. "It is strange," Freud wrote, "that on the very same evening when I formally adopted you as eldest son and appointed you . . . as my successor and crown prince, you should have divested me of my paternal dignity . . . ."

Freud's words foreshadow the fate of their relationship. Freud, for his part, hurried its development by revealing personal aspects of his life to Jung with a disarming openness. He soon began to speak of his own superstitions and irrational fears. "Some years ago," he said to Jung, "I discovered within me the conviction that I would die between the ages of 61 and 62, which then struck me as a long time away." When his dream book was published, Freud received a new telephone number: 14362. Since he was 43 years old at the time, he convinced himself that the rest of the numbers suggested the date of his death. To quote Freud:

> Suddenly method entered into my madness. The superstitious notion that I would die between the ages of 61 and 62 proves to coincide with the conviction that with *The Interpretation of Dreams* I had completed my life work, that there was nothing more for me to do and that I might just as well lie down and die.

Recognizable in Freud's words is the same uncanny thought of "lying down to die" during his visit to the Etruscan graves in Orvieto. A similar feeling of anxiety also spoiled Freud's trip to Athens years later, in 1904, which became the subject of Freud's last self-analytic piece – his famous essay, "A disturbance of memory on the Acropolis" (Freud, 1936). Freud presented several versions of this Acropolis event. In his letter to Jung, he described his experience of derealization at the Acropolis by saying:

> it was really uncanny how often the number 61 or 60 in connection with 1 or 2 kept cropping up in all sorts of numbered objects, especially those connected

with transportation. This I conscientiously noted. It depressed me, but I had hopes of breathing easy when we got to the hotel in Athens and were assigned rooms on the first floor. Here, I was sure, there could be no No. 61. I was right, but I was given 31 (which with fatalistic license could be regarded as half of 61 or 62), and this younger, more agile number proved to be an even more persistent persecutor than the first.

Jung soon began to experience disturbing fantasies and upsetting dreams about prehistoric cemeteries, corpses, and skulls after receiving this letter from Freud. In April, he dreamt his "great dream," the one where Freud appeared to him as a "dead" customs official (Kerr, 1994, pp. 213–214). In Bremen, where Jung joined Freud and Ferenczi on August 20, 1909 to board the steamer ship George Washington for their trip to America, the Swiss psychiatrist began to talk incessantly about "peat-bog corpses" (mummified bodies which were discovered in the marshlands near Bremen). The situation and the topic of conversation distressed Freud, who then fainted (Jung, 1961a, p. 156). Later, as the men were aboard the ship and heading for America, Freud and Jung began interpreting each other's dreams. It was then that Jung dreamed of the house with two skulls.

Freud interpreted Jung's necrophilic fantasies as an expression of a death wish against him, something which Jung strenuously denied. Scholars have for the most part embraced Freud's interpretation of Jung's dream, failing to consider that Jung's death fantasies about Freud were triggered by Freud himself as result of his personal disclosures. Jung was also the first person to engage in a careful study of Freud's text on *The Interpretation of Dreams*. Jung appears to have been deeply affected by Freud's dream of self-dissection, with its shocking and disturbing images. Freud's decision to reveal spicy details about his "Indian summer of eroticism" with his two traveling companions also shaped Jung's feelings and fantasies.[2]

I thus propose that Freud's own behaviors cannot be ignored but played a vital role in evoking thoughts and images associated with his "Etruscan grave" experience in his interlocutors. Freud mentioned his feelings about his visit to the Etruscan grave in context of analyzing his self-dissection dream. His climb down into a death chamber during the visit led Didier Anzieu to fantasize that Freud was accompanied by Minna Bernays into the Etruscan grave. Jung and Ferenczi had each entertained similar fantasies as well.

Ménage à trois

Jung was particularly taken by the idea that Freud had had a sexual affair with Minna, as it can be inferred by his mimetic and provocative response to Freud's questioning about the meaning of the two skulls in Jung's dream. Jung said that they had reminded him of his [Jung's] "wife and my sister-in-law" (Jung, 1961a, p. 159), holding back his true associations for fear that Freud "would have dismissed it as a mere attempt to escape a problem that was really his own" (Jung, 1961b, p. 452; Kerr, 1994, p. 268).

Tensions between Freud and Jung grew increasingly tense after they reached America and disembarked from their ship in New York. Freud soon began to exhibit peculiar psychosomatic symptoms while in the city, something which Ferenczi found revealing. The three men engaged in a sort of psychoanalytic "*ménage à trois*" throughout the trip, interpreting each other's dreams as they crossed the Atlantic and headed to America by ship. The entire trip appears to have transformed into a "significant experience" for each of the three. In Ferenczi's case, it activated his personal "infantile complexes," as he confessed to Freud a year later in a letter on July 9 of 1910.

Ferenczi seems to have remained under the influence of several incidents during this trip to America, and indeed, their effect on him can be seen informing Ferenczi's views on Freud 23 years later. As Ferenczi noted in his *Clinical Diary* (an entry dated August 4, 1932) the two "hysterical symptoms" which overtook Freud during the trip (his fainting spell in Bremen and the episode of urinary incontinence on Riverside Drive as Freud looked out over the Hudson into the Palisades) exposed a "weakness" which Freud "could not hide from us and himself" (Dupont, 1985, p. 184).

The last of Freud's two symptoms, suddenly wetting his trousers as he looked out over the Hudson, was particularly revealing. Freud made his way back to his hotel to clean up and change his clothes. He obviously felt embarrassed by the entire situation but interpreted his symptom as a sign of his senility and advance age. Freud, who was 53 years old at the time, then began to fear that a similar accident might occur during his upcoming lectures at Clark University in Massachusetts.

Jung quickly jumped in to reassure Freud that it was only a neurotic symptom, offering his analytic assistance to help Freud overcome his fears. Freud gladly accepted Jung's offer, but when Jung pressed Freud to provide him with intimate material, Freud refused to go any further, that he could not "risk his authority." Jung had apparently insisted that Freud needed to come clean on details of a possible affair with Minna. The exchange between them has usually been seen as a special moment in the history of psychoanalysis, for it was then, as Jung (1961a, p. 182) later maintained, that he lost respect for Freud.

Various versions of the events in New York can be found in the analytic literature.[3] In a later interview with John Billinsky (1969), published only after Jung had died, we find the Swiss psychiatrist saying that he had learned of Freud's affair with Minna directly from her. When he first visited Freud in Vienna in 1907, he claimed, he was surprised to find that Minna was not only radically different from Martha, her older sister, but that, unlike Martha, she was intimately acquainted with Freud's work. Jung noted that he was shocked to learn of Freud's affair then, indicating that Minna had approached him during his visit to confide to him that she felt guilty about her affair with her sister's husband (p. 42). Numerous Freud scholars have questioned the possibility of Minna sharing such personal details with Jung, a total stranger whom she had just met. Had Jung obtained such information from Minna his attitude during the trip to America two years later would in my opinion been quite different. Jung would not have sought validation for a Freud/Minna affair by pressing Freud to admit to the affair as he had then. Instead, he would have spoken openly of Minna's behavior with Freud.

We met in the "archaic"

Let us now more carefully examine the impact of Freud's personal disclosures on Jung. The psychic entanglement between Freud and Jung was still active, as the sudden interest Jung developed in *archeology* helps reveal. Jung had shown no interest in archeology prior to September of 1909. Immediately following the trip to America, however, he entered a state of discomfort which transformed into a sudden obsession. "One of the reasons why I didn't write for so long," wrote Jung to Freud on November 8 of 1909, was because "I was immersed every evening in the history of the symbols, i.e. in mythology and archeology." Three weeks later, on November 30, he wrote Freud again to say:

> I feel more and more that a thorough understanding of the psyche . . . will only come through history or with its help. Just as an understanding of anatomy and ontogenesis is possible only on the basis of phylogenesis and comparative anatomy. For this reason antiquity now appears to me in a new and significant light. What we now find in the individual psyche – in compressed, stunted, or one-sidedly differentiated form – may be seen spread out in all its fullness in times past. Happy the man who can read these signs!
>
> (McGuire, 1974, p. 269)

It was by reading books like *A Discourse on the Worship of Priapus and its Connection with the Mystic Theology of the Ancients* that Jung became familiar with and attracted to the topic of *self-castration*. The ancient fertility rituals of the great Mother Goddess cults and the celebrations of "the dying and resurgent god" (phallus) suddenly appeared to him as the natural language of "the nuclear complex of neurosis," as he confided to Freud on November 15 of 1909; for Jung, it was the *ritual of self-castration* which remained the central feature of this psycho-mythological complex. "Wasn't self-castration practically unheard of among the Jews?," he asked Freud in the same letter. Jung's communication, which reveals him obsessively focusing on the themes of flagellation and self-castration, represents the climax of Jung's identification with Freud: "I am delighted of your mythological studies," Freud responded on November 21, before adding: "In private I have always thought of Adonis as the penis . . . ."

Jung would feel the "agony and ecstasy over the dying and resurgent god" (February 11, 1910), i.e. of the phallus, as found and represented in fertility cults, from this moment on. He would go on to experience dreams of female mutilations and even enacted a scene of symbolic self-castration by cutting himself (February 20, 1910) before finally losing himself in the "religious-libidinal cloud" of the intertwined symbols of phallic potency, self-castration, and the cross (June 26, 1910). Freud, who addressed Jung as his "dear son Alexander" (March, 6, 1910) during this period, would later say that he and Jung had managed to successfully meet each other in the realm of the "archaic" ("*im Urtümlichen*").[1]

The word "archaic" has a very special meaning here; by addressing Jung as "Alexander" (Freud was likely referring to Alexander the Great), Freud managed to situate Jung in the same position which his own younger brother, Alexander, occupied within his family. All of this occurred during the same period when Emma Eckstein was undergoing her second analysis with Freud. We might therefore conclude that while Jung was rediscovering, through archeology and mythology, the worship of the primeval Phallus, Freud was experiencing a reawakening of memories and fantasies which were quite similar, indeed of material he had experienced years earlier during his self-analysis.

Jung's own *catabasis* (descent) into the "Etruscan grave" was not a product of mere intellectual research but, rather, a product of a lively and compulsive psychic process that he carried out like an "incestuous intercourse" (Hannah, 1976, p. 110). It was in fact a journey with fantasies of dismemberment, intense depressions, and dissociative states. Jung's journey back to "the eternal feminine" progressively took on the form of a conquest of the "figure of terror": the "destructive" or "terrible" Mother imago, threatening the hero back to the sepulchral realm of the Mothers Jung (1912) described in his *Wandlungen und Symbole der Libido* (*Transformations and Symbols of Libido*). Significantly enough, in a chapter entitled "The Sacrifice," found in a work which marked Jung's break from Freud, the hero's act of self-castration was presented by Jung as an offering which served to help appease the "terrible Mother."

The choice

Jung managed to take possession of the "promised land" which had been denied to Freud by conquering the "bad mother imago." This, however, opened the door to the pre-existing and long suppressed theoretical disagreements which existed between the two men. Freud had begun to write *Totem and Taboo* in 1911 in direct response to Jung's theoretical speculations, precisely to reaffirm the primary role of the father at the origins of religion. It was at that point that the relationship between the two men became more difficult.

Freud wrote Ferenczi at the beginning of 1912 to say that he was working to reconcile himself "to the idea that one also has to leave this child to *Ananke*" (February 1). In Greek mythology *Ananke* (*Necessitas*, in Roman mythology) involved a compulsion which was more powerful than the gods. She was mother of the Moirae – the three goddesses of fate (Lakhesis, Klotho, and Atropos) who personified the inescapable destiny of man and sang in unison "the things that were, the things that are, and the things that are to be" (Plato, *Republic 617c*). In his letter to Jung Freud added the following: "I will draw a piece of exposed libido back to myself and cease strenuous efforts to move forward."

This process became particularly painful for Freud in light of the increasing silence that Jung, his most intimate interlocutor during the previous six years, introduced into their relation. On February 25, Jung explained his not writing to Freud by stating that what was keeping him "hidden," distant and away was the "*catabasis to the realm of the Mothers.*" At the beginning of March, Jung again apologized for his prolonged silence, this time explaining to Freud that his inability to maintain their correspondence actively during the previous weeks had partly been due to his heavy workload. This time, however, Jung pleaded with Freud for greater independence between them. Freud replied a week later, on March 5 of 1912:

> Still, if you think you want greater freedom from me, what can I do but give up my feeling of urgency about our relationship, occupy my unemployed libido elsewhere, and bide my time until you discover that you can tolerate greater intimacy?

The silence and decrease in intimacy which now set in between the two men are reflected in a new idea which suddenly came to Freud in mid-June. Freud mentioned it to Abraham and Jones but only fully explained the idea in a letter he wrote to Ferenczi on June 23, 1912. Freud offered it to Ferenczi as a "single thought"; it related to the resemblance which Freud found between the selection scene in the *Merchant of Venice* and the opening scene in *King Lear*. To give expression to his disappointment with Jung, his chosen heir, Freud turned to *King Lear*'s "tragedy of ingratitude."[5] Ultimately, Freud's "single thought" was a meditation on the compulsion to repeat a traumatic attachment in the choice of a new object of love. This meditation, which had both personal echoes and universal application, was described to Ferenczi:

> Three caskets are the same as three women, three sisters. The third is always the correct choice. But this third one is peculiar, she doesn't speak, or she hides (Cinderella!), she is mute. Do you remember the words of the song of Paris in 'Beautiful Helena'?
>
> > And the third – yes, the third –
> > stood beside them and remained mute.
> > I must give her the apple.
> > You, oh Kalchas, you know why.
>
> So, the motif of the choice between three sisters, the third sister being mute. With a few associations I came out with the idea that they are the three sisters of destiny, the third of whom is mute, because she symbolizes death (*Stekel*). The *compulsion* of fate is transformed into the motif of *selection*. Cordelia, who loves and is silent is thus actually death. The situation of Lear with Cordelia's corpse in his arms should be reversed, the old man in the arms of the Fate of death. The three Fates are woman in her three principal manifestations: the one who gives birth, the one who gives pleasure, and the one who spoils; or mother, lover and Mother Earth = death. Later I got out that the Trinity is derived from the *horae*, i.e., from the seasons, of which the ancients at first only distinguished three. Thus, transferred from vegetation onto the destiny of man.

The difficult task of withdrawing his "exposed libido" from Jung, his personally chosen Christian son, might in Freud's case indeed be marked by the "Trinitarian" structure of Freud's "single thought"; many autobiographical elements are conflated within it. The theme of the three sisters of destiny serves to introduce Freud's well-known dream of The Three Fates and, behind it, the "*Kasten* scene" from his childhood. A year later, in 1913, Freud's developed his thoughts on this subject further in his essay on "The theme of the three caskets [*Kasten*]." Insisting on the idea that the scene of Lear holding Cordelia's corpse in his arms should be reversed, Freud (1913b) brought his reflections on the theme to an end by saying:

> it is in vain that an old man yearns for the love of woman as he had it first from his mother; the third of the Fates alone, the silent Goddess of Death, will take him into her arms.
>
> (Freud, 1913b, p. 301)

Freud was here imagining himself as Adonis, a figure who dies in the arms of his Aphrodite. An important question can be raised at this point: How would Ferenczi react to this poetic expression of Freud's emotional trauma and funeral fantasy?

Notes

1 Jung was at the time working as an assistant to Eugen Bleuler, a psychiatrist who later coined the term "schizophrenia" and was the first university professor to support Freud's views (Falzeder, 2007). Bleuler began corresponding with Freud in 1904 and, in March of 1907, sent Jung and Ludwig Binswanger to Vienna to meet with Freud. This unexpected opening, which involved a number of well-known psychiatrists who were not Jews, led Freud to think it could rescue psychoanalysis "from the danger of becoming a Jewish national affair," to quote Freud and his letter to Abraham of May 3, 1908. Above all, Freud hoped to gain the approval of "the civilized world" when it came to his research and findings (see Freud's letter to Jung of March 6 of 1910).

2 In his letter to Jung of February 2 (1910), Freud wrote to say: "My Indian summer of eroticism that we spoke of on our trip has withered lamentably under the pressure of work. I am resigned to being old and no longer even think continually of growing old."

3 I rely mostly on Falzeder (2012b, pp. 326–327) and Rosenzweig (1992, pp. 64–65) for my reconstruction. In an interview Jung granted to Kurt Eissler in 1953, we find him making a veiled reference to Freud's wife Martha and her sister Minna (see Roudinesco, 2014, pp. 296–298). Jung's reference during the interview was in response to Eissler pressing him on the specific material which had led Freud to refuse to respond to Jung's questions.

4 See Freud's letter to Abraham dated July 13, 1917. According to Falzeder (2012a, p. 230), Freud was referring to Jung's statement, found in *The Psychology of the Unconscious* (1917), that the unconscious contains "apart from personal reminiscences, the great 'archaic' [*urtümlichen*] images – the absolute or collective unconscious."

5 Freud had personally appointed Jung President of the just recently founded International Psychoanalytic Association in 1910. He wrote Ludwig Binswanger the next year, on March 14 of 1911 to say: "When the empire I founded is orphaned, no one else but Jung must inherit the lot."

10 Mute correspondence
II. Epopteia

> He [Freud] is the only one who does not have to be analyzed.
> Sándor Ferenczi, *The Clinical Diary*, 4 August 1932

The pendulum

The judgment of Paris has long been a popular theme in art: Paris awarded the apple to Aphrodite, who in turn awarded Helen to him.[1] Paris's real name was Alexandros (in Greek literature, he was only rarely called Paris, or "Defender"). When Ferenczi – himself an "Alexandros" (Sándor) – received Freud's text on the choice of the third, mute sister in June of 1912 he was tormented by the very question of "choice." This was a most difficult period in Ferenczi's life at the time, with the *pendulum* still actively oscillating "between mother and sister" (Ferenczi to Freud, April 23, 1912).

To better isolate the impact of Freud's single thought on Ferenczi, let us consider the important question of Ferenczi's own mother complex. A certain level of misogyny in both Ferenczi and Freud bound the two men together. In Freud, this was rooted in the defensive operations by which he protected an idealized vision of his mother from a split-off bad maternal image. But Ferenczi was not at all free from similar problems. In both men these were rooted in pre-oedipal traumas, finding expression in hypochondriac tendencies, psychosomatic disturbances, and recurrent death anxieties. Differently from Freud, however, Ferenczi gradually and progressively came to accept a less defensive vision of both femininity and androgeny (Vida, 1991, 1999). This should be recognized as one of the crucial factors of his drift from Freud and his doctrine.

Ferenczi became convinced quite early that the origin of his personal neurosis was to be traced to lack of love from his strict, controlling mother, although he was only able to achieve a deeper understanding of his mother complex during the final years of his life. In his *Clinical Diary*, he reasoned that he had developed symptomatically a "compulsive desire to help anyone who is suffering," particularly when it involved "women." Indeed, he noticed that he tended to avoid at all costs situations which required him to respond aggressively and decisively (Dupont, 1985, p. 61).

Ferenczi noticed not only that he had repressed his "infantile aggressiveness" but, in another entry in his diary, that he had also developed an artificial "superkindness" as a product of the split resulting from repression: "heart" had been replaced by "head" (p. 86), with repetition and enactment of certain patterns with his patients. A number of the peculiarities found in his theoretical constructions, Ferenczi reflected, could be explained by this particular constellation.

The main symptom of Ferenczi's "castration hysteria," however, was his unfortunate sentimental life. Ferenczi met Gizella Altschul, his future wife, in 1900. He was 27 and she 35 years old. Gizella was married to Geza Palos at the time and was the mother of two daughters (Elma and Magda, born in 1887 and 1889, respectively). The liaison between Ferenczi and Gizella grew more formal and intense in 1904. Later, in 1909, Sándor's younger brother Lajos wed Magda, a deeply upsetting event. Unable to disentangle himself from this affair with a woman eight years his senior, he wrote Freud to share his feelings of ambivalence: his renunciation of passionate love, his repression of aggression toward the "mother" (Gizella) and the replacement of "heart" with "head" were all themes found present in his letter to Freud of October 26, 1909.

It remains unclear when Ferenczi began falling in love with Elma, Gizella's "difficult child," but this would have been during the period of the replacement of "heart" with "head." Elma experienced difficulty in 1911 and Ferenczi, either offered or accepted an appeal to help her analytically. The analysis soon became unmanageable, when Ferenczi realized that he was now in love with Elma. Marrying Elma, he reasoned, would allow him to realize his desire of fathering children and founding a family. He was tormented with powerful feelings of guilt for wanting to drop Gizella. Instead of following his heart, however, he turned to Freud for help. On November 14 (1911), upset and torn by his situation, he confessed to Freud: "I wanted to commit a terrible act of violence. Dissatisfied with both parents [i.e. Frau Gizella and Professor Freud], I wanted to make myself independent!" In a postscript to his letter, he decided to incorporate and share two poetic lines with Freud:

> I remain a "son"
> Have religion!

"Dear son" – Freud responded on November 20 of 1911: ." . . . Your struggle for liberation doesn't need to take place in such alternation of rebellion and subjugation . . . ." Freud's letter led Ferenczi to drop Elma as his patient and to also put his decision to marry her on hold. It was now decided that Elma should travel to Vienna to undergo analysis with Freud. Her analysis lasted four months, from January to April of 1912.

Ferenczi's dissatisfaction with Frau Gizella remained an object of his autoanalytic reflections for years. In time he concluded that his inability to separate from her was a direct product of his "maternal fixation."[2] Despite his best efforts, he was unable to free himself from it.[3] He considered his wished-for separation as an act of violent cruelty and turned to Freud with the hope of finding a father figure capable of understanding, and helping to liberate himself from this maternal subjugation.

Freud, however, was unable to grasp Ferenczi's need. On the contrary, he became convinced that Elma was dangerous for him and began to regularly express his deep admiration for Gizella's spiritual qualities in his letters to Ferenczi.[4] This in turn reinforced Ferenczi's passive surrender to the "mother." Ferenczi's decision to marry Gizella became the center of his analysis with Freud (in 1914 and 1916). Under "Freud's unrelenting pressure" (Berman, , 2004, p. 517) Ferenczi finally wed Gizella on March first, 1919; in time his decision would feed his bitter accusations against Freud (Berman, 2004, p. 517; Haynal, 1988, p. 44). Less than three months later Ferenczi wrote Freud to say: "since the moment in which you advised me against Elma, I have had a resistance toward your own person" (May 23, 1919). Three years later, in 1922, he wrote a letter to Groddeck where he reflected more deeply on the entire situation: "Prof. Freud . . . persists in his original view that the crux of the matter is my hatred for him, because he stopped me . . . from marrying the younger woman (now my stepdaughter). Hence my murderous intentions toward him . . ." (February 27).

Ferenczi did not react to Freud's ideas about the choice of the "mute sister" in June of 1912. Instead, he became tormented with the question of choice: Did he have to maintain his struggle for liberation from the "mother" (Gizella), he wondered, or give up on his childish desire for revenge against her? At the same time, his attitude began to oscillate towards the "sister" (Elma): Did he have to follow his fantasies of marriage and happiness with Elma or protect himself from his feelings of attraction toward her? Was Elma lovable or dangerous?

Freud's analysis of Elma did not decrease Ferenczi's doubts, but only exacerbated his "strange condition of love." This occurred for a number of reasons, primarily because Ferenczi participated in Elma's analysis, serving as a confidant to Freud during her treatment. Freud himself began his first report to Ferenczi on Elma's analysis by saying: "I can imagine how anxiously you are awaiting news from me." In the same communication he then went on to point out that marriage for Elma represented an occasion for acting-out in "revenge" (January 13, 1912).

In his reply, Ferenczi indicated that he was "*much sooner inclined to renounce the possibility of happiness*" than to afford the dangers of a marriage that had "*too much* risk attached to it" (January 18). However, he then immediately emphasized, within quotes, the strength of his "ambitendency." Freud responded by warning him explicitly of the dangers bound to it. A month later, on February 13, he wrote Ferenczi to say:

> With regard to your indecision, I would like to note that masochistic impulses very frequently take their course in an unfavorable marital choice. One then gets one's misfortune, is punished by God, and doesn't have to worry any more.

Besides her "revengeful" side, Freud also stressed Elma's "genuinely feminine" nature (March 3, 1912). These two aspects of Freud's description of Elma seem to correspond to the two conflicting aspects of the "goddess of Love" and the "goddess of Death." Three months later Freud would interpret Helen's silence in his paper on the choice of the three caskets. Elma's "dangerous attractiveness" was communicated by Freud in his reports to Ferenczi.[5] While Freud underscored her compulsive need for "revenge" (a desire to emasculate men) Ferenczi came to see Elma as "the one who brings death, who spoils" (see below).

After Elma's analysis with Freud ended and she returned to Budapest from Vienna, Ferenczi decided to take her back into analysis. His decision seems a desperate attempt on his part to postpone any decision while making any future action impossible. "In today's hour Elma was quite ill; she didn't say a word," Ferenczi wrote to Freud on June 10. It was just a few days later that Ferenczi received from Freud the "single thought" regarding the choice of the third or "mute sister."

Ferenczi was an extremely attentive reader and correspondent – he would later write Freud to say: "for years I have actually not been able to read anything thoroughly except your writings" (June 4, 1914). This time, he didn't react to Freud's meditation on the choice of the mute sister. Despite this, that meditation is nevertheless silently palpable in the most important moments of their correspondence. Ferenczi's reception of the *three sisters-caskets* motif may also be read in retrospect as the source of a strange "infection" which exploded a few months later, with Ferenczi's nightly fantasies of bleeding to death.

On July 12, 1912, while making his way back to Budapest from Berlin after a short visit to Vienna, Ferenczi wrote a long letter with a high level of self-analytical reflection. For reasons which will become clear later, an extensive quotation now will be useful:

> ... I also have to watch myself so that I don't allow myself to be forced into some unthinking action. My premature decision to marry Elma could become just as fateful to me as my temporarily insincere breaking off of relations with her – or with both women, for that matter! You see, matters have come to a head, and the word now is to watch out until the coast is clear.
>
> The accumulated upsets and stimulations of the last few days have produced in me an almost disagreeable increase in sexual libido. After long vacillation, I decided to get relief by the normal way of prostitution. I also succeeded in overcoming my inhibitions to it, and – despite all the disgust that went along with it – I must say that since then I am thinking and acting more coolly and with less passion.
>
> I just received the news from Fräulein Minna about your summer plans.

Fräulein Minna was of course Freud's own sister-in-law. Like Ferenczi, Minna sometimes accompanied Freud on his summer journeys, as his traveling companion. This association heralds Ferenczi's fantasy of Freud's illicit relation with a "sister" (see below), a fantasy which seems to fuel Ferenczi's sexual excitation and informs his attempt to seek relief from his increased libido "by the normal way of prostitution." Ferenczi's "choice" temps us to link his "long vacillation" with the "pendulum" which in his case oscillated "between mother and sister" (April 23, 1912); it is as if the *pendulum* of the *Horae* had at that moment come to a stop, the time concluding and the choice being made – the fated choice of a speechless Helen . . .

> And the third – yes, the third -
> stood beside them and remained mute.
> I must give her the apple.
> You, oh Kalchas, you know why.

Venus selected and the apple was given, enabling Ferenczi to escape the compulsive tendency to throw himself into the arms – as we read in the next letter of July 18 – of "the one who brings death, who spoils." But it was precisely by his own venereal selection that "the thought of death . . . strongly invested with libido" was embraced. This decision later enveloped Ferenczi, tormenting him with a powerful syphilis-phobia along with fantasies of bleeding to death, and dying. In Ferenczi's letter of July 18, the spoiling qualities of the "mute sister" are impressively echoed in his sudden and new retrospective perception of Elma, who ". . . also played the role of the one who brings death, who spoils. In puberty, the thought of death, which I had evidently strongly invested with libido, was on my mind night after night."

Although Ferenczi was not "yet free of longingly libidinous feelings with respect to Elma," the new link now established between Elma and Death made him realize "more and more clearly how unreasonable" he was when he "thoughtlessly wanted to marry her" (July 18, 1912).

Two days later, on July 20, Freud voiced his satisfaction for Ferenczi's choice in relation to Elma. At the same time, advancing the plot of their mute dialogue, Freud now presented himself as a King Lear who, as in the final scene of the drama, carries Cordelia's dead body onto the stage. This was also the moment when Freud assigned the role of Cordelia, the one who "loves and is silent," to Anna, his "third" daughter, who was now entering her 18th year. It was on his way back to the hotel after a walk that Ferenczi finally put his "(almost realized) fantasy with Elma" "to death." As he wrote Freud on July 26, 1912: "I thought about the misfortune that I may be saving myself by renunciation." The decision finally put an end to Elma's analysis. Two weeks later, on August 7th, after her absence for "a few (-three-) days," Ferenczi "had no other choice but to explain to her" that the analysis "was pointless" (August 8). The silent language of the fated choice is thrice echoed in the letter. Ferenczi's decision to end his analysis of Elma was described as the "severing of the last thread of the connection between us." Atropos – the third Fate, the mute figure who cuts the threads of life – was now speaking.

The infection

It was on the very evening of August 7 that the disease announced itself to Ferenczi in a dream. The somatic symptoms in his anus and inguinal region exploded a month later, in September, immediately after the two men traveled to Italy together. During the trip, Freud visited the Moses of Michelangelo in St. Pietro in Vincoli obsessively, on each and every day he was in Rome. Ferenczi's dream of August 7 was only briefly reported to Freud on October 2: following a scene with Elma and Frau Gizella, Ferenczi suddenly saw himself "climbing a mountain alone." He then discovered a syphilitic hardening of his inguinal gland. What might his climbing the mountain alone possibly mean in the dream? Was Ferenczi climbing the mountain as Freud/Moses had done? Was he now seeing himself as a son finally fulfilling his "crown-prince fantasy"?[6]

Ferenczi began to report to Freud constantly on his symptoms at the end of September of 1912. His letters during the next few months exhaustively described details of his suffering and malaise. He was not only troubled by somatic disturbances localized at the base of his penis but was also reporting his syphilis-phobia as well as hypochondriacal ideas on incurable diseases. These accounts continued for more than three months. Fantasies of bleeding to death and dying also set in at night. Yet Ferenczi remained attuned to Freud during this difficult period, so much so that even while experiencing a relapse of his inguinal pains he predicted Freud's fainting incident in Munich in November. Before turning to Freud's second fainting incident, I want to draw further attention to Freud's habit of expecting and predicting his own death.

Anzieu (1986, p. 427) has interpreted Freud's fainting spells as a repetition of the death anxiety at the heart of his dream of self-dissection. The ceremonial aspects of Freud's attempt to control his *Todesangst* (death anxiety) were earlier discussed in detail by Max Schur (1972). Not enough attention, however, has been given to the effects of Freud's symptoms upon his followers, particularly those most exposed to his needs, urges, and pressures. Because of his close relation to Freud, Ferenczi was more privy to direct and indirect proclamations of his "impending death" and "imminent demise" than any other of his followers.[7] Ferenczi's prediction of Freud's second fainting spell (see his letter to Freud of November 28, 1912) suggests that he had fully internalized Freud's funeral and death fantasies.

Freud's second fainting spell occurred on November 28, 1912, during a scientific meeting at the Park Hotel in Munich, just after a presentation by Karl Abraham on Amenhotep. The young King's neurosis was interpreted by Abraham in light of the Pharaoh's desire to place his mother's embalmed body in a mausoleum where he himself wished to be buried in the future (Abraham, 1912, p. 274). Freud's fainting spell grew even more revealing as he was heard muttering, "How sweet it must be to die" as he regained consciousness (Jones, 1953, p. 147).

Freud immediately set out to analyze the reason for his fainting and "bit of neurosis." Jung, for his part, did not place much trust in Freud's capacity to unravel the logic of his symptoms through self-analysis. The Munich incident must have served to remind Jung of the previous incident in America, when he offered Freud his help in analyzing his symptom of urinary incontinence. Freud, as noted, had stopped cooperating with Jung, refusing to provide him with any more intimate details because, as he explained to Jung, he could not "risk his authority." A week following the Munich incident, on December 3 of 1912, Jung wrote Freud to say:

> As for this bit of neurosis, may I draw your attention to the fact that you open *The Interpretation of Dreams* with the mournful admission of your own neurosis – the

dream of Irma's injection – identification with the neurotic in need of treatment. Very significant.

Our analysis, you may remember, came to a stop [during the trip to America] with your remark that you "could not submit to analysis *without losing your authority*." These words are engraved on my memory as a symbol of everything to come.

Jung grew even more annoyed when Freud tried to reverse the situation by interpreting a slip in one of Jung's letters, not only responding with anger but accusing Freud of habitually reducing his students "to the level of sons and daughters who blushingly admit the existence of their faults" (December 18). This exchange led to a definitive final break between them. Freud wrote to Jung a month later: "I propose that we abandon our personal relations entirely" (January 3, 1913).

Freud kept Ferenczi informed of everything that was happening. The alarming intensity of Freud's neurotic symptoms, the question of the validity of his self-analysis, and the theme of his relations with his followers, all converged toward generating Ferenczi's Christmas dream.

Concerning his fainting episode, Freud wrote Jones on December 8, 1912 to say that he had traced the matter back to "some piece of unruly homosexual feeling" from his previous relation with Fliess. He then wrote Ferenczi the next day to report that he had settled his "dizzy spell" analytically. His fainting episodes, Freud explained, all seemed to point "to the significance of cases of death experienced early in life (in my case it was a brother who died very young, when I was a little more than a year old)."

Sándor kept silent and did not reply until a vision suddenly invaded a dream, his Christmas dream, the dream of a "somewhat small and frail but firmly erect penis" which had been "cut off" and brought in on a saucer (*Tasse*).

The horrible vision (Epopteia)

Ferenczi reported this dream to Freud in a long letter on December 26, 1912. The letter opened with a virulent attack on Jung and a harsh condemnation of "mutual analysis." Ferenczi admitted that he himself had gone through a period of rebellion before adding that he had now realized that mutual analysis was "nonsense." He then added the following in his communication: "You are probably the only one who can permit himself to do without an analyst; but that is actually no advantage for you . . . Despite all the deficiencies of self-analysis, we have to expect of you the ability to keep your symptoms in check."

Jung and Ferenczi had each been shocked by the intensity of Freud's death fantasies. They were disappointed by his vulnerability and skeptical about the capacity of self-analysis to cure and resolve symptoms. Jung, moreover, could no longer tolerate the contradictions between Freud's spectacular requests for assistance and his arrogant refusal of help through analysis. Instead of becoming angry (as Jung did) at Freud's unwillingness to be analyzed by another person, or of confronting Freud openly about his behavior, Ferenczi instead offered himself to Freud as a sick person in need of analysis. Ferenczi's demand to be taken in analysis was his way of assuring Freud of his loyalty, a self-sacrifice, attested to also by his dream that night. Moreover, in requesting that Freud take him on as a patient, Ferenczi offered himself as a substitute for that part of Freud's neurotic illness that required analysis. His dream of the cut-off penis, a visible sign of subjugation, thus announced a change in Ferenczi's desire *vis à vis* the Professor: where there had been an object-relation, an identification had now taken its place.

Ferenczi's identification with Freud had also surfaced during the previous two months, when Ferenczi developed nasal symptoms. A nose specialist recommended to Ferenczi the ablation of a part of his nasal septum, and Ferenczi then considered submitting to a rhinological intervention in Vienna, perhaps during his upcoming visit to Freud at Christmas (see Ferenczi's letter to Freud of December 7, 1912). Freud, we recall, was operated upon twice by Fliess, once in February 1895, when Emma Eckstein was also operated on, and again in the summer of the same year, shortly after the Irma dream. Ferenczi (1919) himself later would suggest that "congestion of the turbinate represented unconscious libidinal phantasies," adding that the connection "between the nose and sexuality was discovered by Fliess" (p. 101).[8] Ferenczi's nose was subsequently operated on in the spring of 1912 and, again, on Christmas day of 1913. A number of nasal symptoms resurfaced as his analysis with Freud progressed during the next few years. In March of 1916 Freud interpreted both Ferenczi's nasal symptoms and his desire to travel to Berlin to consult with a nose specialist (Fliess?) as resistance to analysis, an expression of his fear of the "father."

In December 1912, while entertaining having his nose operated on in Vienna, Ferenczi described for the first time the phenomenon later called "identification with the aggressor": a remarkable theory about fantasies involving both castigation and punishment. Ferenczi proposed that in obsessional neurosis two contradictory opinions regarding the father were typically formed in response to the father punishing the child, the child fantasizing in response that he would one day repeat the punishing gesture on his own offspring (Ferenczi to Freud, December 7, 1912). Ferenczi's nasal symptoms began decreasing after he offered this remarkable speculation to Freud. He then postponed his nasal surgery and had the severed-penis Christmas dream instead.

The dream – Ferenczi awoke from it in a state of fright – contained the following fragment: A small cut-off penis is brought in on a "saucer" (*Tasse*); Sándor's younger brother has just cut off his penis in order to perform coitus. The word "*Tasse*" is probably best translated in English as "cup"; Ferenczi included a drawing in his letter to Freud portraying the cut-off penis on a rectangular tray with eating utensils (a totemic meal?).[9] "The penis," he noted to Freud, had "been *flayed*, its skin had been pulled off so that the *corpora cavernosa* were laid bare. The power of the erection was striking." In a different segment of the dream, "several members of the family are sitting around the table" (the brother clan evoked in *Totem and Taboo?*) conversing on a specific theme: "family resemblances." Commenting on his dream Ferenczi remarked: " 'My younger brother' (= I, myself)."

Although Ferenczi did not analyze this Christmas dream of a cut-off penis, it confirmed his interpretation of another dream from a few days earlier. This earlier dream, which Ferenczi did analyze at length, was reported to Freud in the same letter. This other, earlier dream unfolded as follows: Ferenczi is being attacked by a dangerous little black cat. He responds by forcibly smashing the animal on the floor. Next a poisonous snake appears and raises its head from the blood or entrails of the cat had been smashed to bits on the floor. A woman attempts to protect herself from the snake.

Ferenczi traced the poisonous snake to the "dangerous coitus" he had enjoyed with a prostitute, or whore, back in the first week of September, the event that gave rise to his syphilis-phobia. Ferenczi noted that during intercourse he had "wanted simultaneously to do what is forbidden and get punished." He desired to "marry Elma" and, simultaneously, also wished to be punished for it by a "life-threatening cutting off of [his] penis = syphilis." Ferenczi concludes his report by informing Freud: "*You* and your sister-in-law play a role in this dream."

In Ferenczi's analysis his "dangerous coitus" repeats an incestuous love with a "sister." His very first association is a memory of himself at the age of three caught in an act of mutual sexual touching with his sister Gisela, and "threatened with a kitchen knife (obviously a threat of castration)." His sister and mother were thus aligned for him with Elma and her mother. Just as touching his sister sexually had led to threats of punishment and castration, Gizela was now preventing him from realizing his desire to marry Elma and start a family. Ferenczi concluded: "So, I am not permitted to love a young girl, otherwise my penis will be cut off."

In his analysis of the dream, Ferenczi struggles with many powerful resistances. At a certain point, he informs Freud, he was unable to find how to translate into German a Hungarian word, "an adjective" with which "I wanted to express my inability, my being bound, my inhibited will . . . which also means *impotent*. So: 'my *impotent* rage against my mother.'" Ferenczi was only able to express the depth of his rage by recalling an event of abuse he had experienced during boyhood:

> I envied a young (albeit a year older than I) playmate because of his bravery: his penis was larger . . . and had blue veins. When I was about five years old he tempted me into allowing him to put his penis into my mouth. I remember the feeling of disgust that that produced in me [I was afraid that he had urinated into my mouth]. I didn't permit him a second time. – But the punctuated word still escapes me! Fresh substitute thoughts: raging, Orlando furioso, *hurler*, "*hörögni*" [Hungarian = groaning], whore.

In Ferenczi's associative chain, "whore" surfaced as a censured libidinal word. "My fear of impotence must have been responsible for the strong repression of this word," wrote Ferenczi, recalling how he felt "shocked" to hear his father saying ("unsuspecting of my presence") the word "whore." Ferenczi recalled, as a boy, hearing his father say to his wife (Ferenczi's mother): "that so-and-so had married a whore."

Here we find Freud and Frau Gizella recast by Ferenczi in the role of father and mother. The crucial point, however, is Ferenczi's presentation of his act of dangerous coitus as the enactment of an *acoustic primal scene in which he himself participated as a secret listener*. In the final segment of Ferenczi's analysis of his dream this connection between *hearing and enacting* was condensed in a difficult to decipher formula that he shared with Freud (all brackets in the original):

[Father also said [= acted =] "whore." = You once took a trip to *Italy* with your sister-in-law (*voyage de lit-à-lit*) (naturally, only an infantile thought!).]

Freud-the-Father is in this instance being cast by Ferenczi in the role of the one who, through his words, enacts his illicit desire with a "sister" (Minna). The instances in which Ferenczi himself was cast in the role of a "secret listener" of Freud's words were many, of course, including his role as Freud's confidant during Freud's analysis of Elma, and in that same period, having free access to Freud's letters to Gizela. Yet in my view the main trigger of Ferenczi's strange "infection" and psychosomatic appearance of syphilis symptoms reached back to Freud's "single thought" about his choice of the "mute sister." Consider Ferenczi's very first association, in which is represented a scene with a "sister" and an "apple":

Little black cat. Memories of small sadisms. I was once very shocked when I threw an apple at my little sister Gisela's head so that her eye swelled up and I thought I had blinded her.

Fateful was for Ferenczi-Paris his "small sadism"? Or fateful was his hearing from Freud the words of the song "Beautiful Helena"?

Recall that Ferenczi began experiencing heightened sexual excitation after he received Freud's "single thought" (on June 23 of 1912), which drove him to seek relief from his increased libido "by the normal way of prostitution," while fantasying of Freud's illicit relation with Minna. Ferenczi had apparently instantly "decoded" the poetic expression of Freud's incestuous desire, identifying the "mute sister" with Minna.

Bringing to a close his letter of December 26, 1912, Ferenczi ultimately managed to reverse roles with his "infantile thought." The infantile "wish fulfillment" of the dream, he wrote, "would thus be as follows: "I satisfy my forbidden sexual desires; they won't cut off my penis after all, since 'adults' are just as 'bad' as 'children.'" "Please forgive this *gratis analysis*," wrote Ferenczi to Freud to close his letter.

The incorporation

Four years later, Ferenczi would disclose that his "dangerous coitus" had in truth been carried out with Gizella's younger sister, Saroltà, in September of 1912. Ferenczi only offered Freud this information after the premature end of his analysis in the fall of 1916. The early termination was difficult to accept precisely because there were many important things still to work out, among them this on-and-off affair with his wife's "sister."

In a long self-analytic letter to Freud on November 18, 1916, Ferenczi noted: "I permitted myself intercourse with a prostitute – then with Sarolta – , the syphilophobia came as a punishment." Since Sarolta stood in the same position as Minna in the Freud-Martha-Minna triangle, Peter Rudnytsky (2011, pp. 22–24) has suggested that Ferenczi successfully lived out Freud's incestuous fantasy by sleeping with his own sister-in-law. Gizella's sister had in Rudnytsky's view become the object of Ferenczi's polarized desire shortly after the two men traveled to America with Jung in 1909. It was during the course of the analytic *ménage à trois* on the George Washington that Ferenczi learned that Freud "had gone on a '*voyage de lit-à-lit*' with Minna Bernays" (p. 24). Freud, argues Rudnytsky, did enjoy a sexual affair with his sister-in-law; it was Ferenczi who then became the carrier of this knowledge.

The seeds of Ferenczi's "acoustic primal scene" were certainly planted in the course of Freud's "mutual analysis" with Jung. All in all, I still do not believe that Freud engaged in an actual sexual affair with Minna.[10] I do think, however, that the formula "Father said [= acted =] 'whore'" places Ferenczi in the position of a secret listener of Freud's unconscious. Ferenczi lived out not only Freud's incestuous fantasy but an entire array of fantasies which I have isolated by scrutinizing Freud's self-analysis, including his fantasy of bleeding and dying – Ferenczi experienced such fantasies almost nightly before his Christmas dream – as well as the secret story of Emma Eckstein's nasal surgery at the hands of Fliess.

In Ferenczi's dream this story seems to be inscribed in the *corpora cavernosa* of the penis, which are laid bare. This element is particularly intriguing as it cannot be explained in terms of Ferenczi's own psychological conflicts and, secondly, because it reminds us of Fliess's controversial theories regarding the nose, his nasal reflex theory. Freud himself advanced the hypothesis that the nasal *corpora cavernosa* functioned as a "sense organ" for internal stimuli, proposing this connection to Fliess in Berlin [of] on January 1, 1896, the very letter of the "Christmas fairy tale."[11] That in Ferenczi's Christmas dream his cut-off penis appeared "*flayed*, its skin had been pulled off" is immediately evocative of the Hebrew ritual of circumcision.[12] Ferenczi's Christmas dream of the severed *small* penis[13] on a platter with eating utensils strikes me not only as a demonstration of his powerful identification with Freud but also of *unconscious knowledge* about elements kept secret by Freud, including that in the founding dream of psychoanalysis, the word "*brith milah*," instead of being voiced was represented visually as the scientific formula of trimethylamin. I propose to consider Ferenczi's dream as a sort of "hysterical materialization" which fills a gap in the primal scene of psychoanalysis. Significantly, Ferenczi (1912a) claimed that the "suppressed speech" might reappear as "*Bauchreden*" (discourse of the stomach, ventriloquism) only shortly before (p. 211).

Finally, let us recall Freud's dream of the "break-fast-ship," the only dream in which Freud and his younger brother *Alexander* appear together. Here, the *Tasse* (cup) in Ferenczi's Christmas dream seems to correspond with the Etruscan black pottery that Freud mentioned when analyzing his dream, a piece which had so

Mute correspondence 161

deeply impressed him (1900, p. 465). It is noteworthy that it was during my effort to grasp Freud's psychic shipwreck (*Schiffbruch*= ship-break) that I understood how Emma's circumcision had awakened Freud's memory of Alexander's own *brith milah*, and even further back, the event of Julius's tragic early death.

This mention of Alexander invites further consideration of the names of Freud's two brothers. It was Freud (Sigismund) who, at the age of 10, chose the name "Alexander" for his brother (see Volume I, pp. 241–242). Naming his brother allowed him a symbolic victory over his father Jacob and anticipated his future Hellenism. The more important point, however, is that Alexander the Great was coupled with Julius Caesar and, further, that the name Alexander chosen by Freud rendered his brother a replacement of his dead brother Julius; this is something which Risto Fried (2003, p. 129) also noted. Alexander was thus a "revenant." That children could be "revenants" because of their names was an idea which Freud (1900) himself invoked in context of analyzing his non-vixit dream (pp. 480–487).

In our earlier exploration of the Etruscan "break-fast-ship" the image of Alexander's circumcised penis first intermingled and then merged with the tragic event of Julius's early death. A similar constellation can have informed "Alexander" Ferenczi's Christmas dream. This may be inferred from Ferenczi's remark to Freud in his letter which exposes the identification with his own younger brother; as he noted: " 'My younger brother' (= I, myself)." We only have to remember that Freud, in his letter to Ferenczi of December 9, 1912, explained his fainting spell by invoking his younger brother Julius's death to complete the closing of the circle.

Nachklang

From my first reading of Volume I of the Freud-Ferenczi correspondence, published in 1992, I have carried the impression that Ferenczi's vision of the severed penis served on a saucer or platter had helped to fill a gap. In Ferenczi's letter to Freud of December 26, 1912, the gap in question was signified by a missing word, the word which Ferenczi, in his letter, said had escaped him. Ferenczi even felt a need to symbolize the gap in question by way of punctuation and further attempted

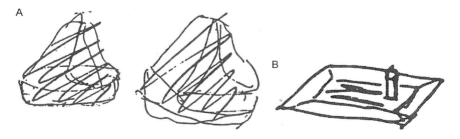

Figure 10.1 Ferenczi's three drawings in his letter to Freud of December 26, 1912.

to fill it by providing Freud's with three drawings, which are unfortunately missing from the English edition of the letters.

Ferenczi was still struggling with thoughts unleashed by Freud's "single thought" on the choice of the mute sister. The third drawing clearly represents the cut-off erected penis on the saucer, while the remaining two represent the strange Italian "four-poster bed" which featured in Freud's dangerous coitus with his sister-in-law Minna. In his associations Ferenczi connected the "four-poster bed" with a "cradle," which may be that of a younger "sister" (his "new-born sister's cradle"). If we put the three sketches in order we find a sister's cradle, the bed of a sister-lover and, finally, a cut off/erected penis, i.e. the three principal manifestations of the three sisters-fates: "the one who gives birth, the one who gives pleasure, and the one who spoils; or mother, lover and Mother Earth = death" (Freud's letter to Ferenczi of June 23, 1912).

In another part of Ferenczi's Christmas dream there was "talk about family resemblance; several members of the family are sitting around a table." This segment of the dream, which Ferenczi failed to comment upon, is highly reminiscent of the peculiar relationship which Freud established with his "analytic family," a relationship undergirding the process which motivated him to write *Totem and Taboo*. This particular work by Freud took shape within an echoing of voices and images of suffering, all made possible by the similarity of Freud's relationship with his analytic family to that which a hero – who "must suffer" (Freud, 1913b, p. 156) – experiences in relation to the chorus in a Greek tragedy.

Freud first announced *Totem and Taboo* by writing to Ferenczi: "Today I am tormented by the secret of the tragic guilt" (May 21, 1911). In the last chapter of that highly controversial text Freud described the Greek chorus as a company of individuals surrounding the tragic hero, hanging upon his words, accompanying him on his journey with feelings of sympathy before mourning his fate when he finally received the punishment he deserved.

A similar communion of voices was one of the functions which colored the exchanges through which Freud maintained contact with his closest followers in correspondence. The mutual sharing of lives and the search for a complete merging of experiences, thoughts, and emotions with his correspondents was part and parcel of Freud's own exchanges with his friends, pupils, and followers. The process began with a friend, Eduard Silberstein. It then proceeded throughout the letters that he and Fliess exchanged before coming to end with Jung, the chosen disciple by whom Freud felt betrayed. Freud did not allow himself such an intimate relationship with any colleague following his disappointment with Jung, who was replaced not by another individual but by a group of persons. A similar "echoing" need was met with a select company of men, their correspondence transforming into a "choral" experience.

The resonating, choral dimension of Freud's communications, as well as his needs, reached their most perfect "unison" sometime between June and July of 1912, when the *Stumm-Tod* (mute-death) symbolism of the "mute sister" reverberated, resounding as a *Nachklang* (echo, repercussion) within the communications of Abraham, Ferenczi, Jones, and Freud with each other. These communications gave birth to the Secret Committee, an imaginary place of burial and preservation.[14]

Freud's speculations in *Totem and Taboo* came to an end a year later. On May 4 of 1913, he wrote Ferenczi that the totem was his "greatest, best, and perhaps... last good thing." Feelings of depression seized Freud as soon as he completed his text: "I am thinking," wrote Ferenczi to Freud on June 23, that your "subsequent vacillation is actually a displaced *retrospective obedience*." He then he added:

> Your work is namely also a totem meal; you are the priest of *Mithras*, who singlehandedly kills the father – your students are the audience to this 'holy' action...

Here we encounter yet another version of the equation "said [=acted=]" which featured in Ferenczi's self-analytic letter, indeed a further identification by Ferenczi with the listener (the "audience") of a *Mysterienspiel*--a "holy play" or "representation of a secret"..

Two weeks later, on July 7, 1913, Ferenczi finally overcame a writing inhibition in relation to Freud. He took pen in hand and two sheets of paper, feeling that he had much to write and share with Freud. The occasion was his fortieth birthday. A "sad enough occasion," because Elma's marriage to another man was now on the horizon and becoming a "reality." Ferenczi's "strange condition of love" was still present, though it had now transformed into a silent struggle "taking place quietly" within his psyche.

In his reply letter two days later, on July 9, Freud reflected on his own 40th birthday in 1896, a time when he was "at the nadir of desolation" and "no one cared" about him. Identifying with Ferenczi, he then remarked: "For each of us fate assumes the form of one (or several) women, and your fate has some rare, precious qualities." Free of inhibitions, Freud then noted that his own "subjective condition of the 'choice of caskets'" had "surely long ago" been successfully "guessed" at by Ferenczi. Freud was again alluding to his younger daughter Anna, situating her in the role of Cordelia, the third sister who "loves and is silent." Finally, as though inspired by the date of Ferenczi's own birthday on July 7 (7/7), Freud then embraced the number seven (7) as a magic number, indeed the source which had patterned his work and fueled his creativity.[15]

> Good things really happen to me in periods of seven years: in 1891 I began with aphasia, 1898/9 the *Interpretation of Dreams*, 1904/5 *Jokes and the Theory of Sexuality*, 1911/12 the Totem thing; so I am probably on the wane and can't count on anything bigger before 1918/19 (if the chain doesn't break before then).

The best and biggest of all the "good things" which materialized during these seven-year cycles (kickstarted with his work on "aphasia") would be the "death instinct." Freud would go on to describe the work of the death drive as both silent and mute.

Freud was 62 years old, the age of his fated death, in 1918. He did not die then but did decide to take into analysis his daughter Anna-Cordelia instead (Young-Bruehl, 1988, pp. 80–90, 103–109, 114–116, 122–125), an incestuous choice enacted by "listening." *Beyond the Pleasure Principle* was itself a work which Freud composed "in the midst of Anna's analysis" (Mahony, 2002, p. 895). As noted by Patrick Mahony, Freud "authored a treatise wherein Anna symbolically emerges in the related themes of repetition compulsion and Thanatos, which in its muteness resembles the very person of Cordelia whose silence is 'a common representation of death.'" (Mahony, 2002, p. 895)[16]

Notes

1. When a dispute between Hera, Athena, and Aphrodite arose, Zeus asked Paris, son of King Priam of Troy, to determine which of three goddesses was the most beautiful. The winner was to be presented with an apple. Helen, wife of Menelaus, the King of Sparta, was known as the most beautiful woman living at the time. Paris's judgment incited the Trojan War.
2. Freud introduced this concept in his paper, "A special type of choice of object made by men," written in 1910.
3. See Ferenczi's undated letter to Freud (n. 306). The letter probably belongs between letters 258 and 259 and was likely written in December of 1911.
4. Indeed, after first meeting Elma, Freud informed Ferenczi that she was a mild case of "dementia praecox." This communication had "a rather depressing effect" on Ferenczi, as he wrote to Freud on February 7, 1911.
5. Apparently, Elma had become especially dangerous for Ferenczi after the suicide of a young man who courted her, precisely during a time when "she badly needed someone to support her and to *help* her in her need" (December 3, 1911). Elma must have experienced the unbearable thought that she had contributed to the death of her admirer. Ferenczi and Freud must have each felt uneasy in relation to her thoughts about the tragedy.
6. In his *Clinical Diary* Ferenczi wrote: "Contrary to all the rules of technique that he established himself, he [Freud] adopted Dr. F[erenczi] almost like his son. As he himself told me, he regarded him as the most perfect heir of his ideas. Thereby he became the proclaimed crown prince . . . " (Dupont, 1985, p. 184).
7. Freud's reaction to Ferenczi's first auto-analytic letter, which concerned a dream about his dead father (of January 4, 1910, erroneously dated January 4, 1909) is paradigmatic and revealing in this regard. Freud responded by saying that the figure of Ferenczi's father in the dream was a mere screen for Freud himself and that it referred to his (Freud's) own death. As he said to Ferenczi on January 10 of 1910: "Whether your harping on the year 1909 (twice repeated) is a compliment for the year just past, or whether it is connected with my imminent demise, I have no way of knowing. Let us nevertheless firmly establish that I myself already decided quite a long time ago not to die until 1916 or 17. Of course, I don't exactly insist upon it." Freud's pressing need to turn the focus of discussion and attention in his own direction, to have his pupils concerned about his death fantasies, seems obvious.
8. In the introduction I have already stressed that Ferenczi became intimately acquainted with details of Freud's traumatic relationship with Fliess after the Palermo incident (see in particular the letters which Freud and Ferenczi exchanged on October 3 and 6 of 1910).
9. Ferenczi's drawing was left out from the English edition of the letters.
10. Should this have been the case, it seems likely, at least to me, that he would have supported Ferenczi's wish to wed Elma; instead he relentlessly opposed it. Moreover,

Ferenczi himself would have felt less conflicted and torn about his prospect of making his way to and even marrying Elma.
11 More specifically, Freud proposed that by means of the *corpora cavernosa* the nose received information on the quantity of the products of sexual metabolism in the blood and, further, that the swelling of the nasal organ was equivalent to "opening the eyes wide . . . straining the ears, and so on" (Masson, 1985, p. 162). I am reminded here to the fact that Freud and Fliess each considered "trimethylamin" a product of sexual metabolism.
12 A further detail: In his self-analytic letter, Ferenczi recalled an incident from childhood in which he was forced to take an older boy's penis into his mouth. This scene reminds me of the *fellatio scenario* and oral theme that encoded Freud's Irma dream.
13 The penis of a newborn child? A penis-clitoris?
14 Freud personally spoke to Jones about the theme of the choice of caskets on June of 1912: "Your telling me of the *Stumm-Tod* [mute-death] symbolism," Jones wrote to Freud from London a month later, on July 30 of 1912, had "an interesting *Nachklang*." The *Nachklang* (echo, repercussion) was a dream interpreted by Jones as representing his dead mother as still "alive." It was precisely in the mutual *echo* between this letter and Freud's immediate reply on August 1 that the idea of the Secret Committee took shape. The burial scene was at the center of Abraham's Egyptian study as well. The study was prompted by Freud and was itself likely an expression of transferential fantasies. Significantly enough, Freud received the manuscript just shortly before the "single thought" about the "*Stumm-Tod*" symbolism occurred to him.
15 Freud's ceremonial use of the number seven in relation to his death anxiety has been discussed by Mahony (1982, pp. 66–67, 1986, pp. 182–183), Schur (1972), and Shengold (1972, 1993). One of the most impressive clues concerning the significance of the number for him can be found in a letter to Ferenczi in 1921. In it, Freud shared his impression that "*seven* of [his] internal organs" were killing him (Jones, 1957, p. 79). Further interesting material associated with the number may be found in his correspondence with Abraham in 1924 where he describes seven as a taboo number. Perhaps not by accident, Abraham felt a strong need to have Fliess operate on his nose in Berlin soon after.
16 Mahony (2002) goes on to say: "In a contextual mirroring of theory and practice, it is important to note that Freud's psychoanalytic treatment of his daughter/death goddess concurred with the publication of the death drive. More than that, while analyzing his daughter/death goddess, Freud desperately avowed that she could be liberated only by his death (Young-Bruehl, 1988, p. 117) – that is, by his return to original sameness" (p. 895). On the incestuous dimension of Freud's decision to analyze his daughter, see Mahony (1992).

11 Thalassa
A reparative fantasy

> Am I trying to behave like a fish, or to enact my genital theory which I won't write down?
>
> Ferenczi to Groddeck, Christmas 1921

Ferenczi's analysis with Freud

In his prophetic dream of the self-dissection of his pelvis, Freud awoke in mental fright at the moment of the thought that "children may perhaps achieve what their father has failed to." In the dream this thought is represented by the image crossing over the chasm not on boards but on the bodies of children. This chapter describes how, after Jung's refusal to serve as a "board-child," Ferenczi took over this role for Freud.

Initially self-analysis was recommended by Freud for budding psychoanalysts.[1] Like Jung, Ferenczi believed that self-analysis was not effective and, in particular, that Freud's self-analysis had not been effective, yet, differently from Jung, Ferenczi did not confront Freud openly on this point. Erich Fromm became acquainted with Ferenczi in the late twenties and commented,

> [Ferenczi] never dared to place himself in open opposition to Freud, and the more he realized that his views on the inadequacies of the Freudian technique had to lead to a personal confrontation with the latter, the more difficult his personal situation became. It was this fear of openly opposing Freud that made him hide the antagonism among assurances of his loyalty.
>
> (Fromm, 2000, p. 159)

Ferenczi's request to be analyzed by Freud on December 26, 1912, was his way to assure the Professor of his loyalty in a very difficult moment. The beginning of the analysis was repeatedly postponed by Ferenczi, however. Only when World War I broke out, in the summer of 1914, did the two men fix a date. According to Judith Dupont (1994), the situation served well "Ferenczi's ambivalence toward his plan to be analysed: Freud asks him to come, but Ferenczi is in a position to be mobilised [into military service] any day" (p. 304).

Ferenczi's analysis began in October 1914. His ambivalence was active from the beginning: he arrived so late to the train station that he missed his first session. Two intensive weeks of analysis (two sessions a day) were interrupted when Ferenczi had to report for military duty. The second period of analysis (two sessions of one hour and a half a day) extended from June 14 to July 5, 1916. This time Ferenczi learned much about the role of repetition but remained skeptical about the question which bothered him the most, his sentimental life (Dupont, 2015, p. 157). The third period took place between September 25 and October 9, 1916. Ferenczi was then deeply troubled by this ending he was not ready to accept, and he pressed to extend the treatment by letter. Freud had to repeat several times that the analysis was finished but not terminated (October 24, 1916), "broken off because of unfavorable circumstances" (November 16, 1916).

Ferenczi was desperate, unable to accept this premature ending of his analysis, partly because he had not yet found the courage to disclose himself. Only when he realized that Freud was immovable, some of the things that he had failed to report began to appear in his letters, such as his sexual enactment with Saroltà, the worsening of his relationship with his mother, and his hostility to Freud. On November 18, 1916, he explained that he was taking out on his mother what he was sparing Gizella, "thereby returning to the original source of [his] hatred of women." "But what is my fate?" he added, "Must I dissociate myself from every woman – like a Flying Dutchman (or, like him, kill the woman and myself)?" Then, in his letter of November 27, he noted that he was sacrificing all women for his "father's sake." One day later, while describing his hostility to "the father," he wrote: "I know only too well that it is here a matter of the repetition of the defiant rebellion in Palermo."

Ferenczi, who had been too frightened to lose Freud's love, would go on to work with the hostility in his relationship with George Groddeck. After the occasion of a session with Freud in 1922, he wrote to Groddeck: "I must admit it did me good to talk for once to this dearly loved father about my hate feelings."[2] In 1930, reflecting on the conflictual character of his relationship with Freud, Ferenczi wrote, on January 17:

> First you were my revered teacher and unattainable model . . . Then you became my analyst, but the unfavorable conditions did not permit carrying out my analysis to completion. I was especially sorry that you did not comprehend and bring to abreaction in the analysis the partly only [Reading uncertain. It could also be "in me," – editorial note] transferred, negative feelings and fantasies. As is well known, no analysand can do that without help . . . .

In "Analysis terminable and interminable" Freud (1937a) would defend himself from Ferenczi's reproach of failing to analyze his negative transference, saying that the latter "was not currently active in the patient himself at the time" (p. 222). Freud's statement is puzzling, since expressions of Ferenczi's "defiant rebellion" can be found throughout the entire correspondence. Yet it probably is misleading to speak of a negative transference generated by the analytic situation, because already long before the beginning of his formal analysis Ferenczi's ambivalence was a specific trait of his relationship with Freud (Dupont, 2015, p. 158). In *The Clinical Diary* Ferenczi wrote of a "mutually castration-directed aggressivity," overlaid by a "harmonious father-son relationship" (Dupont, 1985, p. 185). The intense, too-short analysis did not offer a way out from this entanglement, which had been strikingly anticipated in Ferenczi's dream of the occlusive pessary (Ferenczi, 1915). Even the idea of an incomplete analysis was presaged in this dream.

An occlusive stone

Volume I presented the depiction in popular imagination of the portal to Hell as a mouth. The Hebrew Hell, for instance, was associated to Moloch's yawning mouth, inside which children were to be thrown into the fire as a sacrifice. Similarly, in Virgil's Aenid the starting point of the hero's descent into the world of the dead was a stony cave resembling a wide yawning mouth. Goethe, in his *Faust*, spoke of "the jaws of hell." For Freud it was, of course, the wide-open mouth of the Irma dream, the starting point of his descent into the Hell-Unconscious. In all these situations the mouth is also a vagina; the mystical journey into the beyond is a journey into the depth of the Mother Earth. The same portal is on the top of the erect penis in Ferenczi's Christmas dream: the *corpora cavernosa* laid bare bring in a psychic place which in Freud's dreams had first represented as the wide-open mouth/vagina of Irma and then by Freud's own eviscerated pelvis. This image suggested to me that Ferenczi was resuming the mystical journey in the unconscious, in the precise point where it had been discontinued by the father of psychoanalysis.

The dangerous action of penetration into a cavernous body was the subject of the initial dream of Ferenczi's analysis with Freud in September 1914. Also on this occasion, Ferenczi had sent Freud in advance a detailed self-analysis of a dream, in a manuscript intended for publication in which his dream was presented as a patient's dream. This was the dream of the occlusive pessary (Ferenczi, 1915):

> I stuff an occlusive pessary into my urethra. I am alarmed as I do so lest it might slip into the bladder from which it could only be removed by shedding blood. I try, therefore, to hold it steady in the perineal region from outside and to force it back or to press it outwards along the urethra . . . .
>
> (p. 304)

In the manuscript sent to Freud on September 8, 1914, the analysis of this dream was restructured in the form of a dialogue between doctor and patient. The subject of the dialogue is not the beginning of an analysis, but its termination: the doctor informs the patient that the analysis is terminated and that, from now on, he can rely on his self-analysis alone. The patient doesn't accept the abandonment of this premature ending.

In the manuscript Ferenczi presented himself as the doctor, but in the letter to Freud accompanying the manuscript, he identified himself as the patient and the doctor as Freud. Thus, as remarked by Falzeder (1996), the article resulted in a "masterpiece of ambivalence, meta-discourse and hidden messages" and in something that "can be compared to a *theater play*" (p. 7).

The subject of this hall of mirrors seems once again to be the symbol of Freud's self-analysis: the dream of self-dissection of the pelvis. The extraordinary resemblance between these two dreams has been emphasized by Falzeder: "in both Ferenczi's and Freud's dreams, there is an operation, performed by the dreamer on the lower part of his own body, in both cases the associations link this operation with self-analysis" (p. 9).

The question of self-analysis had a central place in Ferenczi's manuscript. One complaint was of Freud overestimating his capacity to analyze himself. Ferenczi felt quite helpless about this, as he made clear in the last part of the paper:

> I have, as you know, repeatedly tried to analyze myself. I sat at my desk, wrote down my ideas, covered many sheets of paper with associations, without making anything of it. My thoughts flow into the commensurable. I cannot collect them properly, I find no clue to the tangle.
>
> (Ferenczi, 1915, p. 310)

Self-analysis was of no help in overcoming his impasse – the indecision about Gizella and Elma. In September 1914 Elma was married the day before the dream of the occlusive pessary. This reactivated Ferenczi's conflict, which, in the associations, is presented as an incapacity to make a choice between two women, "the woman with the too wide and the bride with the too narrow vagina" (p. 309). The pessary was also a medical treatment, and Gizella made use of this device to treat her prolapsed vagina. This unattractive anatomical feature destroyed Ferenczi's desire, making the mystical journey into the maternal body both revolting and frightening. The womb-fantasy stirred in Ferenczi the idea that "the woman might be damaged as a consequence of the narrowed genital canal" (p. 306). Many repellent images of female genitals – damaged by "perineal tear, operation, abnormal width, etc." – are presented by Ferenczi as an expression of his "strong castration complex" (p. 307), and associated with his too-strict mother, now reincarnated in the analyst who was determined to abandon his patient. In the fictive dialogue the doctor (Freud) tells the patient (Ferenczi) that he exaggerates his "importance and assistance," and that he can now do it alone, as proved by his dream. According to the analyst, the pessary-child represents in fact his own "self-analysis" (p. 310). So Ferenczi's complaint about the inconclusiveness of his self-analysis is also a criticism of Freud's trust in self-analysis. "Mockery and scorn," Ferenczi says in the fictive dialogue, "are concealed behind such nonsense dreams" (p. 309).

Concerning the meaning of the "occlusion," Falzeder (1996) proposed that "the representative of [Freud] in Ferenczi remained to be a hardly digested 'introject'" or "in Ferenczi's own words, Freud represented a 'super-ego intropression'" (p. 269).[3] Today the occlusive pessary looks like Freud's heritage of non-abreacted emotion, which, after having been incorporated, Ferenczi recognized as an obstruction. Ferenczi had forced Freud to take him as patient, but in the moment when he had to place himself in Freud's hands, it was Freud's personality he was most afraid of. Thus the dream, and the way Ferenczi deals with it, also anticipates Ferenczi's idea of the "wise baby," the theory of the patient who must become his own analyst's analyst (Ferenczi, 1923, 1933). The pessary thus brings into representation a role reversal. Remarking upon the failure in the object choice, the doctor says: "Therefore in the dream *you make yourself into the pessary child* . . . In our technology this is called a 'regression' from object-love to self-gratification" (Ferenczi, 1915, p. 309).

In his free associations, Ferenczi was reminded of stuffing small objects into his nose and ears as a child, and of his persistent masturbation. Still, the theme of a *bloody surgical operation* evokes a further line of thought which doesn't surface in Ferenczi's article. At that time the pessary was closely associated with the gynecological treatment of hysteria. As put by Thomas Baskett (2006),

> The 19th century was the golden age of the pessary. Just about any complaint that a woman produced, that could even remotely be connected with the pelvic organs, would potentially fall prey to the use of a pessary to correct 'uterine malalignment.'
>
> (p. 3)

Since in those years castration was still a recommended treatment for hysteria, we must wonder whether Ferenczi discussed this treatment with Freud, including his personal experiences.

In Ferenczi's dream are all sorts of references to a damaged uterus, which the rubber pessary was supposed to repair. Although in Ferenczi's analysis there are no allusions to this reparative fantasy, it is tempting to think of Freud's eviscerated pelvis, itself a representation of a damaged emotional container, and to imagine this as an unconscious target of Ferenczi's reparative fantasy.

A last etymological remark: The word pessary "is derived from the Greek *pessos* and the Latin *pessarium* (Greek 'pessos'), meaning an oval-shaped stone" (Baskett, 2006, p. 1). The etymology of the Greek word πεσσός (*pessos*) is controversial. Besides referring to the treatment for a prolapsed uterus, a suppository, the word "pessos" also was an architectural term for the foundational blocks or pediments that hold up a whole house. For instance, in *De Aedificiis* 1.1.37 (*On Buildings*), Procopius (c. A.D. 500 – c. A.D. 560) used it to refer to the piers at the base of the dome of Hagia Sophia, the famous cathedral in Constantinople (Istanbul) dedicated to the incarnation of Logos in Christ.[1] Ferenczi may not have been acquainted with this very particular meaning of the word "*pessos*," so it is quite striking that for his collected papers Ferenczi chose the title of *Bausteine* [building stones] *der Psychoanalyse*. In truth, his dream of the occlusive "oval-shaped stone" was the starting point of his new foundation of the psychoanalytic building.

Towards a new foundation

What was the fate of this reparative fantasy? For many years, the mutilations of genital organs represented a constant concern for Ferenczi, affecting his research, starting with his observation of Arpad in 1912. Arpad was a five-year-old child whose penis had bled from a bite by a rooster a year and a half earlier. One year later, after returning to the family's summer residence, the child lost his power of speech and began to crow and crackle. Once back in Budapest he began once more to speak, but only of cocks, hens, and chickens. His favorite game consisted in playing slaughtering fowls, and the affects displayed were "plainly ambivalent": he "could dance round the animals' bodies for hours at time in a state of intense excitement"; then "he would kiss and stroke the slaughtered animal" (Ferenczi, 1913a, p. 246).[5] Pierre Sabourin (2011) is one of the few who has emphasized the "founding" character of this case history in which the "a post-traumatic polymorph-perversion is at work" (p. 119).

Sabourin advanced two important points. The first is that the history of Arpad was "the analogic model of the catastrophic consequences that can be caused by an external attack on the sex, here the pecking of a rooster, elsewhere a seduction of a more human character, pedophilic or incestuous, but in any case unpredictable" (p. 119). That is, the two lines of thought that in Freud's work appear disjointed (seduction and castration) are here interwoven. The second is that the case of Arpad is the prototype of Ferenczi's notion of "identification with the aggressor" (Sabourin, 2011).

A further reason for the relevance of the case history of Arpad is that Ferenczi could observe the reaction of Freud and his way of handling the trauma of Arpad when he sent him this material in January 1912. This point will be further explored in the next chapter.

In 1913, Ferenczi began to examine the penis of some of his impotent patients, as described in his note on the "Paresthesias of the genital region in impotence" (1913c). At this time he also had in treatment a patient who would play an important role in Ferenczi's rediscovery of trauma. The patient as a boy had been taken by his father, a Christian country gentleman, to a Jewish butcher of the village, where he was brutally circumcised with "a long and sharp knife" (Ferenczi, 1917b). In 1915, during the war and his suspended analysis with Freud, Ferenczi undertook further research on the real, traumatic aspects of circumcision (Ferenczi, 1917b). In 1917, he wrote two important studies, which represented the first revaluation of trauma after Freud's 1897 abandonment of the seduction theory: on the pathoneuroses (1917a) and on the psychical consequences of "castration" in childhood (1917b). Both were centered on physical wounds to genital organs. Ferenczi was the first to suggest that these injuries could not only be a releasing factor but also specific etiological factor. The second study described this case of the brutally "castrated" Christian country gentleman's son, though in fact, he was only circumcised, and suggested that a trauma of this kind represented a "narcissistic wound" (Ferenczi, 1917b).[6]

Thalassa: A Theory of Genitality was the study in which the full emotional power of the dream of the cut-off penis served on a saucer was finally worked out. This work, published in 1924 in German, represented the zenith of Ferenczi's obsession with genital wounds. When the text was translated into Hungarian, his mother tongue, Ferenczi renamed it *Katasztrofák (Catastrophe)*. The work had been conceived during the years 1913–15, but for many years Ferenczi was unable to put it on paper. He explained in his letter to Groddeck of Christmas 1921 that every time he had tried to put the genital theory in writing, he had suffered back pains, psychosomatic disturbances, and anxiety crises. In the same letter, remarking on his bodily tendency to become very cold, he wrote: "Am I trying to behave like a fish, or to enact my genital theory which I won't write down?" (Fortune, 2002, p. 15)

Structure, function, and meaning of the Thalassa myth

Ferenczi imagined the erect penis as the living memorial of a great catastrophe of cosmic proportions acting as an unresolved and unmastered trauma that is inherited by each generation, partly abreacted, and then passed to the next. This catastrophic event, in Ferenczi's imagination, was the exsiccation (drying up) of the sea ("*Thalassa*" in Greek), which forced the fish, the phylogenetic ancestor of man, to start a process of adaptation and development informed by a desire to restore a pre-traumatic state in real, symbolic, and imaginary ways. Freud considered Ferenczi's genital theory a "most brilliant and most fertile achievement" (Freud, 1933b, p. 228), indeed a "summit of achievement" (p. 229), a "scientific fantasy" containing a truth that remains to be deciphered. Beyond that, I consider it quite a splendid development of Freud's compulsion to repeat as well as of the reparative fantasy at work in Ferenczi's dream of the occlusive pessarium.

Ferenczi's "bio-analysis" of genitality is a work made difficult to read by its violation, as Ferenczi (1924) himself declared in the introduction, of a fundamental principle of keeping natural and mental sciences separate. Hence it cannot be classified either as a biological or as a psychological work. According to the scientist Jay Gould (1977), *Thalassa* carried Haeckel's recapitulation doctrine embraced by Freud "to previously unimagined heights of folly" (p. 163).

Ferenczi's meta-biological speculation did not gain repute even within psychoanalytic circles and today is still considered mainly as an embarrassing oddity. Clara Thompson (1988) saw Ferenczi as impeded in developing his own thinking because "his own original ideas become so clothed in Freudian terminology that he sometimes successfully conceals whatever of himself was in them" (p. 185). *Thalassa*, in her view, was a typical expression of Ferenczi's ambivalent attachment to Freud, which "manifested despite all of his efforts for he would often develop an idea of Freud's to a fantastic degree, thus, in the end, making the situation absurd" (Thompson, 1988). On the other hand, Michael Balint (1949) recognized that *Thalassa* was informed by the main message of Ferenczi, namely that "we subject our children to unnecessary, avoidable, traumata, . . . and subsequently our children, when grown up, pass on similar traumata to their children." (p. 217). That is, the question of "heredity," which is handled through the biological theories of Lamarck and Haeckel, encompasses the problem of *psychic transmission of traumata from one generation to the other*. Clearly, Ferenczi was wrestling with Freud's enigmatic message, an unresolved heritage of emotion.

This is in keeping with the mystic reading of *Thalassa* offered by Norman O. Brown. The deep continuity between Freud and Ferenczi, the idea that the Fall is division and dismemberment, the identity of Penis, Fish, and Christ in the apocalyptic reconstitution of the lost unity in One Body, are all elements which are emphasized in Brown's *Love's Body* (1966):

> The unconscious is rather that immortal sea which brought us hither; intimations of which are given in moments of "oceanic feeling"; one sea of energy or instinct; embracing all mankind, without distinction of race, language, or culture; and embracing all the generations of Adam, past, present, and future, in one phylogenetic heritage; in one mystical or symbolical body.
>
> (pp. 88–89)

In Ferenczi's apocalyptic theory of genitality the sexual act is a historical drama, a symbolic reenactment or recapitulation of all the great traumas in the history of the individual, of the species, of life itself. Psychoanalytic time is not gradual, evolutionary, but discontinuous, catastrophic, revolutionary. The sexual act is a return to the womb. . . .

> Birth really is from water; the womb really is as introjected, incarnate, ocean. . . . In copulation the penis really is a fish in water. . . . Physical, or "real" birth is really rebirth, a repetition of an archetypal birth of the cosmos from the cosmic egg.
>
> (p. 211)

Norman O. Brown's identification of the Fish, the Penis, and Christ is startlingly congruent with the reading of the symbol of Freud's self-analysis in "Necropolis" (Chapter 8). Brown's reference to the "oceanic feeling" is also pertinent: Freud himself, with no direct experience of dreams of flying and floating, was unable to discover the "oceanic feeling" in himself.[7] We have already met this point commenting on Freud's Entombment scene in the self-dissection dream, specifically Freud's failure to be "lifted up" (flying and floating) to the celestial womb in his dream and to make a distinction between a fantasy of being buried alive in a tomb and a successful regression to the prenatal state. A similar confusion attended Freud's attempt at reformulating the tendency to restore an earlier, pre-traumatic state of unity in *Beyond the Pleasure Principle*. Introducing the hypothesis of a "death instinct," which pulls back to an inanimate state of the living matter, Freud (1920) in fact shaped the restored state of unity in light of his funeral fantasy. Ferenczi's Thalassa myth deals with the same theme, but in a way that, as noted by Pierre Sabourin (2011), anticipated what Ferenczi would later describe as the "traumatolytic function of the dream," that the traumatic dream "tries to liquidate the destructive power of trauma by the endless repetition of the same theme" (p. 101). Indeed, according to Balint (1955), the starting point of Ferenczi's phylogenetic theory of coitus were dreams of flying and floating, representing sediments not only of the intra-uterine life, but also of the baby's experience "in its mother's arms, being in love, floating, feeling of oneness with the universe" (p. 231).

The idea of the body as language, and that repetition compulsion is always a "symbolic solution," was called to attention by Nicholas Abraham (1962) as the key of *Thalassa*, Ferenczi's cosmogonic epic. Abraham, an important Hungarian psychoanalyst in the sixties contributed to the rediscovery of this forgotten work, which "evokes in us profound and unspeakable resonances." "It says to us: we are woven by symbols from end to end" (p. 23). Nicholas Abraham also formulated the question that underlies all the work of Ferenczi: "What is the ancestral traumatism that the ontogenesis *repeat* symbolically, what is the repression that manifests itself through this symbolic repetition?" (pp. 21–22)

Thalassa is a creation myth, which, like all creation myths, is about the "Cut," the trauma of division and the fantasy of reunion. The peculiarity of this myth is that it was forged in the language, the ideas, and even the dreams of Freud. That is, it is a myth about the creation of psychoanalysis. This is how I imagine, I contend is, the genesis of Ferenczi's myth. Thanks to his own dreams, Ferenczi entered Freud's dream of the self-dissection of the pelvis, took over the place of the dreamer, and, by looking down at his eviscerated pelvis, was at last able to more completely see what Freud himself had only glimpsed from afar. In Ferenczi's fairy tale there is, fully developed, the connection between the penis, the fish and the compulsion to repeat encountered exegetically in the dream of Freud.

In *Thalassa* Ferenczi did not refer to circumcision, yet the cutting of the prepuce is the template for the unmastered trauma that is passed to the next generation. The core element of Ferenczi's myth became the so-called "womb theory of the prepuce," introducing a formidable series of bio-symbolic equivalences between fish, child, and penis. For Ferenczi, the enveloping of the glans in a mucous membrane represented a reproduction of the intra-uterine life of the child, even as this latter reproduces the aquatic life of the fish before the catastrophic drying-up of the sea. The penis, thus, carries within it the memory of the expulsion of the fish from the mother-sea, which is then repeated in the birth of every child and commemorated through the act of penile erection.

By aiming at penetrating the womb, the genital repeats the fate of the child, who desires to return to the mother-womb, which, in its turn, repeats the striving of the fish, which desires to return to the sea in the regressive attempt to restore a pre-traumatic situation. Finally, the longing for a silent, embracing, and pacifying mother-womb-sea is at bottom nothing but a desire for death, a desire to restore the perfect harmony and rest that existed before the child traumatically enters life and awakes. This is the reason why – as Ferenczi was led to recall in his conclusions – primitive people bury their dead in a squatting or fetal position.

Only after this *requiem* was Ferenczi able to accomplish his inner separation from Freud. Theoretically *Thalassa* was a re-elaboration of Freud's theory of the death instinct, yet, set free from its biological shell, it surfaces as the poetic transformation of the paralyzing vision of an erect penis which is cut off, as in his Christmas dream, offering a cathartic outlet for the occlusive incorporation dramatized in his pessary dream. What was mute, dead, and strange to the ego is here restored and assimilated into a vast, deep, and moving view of the world – ultimately, a silent contemplation of it. Ferenczi's lasting vacillation was not overcome, but better and more simply contemplated as the "perpetual oscillating between the will to live and the will to die" (Ferenczi, 1924, p. 94), mirrored in the analogy between birth and death and echoed by the rhythm of coitus. The "impotent rage" of the letter of December 26, 1912 was now recognized as enraged coitus by which the traumatic "imprisonment in the birth canal" is repeated (Ferenczi, 1924, p. 35). Similarly, horrible mutilations are re-absorbed into a vast reparative fantasy, which, by resuming the pulsing pendulum of the universe, overcomes the blocking effects of repetition-compulsion. The crucial emotion aroused by this myth concerns, more precisely, a maternal fantasy of restoring the peace of a mutilated-penis dead-child. And this is how Ferenczi's theoretical fantasy represents the emotional working-out of pathological mourning encrypted within Freud's phallus cult.[8]

Notes

1 See Freud (1910a, p. 43, 1910b, p. 145). Even when analysis by another person began, Freud (1914a) remained of the opinion that self-analysis "may suffice for anyone who is a good dreamer and not too abnormal" (p. 20). The idea of a regular training analysis, strongly supported by Ferenczi, was introduced only in 1922, in the training program of the Berlin Psychoanalytic Institute.
2 Letter to Groddeck of February 27, 1922. Ferenczi wrote: "[Freud] persists in his original view that the crux of the matter is my hatred for him, because he stopped me . . . from marrying the younger woman (now my stepdaughter). Hence my murderous intentions towards him which express themselves in nightly death scenes (drop in body temperature; gasping for breath) these symptoms are, furthermore, overdetermined by my memories of watching my parents' intercourse."
3 The term "super-ego intropression" was used by Ferenczi in his Clinical Diary (Dupont, 1985, p. 279).
4 See the discussion of "*pessos*" in http://hellenisteukontos.blogspot.it/2009/05/pessos-and-pinsus-pedimental.html
5 Ferenczi (1913a), who met the child and spoke with his parents when the child was five years old, found that in the incubation period he had been threatened with the cutting off of his penis "on account of voluptuous playing with genitals" (p. 248). "Arpad" was also highly interested in the genitals of poultry and treated the other children and the persons in the family as poultry. He would call out that he wanted to cut the head of a girl and "eat it up," or quietly say that his mother "must be put in a pot and cooked." "After expressing these cannibalistic desires, he would at once get an attack of remorse, in which he masochistically yearned for cruel punishment" (p. 249). Recognizing the father as the cock, he said, "Now I am a chicken . . . When I am bigger I shall be a cock." Arpad was also preoccupied with death. On one occasion, he asked, "Why do children die? How long can one live? It was only with great difficulty that he calmed down." It turned it out that the chambermaid had found him manipulating his penis and threatened to cut it off. When the neighbor tried to calm him down by saying that no harm would be done to him and that every child did things of that sort, Arpad cried out indignantly: "That's not true! Not every child! My papa has never does anything like that." Arpad later began to occupy himself with religious thoughts and was very impressed by old, bearded Jews because they come, he said, "from God" (that is, out of the temple). He wanted his mother to invite them home and once he said, "Now I am a beggar-fowl" (pp. 250–251). Finally he once told his neighbor "I shall marry you and your sister and my three cousins and the cook; no, instead of the cook rather my mother." Ferenczi's conclusion was that he wanted to be a real "cook of the roost" (p. 252).
6 Ferenzi announced this case to Freud, in his letter of March 9, 1916, with the following words: "I still want to write a few little things before my departure, among them the interesting case of a man who, in childhood (three years old), was really castrated (circumcised). A counterpart to the Little Rooster-Man. This operation became the fate of this man."

7 The notion was coined by Romain Rolland, but clearly had a "thalassian" resonance. Freud discussed the "oceanic feeling" in his letters to Romain Rolland of July 14 and 20, 1929, and at length in *Civilization and Its Discontents* (Freud, 1930a, pp. 64–73). Concerning Balint's discussion of the sensations and dreams of floating, see Balint (1955, pp. 230–231, 1960, p. 41, 1968, p. 74). Even though Freud introduced this kind of dreams in *The Interpretation of Dreams*, Balint (1955) pointed out that "he personally had no experience of such dreams, a fact which we now might possibly bring into connection with his well-known slight anxiety neurosis, especially his 'Reisefieber.'" (p. 230). Balint derived from this specific aspect of *Thalassa* his theory of the "Friendly expanses – horrid empty spaces." Even though he did not state it explicitly, it is clear that in his view the memories signified by the "friendly expanses" were repressed in Freud, and replaced by "the horrid empty spaces" (Balint, 1955). A discussion of Freud's fear of flying can be found in Fried (2003).
8 This formula was already proposed in my presentation at the International Conference of the Ferenczi Society, *The Talking Therapy: Ferenczi and the Psychoanalytic Vocation*, Budapest, 1993, titled, "Freud, Jung, Ferenczi and the vision of a cut-off penis" (Bonomi, 1994a).

12 A blind spot

> . . . [excision] seemed to Freud a way of seeking to further "feminize" the female by removing this cardinal vestige of her masculinity.
>
> Marie Bonaparte, Female mutilation among primitive peoples and their psychical parallels in civilization (1948a, p. 153)

The founding myth

In *Totem and Taboo* (1913a) Freud presented a new version of the myth of original sin: the collective murder of the father of the primeval family. Assaulted, dismembered, and cannibalized by his own sons, the primal father would arrive to be worshipped as a god through a ritual ceremony which memorialized the crime of incorporation through a totemic meal. The sacramental appropriation of the paternal attributes not only included expressions of remorse and attempts to atone for the horrible crime but also featured a truly festive joy for the triumph over a ruthless despot, brutal tyrant, and rapist.

Freud managed to isolate traces of the original and founding crime in the Christian Eucharist; however, he failed to mention the Hebrew ceremony of circumcision, this despite the fact that it supported the very thesis that he wished to promulgate.[1] Freud filled this omission soon after, introducing the idea that "during the human family's primaeval period castration used actually to be carried out by a jealous and cruel fathers upon growing boys" and by suggesting "that circumcision, which so frequently plays a part in puberty rites among primitive peoples, is a clearly recognizable relic of it" (Freud, 1933a, pp. 86–87).

Freud conceived this idea in January 1912, in response to Ferenczi sharing details of Arpad's case history with him (Arpad was a child whose penis was bitten by a rooster and who reacted to it by later identifying with the rooster). Freud was enthusiastic about the little Rooster-Man. In his reply to Ferenczi on February 1 of 1912, he confessed that "similarly audacious thoughts about castration" had also occurred to him, including those bearing on the jealous, savage father who "castrated the boys before he contented himself with chasing them away."

These "audacious thoughts" quickly transformed into a key structural element for Freud, which he placed at the heart of the founding myth of psychoanalysis.

Freud's reaction was neither totally new nor surprising. As we saw, Emma Eckstein's circumcision scene, which he shared with Fliess in January of 1897, had unleashed similar "audacious thoughts" for Freud regarding the origins of religion. And yet, in the founding myth of psychoanalysis there was no role for women.[2]

The idea that the father of the primal horde castrated his sons was a central theme in Freud's essay, *"Übersicht der Übertragungneurosen"* ("Overview of the Transference Neuroses," renamed "A Phylogenetic Fantasy" when published in English). This metapsychological essay by Freud, written in 1915, was never published during Freud's lifetime. Describing the essay to Ferenczi, Freud wrote to say: "I am dealing with fantasies that disturb me and will hardly be suitable for public expression" (July 12, 1915). Freud believed that "what are now neuroses were once phases of the human condition" and that, further, thanks to the code stored in neuroses, it was possible to re-establish the events that determined early human development. Freud's efforts to synthesize his views were discussed with Ferenczi in detail. This led them to entertain the idea of jointly writing a book based on the Lamarckian hypothesis that individually acquired characteristics were capable of being transmitted to the genetic code and thus inherited. Freud failed to develop his ideas on this particular subject further, relinquishing the entire project to Ferenczi. Even though the idea that the father of the primal family castrated his sons immediately aroused Ferenczi's skepticism (in his letter to Freud of July 24, 1915, Ferenczi noted: "The castrated ones cannot have reproduced and fixated their condition phylogenetically"); *Thalassa*, was in part the outcome of this.

A striking disparity

The decision to feature castration/circumcision in the founding myth elicited a strong interest in puberty rites. Otto Rank was the first to call attention to the puberty rites of primitive societies.[3] Freud then mentioned the need to investigate the puberty rites of primitive societies in context of a well-known footnote in *Totem and Taboo* (1913a, p. 153). It should be noted that while Rank referred to both the circumcision of boys and the excision of the clitoris in girls when broaching the theme of circumcision, Freud only mentioned the "initiation into manhood," thus keeping the female sex outside the circle of ethno-psychoanalytic investigation of puberty rites altogether.

Puberty rites were precisely what Theodor Reik undertook to investigate in his 1915 essay on *"Die Pubertätsriten der Wilden"* ("The puberty rites of savages"). This work, originally published in the journal *Imago*, was later included in his collection *Ritual: Psycho-analytic Studies* (Reik, 1931). Reik found that circumcision was generally understood in these ceremonies as the visible mark of the violence of a terrifying monster, usually identified with an ancestor of the initiate. The ceremony typically consisted of the simulated killing of the initiate; the enactment of terror and dismemberment was then followed by a communion feast through which the initiate was symbolically reborn and provided with new internal organs before being accepted into the brotherhood of men. According to Reik, circumcision during these events represented symbolic castration, having no purpose other than to repress incest. *B'rith milah*, the Hebrew ceremony of circumcision, was in Reik's view merely a "glorified and emended account of an initiation ceremony" (p. 156). Reik's essay was awarded the Imago Prize in 1919. Female puberty rites were however not mentioned and were completely ignored by him in the essay.

This was not just an omission, but rather one of the many striking expressions of the disparity for Freud between males and females with respect to circumcision and castration. In his *Clinical Diary*, Ferenczi would later write:

> The ease with which Freud sacrifices the interests of women in favor of male patients is striking. This is consistent with the unilaterally androphile orientation of his theory of sexuality.

Ferenczi, who wrote this remark on August 4, 1932, that is, a few weeks before his last terrible encounter and conflict with Freud, was referring to Freud's "castration theory of femininity."

While the pioneers of psychoanalysis behaved like the brother-clan described by Freud in *Totem and Taboo* – rebelling against the customs and traditions of their Jewish ancestors, including circumcision – the practice of removing the clitoris of the girl remained largely unchallenged in psychoanalysis until very recently, when the girl's concern for the safety of her own genitals began to be addressed under the rubric of "primary genital anxiety." This led to efforts to distinguish the loss of an illusory phallus from the fear of injuring the genitals.[1]

The destruction of the external and, sometime, internal genital organs carried out in female puberty rites was a widely communicated phenomenon in several ethnological works, in particular, in Ploss and Bartel's (1885) treatise *Das Weib in der Natur- und Völkerkunde*, a book which saw 11 new editions between 1885 and 1927. The book was finally published in English in 1935 under the title *Woman: An Historical Gynaecological and Anthropological Compendium*. Despite many differences in the procedure between different races ("sometimes both labia and clitoris were mutilated, at times only the labia, at other times only the prepuce"), Ploss and Bartel found that the circumcision of girls should no longer be considered only "a specifically African custom" but, rather, that it provided "proof of the resemblances in the mental processes of primitive peoples throughout the world" (p. 342). Sharing the common view that the intention of the procedure was to correct nature, Ploss and Bartels interpreted the Hottentot custom of making the labia longer as an "atavism, a symptom of primitive development" (p. 335). Significantly, at the end of the chapter on "The circumcision of girls," the English translator of this work felt compelled to insert the following note in 1935:

> Removal of the clitoris has long been advocated by certain writers for masturbation in girls and for such female ailments as pruritus. In 1867 and 1868 the English medical world was convulsed by revelations concerning the opinions and practices of Isaac B. Brown who performed the operation at his London Surgical home as a means of curing forms of insanity, epilepsy and

hysteria, as well as masturbation. It appeared that not only was the clitoris excised but the nymphae were clipped to their base, and the whole vulva cauterised. The case excited enormous interest and Mr. Brown was removed from the Obstetrical Society of London. *However, many of his grateful patients, who believed that they had been saved from insanity by his ministrations, combined with others to present him with a silver dessert service in token of his 'singular success in the treatment of female diseases.'*

(p. 353; emphasis added)

Such "psycho-surgical" interventions on the external and internal genital organs of women and young girls were still being practiced at the time when the founders of the psychoanalytic movement began to ponder, digest, and reflect on the meaning of Freud's castration theory of femininity. While Freud cannot obviously be held responsible for how psychoanalysts used his theory, we can at the very least note that he failed to do much of anything to prevent the possible confusion between imaginary (the loss of an illusory phallus) and actual castration (in its various forms).

A similar confusion is also present in Karl Abraham's important essay "Manifestations of the female castration complex." In it, Abraham (1922) presented the following vignette:

> Some time ago a lady who was a stranger to me and who would not give her name rang me up on the telephone and asked me if I could prevent an operation that had been arranged for the next day. On my request for more information she told me she was to be operated on for a severe uterine haemorrhage due to myomata. When I told her it was not part of my work to prevent a necessary and perhaps life-saving operation she did not reply, but explained with affective volubility that she had always been 'hostile to all operations', adding, 'whoever is once operated on is forever afterwards a cripple for life'. The senselessness of this exaggeration is comprehensible if we remember that that operation carried out in phantasy in early childhood makes the girl a 'cripple'.

(pp. 24–25)

I interpret Abraham's description as follows: The lady was perhaps desperately seeking someone who might help save her from a surgical intervention being forced upon her. The intervention might have involved an actual castration procedure that was being proposed to her as a psychiatric (psycho-gynecological) treatment. Abraham's response to the lady's predicament reveals how Freud's theory was used to confuse different things altogether (the fear of being stripped of an imaginary phallus with the fear of actual surgery, for instance) or to even deny the effects of an actual trauma by blaming the victim.

When Abraham wrote his essay, the practice of castrating women was becoming popular for eugenic reasons. While true that Freud did not endorse the views of negative eugenics, the fact remains that the theory of eugenics intersected and overlapped with psychoanalysis in disturbing ways. Commenting in 1961 on a follow-up study of 244 cases of castration carried out for eugenic reasons, for instance, a psychoanalyst reasoned as follows:

> From a psychoanalytic point of view, we must assume that castration in men re-enforces the fear of further loss – the loss of the penis; whereas castration in women *does not interfere with the visible body image and thus has less or no traumatic effect*.
>
> (Gero, 1961, p. 589; emphasis added)

The analyst was in this case directly appealing to Freud's theory of femininity to advance his position. This reveals how Freud's position on women's castration implied meanings which were never fully discussed or explored. These meanings only emerge after we realize that Freud responded to Emma's circumcision trauma by transforming it into a universal theory of "biotrauma."

The curse on female genitals

Ferenczi published his work on *Thalassa* in 1924, during a highly difficult moment in the history of the psychoanalytic movement. The year became highly polarized as a result of Rank's book *The Trauma of Birth* (1924a), which Rank wrote to shift trauma from a phylogenetic scenario back to real-life events. Rank's book recast the "ubiquity of the 'castration complex'" (p. 20) in terms of the ambivalent nature of the infant's relation to the mother, the primal cause of emotional pain to the child during his or her early days. The "primal taboo," Rank argued, "is the maternal genital which from the beginning onwards is invested with ambivalent feelings" (p. 87). This taboo, he argued, resulted in an "insufficient understanding of woman's sexual life" and a systematic devaluation of women "both socially and intellectually" (p. 36). Criticizing the systematic disparagement of women in society, Rank added the following:

> We believe that we shall reinstate the high estimation of woman that was repressed simultaneously with the birth trauma, and [that] we can do this by freeing her from the weight of the curse on her genitals.
>
> (p. 37)

Indeed, Rank could have easily titled *The Trauma of Birth* as "The curse on female genitals," illustrating his thesis with the surgical interventions still practiced in gynecological psychiatry!

Freud was initially impressed by Rank's new perspective on the Oedipus complex. However, not much time elapsed before he refused to accept Rank's idea that the mother, or her genitals, might be feared and hated by the child. In a long letter to Freud on August 9 of 1924 Rank wrote: "I have the definite impression that you don't wish to see certain things or that you can't see them." Later, during his American lectures, Rank proposed not only that the mother featured as an early paradise from which the child had been expelled but as the first "bad" object in the child's life as well.

Whereas Freud viewed the super-ego as a derivative of the father complex and believed that the ego reacted to external trauma by developing feelings of unworthiness and a need to be treated badly by the internal representative of the father, Rank traced the psychic origins of the super-ego back to the child's early relation to the mother. In "The genesis of the guilt-feeling," for instance, he proposed that the attempt to inhibit the sadistic aggression of a depriving mother led the child to turn aggression back towards him or herself. It was from this inhibited sadism, Rank (1926b) argued, that "an image of the strict (punitive) mother" was formed (p. 133). Rank saw Freud as simply incapable of envisioning the mother as a depriving or punitive figure. Freud displaced this personal blind spot, Rank (1926c) further argued, by viewing women as merely "passive and inferior object[s]," indeed as beings who were "castrated" (p. 101).

One powerful cut

The Trauma of Birth remains difficult to assess as it combines brilliant ideas with a hypomanic attempt to shorten the length of clinical treatment, proposing that analysts were "able to sever the Gordian knot of the primal repression with one powerful cut" (p. 213). The use Rank made of the "cut" metaphor reveals that he had successfully assimilated Freud's "basic language" from the founding of psychoanalysis. Rank had served as Freud's right-hand man in Vienna for years. At a more or less unconscious level, Rank grasped that the cut in rites of initiation (circumcision) and psychoanalytic discourse itself was in the end merely a mimetic reproduction of a more primordial cut, that of severing the umbilical cord, the event which allowed all humans to separate from their mother to enter the circle of life (cf. Volume I, pp. 166–171)[5].

Rank also introduced the notion of symbolic adaptation and did so to describe human adaptation as a creative process. Thus, primitive man built huts and houses in order to replace the maternal body lost when separating from the mother, and did so according to a symbolic pattern which informed the building of civilization itself. Symbol formation, in Rank's view, was the most fruitful way humans adapted to reality. To adjust to the external world, man necessarily had to modify it according to the pattern of unconscious desires.

One consequence of Rank's position is the view of humans as never able to fully and completely accept reality, but to transcend it with a continuous remolding and reshaping. Rank was in this case anticipating the shift from past to future introduced by existentialist philosophers only a few decades later. He was also anticipating their rejection of the idea that humans were determined by an "innate program." Rank developed this position further in *Art and Artist* (1932), concluding that writing *The Trauma of Birth* had helped him to better understand how a child's attempt to restore the prenatal condition led to feeling at "one with the world, with a cosmos, floating in mystic vapours in which present, past, and future" were "dissolved." Rank also proposed that the "individual urge to restore this lost unity" was an "essential factor in the production of human cultural values" (p. 113) as well.

Anatomy is destiny

Rank rejected the notion that a human life might be determined by heredity and anatomy. By re-organizing psychoanalytic theory not around the genitals but in relation to the severing of the umbilical cord, Rank was suggesting that the anatomical difference between the sexes was an overvalued if not irrelevant factor for human understanding. Rank's bold interpretation was thus an attempt to rewrite and re-orient our conception of the human being by suggesting a new role for primal repression and for the goal of psychoanalytic treatment as well.

Freud vigorously resisted Rank's new framework for psychoanalysis. He reacted, during the early months of 1924, by writing "The dissolution of the Oedipus Complex," a work emphasizing once again the importance of a phylogenetic approach. Freud (1924a) in fact began his text by stating:

> Although the majority of human beings go through the Oedipus complex as an individual experience, it is nevertheless a phenomenon which is determined and laid down by heredity and which is bound to pass away according to programme when the next pre-ordained phase of development sets in.
> (p. 174)

Freud tried to describe how it was that this "innate program" was "carried out" and in "what way accidental noxae exploit his [of the individual] disposition" (Freud, 1924a). He then went on to trace, step by step, how the threat of castration came to "destroy" a boy's phallic organization, causing the dissolution of his oedipal aspiration and the formation of the super-ego. After describing this inbuilt program, which he argued was a universal underlay of male development, Freud turned to another important question: "How does the corresponding development take place in little girls?" (p. 177). Freud's thesis was that, even though the clitoris behaved just like a little penis, the fear of castration was excluded in the little girl. "The essential difference" he wrote "thus comes about that the girl accepts castration as an accomplished fact, whereas the boy fears the possibility of its occurrence" (p. 178). It was in this context that Freud first proposed his controversial bold statement that "anatomy" was "destiny":

> Here the feminist demand for equal rights for the sexes does not take us far, for the morphological distinction is bound to find expression in differences of psychical development. 'Anatomy is Destiny', to vary a saying of Napoleon's.
> (p. 178)

Freud was here forgetting or denying the essential ambiguity of the clitoris, which both *is* and *is not* a penis. "Anatomy," in this case, appears to be quite undetermined and elastic, challenging a clear-cut dualism of the sexes (see Fausto-Sterling, 2000).

In his work, Rank suggested that women transcended the birth trauma by giving birth, that is to say, by finding the mother within themselves. The process of giving birth, Freud now proposed, allowed women to compensate for the fact of their lacking a penis. Freud argued, in response to Rank, that the girl, in her search for compensation,

> slips – along the line of a symbolic equation, one might say – from the penis to a baby. Her Oedipus complex culminates in a desire, which is long retained, to receive a baby from her father as a gift – to bear him a child. One has an impression that the Oedipus complex is then gradually given up because this wish is never fulfilled.
>
> (1924a, pp. 178–179)

Freud's proposal that the birth of a baby made up for the penis that a woman lacked was another stroke of genius. This idea, however, was in striking contradiction to his bold emphasis on the "innate phylogenetic program." Freud, in fact, saw women no different than did the book of Genesis, namely, as beings "made" and shaped from the body of man. Motherhood as such was left out, not included by Freud in this program. It was Ferenczi who, in an effort to address this omission in 1929, created his own mythology to explain how the female gender came into being during the course of biological evolution. Ferenczi's essay "Male and Female" was first published in 1929, in a journal which just appeared at the time: *Die psychoanalytische Bewegung*. Later, and in response to Ferenczi's own wishes, it was included as part of *Thalassa*, as an addendum to his theory of genitality.

Ferenczi wrote both essays as an adherent of Haeckel's theory of recapitulation, which argued that the developmental history of the individual was a repetition of the developmental history of the species in an abbreviated form. Ferenczi was well aware that his own ideas regarding the tumescent penis constituted "a kind of fairy tale" (1924, p. 99), and he also saw the "Male and female" essay as a fairy tale about an originally undifferentiated creature who was divided and split into two different sexes.

Following Freud's ideas on the primacy of the phallus, Ferenczi's point of departure in his theoretical fantasy was that both sexes had originally "developed the male sexual organ" and, further, that this was recapitulated in the embryological development of the individual. From the embryological point of view, the clitoris was a relatively well-developed penis which had failed to "conspicuously keep pace with the subsequent development of the body." In the case of the male, however, the "*phallus* grows progressively" (pp. 102–103). This embryological identity and biodiversity was the solid rock upon which Freud decided to base his speculations. Ferenczi, however, dismantled Freud's position from within, imagining biodiversity as the product of a "battle" modeled on the struggle preceding amatory activities and which typically ended with woman capitulating to male violence and adapting to male brutality:

> . . . and there came about, perhaps, a tremendous struggle, the outcome of which was to decide upon which sex should fall the pains and duties of

motherhood and the passive endurance of genitality. In this struggle the female sex succumbed, yet gained its compensation in understanding how to fashion out of suffering and affliction the happiness of womanhood and motherhood.

(p. 103)

In the final page of his essay, Ferenczi examined the results of "psychoanalytic ethnology" and the survival of the primitive custom of circumcision. Even though the subject of female circumcision was not mentioned, the genesis of his "fairy tale" on the "tremendous struggle" becomes clearer once we realize that Ferenczi was speaking of a real individual who had been castrated by capitulating to male violence. This will be further elaborated later. For now, let us take stock of Ferenczi first adopting Freud's line of thinking, and then pushing things further by dialectically reversing Freud's views. Instead of seeing women as inferior creatures for having lost a cosmogonic battle for possession of the phallus, Ferenczi saw women as a "more finely differentiated being" than males:

The male has imposed his will upon the female, and in so doing has spared himself the task of adaptation; he has remained the more primitive. The female on the other hand knew how to adapt herself not only to the difficulties in the environment but to the brutality of the male.

(p. 104)

Woman is innately wiser and better than man . . . a creature of finer feelings (moral) and of finer sensibility (aesthetic), and has more "common sense" [than man] . . . .

(p. 105)

Ferenczi was not only speaking of women in general in this instance but directly appealing to all women to advance a position beyond Freud's permanent split and the inevitable oscillation between rebellion and defeat, protest and submission, activity and passivity. Ferenczi was in this instance describing certain "feminine" psychic functions necessary for analytic clinicians, which he was addressing in other papers.[6]

The dark continent

The idea of female sexuality as a dark continent was first suggested by Freud in "The dissolution of the Oedipus complex," an essay admitting that the material available to him remained "obscure and full of gaps" (Freud, 1924a, p. 177). In spite of this, Freud insisted that the fear of castration found "no place in women, for . . . they *cannot have a fear of being castrated [keine Kastrationsangst haben können]*" (Freud, 1933a, p. 87, emphasis added), as he repeated again in his *New Introductory Lectures on Psycho-analysis*, while offering an articulated system of evidences of the fear of castration in boys (threats, ritual circumcision, puberty rites, and the analysis of "American patients" who endured a medical circumcision). This obvious asymmetry met no objections. Claude Dangar Daly (1950) may have been the only analyst to challenge Freud by remarking, in his essay on "The psycho-biological origins of circumcision," that "in female circumcision (the extirpation of the clitoris) the castration of the homologous penis in girls *actually takes place*" (p. 220).

Captain Claude Dangar Daly had lived much of his life in India, where he was exposed to a mythology attributing the primary source for castration anxiety to a fear of the bleeding (menstruating) phallic mother. Daly, it seems, disapproved of the Freudian and Reikian theory of puberty rites in savages, because it did not take into account either the mother complex or the practice of female circumcision. Daly attempted analysis with Freud in 1924 before entering treatment with Ferenczi for a year. During that time, these topics would have been on the minds of all three.

Daly wrote that male and female circumcision each surfaced during the course of human evolution in order to promote heterosexual development by removing the female element in a boy (prepuce) and the male element in girls (clitoris), which left both boys and girls with an unconscious wish to reestablish their original bisexual unity (as in the Platonic myth of the Androgyne). Daly corresponded with Freud about this. Since Freud never disclosed his thoughts on female puberty rites in public, their exchanges would have served as an important source of information, but unfortunately, their correspondence was destroyed in a hotel fire in London during the Second World War (Lupton & Lupton, 1990; Rickman, 1950).

Daly's objection to Freud is puzzling for a number of reasons. Freud was obviously acquainted with female circumcision as a puberty rite. Despite his never making his views public, however, it may be assumed that it not only raised his curiosity but that it had done so from the time of Emma Eckstein's analysis, if not before. Freud's description of female sexuality as a "dark continent" (original in English) was first proposed in his defense of lay analysis in 1926, which I strongly suspect was inspired by the "female circumcision controversy" – a subject debated heavily in the British colonial empire circa 1920, as Protestant missions in Kenya actively challenged the practice of circumcising females, and the colonial administrators had a policy of not interfering with local customs (Fredericksen, 2008).[7]

A strange tribal custom

The first to broach the topic of female circumcision from a psychoanalytic perspective was Geza Róheim, a distinguished Hungarian anthropologist and psychoanalyst.[8] Princess Marie Bonaparte in 1928 proposed to Róheim that he conduct research among native tribes. Psychoanalysis was after all able to explain many aspects of the life and mental state of primitive man despite the fact that neither Freud, nor any of his followers, had "ever seen a savage" (Róheim, 1932, p. 6). To address this gap, Bonaparte financed Róheim's expedition. Freud was particularly enthusiastic about this plan, and one of the goals of the expedition, as he wrote to Bonaparte on January 16 of 1928, was to seek "indications of a masculine complex among the primitive women" (Jones, 1957, p. 147). Chapter 3 has already explored the 19th-century belief that African women had a larger clitoris.

Róheim delivered several lectures following his expedition and, in 1932, published a long essay on the topic in a double issue of *The International Journal of Psychoanalysis*, which unfortunately had little to say about the subject that most interested Bonaparte. Róheim quite simply did not know how to explain the practice of extirpating the clitoris in the Somali tribes. He suggested that it might involve the displacement of the father complex (the clitoris representing the father's penis in the mother's vagina) (p. 219). His most interesting comment, about infibulations, can found in this passage:

> This story shows that infibulation in this form really signifies to the man the destruction of the sexual object. After it is sewn up, the vagina disappears; after the clitoris is cut, the woman's penis is gone. Hence the strong traumatic element in the whole operation. The man forces coitus on the woman in an extremely painful form; he uses the penis and a knife. Before we ask, however, why he needs thus to destroy the sexual object, we must try to understand what the operation means to the woman. *First of all, however, we must note that it is really a dramatically abridged repetition of biogenetic and ontogenetic development.* For women have to give up their original erotogenicity based on the clitoris and advance to the vaginal type. They must also accept their 'defeat' (Ferenczi) and preserve the feminine-masochistic attitude. All this and also the biological 'innovation' of the hymen is represented in the operation. We might therefore suppose that it fosters the right attitude of women in sexual life.
>
> (p. 202; emphasis added)

Róheim's words vividly capture the horror this tribal custom elicited in a civilized and educated European man. Róheim was able to fully recognize the brutal "destruction of the sexual object." His conclusion, however, is bewildering: how does the destruction of the female genital organ foster "the right attitude of women in sexual life"?

Seeking to "feminize" the female

Marie Bonaparte was one of the few who found appealing Ferenczi's description of coitus as a vestigial remain of the primitive biological struggle between male and female. In her book on *Female Sexuality* (1951), for instance, she described an imaginary "battle between two males":

> The coitus of a clitoridal woman with a male is, in effect, comparable with a battle between two males in which the weaker is defeated, penetrated and transfixed; one in which the victor, and he alone, wins the trophy of orgasm, in the return to the "womb."
>
> (p. 61)

Like Freud and Ferenczi, Marie Bonaparte alternated between moments of fierce rebellion and severe masochistic enactments. As soon as she became interested in psychoanalysis, she developed a special interest in the anatomical causes of frigidity. She believed that the clitoris played an essential role in normal sexual intercourse and found that its position varied in women in relation to their height. In 1924, under the pseudonym of A. E. Narjani, she published a series of observations in support of the theory that a large gap between the clitoris and the vagina functioned as a specific cause of frigidity in women. Dr. Narjani, as Bonaparte called herself, also recommended that a small operation be performed on certain women to lower their clitoris and to enhance its direct contact with the penis during intercourse.

Three years later, in the spring of 1927, she herself submitted to the operation to improve her own experience of pleasure during vaginal intercourse. The surgery, performed by a Dr. Halban, consisted of severing the suspending ligament of the clitoris to relocate it to a lower, closer position to her vagina; there was most likely also a reduction in the size of her labia minora (Bonaparte, 1951, p. 151). When the operation failed to produce the desired results, Bonaparte entertained the idea of a second operation in 1929. Given that a certain level of sensitivity remained in the area where her clitoris once stood, she decided, on the advice of her gynecologist, to undergo a resection of the nerves on her external genitals and a complete hysterectomy. This procedure, a complete castration, was performed at the American hospital in Paris on May of 1930. Max Schur, an internist also trained in psychoanalysis, traveled from Vienna to Paris on that occasion to provide her with support and assistance.

Just a year earlier Bonaparte had persuaded Freud, who was struggling with cancer of the mouth at the time, to appoint Schur as his personal physician. The results of the massive surgical procedure performed on her in 1930 were once again less favorable than she hoped. A third operation was performed a year later, in 1931. Her biographer (Bertin, 1982) did not provide details on this final procedure (see also Moore, 2009; Thompson, 2003).

Marie Bonaparte is currently known in psychoanalytic and feminist circles as a thinker who remained overly close to Freud's views on feminine sexuality. In "Some psychical consequences of the anatomical distinction between the sexes," Freud (1925b) claimed that "the elimination of clitoridal sexuality" was a "necessary precondition for the development of femininity" (p. 255). It is generally thought that Bonaparte took Freud's theory at face value, submitting herself to repeated surgical interventions during the period of her analysis with Freud. "Marie," claimed Appignanesi and Forrester (1992) in an echo of a text by Derrida, turned herself into "Freud's postman to France . . .":

> As such, Marie Bonaparte was a thoroughly loyal if not always reliable postman. In her capacious sack, Freudian 'truth' was transformed into a biological message, anatomy into a castrated destiny. Rather than into a dynamic symbolic structure.
>
> (p. 329)

Appignanesi and Forrester seem here to forget the great importance assigned by Freud to the "biological bedrock," and fail to take stock of the serious theoretical gap existing between Bonaparte and Freud on the question of female sexuality. Marie Bonaparte met regularly with Freud for her analysis between 1925 and 1928, and after that, sporadically for treatment. Freud helped her significantly to decrease her suicidal tendencies and also kept her from acting out other self-destructive behaviors, though he could not prevent her from undergoing the various vaginal surgeries described above.

Elisabeth Roudinesco (2014) has suggested that since "Freud was himself enduring painful medical interventions at the time [as a result of his cancer], the transferential situation [which existed between him and the princess] killed any possibility of his being able to interpret the *jouissance* that Marie experienced while under the scalpel." Freud, Roudinesco suggests, was apparently "fascinated by the history of women whose clitoris were cut off and must have found, in Marie's surgical obstinacy, the 'biological echo' of his own theses" (p. 390).

Can it be that Freud experienced Princess Bonaparte as a revenant of Emma Eckstein – a masculine woman who, as Freud noted in 1937, ended up falling "in love with" her "surgeon"?

Freud, oddly enough, presented the Princess with Felix Bryk's *Neger-eros* in 1928, which had just been published.[9] Bonaparte mentioned Freud's gesture in a paper crafted 13 years later, between 1941 and 1942, and not published until 1948 under the title "On Excision" ("*Notes sur l'Excision*"). In his book Bryk described a ceremony practiced in East Africa by the Nandi: cauterizing the clitoris in girls with a red-hot stone. Bryk interpreted the meaning of the procedure, wrote Bonaparte (1948b), as involving

> an attempt by the Nandi males to maximally feminize their females by doing away with this penile vestige, the clitoris, which, he adds, must result in encouraging the transfer of orgastic sensitivity from the girl's infantile erotogenic zone, the clitoris, to the adult erotogenic zone of the woman, which must necessarily be the vagina at puberty.
>
> (p. 191)

When Freud presented Marie with Bryk's book he also drew her attention to "the fact that Bryk must have been familiar with his own theory of the transfer," with Freud's ideas concerning the "erotogenic sensitivity from one zone to the other" during puberty. According to Marie Bonaparte, Freud felt that Bryk's hypothesis was "worth examining, and checking, in light of the facts." As she explained:

> In any case, he [Freud], said [that] this operation should not suppress the erotistic or orgastic potentiality in the woman; otherwise the Nandi men would never have allowed a custom which deprived them of mutual participation in voluptuous pleasure, which all men prize in all climes.
>
> (pp. 191–192)

Freud might have presented her with Bryk's text because she was financing Róheim's ethnological expedition. Yet, it remains unclear why he presented someone who had recently undergone a resection and relocation of her clitoris and who, moreover, was disappointed with the results of the surgery, with such a gift. Perhaps Freud wanted to minimize the lack of success and, at the same time, to reassure her that her "erotistic potentiality" had not been completely damaged or lost. Bonaparte was unconvinced by Freud's explanation and, in 1948, saw it as an expression of the male point of view, the "worst observer of all in whatever concerns feminine psycho-sexuality" (p. 192). Indeed by then, Marie Bonaparte had arrived at the conclusion that men were either "enemies" or "friends" of the clitoris, either repelled by anything unfeminine in a woman or else devotees of the phallic mother (p. 207).

Marie Bonaparte began visiting hospitals in 1929 to collect data on cases involving young German women whose habit of compulsive masturbation were "cured" through a variety of surgical interventions. In her later article she (1948b) identified the following procedures: resection of the nerves of the genital region, cutting of the *labia minora*, excision of the clitoris, removal of fallopian tubes and of the ovaries. This report should be read today, as it provides an excellent description of the cruelty of these treatment procedures still being practiced in central Europe at the time. Marie Bonaparte personally discussed these surgical procedures with Freud, but unfortunately failed to mention his responses.

Marie Bonaparte later became the first female psychoanalyst to research the topic of female genital mutilation among primitive tribes, and the first to discuss the similarities found between these tribal practices and modern surgical attempts to "cure" women and young girls from the habit of excessive masturbation. Although she is typically portrayed in the analytic literature as a vigorous defender of Freud's position, this was certainly not true with this particular topic, and in fact viewed the excising of the clitoris to reduce female desire as a barbaric practice. She remained so unconvinced by Bryk's theory, and by Freud's own, that she pursued research on the effects on women of tribal genital mutilations. The removal of the clitoris, she concluded, neither inhibited masturbation nor facilitated the transfer of sensitivity from the clitoris to the vagina. Her research thus failed to confirm Freud's "qualified opinion" that "excising the clitoris might help to internalize the erotogenic zone, and in some degree intensify internal vaginal sensitivity" (p. 204):

> The physical intimidation of the girl's sexuality by this cruel excision would not achieve the aim of feminizing, vaginalizing her, any better than the psychical intimidation of the clitoridal masturbation of European little girls.
>
> (p. 204)

In another article, entitled "Female mutilation among primitive peoples and their psychical parallels in civilization," Marie Bonaparte (1948a) suggested that the excision of the clitoris, a custom which was practiced by many tribes,

> seemed to Freud a way of seeking to further "feminize" the female by removing this cardinal vestige of her masculinity. Such operations, as he once said

to me, must be intended to complete the 'biological castration' of the female which Nature, in the eyes of these tribes, has not sufficiently effected

(p. 153).

This passage is illuminating and disturbing because it exposes Freud's blind spot, his failure to see these tribal practices as involving a hostile procedure, a direct attack on the female genitalia. Marie Bonaparte's description also affirmed Róheim's suggestion that Freud, as well as his early followers, viewed clitoridectomy and infibulation as "a dramatically abridged repetition of biogenetic and ontogenetic development." Despite the fact that Freud abhorred these tribal practices (Freud, 1918b, p. 197), he nevertheless seems to have interpreted them as attempts to help complete and fulfill the action of Nature ("biological castration"). Freud's position recalls a motto from negative eugenics declaring that what Nature performed slowly, man was able to achieve faster (Kevles, 1986).

Returning to the Princess and her article (1948a), we find her mention of clitoridectomy, until recently practiced in Europe as a mean of curing girls of their habit of masturbation: "We know that for fifty years, European surgeons did not hesitate to resort to it at times. Yet the children and adolescents who underwent this operation, continued to masturbate as much as before" (pp. 156–157). "The more or less unconscious motives for excision," she added, suggested "a factor" present which tended to "repress the feminine sexuality" (pp. 157–158).

Freud's biologically-based stance, his decision to explain the operation as aiming to "feminize" females by depriving them of their small penis, was in Marie Bonaparte's view insufficient to explain the phenomenon. Instead she proposed that "something in man wants his partner to be 'chaste'" (p. 158). The barbaric practices whose aims were to castrate women were as such seen by the Princess as an expression of a *cultural* tendency "to reduce female desire" (p. 158), an *intentional* attempt by men to repress the "sexual licence in women" (p. 159).

These conclusions, which can be taken for granted today, were long ignored by the vast majority of psychoanalysts. Moreover, as Alison Moore (2009) noted, Marie Bonaparte was "patently vilified" by feminists and sophisticated psychoanalytic thinkers since the 1960s, largely because of her masochistic enactments to castrate herself through surgery. Moore has recently attempted to redeem Marie Bonaparte by emphasizing her divergence from Freud as well as her desire to "relocate" her clitoris, both physically and symbolically, though she failed to notice the other important aspect of the Princess's lonely struggle, namely, her attempt to address the actual castration of women in modern civilized countries. Marie Bonaparte had the courage to tackle topics related to women and female sexuality, to which few in our field have paid much attention or wanted to hear about.

Symbolic cuts

Marie Bonaparte purchased Freud's letters to Fliess from a book dealer in Vienna in 1936. Any reconstruction of the origins of psychoanalysis would have been impossible if not for her resistance to Freud's ardent plea to destroy those letters.

As Max Schur (1963) noted in her obituary: "On one occasion only did she act against Freud's wishes: she refused to destroy the Fliess letters, which she saved for posterity" (p. 99).

Marie Bonaparte carefully studied Freud's letters to Fliess from February to November of 1937. Given her interest on the theme of female genital mutilation, she must have grown particularly curious when reading Freud's letter describing a "scene about the circumcision of a girl" from one of his female analytic patients. Since by then Bonaparte had formulated her own views about female genital mutilation, views diverging considerably from Freud's, and she was moreover also in the habit of discussing openly such topics with Freud, she might plausibly have inquired from Freud about the identity of the patient, perhaps even questioning him on the actual circumstances surrounding the event. While this remains mere conjecture, what strikes me as more certain is Freud's recollection of Emma Eckstein's case history after Bonaparte purchased the letters, giving rise to his featuring Emma Eckstein's case history in "Analysis terminable and interminable" (1937a, p. 222), one of his final texts.

Freud's letters to Fliess were delivered to Anna Freud after the war, and were published in abridged form in 1950 under the title *Aus die Anfänge der Psychoanalyse* (the English translation, *The Origins of Psychoanalysis*, appeared in 1954). The passage in the letter with a "scene about the circumcision of a girl" was however cut out, left out, and suppressed along with other vital material in the letter. We do not know what Marie Bonaparte thought about this decision, but before dying in 1962, she asked Anna Freud to verify her copy of the original letters and to forward them to Max Schur, who was then working on his book on Freud.[10] Schur, who assisted the princess when she underwent her double operation in Paris in 1930, then decided to publish the "circumcision scene" Anna Freud had left out when including some letters in his 1966 article on the "specimen dream of psychoanalysis." He introduced an unusually long note when citing the passage Anna Freud left out, with Freud's description of Emma Eckstein's circumcision scene to Fliess:

> . . . **a scene** [The use of the word "scene" here and in Freud's two previous letters is highly significant. We know from Freud's correspondence with Fliess that he still believed in the "seduction etiology" of hysteria. However in the published portion of this letter and the preceding one he clearly describes what he later called fantasies. This holds true for Emma's "scenes." It would therefore seem that Emma was one of the first patients who offered Freud a clue to the crucial realization that what his patients had described to him as actual seduction episodes were fantasies. As we know, this realization opened the way to the discovery of early infantile sexuality and its manifestations in infancy] **about the circumcision of a girl** . . .
>
> (1966, p. 114)

How can we understand Schur's gloss on Emma Eckstein's circumcision scene? Was he proposing that the entire mystery of Freud's grand turn, the decision to abandon his theory of seduction, was somehow encysted in Freud's description of

Emma Eckstein's circumcision scene? More specifically, in Freud's words: "a scene about the circumcision of a girl"?

Notes

1 As Nunberg (1947) noted, during the circumcision ceremony the son functioned as a "reincarnation of his father's father" while the act of "sucking blood" from the child's penis remained a "relic of the totem meal" (p. 172).
2 In private Freud saw the mother as the agent who intervened to persuade the primal father to spare his sons and thus to accept the younger generation (Rank, 1924b, p. 169).
3 Otto Rank (1912, pp. 304–305) found the idea of circumcision as an equivalent to castration (Freud, 1909a, p. 36, footnote) so inspiring that he suggested it revealed a new angle to the historical origins of the old Hebrew custom of circumcising male children eight days after birth. Rank, who was serving as Freud's secretary in those years, also argued that the story of the near-sacrifice of Isaac, the event which the Bible related to the establishment of the covenant between God and Abraham and the mandate to circumcise all male Jews, was structurally connected with the story of Oedipus, the binding of Oedipus' pierced foot by his father Laius in particular. Rank proposed that various aspects of Oedipus's trauma issued from the myth of Kronos where the threat of castration was directly represented (p. 304).
4 On this point, see "Castration anxiety or feminine genital anxiety?" (Dorsey, 1996). During the last two decades, however, psychoanalysts have grown increasingly aware of the fact that psychoanalysis has for nearly a century failed to consider girls' fear of injuring their genitals and the anxiety to which such fear gives rise. Reviewing the question of primary genital anxiety in females, Ruth Lax (1994) proposed that "this 'neglect' was largely due to the phallocentric concepts and orientation found at the heart of Freud's psychoanalytic theory," his misunderstanding of early female psychosexual development, and "the impact of the general disavowal of feminine sexuality in little girls" (p. 283). The fact that Freud's main patient during the founding of psychoanalysis was a woman who was circumcised as a child leads us to invert the question: the disavowal of the girl's fear about the safety of her genitals was not a consequence but rather a premise of Freud's phallocentric system.
5 After the publication of Volume I, I found that Devereux came to a similar conclusion. Daniel Prager (1960) reports in a footnote the following: "Dr. George Devereux, in a personal communication, offers the hypothesis that circumcision duplicates the cutting of the cord at birth. He supports his hypothesis with the anthropological finding that the circumcision takes place at puberty as part of a rite that is regarded as a rebirth. Where penis symbolizes cord (rather than cord symbolizing penis), cutting the penis in circumcision at puberty is equated with cutting the cord at birth." (p.53)
6 In a way Ferenczi anticipated Emmanuel Ghent's (1990) ideas on masochism, submission, and surrender. Commenting on the masochistic processes which often feature in our profession, Ghent (1990) observed: "I suspect that a deep underlying motive in some analysts at least, is again that of surrender, and their own personal growth. It may be acceptably couched in masochistic garb or denied by narcissistic and/or sadistic exploitation. When the yearning for surrender is, or begins to be, realized by the analyst, the work is immensely fulfilling and the analyst grows with his patients" (p. 133).
7 I found some confirmation for my suspicion in Anna Freud's essay on "Insight," a brief piece describing various forms of unbalance between a person's orientation to the outer world and the process of gaining insight into the inner psychic world. Anna Freud (1981) ended her essay by noting that these two opposing attitudes might be combined in rare individuals who "investigate what lies beyond consciousness in the spirit of examining *strange tribal customs in a dark continent.*" Her father, she noted, saw himself "as an explorer of this kind" (p. 249; emphasis added).

8 Ferenczi wrote Freud on March 23, (1916) to say: "I am analyzing a young and very talented ethnologist, who will perhaps be a gain for psychoanalysis." Róheim, who later analyzed with Vilma Kovács, became a member of the Hungarian psychoanalytic society during the decade of the twenties, presenting many papers with ethnological content before its members. About Róheim, Freud (1925a) said the following in his autobiographical study: "Theodor Reik and G. Róheim, the ethnologist, have taken up the line of thought which I developed in *Totem and Taboo* and, in a series of important works, have extended it, deepened it, or corrected it" (pp. 68–69). Róheim's (1943) basic thesis was that "culture is due to retardation, that is, to a slowing down of the process of growth to a prolongation of the infantile situation."

9 Félix Bryk's *Neger-eros; ethnologische Studien über das Sexualleben bei Negern* first appeared in (1928). An English translation was released in 1975 under the title *Dark Rapture: The Sex Life of the African Negro*). Mary Daly (1978) described Bryk's text as a manifestation of "crass indifference" (p. 475); see her book *Gyn/Ecology. The Metaethics of Radical Feminism*, the chapter "African Genital Mutilation: The Unspeakable Atrocities" in particular.

10 Letter from Bonaparte to Schur on January 23 of 1961; see (Stouten, 2012, p. 129). Schur's book, *Freud: Living and Dying*, appeared in 1972.

13 Nightmares are real

> What is the content of the split-off ego? Above all a tendency, probably *the* tendency, to complete the action interrupted by shock.
>
> Sándor Ferenczi, *The Clinical Diary*, 24 January 1932

Both Clara Thompson (1988, p. 185) and Erich Fromm (2000, p. 159) felt strongly that Ferenczi stayed too much with the language of Freud, not daring to place himself in open opposition to the master. This chapter will take up how Ferenczi was nevertheless able to transform Freud's conceptual system, focusing on a few selected points: 1) his reorganization of the fulcrum of psychotherapy; 2) his creation of a new language for trauma; and 3) his mutual analysis with Elisabeth Severn.

A new fulcrum of psychotherapy

From the very beginning Ferenczi found that active interference was sometimes necessary to release an emotional reaction. For example, the use of "scientific language" for discussing sexual matters with patients could easily bring the analysis to a standstill. In his 1911 article on obscene words, he wrote that this type of resistance ceased only when the analyst discovered the original proscribed obscene words for which scientific terms had been substituted. The utterance or hearing of these magic words – like "whore" in his letter to Freud of December 26, 1912 – was accompanied by shame, intense emotional reaction, and motor agitation, which often resulted in unexpected disclosures.

Encouraged by Freud, Ferenczi introduced a method for these times when analysis stagnated.[1] It was called "active" (Ferenczi, 1919, 1920, 1924), but should more properly have been called "reactivating."[2] This method was at the center of Ferenczi and Rank's (1924) joint revision of the relationship between theory and technique, which viewed Freud's technical papers as incomplete, even "antiquated with regard to certain points" (p. 2).

When Freud introduced the notion of repetition, he considered it a manifestation of resistance to remembering (Freud, 1914c, p. 151), but then, the study of traumatic war neurosis convinced him that repetition could be in itself a therapeutic factor, since it offered an occasion to achieve mastery of a psychic trauma (Freud, 1920). Capitalizing on Freud's new vision, Ferenczi and Rank (1924) claimed that the tendency toward repetition could no longer be regarded as a disturbing secondary phenomenon to be suppressed. On the contrary, the primary work of analytic technique should be attributed "to repetition instead of to remembering" (p. 4).

In particular, the priority given to remembering over repetition was presented by Ferenczi and Rank as a defense, as a way to ward off emotional experience, and supported a tendency to replace analysis with instruction. The overvaluation of theory gave rise to an overly rigid attitude, which at that time was justified by the "scientific" nature of the task (pp. 39–51). They pointed out that the knowledge acquired in this manner did not stick with the patient, who was then forced to identify himself with the analyst. The classical analyst was depicted as trying to prevent repetition by distancing from emotions, cooling down the temperature of the relationship by deflecting the hot here-and-now aspects of the transference into the past, thus achieving a merely intellectual awareness of genetic influences.

In contrast, Ferenczi and Rank proposed to transform remembrance into dramatic re-enactment, intellectual literalism into reincarnation. They introduced the notion of the "psychoanalytic situation" and wanted to revive and update the cathartic method, emphasizing that the abreaction of affects and discharge of libido was taking place within a "social" frame. In Freud's (1920) own revision, repetition was linked to the force of instincts and considered an "economic" (intrapsychic) factor, whereas both Ferenczi and Rank emphasized the "social" dimension of analytic therapy, that is, the difference between repeating by oneself and repeating in the presence of another person. The notion of repetition was thus transformed, shifting from an intrapsychic to an interpersonal meaning. Ferenczi and Rank's contribution was a "New Testament" – a "Second Coming" in the here and now of the psychoanalytic situation.

These views of Ferenczi and Rank polarized the debate on technique (Bonomi, 2010). Since the 1924 Salzburg Congress Ferenczi and Rank were criticized for many reasons, and especially for unduly emphasizing abreaction. Rado (1925), for instance, characterized cathartic hypnosis as a violent discharge of libidinal excitation which was useless because "entirely governed by the pleasure-principle" (p. 40). The revision proposed by Ferenczi and Rank appeared dangerous because it exacerbated the transference and led to discharge and regressive satisfaction, rather than the education of the patient's ego.

In his review of *The Development of Psychoanalysis*, Franz Alexander (1925) – who later changed his view radically – said that Ferenczi and Rank's error was to convert an "internal conflict" into "an external one" (p. 494), whereas "the aim of psycho-analysis is to subordinate the affective processes to the intellect" (p. 495). It was in this context that a new model of the therapy, conceived as an application of the structural theory, began to emerge, later systematized by Strachey (1934), that the super-ego was "the fulcrum of psychotherapy" (p. 279).

Ferenczi was especially dissatisfied with the tendency to base therapy on "the substitution of one super-ego for another," since the latter failed "to attain the final aim of therapy, the dissolution of the transference" (Ferenczi, 1928, p. 98). Moreover, the analyst who aims to "convince" has to rely on "reputation and infallibility" and tends therefore to be experienced as "omniscient and omnipotent" (p. 94), but a "schoolmasterish" or "authoritative" attitude by the analyst is ultimately "harmful to analysis" (pp. 94–95). Finally, by pretending an unattainable objectivity, the analyst covers up his subjectivity by means of a sophisticated, inaccessible theory, making it more difficult for the patient to express objections. A consequence of this intellectualization is that the patient isn't allowed to criticize the analyst. In fact, even when dissatisfied, patients do "not dare to rebel openly against the didactic and pedantic attitude of the analyst" (Ferenczi, 1930, p. 113).

The typical analyst's polite coolness and tolerant attitude ("professional hypocrisy") became a main target of Ferenczi's criticism. Ferenczi (1933) found that dissimulation of real feelings by the analyst forces the patient's mind to remain split, pushes the patient to "identify" with the analyst (p. 158), and makes repetition of the trauma "unbearable" (p. 159).

Ferenczi's meditation on re-traumatization of the patient by the analyst began by revising the active technique, which he associated with circumcision (Ferenczi, 1925, pp. 227–228). Ferenczi became progressively aware that his active technique was in part an attack on Freud, enacted by "exaggerating and exposing" its "sadistic-educative methodology" (Dupont, 1985, p. 94). Ferenczi was very much supported by Groddeck in this separation from Freud. Since Groddeck believed that circumcision in Hebrew religion was mainly aimed at suppressing man's original bisexuality and rejecting the feminine side of his soul, he may have had some influence on Ferenczi also in this regard. Groddeck, Erich Fromm once remarked (1965, p. 84),

> did not share the belief in the patriarchal overevaluation of the male, current among psychoanalysts. He was impressed by the significance of the mother, by man's fear of women, and by man's wish to be a woman – facts which did not fit at all into the Freudian concept of the relationship between the sexes.

Ferenczi (1925) also noted that the active method could result in a re-traumatization of the patient based on a "repetition of the parent-child situation" (p. 220). He then began to appreciate elasticity, tact, and the analyst's capacity to adapt to the patient. By acknowledging analysis as "a process of fluid development unfolding itself before our eyes rather than as a structure with a design pre-imposed upon it by an architect" (1928, p. 90), Ferenczi was discovering a living relationship between two persons as the fulcrum of psychotherapy.

While adhering to the idea of curing a neurosis by way of re-experiencing the pathogenic trauma, Ferenczi came to realize that repetition had a totally different outcome depending on the quality of the living relationship between patient and analyst; only a relaxed, non-frustrating, and receptive atmosphere would convert the repetition tendency into recollection. In his paper on neocatharsis, Ferenczi put forth this repeat-repair principle, which later became a cardinal tenet of the so-called "dynamic psychiatry": "While the similarity of the analytical to the infantile situation impels patients to repetitions, the contrast between the two encourages recollection" (1929, p. 124). Only "feeling" this contrast and knowing himself "safe," the patient can "let himself sink down into a reproduction of the painful past" (1931, p. 132).

A new language for trauma

When Freud asked Ferenczi and Rank to collaborate to work on the gap between practice and theory in psychoanalysis, Rank wrote to Freud that they had "decided first to start a scientific campaign against overestimation of the castration complex" (August 22, 1922). An alarmed Freud discouraged them from this, and the theme was then removed from their agenda. But as we know, this theme would feature prominently in Otto Rank's *The Trauma of Birth* (1924a). With the crisis of 1924, Rank was forced to leave the psychoanalytic movement. Ferenczi separated himself from Rank, but was no longer welcome in the mainstream.

Reacting to Rank's attempt to move beyond the castration complex, Freud (1926a) reorganized his theory to postulate the trauma of castration as a synthetic *a priori*: whatever the danger or loss experienced by the ego, Freud argued, the unconscious represents it as the ablation of the penis.[3] Thus was castration once again reaffirmed by Freud as the natural language of trauma. This assumption abounds throughout the entirety of Freud's work and has a systemic and all-embracing structure impermeable to compromise: accept it and remain in the system, or reject it and be cast out forever.

Whereas Rank challenged the system frontally, Ferenczi embraced the language of Freud adhesively and proceeded slowly to deconstruct the system from within. *Thalassa* was the starting point of Ferenczi's toppling of Freud's pillar, the transcendental Phallus. Following and interpreting Freud, Ferenczi (1924) presented the erect penis as the place of "perpetual repetition of the painful situation" (p. 66). He focused on the phallus as the embodiment of an impulse to "self-castration,"[4] proposing self-castration as the biological prototype of the repression by which the original trauma is preserved (1924, pp. 29, 83, 87, 89), and as a manifestation of *Todestrieb* (p. 66), the death instinct postulated by Freud in *Beyond the Pleasure Principle* to explain the compulsion to repeat. Ferenczi's meditation bears the clear traces of the introjection of Freud's intimidating dream of self-dissection, and can be read as an effort to metabolize the uncanny symbol of Freud's self-analysis.

Ferenczi's further move traced self-castration back to the biological law of "autotomy" – a Greek neologism that means self-cut or self-dissection. Within biology the notion referred to the behavior of certain animals who cut out a part of their own body to survive when life was in danger. Ever since 1916,[5] Ferenczi had used this autoplastic reaction to understand how the human psyche reacted to traumatic experiences, and considered "this sort of sequestration a physiological prototype of the process of repression" (1926, p. 375). Initially Ferenczi used the notion of autotomy as a kind of autoplastic adaptation (Ferenczi, 1916–1917, 1921, 1926), to explain how the memory of an external trauma was inscribed, preserved, and reproduced in the reaction of an organism. Later on, he conceived of it as the automatic response to an experience of annihilation (1930–1932), prospecting the effect of psychic trauma as a "partial death" involving the destruction of certain parts of the psyche which become insensitive. An entirely new universe opened up for Ferenczi as a result, one in which the fragmentation of mental life appeared before him for the first time. It ultimately led him to formulate a new metapsychology and to create an altogether new language to describe the effects of trauma on the human psyche. The castration complex obviously maintained its clinical relevance, but was no more the foundation stone of the psychoanalytic building.

Further light is shed on Ferenczi's deconstruction by Karl Menninger's (1935) study of self-mutilations. Menninger concluded a section on "Religious self-mutilation" by extrapolating a structure common to all sacrifices. While the contents can vary, sacrifice is always, he said, "a technique of giving up a part in order to preserve the whole" (p. 437). This is exactly what Ferenczi had in mind when he began to explain trauma by appealing to the biological function of autotomy. That is, by focusing on the phenomenon of animal autotomy, Ferenczi extrapolated a formal structure of sacrifice in general, *common to both animal kingdom and religion*, which manifests itself in an especially transparent way in the ceremony of circumcision.[6] This formal structure, which is all embracing, designates the *a priori* of trauma, in the form of an inborn automatic response. Thus did Ferenczi succeed in deconstructing the Freudian system from within and in creating a new language for trauma, simply by liberating it from fixation to a single specific anatomic part of the body, the penis. This was made possible by Ferenczi's full realization that the key to Freud's reductionism was the tendency of the ego, or total person, to identify with the penis.

We can here admire the elegance of Ferenczi's ongoing meditation, for its deep continuity with the Freudian system, which is not discarded, but rather liberated from an idol and fetish, and made less rigid and more abstract and flexible. Since Ferenczi saw the phallus as a miniature, a duplicate of the total ego, the new language was now about the total ego, or self. Indeed, the most important element of that new language was the notion of "narcissistic split of the self," which was introduced in Ferenczi's (1931) article, "Child analysis in the analysis of adults." It is as though, he wrote,

> Under the stress of imminent danger, part of the self splits off and becomes a psychic instance self-observing and desiring to help the self, and that possibly this happens in early – even the very earliest – childhood.
>
> (p. 136)

Since the idea of "narcissistic split of the self" clearly was a further development of the notion of "autotomy," (literally: "self-dissection"), we can trace it back to the very symbol of Freud's self-analysis, which had so deeply troubled Ferenczi. The father of psychoanalysis, in that most revealing dream, was in fact divided, split in two, and left observing himself as a spectator from the outside, without feeling.

In *The Interpretation of Dreams* Freud (1900) identified this lack of feeling as involving a "suppression of affects," and also interpreted it as a neurotic attempt at defense, this despite having described it in another part of the dream book as "the peace that has descended upon a battlefield strewn with corpses" with "no trace" being "left of the struggle which raged over it" (p. 467). Ferenczi in 1931 provided a new reading of this kind of traumatic insensitivity, tracing it to the splitting of the self into a "suffering brutally destroyed part" and a "self-observing" part that "knows everything but feels nothing" (pp. 135–136). This theme was so important that it became the opening page of Ferenczi's *Clinical Diary*, titled "Insensitivity [*Fühlosigkeit*] of the analyst" (January 7, 1932).

Insensitivity, a generic hallmark of trauma, had been embedded in psychoanalytic technique since the very beginning. Even though Freud's concrete way of working was lively and unpredictable, still emotional coldness was praised as the state of mind required for an analyst if the emotional embroilment between doctor and patient was to be kept in check and the interpersonal dimension of the analytic situation rendered neutral. Freud spoke, in this regard, of "indifference" ("*Indifferenz*," rendered as "neutrality" in the Standard Edition) (Freud, 1915, p. 164), imagining the analyst as a "surgeon" within the analytic setting.[7] In this view emotional coldness created "for the doctor a desirable protection for his own emotional life" (Freud, 1912b, p. 115), and was required to perform analytic "operations" with the balance and clarity of a scientist.[8]

Ferenczi was not satisfied with this model, and tried to move beyond it in many ways, for example, proposing the "obstetrician" instead of the "surgeon." At first he tried to manage this problem technically, that is, by intentionally creating a benevolent atmosphere, but he soon realized that the quality of the relationship was not defined by its exterior aspects, but involved a participation on the part of the analyst that could not be planned in advance because, as he wrote in *The Clinical Diary*, "the patient makes use of our sensitivity to repeat a past injury" (Dupont, 1985, p. 120).

In spite of goodwill, the analyst's unconscious is an attractor for and a trigger of the patient's tendencies to repeat. Freud's solution was stepping back from the relationship and dissociating his persona from the subjective experience of the patient ("*Indifferenz*"). Ferenczi, in his turn, came to see that the standardization of the analyst's position amounted to an abandonment of the patient by the doctor. The insensitivity of the analyst, as he wrote in the opening page of his diary, only contributed to unconscious re-enactments and repetitions by patients. To avoid this, Ferenczi encouraged the expression of the patient's perplexities and objections by means of the analyst frankly admitting certain errors, taking seriously the patient's reproaches, and even disclosing some negative feelings (Ferenczi, 1931, p. 130, 1933, pp. 158–162). Ferenczi learned most of these unconventional principles through his experiences of "mutual-analysis" as described in his diary.

Ferenczi's great desire was to achieve a completely analyzed case. Perhaps sensing the impossibility of this aim, in 1932 he crafted his *Clinical Diary* as a memorandum on his last experimentation, as well as a testimony of his conflicts and differences with Freud. Doing so not only provided him the chance to present his own clinical views, but also to pinpoint what he saw as the faulty path of psychoanalysis so far.

Mutual analysis

In his last years Ferenczi was deeply influenced by Elisabeth Severn (R.N. in *The Clinical Diary*), a woman who Freud called "Ferenczi's evil genius" (Jones, 1957, p. 436), blaming her for turning Ferenczi away from psychoanalysis.

After several failed attempts with American analysts, in 1924 Elisabeth Severn tried an analysis with Rank, but found him "completely wrapped up" in his idea of "the birth trauma," and "incapable of thinking anything else" (Eissler, 1952; Rachman, 2015). She then traveled to Budapest to have an analysis with Ferenczi, which lasted more than eight years, terminating only with Ferenczi's illness and death in 1933.

In 1924 Severn was 45 years old, suffering from exhaustion, headaches, severe depression, and suicidal impulses. She did not have memories before the age of 12. To Ferenczi her willpower appeared "exceedingly strong" and endowed with the "majesty superiority of a queen" (Dupont, 1985, p. 97), but instead of making himself aware of these unpleasant impressions, he covered his anxiety with the attitude of medical superiority. This professional pose did not last long. As he became more deeply involved with the analytic work, he "gave in to more and more of the patient's wishes" (Dupont, 1985, p. 97). Ferenczi's medical "superperformances" included double and triple sessions, weekend sessions, at night, during vacations. Finally, in 1928–29, after four years, the story of a traumatic childhood began to emerge, "in the form of states of trances, or attacks" (Dupont, 1985, p. 97). Yet, each attack ended with the statement: "And still I don't know if the whole thing is true" (p. 98).

Exhausted and alarmed by Severn's fantasies and requests, Ferenczi began to reduce his attentions, which increased Severn's imperiousness. She then began to say that "her analysis would never make any progress" unless he allowed her to analyze the feeling of hate that she was sensing in him. To his "enormous surprise," Ferenczi had to concede that "the patient was right in many respects" (p. 99). Thus began the experiment of mutual analysis. Unlike Freud, Ferenczi allowed himself to "risk his authority."

Ferenczi realized that the excessive friendliness he displayed was "identical with the feelings of the same kind" he had for his mother, when he forced himself to be obedient while repressing terror and hatred. Ferenczi also grasped that his hatred was not only sensed by Severn, but also experienced, by her, as a repetition of the hatred of her criminal father. Mutual analysis liberated the anxiety in both participants, transforming a vicious circle into a virtuous one. Ferenczi's expression of his antipathy had "a tranquillizing effect" on the patient, who began to reduce her demands on him. In his turn, Ferenczi began to find Severn "less disagreeable" (Dupont, 1985, p. 97). In the last page of his *Clinical Diary* he wrote: "I released

R.N. from her torments by repeating the sins of her father, which then I confessed and for which I obtained forgiveness" (p. 214).

Nowadays this therapeutic relationship is widely acknowledged as a pivotal point in the history of psychoanalytic technique which radically expanded its bounds (Fortune, 1993, 1994; Haynal, 2002; Rachman, 1997, 2015; Rudnytsky, 2015; Smith, 1998; Wolstein, 1997). Described by Ferenczi as his "main patient," "colleague," and "teacher," Elisabeth Severn was the catalyst for Ferenczi's recognition of the significance of countertransference, his theory on the fragmentation of mental life, and several technical innovations.

The incarnation of the "bad mother"

Denied by Freud, theorized by Rank, the incarnation of the "bad mother" in the psychoanalytic situation was experienced *in vivo* by Ferenczi. From the very beginning, Ferenczi was convinced that the lack of love from his strict mother was at the origin of his neurosis, but Freud was deaf to this. In his auto-analytic letter of December 26, 1912, Ferenczi recalled the episode when, at the age of three, he had been caught in mutual touching with a sister and threatened with a kitchen knife. It was at that point that the theme of "impotent rage" against his mother broke through. The same theme surfaced in his analysis of the dream of the occlusive pessary. It is not clear how Freud handled this theme in the course of his analysis with Ferenczi. Certainly it was only in his mutual analysis with Elisabeth Severn that it became a *real* experience for Ferenczi. In *The Clinical Diary*, Ferenczi described R.N. as the reincarnation of his strict and frightening mother. In R.N., he wrote, "I find my mother again, namely the real one, who was hard and energetic and of whom I am afraid" (Dupont, 1985, p. 45).

In spite of this great fear of Elisabeth Severn, Ferenczi slowly began to trust her, creating the situation in which repetition could be transformed into reproduction and then, eventually, into recollection. In one of the sessions in which he was lying on the couch, Ferenczi plunged himself deeply into emotionally vivid reproduction and recollection of infantile experiences. The most evocative element, he wrote, was

> the image of a corpse, whose abdomen I was opening up, presumably in the dissecting room; linked to this the mad fantasy that I was being pressed into this wound in the corpse.
>
> (Dupont, 1985, p. 61)

In Ferenczi's own reconstruction a housemaid allowed him to play with her breasts, but then pressed his head between her legs, so that he became frightened and felt that he was suffocating. Ferenczi used the adverb "probably" to indicate the effort at interpretation. Elisabeth Severn, in her turn, wrote the following in a transcript of the sessions: at the age of six, Ferenczi endured "another serious trauma," an "unscrupulous attack by an adult person . . . which was ruinous to his mental integrity and subsequent health." The offender was his housemaid, "a comely young woman of voluptuous type who, for the satisfaction of her own urgencies, seduced the child, i.e. used him forcibly as best she could in lieu of an adult partner." According to Severn, the child was "horrified, frightened, and emotionally shocked," and, at the same time "seduced," in that "a *desire* was aroused in him which was beyond his years and capacity," acting as "a constant excitation" and determining "an inclination to a repetition of the experience."[9]

Ferenczi's inference about what really occurred when he was a boy of six was based on a hallucinatory reproduction in the course of his analysis with Severn. Yet, he was convinced that this trauma had a general meaning, representing, he wrote, "the source of my hatred of females: I want to dissect them for it, that is, to kill them." This is why, Ferenczi went on to say in his diary, his mother's accusation, "You are my murderer," cut him to the heart. Her words led him to develop what he described as "a compulsive desire to help anyone who is suffering, especially women" (Dupont, 1985: 61). He also described a strong urge to flee from situations whereby he was forced to show aggression.

According to Ferenczi the traumatic origin of his "castration hysteria" was inscribed in this "mad fantasy." In the latter was condensed not only the (hypothetic and plausible) event of his shocking seduction by the housemaid, but also the quality and emotional color of his relationship with his mother, which was described by Severn as "an angry, hysterical woman, often scolding and threatening her child."

As part of the overdetermination for selecting 'the cut' as the key to the story of the foundation of psychoanalysis, Ferenczi's hallucinatory reproduction is especially significant because his "mad fantasy" of being pressed into the dissected pelvis of a woman's corpse was anticipated by his psychosomatic symptoms (in October–December 1912) and in his dreams. But what is even more impressive is that the image of opening the abdomen of a corpse in a dissecting room was repeating the opening scene of Freud's own crucial dream of the self-dissection of the pelvis. How should we value this coincidence? It could seem that Ferenczi's hallucinatory recollection was just one of the many expressions of Ferenczi's identification with Freud, that is the result of a suggestive influence, until two facts are taken into further consideration. The first is that the nightmarish scene in Freud's dream was a repetition on Freud's own body the castration trauma of Emma Eckstein. The second is that Ferenczi experienced his emotional recollection within the living relationship with Elisabeth Severn, a woman who herself had endured a traumatic castration.

Emotional recollection

Ferenczi's case appeared anonymously as Chapter 5, "Nightmares are Real" in *The Discovery of the Self*, which Severn published in 1933, after Ferenczi's death. Ferenczi saw and approved the manuscript before he died (Rudnytsky, 2015, p. 141). Severn (1933) credited Ferenczi for convincing her that trauma was an almost universal cause of neurosis; she, in turn, taught him the importance of re-living the dissociated emotion with the dramatic participation of the analyst in the here and now of the analytic situation. The idea that the essential core of psychoanalysis was an "*emotional recollection*" of traumatic experiences was the result of their collaboration. According to Severn, the patient "*always tells the truth*, even though in a distorted form" (p. 126). A "hallucination" is a memory that has been kept alive in the unconscious and is projected outward into the objective world (p. 97). Apparently Severn helped Ferenczi not only to experience his frightening hallucination – the mad fantasy of being pressed into a pelvic wound – but also to believe it was a distorted representation of a real memory (or of the conflation of a series of real memories). Ferenczi himself in his *Clinical Diary* noted that the hallucination of the mentally ill perhaps were "no hallucinations, but only an illusionary working through of real events" (Dupont, 1985, p. 140).

Severn's description of the therapeutic process is also very interesting. Ferenczi's attitude of superiority, his professional pose, and his façade of a balanced, calm, and well-adjusted person collapsed, and Ferenczi went through a psychotic crisis in the course of a session. Analysis, Severn said, disclosed "a clearly outlined psychosis" (p. 135). In her reconstruction the shocking sexual attack by the housemaid, which was completely absent from his memory, was the endpoint of a series of traumas endured by Ferenczi from the age of three to the age of six. After this trauma Ferenczi was able to preserve his sanity but at the cost of a fragmentation: "the exploded bits" of his psyche "continued to exist, spatially speaking, outside of him: where we had to 'catch' it, so to speak, before it could be restored" (p. 140). Ferenczi, remarked Severn, "was deprived of both happiness and health for most of a life-time, for it was fifty years after its occurrence, that this trauma came under observation and treatment" (p. 140). Severn's diagnosis was corroborated by Ferenczi himself, who, in his *Clinical Diary* wrote: "Psychoanalytic insight into my own emotional emptiness, which was shrouded by overcompensation (repressed – unconscious – psychosis) led to a self-diagnosis of *schizophrenia*" (Dupont, 1985, p. 160).

Orpha

Elisabeth Severn was born Leota Loretta Haywood in a small town in the American Midwest. Her own case history in disguise concludes the chapter "Nightmares Are Real." Apparently she was repeatedly sexually abused by a "criminal father" while her mother "closed her eyes to all what took place" (Severn, 1933, p. 153). The scene of abuse by father was reenacted in a dream titled, "This is how it feels to be murdered." Severn notes that they considered the possibility that it was only a fantasy. However, after many reproduction of the same scene, Severn (1933) wrote, "the amount and terrific intensity of the emotions . . . finally convinced both of us beyond any question that it was a historical reality" (p. 155).

Commenting upon another dream, titled "I attend my own funeral" (p. 156), Severn claimed that it was possible for a person to be psychically "killed" while she continues to live in the flesh. This was exactly the theory of Ferenczi. The dream, according to Severn, was a faithful reproduction of what had been recorded in the patient's (Severn's) mind: a part of herself had been destroyed, while another part was observing the murdered self. This reading can also apply to the funeral scene dreamed, enacted, and dramatized by Freud. Severn called "Orpha" this self-observing and disembodied intelligence, which is so clearly represented in Freud's self-dissection dream and, as asserted by these two volumes, created psychoanalysis.

Ferenczi introduced this notion in one of the first pages of the diary (January 12, 1932), where the three main traumas of Elisabeth Severn (R.N.) are reconstructed. After having been "drugged and sexually abused" by an adult at the age of one and half years, Severn experienced a "renewed brutal attack" at the age of five. This was the moment when, according to Ferenczi, the enormity of suffering, plus helplessness and despair of any outside help, propelled her toward death, and the life-organizing instincts ("Orpha") awoke, producing wish-fulfilling fantasies, and anesthetizing the consciousness and sensitivity "against sensations as they become unbearable" (Dupont, 1985, pp. 8–9).

This anesthetizing effect is further described by Ferenczi as a disintegration which "is not perceived at all or is regarded as an event happening to another person, being watched from the outside" (p. 9).

The "last great shock" occurred at the age of 11-and-a-half. "Being hypnotized and sexually abused," says Ferenczi, became a *Lebensform*, a style of life: the "indefatigable Orpha" could not help itself any longer and a "complete atomization of psychic life" was the only form of existence left available,

> But the life of the body, compelled as it was to breathe and pulsate, called back Orpha . . . She managed . . . to get this being back on its feet, shattered as it was to its very atoms, and thus procured a sort of artificial psyche for this body forcibly brought back to life.
>
> (pp. 9–10)

Ferenczi also described Severn's "incessant protestations that she is no murderer, although she admits to having fired the shots" (p. 17). Referring to "the most abominable cruelty that the patient was subjected to," in another passage Ferenczi said that she was "forced to swallow the severed genitals of a repugnant black man, who had just been killed" (p. 140). Severn's hallucinatory memories of this event seem implausible until we consider what Karl Menninger (1935) wrote in his study on self-mutilation:

> In American lynching episodes a common preliminary to the burning or hanging of the victim is the amputation of his genitals. In a recent article (*American Spectator*, March 1933) fictional in form but based upon actual occurrences a female relative of the injured girl is permitted to burn off the penis of the still living negro with a gasoline blow torch.
>
> (p. 450, footnote 40)

As adolescent Severn suffered a number of nervous breakdowns from which she recovered in mental sanatoria. At the age of 22 she married and gave birth to her only child, a daughter. Four years later, in 1905, her marriage ended. She then went through a further major breakdown. Apparently, it was at this point of her life that she was treated against her will with castration (removal of ovaries). After this shock, Leota Loretta Haywood Brown put then herself under the care of a medical doctor whose practice incorporated the "power of positive thinking with a theosophical turn" (Fortune, 1993, p. 103), and, when she emerged from treatment, in 1907–09, obtained a divorce, legally changed her name to Elisabeth Severn, and became a "Metapsychician and Healer."

In 1912 Severn sailed for England, and the following year she published her first book, *Psycho-Therapy: Its Doctrine and Practice*. It includes a clinical case which William Brennan (2015) has recently identified as autobiographical:

> In a third surgical case, a severe ovariotomy had been performed, two years previously, and a cystic tumour removed. It was another "successful" one, but the patient had grown steadily worse until she was physically incapable of any effort, never free from pain, and her mind so affected as to develop suicidal tendencies. She was of a sensitive, high-strung nature, susceptible to many impressions, and the operation had been a serious factor in disturbing her psychic poise. . . . After discovering her new powers, she needed some restraining until the deeper forces could be securely built up to sustain them. The abdominal pains which had been constantly present for so many years disappeared in the first few weeks of the treatment and also the convulsive attacks, but a year was required to put in order the tangled threads of a complex mind. During this time there were many set-backs and discouragements, but in the end the patient said she was "all made over."
>
> (Severn, 1913, p. 173)

In Volume I it was presented that these gynecological operations were recommended and performed as treatments for conditions of mental illness. That a "cystic tumour" had been removed says nothing about the real intention of the operation. The detail that the castration had been performed without her consent derives from another source (see below).

While Freud was finding a revenant of Emma Eckstein in Princess Marie Bonaparte, Ferenczi too had found his own soul mate and "Queen." Ferenczi let himself be analyzed by Elisabeth Severn in approximately the same period that Marie Bonaparte was submitting herself to a resection of her clitoris and a complete hysterectomy (May 1930). Ferenczi's "evil genius" was also a revenant of Emma Eckstein: both women suffered abdominal pains and both developed new powers after their castration: Emma began to have fantasies and dreams of gigantic snakes, and Elisabeth a fantasy of immensely strong willpower and invulnerability.

Reading Severn's first book, Nancy Smith (1998) found it full of references to a "Greater Self," which is repeatedly described as "Infinite Supply," "Infinite Intelligence," and so on. Smith, observing that these repeated phrases induced in her a sleepy trance-like state was reminded of Ferenczi's description of the obscure phenomenon labeled "Orpha" in his *Clinical Diary*.

Severn's second book, bearing an extremely long title, was published in 1917. Reading these texts, seeming so different from *The Discovery of the Self*, Nancy Smith (1998) grasped that the key to understanding Severn and her early work was Orpha, whose major function consisted in

> the revival and preservation of remaining fragments of self after traumatization has occurred. Thus Orpha is "reviving." Severn's first two books must be understood as fundamentally about this traumatized woman's "Orphic" attempts to create and maintain some sense of self in the midst of severe fragmentation due to early and repeated sexual and physical abuse.... Orphic functioning drew on consolidation fantasies to create a self for Elizabeth which was strong, sure, and determined instead of shocked, frightened, and vulnerable.
>
> (pp. 242–243)

According to Smith, this explains Ferenczi's first impression of Severn's "immensely strong willpower as reflected by the marble-like rigidity of her facial features" and "majestic superiority of a Queen" (Dupont, 1985, p. 97). Smith thought that her change of name from Brown to Severn "was an Orphic attempt at severing herself from her traumatic past" (p. 243). The recent discovery that Severn underwent a forced castration, suggests to consider the possibility that her trauma, the fact that her internal genital organs had been "severed," might also have been inscribed in her new name and personality.

Perhaps this inscription "Severn" condensed many symbolic and literal cuts. Did Severn's injury (the removal of the ovaries) serve as an attractor for Ferenczi's unconscious – his hallucination of cutting an abdomen in a dissecting room and his mad fantasy of being pressed inside of a pelvis? The notion of Orpha becomes, further, evocative of Orpheus's descent into the "*corpora cavernosa*," simultaneously the deepest regions of the body and of the dead, to reach his severed half, Eurydice. It is also evocative of Severn's "reunion" fantasy, her conviction that Ferenczi was her "perfect lover" and that ever since she and Ferenczi had been in telepathic contact. At the time of her principal trauma, Ferenczi wrote in his diary, she, so to speak, scoured the universe in search of help with the aid of an omnipotent intelligence (Orpha),

> Thus her Orpha is supposed to have tracked me down, even at that time, as the only person in the word who owing to his special personal fate could and would make amends for the injury that had been done to her.
>
> (Dupont, 1985, p. 121)

It is tempting to associate Severn's mad hallucination of being "forced to swallow the severed genitals of a repugnant black man" (Dupont, 1985, p. 140) with

Ferenczi's visionary dream of the cut-off penis served on a saucer. Further reflecting on mutual analysis, Ferenczi wrote:

> it is as though two halves had combined to form a whole soul. The emotions of the analyst combine with the ideas of the analysand, and the ideas of the analyst . . . with the emotions of the analysand; in this way *the otherwise lifeless image become events*.
>
> (p. 14; emphasis added)

According to Ferenczi patients cannot believe that certain terrible events really took place "if the analyst, the sole witness of the events, persists in his cool, unemotional, and . . . purely intellectual attitude" (Dupont, 1985, p. 24). While reviving Freud's initial theory of trauma as a "gap in the psyche"—for instance in the *Clinical Diary* he wrote ". . .a part of our personality can 'die', and if the remaining part does survive the trauma, it wakes up with a gap in memory, actually with a gap in the personality. . ." (p. 179)—Ferenczi found that a mere intellectual "mosaic-like reconstruction of the whole picture" failed to attain the feeling of conviction in the patients, He thus advocated a dramatic participation of the analyst in the process (pp. 2[1-9]-[1-9]5).

Incarnation – the becoming alive of the "lifeless image" – can only occur in a meeting of minds, or in an intersubjective field. This important passage represents a further development of the shift from remembering to repetition promoted in the 1924 book with Rank. This is beyond a cognitivist paradigm in psychoanalysis, namely the idea – later developed by authors such as Alexander and French (1946) and Weiss and Sampson (1986) – that by repeating early traumas and conflicts in a social context, the patient is enabled to repair or, in the cognitive version, to master them. In this passage of Ferenczi, the social dimension is not just reparative but rather constitutive of the "*Erlebniss*." This also turns the question about suggestive influence – an objection that Freud advanced to Ferenczi, after Ferenczi's death, in "Analysis terminable and interminable" (1937a, p. 230) – into a false dilemma. In this respect Ferenczi and Severn's mutual analysis anticipated the relational turn in psychoanalysis and the rediscovery within a relational frame of the dialogue between unconsciouses. This is reminiscent of Baranger (1993; Madeleine Baranger and Willy Baranger's 1961–1962) notion of "dynamic field." Further developing the notion of "analytic situation" (introduced by Ferenczi and Rank in 1924), these authors suggested that the two persons involved are taking part in the same dynamic process and that all the significant phenomena within that field must be considered in a bipersonal dimension. The dynamic field (a notion derived from Gestalt and phenomenology) is thus organized by an "unconscious fantasy of the couple" created by both participants, and not just by the patient. The "*otherwise lifeless image*" (Ferenczi) is allowed to "*become events*" in a dynamic field structured by many factors, including society, history, and language. In "Construction in analysis," Freud (1937b) resumed his own initial focus on actual trauma, reducing his distance from Ferenczi. In this rather impressive essay, Freud reflected on the analyst's attempt to deal with the patient's destroyed psychic objects by filling the gaps with "constructions" (forgotten pieces of the patient's early history), which are similar to delusions and ultimately owe their power to the element of "historical truth." Extending his consideration from the single human individual to mankind as a whole, Freud concluded by saying that mankind as well has developed delusions which "owe their power to the element of historical truth which they have brought up from the repression of the forgotten and primeval past" (p. 269).

Again here is the idea that to fully understand "incarnation" we need to transcend contingencies, to go beyond the history of the individual and to make possible a general morphology of the psyche understood as sediment of a deep and catastrophic time in the evolution of the human species, this a goal which Freud and Ferenczi had in common. Even though Ferenczi realized that in composing his theory of genitality he was clinging "too closely to the words of the master" and that "a new edition would mean a complete rewriting" (Dupont, 1985, p. 187), still he never discarded the study of the "eternal return of the same." On the contrary, the more microscopic was his description of the "here and now," the more he found himself in the role of a compiler of a general morphology and grammar of trauma. Conscious of this timeless dimension, Ferenczi asked himself: "Is the purpose of mutual analysis perhaps the finding of that common feature which repeats itself in every case of infantile trauma?" (p. 15).

An egg, or a penis, or a piece of rotting flesh

The central page of *Totem and Taboo* comes back into view, where Freud (1913a) wrote:

> The doctrine of original sin was of Orphic origin. It formed a part of the mysteries, and spread from them to the schools of philosophy of ancient Greece. . . . A fragment of Anaximander relates how the unity of the world was broken by a primaeval sin . . . .
>
> (p. 153)

Ferenczi and Severn's mutual analysis was an attempt to recombine the different planes in which the unity of the self had been crushed. To do so, their souls traveled through the entire universe searching for the scattered fragments. Believing in their dreams, mad fantasies, and hallucinations, Severn and Ferenczi explored the atomization of the psyche as previously only pre-Socratic philosophers, Buddhists, and mystics had done.

Ferenczi did not live long enough to systematize the different lines of thought that emerged from his experiment of mutual analysis. Terminated by Ferenczi's premature death, the treatment proved to have long-term beneficial effect on Elisabeth Severn. The worst symptoms were allayed or disposed of, and even though her nightmarish dreams never ceased, Severn remained capable of functioning at high level. Her recovery was reflected in the title of the book she published in 1933, *The Discovery of the Self*.

The event of Severn's castration does not surface in Ferenczi's diary. William Brennan (2015) found a reference to this event in Margaret Naumburg's papers, more precisely in the transcript of a spiritist séance Severn gave with Margaret Naumburg, an art therapist and teacher at the Walden School. The sitting, which took place on July 16, 1934, begins with Severn recalling a dream of eggs and a broken eggshell, her associations are to the operation where her ovaries were removed:

> "They did not tell me they were going to do it," Severn states. "It was done against my will. I was victimized. I was indignant." Severn then begins to see a Greek Temple and states, "I am chosen. I must undertake the sacrifice" . . . Severn is seeing something. But not clearly. There is a pause. Then she utters the name of Orpha.
>
> She then says, "One must accept the pain . . . Pain is given for the wider understanding of humanity. When one can absorb it there is release." She states, "The word is absorption." Next she sees cannibalistic rites, and states that Incorporation is the rite. "Whether it is an egg, or a penis, or a piece of rotting flesh, that it is the interpenetration of the different planes."

Notes

1 Freud himself called attention to the ineffectiveness of mere intellectual knowledge, remarking that with obsessional neurotics "analysis is always in danger of bringing to light a great deal and changing nothing" (Freud, 1919d, p. 166), and further, requiring that phobic patients seek the avoided situation in order to free up affect.
2 As pointed out by Glover (1924), because the method of Ferenczi was based on the reactivation of "the links formed at the earliest stages between the ego and the object along 'regressional' paths" (pp. 296–297). In other words, an emotional reaction is released when the analyst steps into the role of an archaic object of the patient's internal world.
3 A crucial argument concerned the feeling of annihilation caused by a traumatic event. Freud (1926a) was convinced that, since "nothing resembling death can ever have been experienced; or if it has, as in fainting, it has left no observable traces behind" (p. 130), the annihilation of life was necessarily represented in the unconscious by castration.
4 Ferenczi described the erection as an impulse which aims at a complete separation of the genital from the body. The latter is hallucinatory achieved by the elimination of fluid and the event of fertilization. Perhaps this impulse is the root of the universal fantasy of the erect penis as a flying "bird." In ancient rituals the bird is a soul symbol.
5 Ferenczi first referred to this notion in a letter to Freud of April 27, 1916, where he wrote: "*scratching oneself* seems to me to be the primal image of the reaction to an external unpleasurable sensation . . . so really the repetition of the *autotomy* prevalent in animals – the reflex tearing off and letting go of painful parts of the body. . . . I will naturally also connect this special part of coitus with the unaccustomed dermal sensations during birth (after the water breaks) – and phylo-genetically with the time in which our animal forebears were 'put on dry land' out of the water."
6 As put by Menninger (1935): "Instead of cutting off the entire penis, a part of it is cut off, a part standing for the whole just as it does in all sacrificial offerings" (p. 437).
7 The analogy between psychotherapy with surgical intervention [is] was first developed by Freud in the chapter on psychotherapy of the *Studies on Hysteria* (Breuer & Freud, 1895, p. 305); It would then reappear in several places, among which Freud (1910a, p. 52, 1910b, p. 146, 1912b, p. 115, 1916–1917, p. 459).

8 According to some authors, the so-called Freudian technique was largely an artifact. The contention that Freud did not rely on the "Freudian technique" has been first advanced by Samuel Lipton (1977), and then supported by personal reports of many former patients of Freud (Nissim Momigliano, 1987; Roazen, 1995). According to Lipton, the formalistic redefinition of technique in terms of a non-interfering, constant, uniform, and predictable external behavior began only after Freud's death in 1939. Yet, Ferenczi's criticism of the "insensitivity" and of the "professional hypocrisy" of the analyst suggests that the problem already existed long before. Ernst Falzeder has offered an excellent reconstruction of the difficulties met by Freud and of the solutions he found (*"Indifferenz"*) in his 1994 paper, "My Grand-Patient, my Chief Tormentor."

9 Severn (1933, pp. 136–138), quoted in Rudnytsky (2015, pp. 142–143). The patient described by Severn was identified as Ferenczi by Rudnytsky in "The other side of the story," which is the main source for Severn's analysis of Ferenczi.

14 Freud and Ferenczi on the Acropolis

> A man who has grown rational and skeptical, even, may be ashamed to discover how easily he may for a moment return to a belief in spirits under the combined impact of strong emotion and perplexity.
> S. Freud, *Delusions and Dreams in Jensen's Gradiva*, 1907a, p. 71

Freud's posthumous dialogue with Ferenczi

Around 1930 the discovery and interpretation of traumatic memories had ceased to be a central goal, as classical psychoanalysis was being transformed into an ego-psychology of adaptation. Ferenczi (1929), however, proposed that "no analysis can be regarded . . . as complete unless we have succeed in penetrating the traumatic material" (p. 120). He was embracing "an earlier direction," which had been, in his words, "undeservedly abandoned" (p. 108), yet, according to his new perspective, the "traumatic material" was not to be sought in the neurotic reactions (the "masculine protest") and adaptive solutions of the ego (repression). Rather, it could be observed in more primitive reactions, such as splitting, fragmentation, and the psychotic turning away from reality – all clinical elements which, as we have seen, informed Freud's early theory of "a foreign body and the splitting of consciousness."

How did Freud react to Ferenczi's new metapsychology? Freud immediately grasped the deep continuity between Ferenczi's Thalassa myth and his reformulation of the trauma theory. In his letter of September 16, 1930, Freud wrote to Ferenczi to say that his "new views about the traumatic fragmentation of mental life" had "something of the great characteristic of the Theory of Genitality." However, Freud added:

> I only think that one can hardly speak of trauma in the extraordinary synthetic activity of the ego without treating the reactive scar-formation along with it. The latter, of course, also produces what we see.
> (Falzeder & Brabant, 2000, p. 393)

This response defines the bones of contention in the Freud-Ferenczi dispute. Freud's appeal to the "extraordinary synthetic activity of the ego," in particular, recalls Freud's old disagreement and dispute with Pierre Janet. Freud, in fact, appealed to the same argument when he began to oppose Janet's theory of a primary mental dissociation (*désagrégation psychologique*).[1] Summarizing the difference between his view and Janet's, Freud (1910a) stated in his American lectures:

> We do not derive the psychical splitting from an innate incapacity for synthesis on the part of the mental apparatus; we explain it dynamically, from the conflict of opposing mental forces and recognize it as the outcome of an active struggling on the part of the two psychical groupings against each other.
>
> (pp. 25–26)

Thus "Resistance," a force that prevented unconscious traumatic memories from becoming conscious, was the pillar of Freud's dynamic model of intrapsychic struggling and conflict.[2] Since Freud's discovery of resistance was made possible by his moving away from hypnosis, Freud could claim that "the history of psycho-analysis proper . . . only begins with the new technique that dispenses with hypnosis" (Freud, 1914a, p. 15).

Like Freud, Ferenczi also opposed the idea that hysterics possessed an "innate" incapacity for synthesis. Yet, in 1930 Ferenczi was challenging all these points. He had resumed attempts to recover unconscious traumatic memories and he was working to overcome resistance by creating a warm and facilitating atmosphere, one which he himself compared to hypnotic catharsis. He had returned to an awareness that trauma operated like a foreign body in the psyche, and, finally, had challenged the core assumption upon which the dynamic model of defense of the mental apparatus based on resistance and repression was built, namely the idea that the psyche has the capacity to preserve an internal equilibrium and organization in the process of post-traumatic adaptation. It took eight more years for Freud (1938b) to realize that by taking "for granted the synthetic nature of the processes of the ego," he was "clearly at fault" (p. 276).

In 1930 Ferenczi was disappointed by Freud's reaction. "I was pleased to hear that you find my new views 'very ingenious'" he wrote to Freud on September 21st, but he added "I would have been much more pleased if you had declared them to be correct, probable, or even only plausible." It was shortly thereafter that the long-simmering conflict between the two men burst into the open.

Interestingly, several years after Ferenczi's premature death, Freud began to reconsider his views. As André Haynal has pointed out (2005):

> The issues and conflicts aroused by this relationship continued to exert an influence in Freud's mind even after Ferenczi's death. After a few years' mourning (from 1933 to 1937), he returned to the theme of trauma in 'Analysis terminable and interminable' (1937). He noted – almost as if he had thought through Ferenczi's ideas again – that the effect of the castration threat represented the greatest trauma of all. He was here manifestly seeking to bring

his own theory of the Oedipus complex and of the threat of castration, which meant so much to him, into harmony with trauma theory.

(p. 464)

Freud's attempt to assimilate Ferenczi's new metapsychology of the fragmentation of mental life within his system informed some of his last works. Ferenczi's influence is palpable in a passage found in *Moses and Monotheism* wherein Freud speaks of "sequestration" and "fragmentation" of the ego (Freud, 1939, pp. 76–78). Freud's last piece of self-analysis was also informed by this posthumous dialogue with Ferenczi, especially by Ferenczi's idea that the "traumatic material" was not to be sought in the neurotic reactions but, rather, in splitting, fragmentation, and the psychotic turning away from reality. This was exactly the material that Freud revisited in an essay of far-reaching significance, "A Disturbance of Memory on the Acropolis," written in 1936 in the form of meditative open letter to Romain Rolland, the Nobel Prize–winning novelist and scholar of Eastern religions, who Freud had already notably addressed in *Civilization and Its Discontents* (Freud, 1930a, pp. 64–73).

Disbelief on the Acropolis

Freud's agenda is immediately made clear by the title, a tribute to his old Signorelli parapraxis and memory disturbance. We are transported into the midst of Freud's self-analysis, recalling his visit to the Orvieto necropolis, and reminded of his earlier inhibition regarding travel to Rome, which was for Freud the comprehensive symbol for the most intimate goals he was forbidden to achieve. Freud finally overcame this phobia in 1901 and was so enthusiastic about the "eternal city" that he later made six return trips. Entering Rome for the first time he felt that he "could have worshipped the abased and mutilated remnant of the Temple of Minerva [the Roman goddess Athena]" (letter to Martha, September 3, 1901). Yet, Freud experienced a severe return of the same phobia three years later, when he visited Athens for the first and only time in his life. Freud, we know, first disclosed some of the uncanny aspects of this event in his letter to Jung dated April 16, 1909. Risto Fried (2003), who has provided the most comprehensive study of Freud's "incident" on the Athens acropolis, wrote:

> It was three years later, in September 1904, that Freud arrived in Athens for the experience that surpassed even Rome and Orvieto. One might have expected that of the three cities, Athens would prove to be the purest source of pleasure, least mixed with anxiety. In Orvieto the Etruscan tombs and Luca Signorelli's *Day of Judgement* murals were heavy with the odor of death. Rome represented the power of Caesars and Popes who inflicted suffering on Jews over the centuries, and the Catholic dogma that to Freud was an affront to reason. Athens was free of such burdens.

(p. 24)

Since Freud was deeply involved in classical culture, the walk uphill to the Parthenon promised to deliver the highest degree of pleasure, but this would turn out to be spoiled by a strange feeling of incredulity. In fact, the experience was so uncanny that he never returned to Athens. The "incident" – as Freud (1936) called it – would trouble him for the rest of his life (p. 248). The German expression Freud used was "*heimgesucht*," which, according to Niederland (1969), indicated an extremely painful affect such as "tormented or tortured," while, according to Bettelheim (1982), it holds a religious connotation. "*Heimsuchung*" is, in fact, the Viennese name of the holy visitation of the Virgin Mary (an equivalent of the virgin goddess Athena). Moving between the two readings, and taking into account that references to the Acropolis incident appear in Freud's 1919 essay "The uncanny" [*Das Unheimliche*], Risto Fried has suggested that "troubled" should be replaced by "haunted."

The initial title Freud chose for this last piece of self-analysis was "*Unglaube auf der Akropolis*" (*Disbelief on the acropolis*), a name suggesting that he was broaching the theme of skepticism about religious belief. He had already considered this subject in *The Future of an Illusion* (Freud, 1927b). In 1936, working on *Moses and Monotheism*, Freud was, in Rice's (1990) felicitous expression, on the way to his "long journey home." Following a suggestion by André Haynal, the word "*Heimsuchung*" can be heard as an echo of Freud's troubled "search for" a "home" (*Heim*). His Hellenic meditation was indeed a detour from the Judaic religious beliefs of his father Jacob and his paternal ancestors.

In reconstructing Freud's self-analysis, it is necessary to recall that conscious and unconscious memories of the circumcision of Alexander and the death of Julius haunted Freud's 1897 visit to the Etruscan necropolis in Orvieto. Recall also that the name Alexander, inspired by Alexander the Great, made him a revenant of Julius, a name associated with another great conqueror, Julius Caesar. In Athens, Freud was again accompanied by his brother Alexander. Remembering the event in 1936, Freud identified himself with Napoleon, thus reconstituting a trio of the most famous "conquistadors": Julius Caesar, Alexander the Great, and Napoleon Bonaparte. Freud noted that he might have said to his brother, as they stood together looking over the city,

> "Do you still remember how, when we were young . . . And now, here we are in Athens, and standing on the Acropolis! We really have gone a long way!" So too, if I may compare such a small event with a greater one, Napoleon, during his coronation as Emperor in Notre Dame, turned to one of his brothers – it must no doubt have been the eldest one, Joseph – and remarked: "What would *Monsieur notre Père* have said to this, if he could have been here to-day?"
>
> (p. 247)

The pleasure of this crowning achievement was spoiled, however, by the strange "*Erinnerungsstörung*" (disturbance of memory), which, after it was analyzed, appeared to Freud as a feeling of alienation and incredulity, involving a "falsification of the past," as though what Freud was seeing in Athens, the Acropolis, was *"not real."* Such feelings of "derealization," Freud explained, arise "very frequently in certain mental diseases, but they are not unknown among normal people, just as hallucinations occasionally occur in the healthy" (p. 244).

This remark leads directly to the central theme of Freud's essay, that is, the meaning of *hallucinations* in a broad, non-psychiatric sense. From the beginning of his practice, Freud found that kind of sensation frequently occurred in the regressive setting of analysis. In his last years Ferenczi came to the conclusion that such hallucinations were an "illusionary working through of real events" (Dupont, 1985, p. 140; see also p. 58).

In this meditative essay, Freud traced his strange feeling of incredulity back to the idea that he did not "deserve" and was not "worthy of such happiness." Standing in Athens and looking out toward the Acropolis thus represented an oedipal achievement, the realization of his desire to supersede his father Jacob. Indeed, it was by adopting a Greek vision of the world, by making the Oedipus myth the key to understanding mankind, that Freud had superseded his father.

In his analysis of the incident, Freud (1936) conveyed his "disbelief" with a provocative simile: it was as if, while standing on the Acropolis, he had been "forced to believe in something the reality of which had seemed doubtful, just as if walking beside Loch Ness the sudden sight of the famous ["*vielberedeten*," much discussed] Monster stranded upon the shore would force the startled walker to admit: 'So it really does exist – *the sea-serpent* we've never believed in!'" (p. 241)

The insertion of the Scottish sea serpent into the midst of classical Greece is something of a narrative shock. What does it communicate? This last piece of Freud's self-analysis has been commented on by many eminent psychoanalysts, most of whom have sensed in this passage the echo of a shocking castration. Some of the responses elicited were highly stereotyped psychoanalytic interpretations. For instance, Vermorel and Vermorel (1993) wrote:

> It is the sight of the feminine sexual organ by the little boy which, because of the absence of the penis, causes a feeling of horror. It is therefore the denial of the castration of the mother which is at the origin of the phenomenon of splitting and *double conscience*: a part of the ego accepts this void, while the other denies it.
>
> (p. 476)

Risto Fried (2003), on the other hand, provided a different reaction to the facetious metaphor. Fried saw in the image of the unbelievable sea serpent, first and foremost, a resurfacing of the provocative question of *what is real*, a concern at the heart of psychoanalysis itself. At the time of his self-analysis, Freud was haunted by such a question: Was he sexually abused when he was a child? By his father or by his Catholic nursemaid? What is true? What is real? Can childhood memories be trusted? For Risto Freid, these questions are "at the heart of the Acropolis mystery" (p. 289).

In Freud's letter I myelf also sense a rather precise allusion to the key question at the heart of his disagreement with Ferenczi, namely: are hallucinations reproductions of traumatic memories, or are they fantasies, products of the synthetic activity of the ego? Like Ferenczi, Elisabeth Severn believed that hallucinations are dissociated memories projected into the external world, and it is highly likely that she discussed this point with Freud when visiting him in Vienna. Freud, in turn, would call Elisabeth Severn Ferenczi's "evil genius," in reference to an argument advanced of Descartes. The French philosopher hypothesized that his bodily sensations and his perceptions of the external world were mere hallucinations created by a deceitful demon, an "evil genius." Descartes, in his famous first meditation, came to the conclusion that the only way to defend himself from this misleading demon was to doubt everything. That is, *skepticism*, *disbelief*, was assumed to be the foundation of rationality, an assumption which Freud shared. Ferenczi, on the other hand, chose "to take really seriously the role . . . of the benevolent and helpful observer," that is, as he explained in his *Clinical Diary*, "actually to transport oneself with the patient into that period of the past (a practice Freud reproached me for, as being not permissible), with the result that *we ourselves and the patient believe in its reality, that is, a present reality, which has not been momentarily transposed into the past*" (Dupont, 1985, p. 24; emphasis added).

Despite Freud's criticism at the time, the question was far from settled, as evidenced by his later meditative essay on the Acropolis. In fact, Freud took as his starting point in that essay the peculiar sentiment of disbelief and skepticism incorporated in the mind of modern man. After Descartes, this is no longer a medieval world populated by monsters and ghosts, nor do we believe in our everyday hallucinations. We have become skeptical, disenchanted. As educated persons, we are supposedly free from superstitions and do not believe that the Loch Ness monster exists, even though, from time to time, someone reports having seen it.[3] The belief that sightings of the monster are hallucinations is generally well rooted in modern consciousness. Freud, however, in a fictional, postmodern scene, imagined that, while walking on the shore of a Loch, he, a modern and skeptical person, actually met his hallucination in the external world, in direct observation of the Loch Ness monster.

This scene is especially intriguing because this is exactly what can occur in an analysis when a patient is enabled to fill gaps in the psyche by meeting a hallucination. Freud, the originator of this situation, could not directly take advantage of it, yet he found a surrogate in his *Reisefieber* (travel nerves). Moreover, on the occasion of his journey to Greece, Freud found himself sailing towards Athens "like an automaton," says Maynard Solomon (1973), "possessed by his Dybbuk" (p. 153).[1] The view that hallucinations are traumatic memories that cannot be remembered, was initially endorsed by Jeffrey Masson in the article, "Buried memories on the Acropolis" (Masson & Masson, 1977), in which the monster of Loch Ness is presented as the return of the monstrous experience of being abused: "the banished monster of childhood returns from its lair" (p. 204).[5]

Risto Fried found in the Loch Ness metaphor the echo of a puzzling memory which also surfaced in Freud's Hollthurn dream (July 1898). In his youth, while in England to visit his family, Freud spent a whole day on the shore of the Irish Sea, collecting marine animals among which were holothurians, which have a remarkable phallic size and shape. On that occasion a charming little girl came up to him, and he made a grammatical error which served "as the most innocent possible example" of his "bringing in sex . . . where it did not belong" (Freud, 1900, pp. 519–520). In Fried's opinion (2003, pp. 424–426), the scene was not at all "innocent," but rather an act of phallic exhibitionism. This invites a new perspective on Freud's Loch Ness fantasy, suggesting that the "sea-monster" (which Fried read in English as: "see [the] monster!") was "neither father's nor mother's phallus, *but his own*" (p. 426 emphasis added).

Fried thought that the image of "the sea-serpent we've never believed in" fits perfectly with the peculiar feeling of being castrated as experienced by the exhibitionist who, doubting the existence of his own penis, has to display it in order to obtain a woman's confirmatory response to believe in his masculinity. "In real life," Fried noted, "a man overcomes his dread of the adult female genitals sufficiently to father children and live together with his wife, day in, day out. But somewhere, in a timeless alternative reality, the old fear and the old fixation survive. And at times, prevail" (p. 423).

These thoughts of Fried are very convincing, even though they do not sufficiently explain Freud's feeling of alienation ("*Entfremdungsgefühl*"). Freud in fact said that in these situations the subject "feels either that a piece of reality or that a piece of his own self is strange to him" (Freud, 1936, p. 245). To illustrate his own attempt "at keeping something away from the ego, at disavowing it" (p. 245), Freud introduced the figure of the infamous Boabdil, who overthrew his father to become Sultan and King of Granada. When Boabdil received the news of the fall of his home city of Alhama, he burned the letters and killed the messenger, combating his feeling of impotence by treating the news as "*non arrivé*."[6]

What remains unclear is how this situation applies to Freud's own experience on the Acropolis. Risto Fried thought that the figure of Boabdil helped to establish a rather precise connection between Freud's experience on the Acropolis and his dream of self-dissection of the pelvis.[7] Yet, he couldn't explain this pulling back to the very symbol of Freud's self-analysis, or why the walk to the Parthenon should have provoked Freud's sudden collapse, that intense experience of fragmentation. Obviously, Fried was not content with generic formulations in terms of either oedipal wish or pre-oedipal awe, and knew that, even though travel phobias are traceable to unresolved dependency conflicts in early childhood, "they can only be explained in terms of ongoing events" (p. 427). For him the *current crisis*, not its ultimate origin, was the essential point, but in vain did he search for the actual conflict that triggered Freud's crisis.

The terrifying irrational

There is another element of Fried's analysis of the Acropolis incident that deserves highlighting, that is, Freud's powerful idealization of classical Greece. In 1926, Freud said to Marie Bonaparte, Princess of Greece, that the "amber-colored columns of the Acropolis were the most beautiful things he had ever seen in his life" (Jones, 1955, pp. 26–27). The same attitude can be found in his self-analysis: Freud chose classical Greece as his source of "perfect beauty," as evidenced by his Hella dream of May 1897.

The Greek spirit that Freud learned about at school, under the influence of Winckelmann and neoclassical culture, valued democracy, reason, harmony, the beauty of the body, and the human individual as the center of the universe, the measure of the cosmos. Six years before Freud's meditative essay on the Acropolis, this view was made popular by Edith Hamilton (born in 1867) in her influential 1930 book *The Greek Way*, which claimed that there was no place in Greek spirit for the "terrifying irrational." In a later work (1942) she wrote:

> That is the miracle of Greek mythology – a humanized world, men freed from the paralyzing fear of an omnipotent Unknown. The terrifying incomprehensibilities which were worshiped elsewhere, and the fearsome spirits with which earth, air and sea swarmed, were banned from Greece.

All this Freud learned at school. Only later did archeologists find the traces of the "terrifying irrational" in the buried remnants of ancient Greece. Right on the Acropolis, archaeologists discovered statues with their original paint still intact, housed in the Acropolis Museum where Freud later saw them.[8] They were strikingly different from what his teachers taught about Greek art, just as the 12-meter-high statute of the virgin goddess Athena with a gigantic snake, which originally stood at the center of the Parthenon, was very different from the classical Athena. Fried sensed that Freud's image of classic Greece as a world of beauty was shattered after an overwhelming exposure to vestiges of ancient Greece, especially the breathtaking power of the cult of the snake. The snake then became the "concrete factual basis" for the image of the Loch Ness monster, itself a symbol for the "terrifying irrational" banned from classic Greece and displaced in the Scottish Loch (or in the Irish sea shore).

Fried himself idealized classical Greece and was shocked when he first set foot in Athens. He was also powerfully affected by the numerous effigies of snakes in the Acropolis Museum:

> There were snakes of natural and gigantic proportions, realistic and fantastic, terrestrial and oceanic, with one or several heads or with human upper and snakelike lower bodies. Living snakes formed Medusa's head and the fringe of Athena's garment. I had stumbled upon something that none of the critics of Freud's Acropolis paper had been aware of: the concrete factual basis for his playful and richly symbolic comparison of the Acropolis with the Loch Ness monster.
>
> (p. 610; see also pp. 409–411)

Although he couldn't identify the *current crisis* that triggered Freud's breakdown, Risto Fried was convinced that, after setting set foot in Athens, Freud felt himself surrounded and even persecuted by a multiplication of snakes. The Loch Ness monster was not a metaphor: Freud actually met his hallucination embodied in the form of a gigantic snake.

The trigger

The gap in Risto Fried's analysis can be filled using the following evidence provided by Max Schur, which becomes even more significant when we consider that in 1904 Emma Eckstein published her 38-page essay on the dangers of masturbation titled, "*Die Sexualfrage in der Erziehung des Kindes*" ("The Question of Sexuality in the Rearing of Children," an event which would have reminded Freud of her childhood trauma.[9]

Exploring the background of the Acropolis incident, Schur (1969) thought that Freud's feeling of derealization was precipitated by a letter he had received from Fliess "only a week or so before" he started on his trip to Athens (p. 130). Schur described it as "a violent blast from Fliess accusing Freud of plagiarism" (p. 129) regarding the idea of a universal bisexual constitution. This idea had originally been introduced by Fliess on Easter 1897, at the Nuremberg meeting. Since Freud tended to "forget" again and again his discussion with his friend (see Volume I, pp. 219–220), Fliess reminded him of the specific circumstances under which the discussion took place occurred. Here is the passage in question:

> Until now I did not know what I learned from your letter – that you are using [the idea of] persistent bisexuality in your treatments. We talked about it for the first time in Nuremberg while I was still lying in bed, and you told me *the case history of the woman who had dreams of gigantic snakes* [*riesigen Schlangen*]. At the time you were *quite impressed* [*sehr betroffen*: very struck] by the idea that undercurrents in a woman might stem from the masculine part of her psyche. For this reason I was all the more puzzled by your resistance in Breslau to the assumption of bisexuality in the psyche. In Breslau . . . you rejected left-handedness itself and, as you yourself admitted most candidly, forgot our bisexual discussion for some time.
> (Masson, 1985, pp. 465–466; emphasis added)

The content of this letter validates Risto Fried's "snake" hypothesis, which had been formulated without taking into account what Fliess had written to Freud one week before this "incident." It also explains why Freud called his Acropolis incident "a memory disturbance" and makes more understandable why Freud (1936) introduced the figure of the infamous Boabdil to illustrate his own feeling of derealization. Just as Boabdil burned the letters, treating the news of the fall of Alhama as "*non arrivé*," similarly, Freud destroyed all or most of the letters that Fliess had sent to him "at same point after 1904." This, at least, is what Freud wrote in December 1928, after the death of Wilhelm Fliess, to his widow, Ida Fliess (Masson, 1985, p. 5).

Who was Freud's woman patient whose dreams caused such a reaction in the founder of psychoanalysis? Why did Freud repeatedly "forget" his discussion with Fliess in April 1897? It was immediately after his Nuremberg meeting with Fliess that Freud had his "secerno" dream, a word which "means 'I hide' or 'secret' in Italian" (Anzieu, 1986, p. 218; see Volume I, p. 180). It seems that Freud did not inform Fliess that the female patient who had recurrent dreams of gigantic snakes was Emma Eckstein. It was not the first time that Freud was secretive with Fliess in this regard: when he wrote to his friend to inform him of his new brilliant ideas about religion which had been stirred up by a "scene about the circumcision of a girl," he didn't say that the girl in question was Emma Eckstein. Similarly, Freud did not say anything to Fliess when he had his Irma dream. As Harold Blum (1996) put it, "the Irma dream was originally a secret dream. This special dream was kept secret from Fliess, Freud's proto-analyst and supervisor, for virtually five years" (p. 514). Why? Blum does not offer any significant insight.

What is certain is that, in the summer of 1904, Fliess's letter breached Freud's defenses, though not immediately.[10] Freud was seized by intense anxiety only a few days later when he embarked from Trieste with Alexander. The original plan was to go to Corfu, but the two changed destination at the last moment. While sailing to Athens on the ferryboat Urano (*Uranus*), Freud became anxious and was persecuted by numbers pointing to his fated death, such as 61–62 and 31 (the half of 62). To Schur (1969) Freud's superstitious preoccupation with numbers had the character and intensity of an "obsessive compulsive symptom" and "the derealization on the Acropolis was only the culmination of this neurotic episode" (p. 132).

Freud received Fliess's stunning communication on the day of Martha's birthday (July 26), a festive event celebrated in the dream of Irma's injection. Reprising from Volume I: Freud found in analyzing his dream a reaction to the disgusting smelling of "amyl" and that the repressed element fell under the influence of the Greek spirit and vision of beauty. The vision of beauty was represented by the verbal complex "Propyls – Propylaea," which hints of classical Greece as the cradle of universal culture and a paradigm of the transformation of the horrible into the beautiful. Indeed, in Freud's own analysis "amyl" was *the signifier of the horrible which is transformed in beautiful* by dream work. This analysis becomes more transparent once 'amyl' is read as a transcript of "*milah*" (the Hebrew word for cut). In other words, Freud employed the idealization of Greek beauty, culture, and civilization to keep dissociated the deep-seated memories that the "cut" of Emma Eckstein had evoked in him. The very same reaction was repeated in 1897 when, after the reproduction in analysis of Emma Eckstein's circumcision scene, Freud had the Hella dream.

In service of this defensive function, however, classical Greece had to remain a remote and abstract idea.

Dragons and dinosaurs

Freud, we recall, had composed his meditative essay on the Acropolis as an open letter to Romain Rolland, with whom he discussed the "oceanic feeling" as a basis for religious sentiment (Freud, 1930a, pp. 64–72). Religion itself was associated by Freud with the worship of woman's primordial penis. Once, in a letter to Jung (of November 21, 1909), referring to the "long-lost and ardently longed-for woman's penis of the primordial age of infancy," he wrote: "Evidently some people search as passionately for this precious object as the pious English do for the ten lost tribes of Israel."

Perhaps the image of the marine animal stranded upon the shore of the Loch contained an allusion to the myth of the drying up of the sea exposed by Ferenczi in *Thalassa*, the ingenious theory of the fish/phallus admired so much by Freud. In *Thalassa* Ferenczi (1924, p. 44) said that the symbol of the fish was the point of departure of all his speculations on the Phallus as memorial of a catastrophe of cosmic proportion. He appealed to Haeckel's law of recapitulation, and, on another page, Ferenczi suddenly remarked that the distinctly fishy odor of the vagina "comes from the same substance (trimethylamin) as the decomposition of fish gives rise to" (p. 57, note). Ferenczi would have been well acquainted with the trimethylamin formula as a core element of the founding dream of psychoanalysis, the dream of Irma's injection. Thus Ferenczi's scientific fairy tale on the phallus-symbol can be seen as an unconscious re-elaboration of an element kept secret and dissociated, an element which managed, nevertheless, to be deeply inscribed in the dreams of Freud. Like a good analyst, Ferenczi used his imagination to fill the gap with his imagination, in an effort to help Freud to face his dissociation.

Freud's meditation on the Acropolis was an elegant attempt to give representation to the same unmastered trauma, first played out in the Irma dream and then in the dream of self-dissection. The Loch hints to the gaping hole (Irma's mouth/vagina), while Nessie, the sea-monster stranded on the shore of the Loch, brings into visual representation the vague allusion to a "fish" that Freud glimpsed in the deep of his eviscerated pelvis. The same Big Fish and monster of the deep would resurface shortly after in "Analysis Terminable and Interminable."

In December 1936, Marie Bonaparte informed Freud that she was in the process of purchasing his letters to Fliess. Freud immediately told her that he didn't want any of them "to become known to so-called posterity" (Masson, 1985, p. 7), and urged her to burn them (p. 9). When Freud realized that she would have disregarded this injunction, he began to work on "Analysis Terminable and Interminable," where Emma Eckstein's case history is discussed anonymously (Freud, 1937a, pp. 221–222). Indeed the only two analyses discussed by Freud in this essay were those of Emma Eckstein and Sándor Ferenczi, as though this meditation on what analysis can and cannot achieve was a continuation of his Acropolis essay.

The Leviathan, a close symbolic cousin of the Loch Ness monster, resurfaced in Freud's (1937a) caution against Ferenczi's belief that it was easy to gain access to traumatic memories (p. 230), an illusion fostered, Freud said, by the belief that the hypnotic method was a splendid way of achieving this end.[11]

The dragon resurfaced at this precise point in the text as a signifier of all that should be surmounted and dead, yet clings tenaciously to life. Discussing the persistence of libidinal fixations and superstitious beliefs, Freud wrote: "One feels inclined to doubt sometimes whether the dragons of primeval days are really extinct" (p. 229). Mark the wording: Freud does not say "extinct dinosaurs" or "non-existent dragons" and instead speaks of never extinct dragons, blurring the distinction between *legends* and *fossils*, fiction (dragons) and reality (dinosaurs). This is a dramatic way of asserting that the interplay between external reality and unconscious fantasy, trauma and defenses, life events and predisposition, cannot be disentangled. It offers a precise response to Ferenczi.

Leaving aside the controversy regarding the technical measures used by the two men in the pursuit of traumatic memories (indifference and emotional coolness versus emotional participation and dramatization), further exploration of the interconnected images of the dragon (fiction) and of the dinosaur (reality) will help to understand Freud's call to the *extraordinary synthetic activity of the ego*.

The Saurian code: Dragon Lady, Ichthyosaura, and Melusine

When Freud abandoned his theory of real trauma, the seduction theory, in 1897, he grew convinced that traumatic unconscious memories are condemned to remain forever opaque and that what is allowed to resurface are only *composite structures* composed of elements "which could never have been objects of actual perception." To illustrate this point, Freud invoked the images of "a centaur or a dragon [*Drachen*]" (Freud, 1900, p. 324). In investigating this image he acted as one of those medieval cartographers who inserted in their maps images of dragons and sea serpents to fill the voids of *terra incognita* they drew.

The image of the dragon then resurfaced in Freud's later paper, "The Disposition to Obsessional Neurosis" (Freud, 1913c), in a context closely related to our discussion: he formulated the theory that the choice of the neurosis is independent of the traumatic experience, arising instead from the nature of the individual's disposition. The latter was explained by Freud as a "point of fixation" to which the function may regress if the subject falls ill through some external disturbance.

Referring to the "well-known fact" that women become "quarrelsome, vexatious and overbearing, petty and stingy" when they lose their genital function, Freud made his point referring to the satirists who, in all ages, have directed their invectives against the "old dragon" (*alten Drachen*) into which the charming girl, the loving wife, and the tender mother transform. Since in order to gain their charm, female children must jettison their masculine sexuality, Freud explained the alteration of character as a regression to a masculine libidinal disposition, which had been only temporally overcome. In short, "Old Dragons" are unloving women whose sexuality is not only regressed on the sadistic anal-erotic stage, but also fixated on their imaginary masculine organ – a sort of gigantic snake or dragon, as "satirists" have unconsciously well understood.

Freud did not consider, however, that the transformation of a tender love object into a vexatious dragon might rather be the outcome of misogynistic attacks. The relevance of this objection becomes transparent as soon as related to the object of Freud's first infatuation.

In the summer of 1871, the 15-year-old Freud made his first and only return to his native Freiberg, in Moravia, and immediately fell in love with Gisela Fluss, then aged 11. He was too young and too shy to express his feelings, however, and Freud's infatuation turned into bitter spite. Some six months later she would surface in the correspondence between Freud and Silberstein, taking up the central place in their mythological web with the code name "Ichthyosaura" (fish-lizard).[12] The beauty that he admired was turned into an ugly reptile – a 15-meter-long "aquatic reptile of dinosaurian proportions" (Eissler, 1978, p. 470), which had been reconstructed by paleontologists just a few decades before, and inspired a humorous poem popular in student circles about an "Ichtyosaura" who lets herself be kissed by an Iguanodom.

According to Eissler, this experience had "an almost unique position in his memory" (p. 469). Freud briefly saw Gisela again only once, in 1872. Three years later, in 1875, when Freud was informed (or misinformed) of Gisela's marriage, he wrote a nuptial poem, dedicated to Ichthyosaura's beauty, imagining the bridegroom's disappointment at seeing her on the blissful evening of the wedding night. As Boehlich (1990, p. xx) put it, the "Saurian age" had come to an end. Hostility, debasement, and ridicule was the strategy used to break hold on his affections. Freud's love for Gisela turned into disgust and horror towards women. In Eissler's (1978) view, Gisela's nickname suggests an unconscious fantasy that "women are dangerous monsters, a fear-arousing species whose phallic nature seems obvious" (p. 471).[13]

Reviewing Freud's "Saurian age," Risto Fried (2003, pp. 414–427) concluded that the transformation of love object into attractive monster was a recurrent pattern in Freud's life and work. As a child, the initial moment of his sexual life was marked by his strict "prehistoric" nanny, the prototype of all the disapproving and exciting Dragon Ladies of his dreams. As an adolescent he turned his love into disgust, debasing the tender love object as an ugly reptile, and on the occasion of his secret betrothal with Martha he called her "Melusine," giving her the name of a medieval water nymph, a woman from the navel up, and a serpent or fish from the navel down, like a siren or mermaid. The supposedly surmounted "Saurian age" was not letting go.

The theme of the wedding night was overdetermined: a few weeks before, Freud had been in England, and he got very angry at his father's plan to have him marry Pauline. In his paper, "Screen Memories," written in 1899, at the age of 43, Gisela and Pauline were condensed in the nearly hallucinatory intensity of the memory of the yellow dandelions. The yellow was the color of the dress of Gisela, while the dandelion stemmed from the meadow near Freiberg, where Sigmund, John, and Pauline picked flowers and the two boys knocked Pauline down, "snatching away the little girl's bunch of flowers" (Freud, 1899, p. 310).

The wedding night theme joined forces unconsciously with a Melusine fantasy[14] on the occasion of Freud's secret betrothal with Martha. In the story of Melusine, a popular legend in 14th-century France, Count Raymund finds a beautiful maiden in the woods and falls in love with her. Melusine consents to marry him on the condition that he never tries to see her naked; but he breaks his promise and sees her in the form of a part-woman part-serpent. At this point, she forgives him, but when, during a disagreement with her, he calls her a "serpent" in front of his court, she assumes the form of a dragon and flies off, never to return. In 1801, Goethe wrote a new version of the tale, reflecting the conflict between the individual and the family in the choice of a life partner.[15] The tradition of marriage formation was changing from one of parental arrangement into an individual choice based on love. Goethe was one of the novelists of the time who dramatized the conflict between the individual and the family, including the often tragic consequences of allowing one's passion to determine one's choice.

In Goethe's novel *The New Melusina*, the heroine was neither a serpent nor a mermaid but an insect-size dwarf, living in a small box and able to assume human proportion for limited periods. The story was changed, but the themes of the shocking vision and the broken marriage were retained in inverse form. When the male protagonist breaks his promise, Melusine gives him a wedding ring to shrink him to her size, but when he is unable to adjust himself to the constraints of marriage, he breaks the ring, regains his size, and escapes.

Martha had given Freud a little box – a *Kätschen* – with her portrait, and Freud became obsessed with the idea of a man who carried his beloved in a box. Finally he realized that Goethe's version of the Melusine saga was giving expression to his fears about his betrothal.[16] The detail of the ring proved prophetic: inadvertently Freud was to break the ring Martha had given him as a token of their engagement, not once but twice. "He was to spend the rest of his life denying, with remarkably few lapses, the unhappiness of his marriage" (Fried, 2003, p. 422).[17]

Propionsäure

Dragon Lady, Ichthyosaura, and Melusine form a consistent chain of private metaphors which, in Freud's final meditation, surfaced in the interconnected images of the stranded Loch Ness monster and of the never-extinct dragon. These creatures represent the story of Freud's own libidinal fixation and superstitious beliefs, now embedded in the Saurian code.

The same code informed the magic words of the founding dream of psychoanalysis. The repressed element in the dream of Irma's injection (amyl) was pushed in the direction of a line of signifiers (the preparation of propyl . . . propyls . . . propionic acid) that contributed to the eventual emergence of trimethylamin within the dream. Most of these magic words were decoded in Volume I. Only "propionic acid," in German "*Propionsäure*," remains to be understood. To Erikson (1954), "propionic" hinted at "priapic – phallic" (p. 26). I agree. A more precise survey, however, suggests that "propionic acid," in German, was a composite structure (*Propion-saur*) fabricated on the model of "*Ichthyo-saura*" and based on the replacement of "*Ichthyo*" (fish) with a phallic symbol. By recapitulating in abridged form the story of Freud's libidinal fixation, this replacement illustrates to a remarkable degree that "extraordinary synthetic activity of the ego" advocated by Freud. The same Big Fish and sea serpent resurfaced in Freud's final meditation, first as the Loch Ness monster, and then as the image of the "dragon of primeval days." In "Analysis Terminable and Interminable," Freud then traced back the "erroneous and superstitious beliefs" that persist in spite of civilization, attached to humanity's biological "bedrock" (Freud, 1937a, p. 252). In the same context, Freud evoked Fliess's theory of bisexuality and repression from Nuremberg (p. 251): he was specifically thinking of Emma Eckstein's *recurrent dream of a gigantic snake* and her hallucination at having a penis. The same element stood behind Freud's conclusion regarding "the great riddle of sex." Freud, we know, repeatedly identified and commented on the futility of persuading a woman during analysis "to abandon her wish for a penis . . ." (p. 252).

Exploring the image of the "bedrock" (*gewachsene Fels*, growing or living rock), Jay Geller (2007) found it evocative of Freud's claim, in *Moses and Monotheism*, that circumcision served him once again as a "key-fossil" (*Leitfossil*) (Freud, 1939, p. 39). Linking together "petrified life" and "living rock," Geller was reminded of Jesus in the gospel of John, and of the scene in Exodus of Moses striking water from a rock (*Felsen*) for the thirsting children of Israel, and many other biblical passages. "I am struck," Jay Geller wrote,

> by a chain of signifiers that connect these texts from the Bible to *Interpretation [of Dreams]* to 'Analysis Terminable and Interminable' to *Moses*, and points in between: in particular, "*Fels*" and "*Stück*" (rock and piece) – those traces of remains of castration and circumcision as well as Freud's repressions and disavowals.
>
> (p. 213)

Finally, again noted by Geller, Freud's description of "bedrock" as "the unplumbable point of an analysis, where analyst and analysand can penetrate no further," takes us back "to the navel of Freud's Irma dream" (p. 212). Here it is good to recall that in his reading of the Irma dream, Erikson (1954, p. 35) imagined this unplumbable spot as a petrifying Medusa's head. More precisely, Erikson imagined that while he was peering down into the gaping cavity of Irma's mouth/vagina, Freud stumbled on "a terrifying discovery which stares at him like the head of the Medusa" (p. 35). Glossing this point, Lacan (1954–1955) wrote: "There's a horrendous discovery here, that of the flesh one never sees, the foundation of things" (p. 154).

The foundation of things?

How can we understand this amazing proliferation of fantasies, images, and symbols, all related to the unplumbable "omphalos" of the psychoanalytic building, its corpus?

When I began my research, in 1992, my impression was that Freud had been either directly involved in the psycho-surgical methods of curing hysteria (castration), or traumatized by especially shocking images of genitals in girls who had been "cured" by his colleagues. Only later, did the case history of Emma Eckstein become significant to me. Since in "Analysis Terminable and Interminable," Freud (1937a) stated that her hysteria had "defied many kinds of treatment" (p. 222), I considered the possibility that, after her circumcision, she endured further psycho-surgical treatments. Previously, in Volume I, I advanced the suspicion that Emma Eckstein had endured a castration (removal of ovaries) as a young woman. Sometimes, the thought surfaced in my mind, that one of the "many treatments" she had undergone was the ablation of her clitoris. I resisted this fantasy and it didn't take hold. But now, at the end of this long journey, I have grown increasingly convinced that her clitoris was actually ablated. I cannot say when this occurred, whether as a girl, an adolescent, or a young woman, but in any case, the heuristic power of this final reconstruction is very strong. It explains Emma Eckstein's dreams and hallucinations, which attest to her non-acceptance of castration, and sheds light on many aspects of Freud's reaction, starting with his emotional reaction when she nearly died after the botched operation by Fliess. On March 8, 1895, Freud in fact wrote to Fliess: "I do not believe it was the blood that overwhelmed me – at that moment strong emotions were welling up in me." Likely, up until that moment, Freud had not been affected by her castration – *it was routine, after all* – but now, because of the fright and the repetition entailed in her nasal surgery, Freud was touched deeply, *après coup*, and began to react emotionally through identification, memories, and unconscious fantasies.

This hypothesis is in keeping with Freud's "dishonesty" dream in which "something had been missed," with Freud accused of having "appropriated the missing article" (Freud, 1900, p. 336; Volume I, p. 201). It also fits with the tentative conclusion that the act of self-sacrifice staged in Freud's self-dissection dream might be read as follows: "*What I have taken away from you, i.e. the penis, I am restoring to you.*"

Freud must have been very puzzled by the contrast between the missing clitoris and the intensity of Emma Eckstein's hallucinatory sensation of having a penis. This phantom-penis, which persisted in reappearing in spite of its having been removed, stood at the very center of Freud's speculations in the matter of biology and religion. Even Freud's idea that the broomstick witches ride was the "great Lord Penis," which we have found as a mark of Emma Eckstein's imaginary penis (in Freud's letter to Fliess of January 1897), becomes more intelligible if we can think of it as her lost clitoris. Finally, we can better understand why Freud moved away from common sense and linguistic usage, imagining "castration" as an ablation of the penis, instead of an ablation of the testes. We might speak here of a mimetic reaction, the ablation of the clitoris serving as both imprint and model.

Freud's special sensitivity to "gaps" might stem from the same situation. Emma Eckstein's missing clitoris could have been the somatic model for the idea of a *gap* in the psyche (*psychischer Lücke*), introduced by Freud in his Christmas fairy tale of December 1896. This, in its turn, would help to explain how, in Freud's Signorelli slip, a gap in the memory became a signifier of symbolic castration. It is also striking, in this context, that the first name of the Italian artist, Luca, is a homophone of the German word for gap, "*Lücke.*"[18] The same "Lücke" was inscribed in the "Loch" (hole) of the image of the "Loch Ness monster" proposed by Freud in his Acropolis meditation, attesting to the continuity and deep identification of Freud's "memory disturbance" in both instances. Did psychoanalysis, as a system of equations and replacements, spring ultimately from Freud's capacity to observe his own hallucinatory attempts to fill this horrid empty space in the material body of Emma Eckstein, and, further, from Freud's assumption that this kind of automatic reaction was a universal phenomenon? Certainly he found that his own imagination had "created the same product as the imaginative activities of primitive man, of which myths [such as the Uranus-Kronos myth] and fairy tales are the precipitate" (Freud, 1926b, p. 212) – just to paraphrase what Freud wrote in *The question of lay analysis*.

We have also located a similar attempt to fill the same gap in a series of important dreams, scientific fairy tales, and theoretical fantasies continued within the works of Sándor Ferenczi. I always wondered why, in Ferenczi's dream of the cut-off erect penis served on a saucer, the penis was "small and frail." Was it the lost small penis (clitoris) of Emma Eckstein that Ferenczi saw in his Christmas dream?

Freud's reaction to Ferenczi's views held on many years after Ferenczi's death, prompting him to review his uncanny "memory disturbance." Freud's meditation was still organized around the assumption that traumatic memories cannot be disentangled from fantasies (reactions based on the synthetic activity of the ego), although this assumption was partly reconsidered first in "Constructions in Analysis" (Freud, 1937b) and then in the unfinished note on the "Splitting of the ego in the process of defence" (Freud, 1938b). In the first essay Freud reflected on the analyst's attempt to deal with the patient's destroyed psychic objects by filling the gaps with "constructions" similar to delusions, ultimately owing their power to the element of "historical truth." In the second, unfinished note Freud made the important admission that, in taking "for granted the synthetic nature of the processes of the ego," he was "clearly at fault" (p. 276).

In this delayed attempt to assimilate Ferenczi's notion of the "narcissistic split of the self," Freud acknowledged that the ego could be split in two, and that the rift "never heals" but "increases as time goes on." Freud went on to illustrate the split by sketching a theme which never ceased to torment him: the reaction of a three-year-old boy to a tremendous fright of castration. *The scene was always the same.* In this schematic disquisition, Freud turned once again to the myth of Kronos, which had guided him since the very beginning, and which he had appealed to a number of times. But this time, he was unable to go further.

Notes

1 In 1894 Freud abandoned Janet's notion of "splitting of consciousness," claiming that [the] patients whom he had analyzed showed no "innate weakness" in their capacity for "psychical synthesis" (1894a, p. 46). The topic resurfaced in his American lecture, where Freud (1909) recalled that, according to Janet, "hysteria is a form of degenerate modification of the nervous system, which shows itself in an innate weakness in the power of psychical synthesis. Hysterical patients, he believes, are inherently incapable of holding together the multiplicity of mental processes into a unity, and hence arises the tendency to mental dissociation" (p. 21). Freud's hostility to Janet was so strong that in 1937 he refused to see Janet, when the latter wanted to visit him in Vienna. "Freud explained this inhospitality in a letter to Marie Bonaparte, telling her that he could not forgive Janet for not having disavowed the French authors who accused him of plagiarism" (Lebovici, 1976, p. 134).

2 In his recantation letter of September 21, 1897, Freud gave a fourth motive for abandoning his etiological theory of hysteria: "the consideration that in the most deep-reaching psychosis the unconscious memory does not break through, so that the secret of childhood experiences is not disclosed even in the most confused delirium. If one thus sees that *the unconscious never overcomes the resistance of the conscious*, the expectation that in treatment the opposite is bound to happen, to the point where the unconscious is completely tamed by the conscious, also diminishes" (Masson, 1985, p. 265; emphasis added).

3 It seems, however, that the sightings of the Loch Ness monster became more frequent in the scientific era, after the popularization of the paleontological findings about dinosaurs. Only a year and a half before Freud's essay the first scientific investigation of the monster was undertaken with sonar and divers by a team of 20 conducted by Sir Edward Mountain (Fried, 2003, p.). We can easily imagine how fervently these zealous scientists hoped to find Nessie.

4 According to Solomon (1973), Freud and his brother were both driven by the "the revival of an early fantasy of pederastic sexual satisfaction by the father" (p. 145), a fearful scene of "penetration via pederasty or fellatio," which was close to the surface (p. 152). Solomon, though referring to "fantasies" and "wishes," and not to sexual abuse, is still one of the very few commentators on the Acropolis essay who emphasized that when Freud formulated his seduction theory he was obsessed by the idea that he had been sexually abused by his father, and that by theorizing the Greek myth of Oedipus he got (partially) free from his "pederastic" obsession.

5 In the Acropolis paper Masson and Masson (1977) suggested that the abuser (the Loch Ness monster) was the Catholic nurse. But then, in *The Assault on The Truth* (Masson, 1984), the seduction by the nurse was mentioned only in a footnote. "Masson," wrote Risto Fried (2003), "berates Freud for denying the reality of his patients' accounts of sexual abuse in childhood. Yet when Freud confesses that he himself was just such a 'miserable victim,' Masson takes the role of the overcautious physician . . ." (p. 284).

6 The notion of "disavowal" (*Verleugnung*) had already been used by Freud to describe the loss of a piece of reality in psychosis (1924c) and fetishism (1927a).

7 According to the legend, as fugitive the "*el rey chico*" (the boy king) stood atop a hill, looked back at his beautiful city, and began to weep. It was in that moment that his mother, Queen Ayesha, said: "Weep, weep like a woman for the throne you could not defend like a man, nor like a king." Since she had been the one who had set Boadbill up as a rival against his own father, Risto Fried (2003) remarked: "If ever there was a 'castrating woman,' it was *El Chico*'s mother, Ayesha" (p. 441) – a detail which takes us back to the figure of the "eternal woman" of Freud's favorite novel *She*, whose name also was Ayesha. Indeed, Fried (2003) further speculates that the figure of "She-who-must-be-obeyed" had been actually modeled by Rider Haggard upon the historical figure of Boadbil's mother Ayesha. Whatever it is, we have come once again to "the attraction and repulsion exercised on Freud by a *phallic* woman on whom he remained fixated without regard with the passage of time" (p. 441).

8 Fried didn't know that the day that Freud arrived in Athens, the Acropolis museum was closed. Freud visited it only after his visit to the Acropolis, on September 5, 1904.

9 Freud had assisted Emma Eckstein in the bibliographic research as well as in the composition of the paper, as attested by his letters to Emma of October 11, 1902; March 23, 1903; and April 17, 1904.

10 Freud's long answer, crafted on July 27, 1904, was well balanced. It began with the admission "I see that I have to concede to you more right than I originally was prepared to," and acknowledged that Fliess's "novum" was the step from the bisexual disposition "of some individuals to . . . all of them."

11 Freud (1937a) wrote: "Hypnotic influence seemed to be an excellent instrument for our purposes; but the reasons for our having to abandon it are well known. No substitute for hypnosis has yet been found. From this point of view we can understand how such a master of analysis as Ferenczi came to devote the last years of his life to therapeutic experiments, which, unhappily, proved to be in vain" (p. 230).

12 Freud and Eduard Silberstein attended the same gymnasium. By 1871, when the boys' regular correspondence began, they had already founded the "Spanish Academy," communicating in Spanish with the "academic" names of two dogs, Cipión and Berganza. Sometimes they coined words that do not exist in Spanish, creating funny neologisms from Latin and French words, further disguising their communications from others by

giving them secret names. "Thus they referred to the girls to whom they felt attracted as 'principles,' and developed a private mythology whose beginnings seem to go back to a shared journey from Roznau to Freiberg in the summer of 1871" (Boehlich, 1990, p. xvii). Freud's wedding night poem was included in a letter that he sent to Eduard Silberstein on October 2, 1875.

13 In order to illustrate this point, Eissler recalled that shortly afterwards, Freud spent the Easter holiday of 1876 in the marine laboratory of Trieste, where the 20-year-old student in medicine had been assigned the task of dissecting eels. Here, in Trieste, young Freud was struck by the beauty of Italian women, but to his friend Silberstein, he wrote that since "it is not allowed to dissect human beings," he had "nothing to do with them." In reality, what he was dissecting were eels, namely "descendants of ichthyosauri" (Eissler, 1978, p. 471).

14 Reviewing the Melusine saga in his essay on "Nakedness in saga and poem," Otto Rank (1913) traced the motive for the transformation of the lower half of the body into a serpent to the twofold feeling of fear and desire in regard to the sexual embrace, being evocative on the one hand of the disgust and repulsion felt towards the female genitals at the time of menstruation, and, on the other hand, of the hallucination of the woman's penis.

15 The first German version of the tale was written in 1474 by Thüring von Ringoltingen, in the increasingly misogynistic spirit of the Church and of society at the time. In this version Melusine is called *Minne* (the medieval Aphrodite) and exposed as a disgusting monster, thus validating the husband's suspicions about his wife's trustworthiness and reliability.

16 Freud's letter to Martha, 19 June 1882 (Freud, 1960). See Fried (2003, pp. 419–422), and the excellent exploration of the Melusine phantasy in Freud in Rosenberg (1978). For comments on both Ichtyosaura and Melusine, see Eissler (1978). Abraham (1982), Doria-Medina (1991), and Harrison (1988). A significant feature of Freud's Ichthyosaura fantasy is that the disparaging name with which his object of love was ridiculed, was from time to time abbreviated to "Ichth." or "Ich" (that is "I") (Boehlich, 1990, p. 11).

17 "When Freud proposed to Martha without informing anyone, he was still in revolt against the families that had wanted to plan his life for him. But then came the great disillusionment: with his wife and with his own ability to make life decisions. He must have been terribly unhappy if he habitually fantasised what life would have been like if only he had not so abruptly broken off with Gisela. And he must have been badly shaken in self-esteem when, in addition to conceding that his father and brother meant well, he even thought that the choice they made for him could have been better than his own" (Fried, 2003, p. 423).

18 See Michael Molnar (1994). In particular, Molnar noticed that the missing name was replaced by an ultra-lucid vision of the portrait of Signorelli, and that the artist's look (in his portrait) was "at the same time *eine Lücke 'a gap'* – or *eine Luke 'a hatch'* – in the frame of the representation" (p. 86).

15 Flight into sanity

> Freud's flight to sanity could be something we psychoanalysts are trying to recover from.
>
> D.W. Winnicott (1964, p. 450)

Jones's allegation

Sándor Ferenczi died on May 22, 1933, at the age of 59. He was afflicted with pernicious anemia, which had been first diagnosed in September 1932, a few weeks after the Wiesbaden congress. In his obituary, Ernest Jones (1933) wrote:

> in his still later writings Ferenczi showed unmistakable signs of mental regression in his attitude towards fundamental problems of psycho-analysis. Ferenczi blazed like a comet, but did not shine steadily till the end. In this course he illustrated one of his own most important teachings – the astoundingly close interdependence of mind and body.
>
> (p. 466)

What Jones meant becomes clearer when we examine his correspondence with Freud of that period. As Jones put it, he had followed Ferenczi's "pathological evolution" for years, till the "denouement" occurred. This "denouement" consisted of Ferenczi's conflict with Freud in the days before the Wiesbaden congress, in Ferenczi's pale, sick appearance during the congress, and in his "paranoia," which, according to Jones, became "obvious to all analysts from his . . . paper" (Jones to Freud, September 9, 1932, and June 3, 1933).

Two elements here have to be stressed. First, Jones was convinced of Ferenczi's "mental regression" before, independently of the neurological symptoms that appeared in the last two months of Ferenczi's illness, characteristic of organic brain disease. Second, the belief in Ferenczi's "mental regression" was shared by a group of people, to which Freud belonged as well (see Freud's letter to Jones of May 29, 1933). This belief depended strictly on Ferenczi's conflict with Freud (Roazen, 1975, pp. 363–371), and tended to disappear during the years to follow. Since this belief did not reach the official level of pronouncement, its formal consequences were limited to the withdrawal from publication of the English version of the Wiesbaden paper after Ferenczi's death. However, the treatment of Ferenczi's last contributions remained informal and inaccurate, a kind of *de facto* censure. His final theory and technique were neither studied nor considered critically, either in public discussions or published papers – with the sole exception of Franz Alexander (1933, 1950), who, by the way, would later approach more and more a position closer to Ferenczi's. In the long run this led to a recovery process through the revived publication of his works. A very significant moment was the so-called "Ferenczi issue" of the *International Journal of Psycho-Analysis*, in 1949. In his introduction, Michael Bálint observed that "Psycho-analytical thinking is now beginning to re-examine Ferenczi's ideas" (1949, p. 219). In this issue, the Wiesbaden paper was finally published (under the title "Confusion of tongues between the adult and the child"), without meeting Jones's open opposition.[1] The works on Ferenczi's technique by his pupils – beyond Balint there were Izette de Forest (1942, 1954) and Clara Thompson (1943) – and the ongoing publication of Ferenczi's collected papers in German and in English became part of a progressive rehabilitation, which also included a plan to publishing selected portions of the Freud-Ferenczi correspondence and of Ferenczi's *Clinical Diary* (Balint, 1969; Haynal, 1992). In particular, summarizing Ferenczi's last contributions in the *International Journal of Psychoanalysis*, Izette de Forest (1942) remarked that: "To use the counter-transference as a technical tool, as one uses the transference, dreams, association of ideas, and the behaviour of the patient, seems to many analysts exceedingly dangerous" and presented a detailed account of objections to Ferenczi's technique, which included objections "to the use of counter-transference as a technical instrument; to the analyst's attitude towards the patient's resistance; to the necessity of reliving early traumatic experience; and to the dramatic tone of the process" (p. 136). This progressive rehabilitation coincided with an enlargement of the conception of psycho-analysis, which became immediately apparent in the review of the *Final Contributions* (Ferenczi, 1955) by Margaret Little (1957). Little understood that Ferenczi's final work was confirmed by Winnicott's latest developments. She also observed that Ferenczi "went further than his colleagues in ways they found unacceptable for unconscious reasons" (p. 123).

However, this trend would be counteracted with the arising of another spirit within the psychoanalytic community: reviewing the same volume in the same year, Alexander Bromley insisted that Ferenczi abandoned psychoanalysis "in favour of what might be described as rapport therapy" (1957, p. 113). Such a way to describe Ferenczi's evolution was new, making retrospective use of a new and growing distinction being drawn between psychoanalysis and psychotherapy. The astonishing result was to situate Ferenczi outside of psychoanalysis – something that even for Freud would have been absurd. What was happening? "Exact interpretation" was becoming a battle cry, since psychoanalysis "no longer had a monopoly on dynamic treatment. Consequently, as a profession it had a vested interest in advertising what was superior in its approach" (Friedman, 1978, p. 536).

In the same year, 1957, the third volume of Freud's official biography appeared, in which Jones (1957) explained the third wave of dissension (after that with Adler and Jung), as an effect of the progressive mental deterioration of two members of the Committee that governed the psychoanalytic movement:

> Two of the members, Rank and Ferenczi, were not able to hold out to the end. Rank in a dramatic fashion presently to be described, and Ferenczi more gradually toward the end of his life, developed psychotic manifestations that revealed themselves in, among other ways, a turning away from Freud and his doctrines. The seed of a destructive psychosis, invisible for so long, at last germinated.
>
> (p. 47)

The "heresy" at the center of the crisis of 1924 consisted in the emphasis put by Rank and Ferenczi on experience (*Erlebnis*) in the psychoanalytic situation or, as put by Jones (1957), in "the theory that study of repeating experience could supersede the need for a deeper genetic analysis: that *Erlebnis* therapy could replace psychoanalysis" (p. 77). By reflecting the contemporary "battle cry," the opposition between *Erlebnis* and intellectual analysis transformed a historical burning question into a contemporary issue of self-definition. According to Jones's historical reconstruction, the crisis of 1924 ended two years later with Rank's mental troubles and defection (p. 81), while Ferenczi's mental troubles became apparent later when, after the disappointment for not having been made president, he withdrew from the concerns of the International Association and "began to develop lines of his own which seriously diverged from those generally accepted in psycho-analytical circles" (p. 156). Jones declared that Ferenczi had "delusions about Freud's supposed hostility" (p. 190), that his illness "exacerbated his latent psychotic trends" (p. 188), that "the mental disturbances had been making rapid progress in the last few months" (p. 190), finally culminating in "violent paranoic and even homicidal outbursts, which were followed by a sudden death" (Jones, 1957).

Reactions

Ernest Jones's allegations about the mental troubles of both Rank and Ferenczi were accepted without scrutiny.

On October 13, 1957 Lionel Trilling's review of *Freud, Volume III* was published by *The New York Times Book Review*, which exaggerated Jones's allegations even further. In November an article by Morton M. Hunt titled "How the analyst stands the pace" appeared in the Sunday Section of *The New York Times*, which reported Jones's statement that Ferenczi died after having developed a severe psychosis. Marjorie Brierley then reviewed the third volume of the Freud biography in the *International Journal of Psychoanalysis*, mentioning the "stories of Rank and Ferenczi" in a way that implied a total belief in Jones's assertions. She also stressed Freud's openness to criticism while reproaching him for having tolerated such persons (Brierley, 1958, p. 423). Only a few protested. However, since they were pupils, relatives, or friends of Rank or Ferenczi, they were quickly identified with "partisans" of the "dissidents Rank and Ferenczi," thus divesting their voices of value.[2]

On October 22, 1957, Izette de Forest sent two recent reviews of Jones's *Volume III* to Erich Fromm, pointing out the inconsistencies of Jones's assertions, and inviting him to write a criticism of Jones's fallacy.

De Forest was in analysis with Ferenczi in 1925–27 and again in 1929, during the period when "he was becoming acutely aware of his dissatisfaction with some of the crucial aspects of the Freudian approach," as she wrote in the introduction of *The Leaven of Love* (1954, p. xi), a book dedicated to the theory and technique of Sándor Ferenczi. In his review of the book, Jones (1956) claimed that by presenting Freud's attitude as hostile to Ferenczi, de Forest had given a false report, based on "her extraordinary view of Freud's imagined hostility" (p. 488). In *Freud, Volume III*, Jones (1957) then spoke of the "myth of Freud's ill-treatment of Ferenczi" sustained by Ferenczi's former pupils, in particular Izette de Forest and Clara Thompson, further insinuating that the myth was created by Ferenczi himself in his "final delusional state" (p. 188). De Forest's voice was crushed by Ernest Jones not as an individual but in his institutional role. Jones was president of the International Psychoanalytic Association (IPA) in 1920, 1922, 1932, 1934, 1936, 1938, and held the post till 1949, when he was appointed honorary president for life. He was the highest authority of the IPA.

After the death of Ferenczi, Izette de Forest became a pupil of Erich Fromm and considered Fromm's theory of the development of the patient's integrity of personality a continuation of the teaching of Ferenczi. When she was so heavily attacked by Jones, she appealed for help from Fromm, who was at that time collecting the material for his book *Sigmund Freud's Mission* (1959). De Forest was already providing him with information about Freud's life, since through her cousin Dorothy Burlingham she had been part of the intimate circle of Professor Freud and his daughter Anna. Fromm, who never had the opportunity of meeting Freud, was searching de Forest's memories for a confirmation of his hypothesis about Freud's having transferred on to his pupils his dependence on his mother, thus experiencing signs of independence from his closest pupils as a traumatic abandonment and a betrayal.

Fromm met Ferenczi several times in Baden Baden, at Groddeck's sanatorium, and was very impressed by him, even shocked. In a letter of July 20, 1979, addressed to Paul Roazen, he reported:

> What I meant to tell you is a scene in which Groddeck, in his masterful and outspoken way, criticised the official psychoanalytic organisation and its training program and tore it to shreds. I was then a young analyst believing in the authority of Freud and the analytic hierarchy, and I remember my shock and surprise to hear all this blasphemy remaining unanswered by Ferenczi. He sat there, listened, and as far as I remember, did not say a single word.

In later years, Fromm would modify his attitude towards the analytic hierarchy. As a consequence of his many disappointments, among which his exclusion from the IPA, he began to wish for the creation of a non-bureaucratic psychoanalytic organization in which moral integrity could coexist with intellectual courage.[3]

When Erich Fromm received de Forest's invitation to react to Jones's allegations, he was already taking steps to move in this direction and, on October 31, 1957, replied to her: "I had the same idea, and I have asked *The Saturday Review* whether they would publish it. I think the point you make is very well taken, and should be mentioned." He then wrote:

> I believe the main point is the typically Stalinist type of re-writing history, whereby Stalinists assassinate the character of opponents by calling them spies and traitors. The Freudians do it by calling them "insane." I think even Freud would not have approved of this vicious treatment, and incidentally, Jones does not seem to be aware of the disservice he does to psychoanalysis. The picture he gives of the Secret Committee is, then, that two members, and the most trusted ones, became insane. Of one, Dr. Sachs, he says that Freud said he should not have belonged in the first place. Of Eitingon he says that he was not too bright. There remain Abraham and Jones, who were, according to Jones' own testimony, constantly engaged in the pettiest quarrels with all the other members. A beautiful picture of the group of those who claim to represent the sanity which follows from psychoanalysis!

With the assistance of Izette de Forest, Fromm led an independent inquiry and collected various statements about Ferenczi's mental state by witnesses of his last period of life, all contradicting Jones's assertions.[1] The witnesses were the members of Ferenczi's family who assisted him till his last days (Elma Laurvik, Ferenczi's step-daughter, and Sophie Erdös, Ferenczi's sister), and patients who remained in analysis with Ferenczi till two or three months before his death (Clara Thompson, Alice Lowell, and Elizabeth Severn). Especially important is Thompson's testimony, because she was a physician and visited Ferenczi till his death. The following passage is taken from her long report:

> I went to visit him regularly and we talked, naturally not about deep or disturbing subjects, although he really tried to prepare me for the fact that he was dying. It was I who wouldn't face it . . .
>
> What I believe is that in the last two months of his life there was some organic mental deterioration. That is, he showed memory defects and forgetfulness characteristic of organic brain disease, but I think it was minimal and a part of the death picture. To try to push it back into preceding years and explain his thinking by this is to say the least – criminal. I think he was a disturbed man and some of his procedures could be criticized, but I do not believe they were evidence of psychosis. . . . Certainly he was never maniacal and homicidal. To call his belief that Freud was treating him badly, paranoid, is obviously to deny the facts.

Based on this evidence, and pointing out that Jones didn't "claim any first-hand knowledge nor is any proof or evidence whatsoever offered of Ferenczi's psychosis," Fromm (1958, p. 13) came to the conclusion that "Jones's assertions . . . must be judged to be untrue" (p. 55). Ultimately, according to Fromm, the treatment of Rank and Ferenczi in Jones's work was an expression of a party-line spirit, which manifested itself not only in the "grotesque, posthumous attacks against men who disagreed with Freud," but also in the fact that "many reviewers of Jones's book have accepted his data without criticism or question" (p. 11). Thus, this specific question was essentially coupled with the more compelling general question: "how was it possible that psychoanalysis, a theory and a therapy, could be transformed into this kind of fanatical movement?" (p. 55).

This question was at the heart of *Sigmund Freud's Mission*, in which Freud's relationship to Ferenczi – his "most loyal, unpretentious pupil and friend" – was presented as "The most drastic example of Freud's intolerance and authoritarianism" (Fromm, 1959, Chapter VI, Freud's authoritarianism). This – intolerance and authoritarianism – was responsible for killing the radical, non-conformist, revolutionary energy of early psychoanalysis. Like religion, psychoanalysis disintegrated from its beginnings as a living system into a dead ideology, a bureaucratic system administered through rituals by priests rather than prophets (see also Braune, 2014). Fromm (1959) accused psychoanalysis of having become "the substitute for radical philosophical and political interests, a new creed which demanded little from its adherents except learning the nomenclature" (p. 56). In short, for Fromm, psychoanalysis was now governed by a sterile bureaucracy, occupied in petty intrigues and machinations, which had inherited little of Freud's greatness and of his real radicalism. Thus, the "official" myth about Ferenczi and Rank was functional to this kind of bureaucratic leadership because it served "to eliminate the only two productive and imaginative disciples among the original group" after Adler's and Jung's defections.

Fromm's (1958) article, originally titled "Psychoanalysis – science or party line?" was published in *The Saturday Review* of June 14, 1958 under the editorial title "Freud, friends, and feuds. 1. Scientism or fanaticism?" together with Jacob's Arlow's reply, "Freud, friends, and feuds. 2. Truth or motivations? Towards a definition of psychoanalysis." Arlow (1958) strongly objected to the idea that Jones's assertions about Rank and Ferenczi were the expression of a "party line," because psychoanalysis couldn't be compared to "a movement which promulgates a rigid policy line," and because it was ludicrous to regard Jones as the enunciator of a dominant party line (p. 14). Moreover, according to Arlow,

> The technical innovations which Ferenczi introduced in keeping with his theory about unloving parents went beyond psychoanalytic concepts. Ferenczi did give his patients more than interpretations. He sat them on his lap and caressed them. This may be effective therapy – but it is not psychoanalysis.
>
> (p. 14)

"The trustworthy evidence of an eye-witness"

Although Fromm succeeded in collecting many testimonies, he failed to reach the most important ones: Michael Bálint and Lajos Lévy, Ferenczi's literary executor and his physician. Different from colleagues living in America, Levy and Bálint were

Hungarian Jews living in England after the Nazi era, the war, and the invasion of Hungary. They depended very much for their living on their good relations with the psychoanalytic establishment in England. In a letter to Elma Laurvik of November 13, 1957, Bálint had written that his and Lévy's intention was to write a joint letter to the editor of the *International Journal of Psychoanalysis* to express their criticism of Jones's assertions. The letter (Balint, 1958, p. 66) appeared together with Jones's reply, in which it was claimed that what he "wrote about Ferenczi's last days was based on the trustworthy evidence of an eye-witness" (Jones, 1958, p. 66). For unknown reasons, the letter was not co-signed by Lajos Lévy. Since this silence fit with Jones's assertion of an anonymous eyewitness, Lévy was suspected to be the secret proof claimed by Jones (letter of Izette de Forest to Erich Fromm of May 25, 1958).

Jones died in February 1958. In June, Fromm's article was published along with a reply by Jacob Arlow, in which it was acknowledged that Jones's claims about Rank and Ferenczi were "weighty ones" and that, "if proven unjustified, would constitute grievous errors" (Arlow, 1958, p. 14). Shortly thereafter, Anna Freud addressed the question to Lajos Lévy, probably exploring the possibility of writing a reply (obviously not in first person) to Erich Fromm's article. Finally, in October, Lévy made a detailed report and addressed it to Robert Wälder, who was very close to Anna Freud. Lévy stated that, before the onset of pernicious anemia, Ferenczi never displayed any trace of paranoid manifestations. A few weeks after the Wiesbaden congress the diagnosis of pernicious anemia was made by Lévy himself. With currently available treatment, there was every possibility that Ferenczi would rapidly recover. However, in March 1933, the symptoms of funicular myelitis began to spread rapidly. Walking disorders, ataxia of the upper limbs, sight disorders, and incontinence appeared, and these symptoms were followed by relational and persecutory delusions ("*Beziehungs- und Verfolgungswahnvorstellungen*"), which also resulted in aggression directed toward his wife. He died of respiratory paralysis. Lévy explained that paranoiac manifestations are frequent in severe anemia at this point, and had to be carefully distinguished from paranoia proper. In his medical opinion, Ferenczi did not have a predisposition to paranoia.

On October 20, 1958, Anna Freud wrote to Lajos Lévy saying that she had been very impressed by his report and regretted the fact that Jones had not consulted him before writing the biography.

Conclusions about Jones's allegation

None of these documents support Jones's allegation of Ferenczi's insanity. At the same time, they show that Jones's allegation was not a solitary fabrication, but reflected a shared belief that originated and spread in two phases. In the first phase, the main elements making such a belief possible were Ferenczi's previous collaboration with Rank (who became a dissident and was banished), his growing isolation and alienation from Freud, the theoretical and technical divergences from Freud, and finally Ferenczi's refusal of the IPA presidency, which Freud offered him as a "forcible cure," a pressured identification with the common cause.

The second phase of pathologizing Ferenczi was characterized by the shift of the belief to a formal level and its spread within the psychoanalytic mainstream.

The vehicle was Volume III of Jones's biography of Freud, in which this latest arising of "the evil spirit of dissension" was discussed in the chapter "Disunion." It is likely that reading the various correspondences in preparation for the biography reactivated Jones's old envy and jealousy of Ferenczi. However, the myth of Ferenczi's insanity cannot be explained solely on the basis of Jones's individual psychology. The lack of scrutiny with which this myth was accepted by reviewers, its rapid spread, as well as its persistence, indicate that it performed some unconscious function within the psychoanalytic community.

My decades-long immersion in psychoanalytic research persuades me that the myth was functional to the "union" of this community, i.e. to the moral definition of its boundaries and obligations. After Freud's death, a test of doctrinal loyalty became increasingly important for identifying one's respect for and dedication to the psychoanalytic cause. Moreover, Ferenczi's emphasis on the analyst as a real person was incompatible with the strict conception of psychoanalysis, based on the theoretical rejection of affective factors, which was becoming dominant in those years. This conceptualization created a protection from analysts' fear of remaining "captives of their patient's emotional structures," "embroiled in their patient's affective net" (Friedman, 1978, p. 538). As pointed out by Friedman, the analysts "wanted to be above it, looking at it. If they were caught inside it, they thought both patient and analyst would be thrown together in a position designed by the patient's neurosis" (p. 538). In 1964 Winnicott stated that "Freud's flight to sanity could be something we psycho-analysts are trying to recover from" (p. 450). Now, if we call recoiling from being caught in the patient's neurosis a "flight into sanity," the narrative of Ferenczi's "insanity" becomes visible as its mirror image. The narrative arc of Ferenczi's case history, tragically ended in isolation, mental deterioration, self-destruction, and blame, represented an admonition and had normative value: "see what happens if you let yourself enter into a relationship with your neurotic (or even psychotic) patients!"

The freedom of dissidents from this kind of boundary might explain why it was possible for them to protest Jones's false allegations. Gratitude is owed to Izette de Forest and Erich Fromm for collecting the documents which allow a validity-check of Jones's assertions in those years, all in an effort to bear witness, restore an piece of truth, and preserve a humanistic, non-authoritarian idea of psychoanalysis.

The story of Anna Freud shows that, even at the center of psychoanalytic orthodoxy, it was possible to ascertain the validity of Jones's assertions. Thanks to the report of Lajos Lévy, Anna Freud came to the conclusion that Jones's allegation was false. Yet even she did not do anything to modify the impression created by Jones. Why? Perhaps admitting such a serious error in relation to the person of Ferenczi would have inevitably led to re-open the question of Rank as well, i.e. the re-opening of a chapter in the history of the psychoanalytic movement which was, if possible, even more miserable than was currently known. And since Jones's assertions about the insanity of Rank and Ferenczi were not limited to their private life, but were synchronized with the story of the Secret Committee, the crisis of 1924, and the verdict about their theoretical positions and technical innovations, the admission that Jones's allegations were false would have fueled criticism on the dogmatic aspects of mainstream psychoanalysis, destroying the credibility of large portions of Freud's official biography. Thus, Anna Freud could easily have come to the conclusion that preservation of the credibility of the whole deserved the sacrifice of the part. But this choice represents, clearly and precisely, an expression of totalitarianism, a further confirmation that the analysis made by Fromm was basically correct.

As a consequence, the rehabilitation of Ferenczi promoted by Balint was held back for nearly three decades. The publication of Ferenczi's *Clinical Diary*, as well as of the Freud-Ferenczi correspondence, was postponed continuously, becoming possible only in 1985 – a year that represents the beginning of new interest in Ferenczi, as reflected in the increased number of articles devoted to his work. Such interest has been facilitated by the decline of formal and dogmatic definitions of psychoanalysis, the overcoming of authoritarian (one-sided) modes of interaction, new respect for the phenomena explored by Ferenczi such as trauma, psychic pain, countertransference, regression, and mutuality. The myth of Ferenczi's insanity did not gain traction in this new climate, and has tended to disappear with the same indifference and lack of scrutiny that accompanied its onset.

We should finally wonder why Ferenczi was experienced as dangerous, when he had no intention of founding an alternative psychoanalysis, had no interest in power, and as a man was defenseless and extremely vulnerable. My research supports that it was Ferenczi's critical attitude toward the psychological process of identification, which was experienced as a threat by the members of a group functioning primarily on the basis of identification. In spite of his lifelong commitment to the psychoanalytic movement, Ferenczi kept a part of his personality separate from "blind belief" in the cause; this was the part that corresponded to his social role of "*enfant terrible*" and his private vocation of "wise baby." His refusal to use the technical language of psychoanalysis and his preference for everyday language communicated his skepticism for the ritualized means of identification that keep a group together. Moreover, large parts of his theory were based on the conception of the super-ego as a more or less traumatic "intropression" of an alien will, and he carefully avoided basing his technique on an identification with the analyst. Even his restless experimentation, the ups and downs, the forcefully pushing everything beyond limits, show a lack of the compliancy and accommodation which is commonly associated with identification (as well as with sanity). Identification is a protective device, and Ferenczi was refusing it. *The Clinical Diary* offers a glimpse into a world as it would look if devoid of this protective device, as well as into Ferenczi's own dissolution when, by refusing the benevolent protection of Freud's idealized imago, he decided to enter it.

However, none of this is the real point. The real point is that Ferenczi's personality, discoveries, and teachings were in contrast with, and made ridiculous, the mimesis required to sustain a psychoanalytic community that had become a bureaucracy intent on securing its own survival.

Bearing witness

Reading the many testimonies of the group of persons who were close to Ferenczi when he was sick and dying, I am moved by what these people, mostly humble, without homeland or voice, were trying to do: bear witness.

What is the meaning of bearing witness? Is this relevant to psychoanalysis or not? According to Clara Mucci (2015), psychoanalysis is itself a practice of testimony, since what Freud did since the beginning was "being a witness" to the story of the patients. The refusal to be silent, the commitment to perform and receive testimony, in ourselves, and outside, in our practice, in the community, and in society at large, is the present tense of testimony: "Testimony resides in the ethical necessity to speak and restore memory and truth in the individual and in society." In her view the psychoanalytic community needs to become a "testimonial community," an expression used by Dori Laub in his work on the *Shoah* and the survivors. In his seminal article, "From Speechless to Narrative," Laub (2005) says that what he realized

> was that the breaking of the silence, the lifting of the muteness, that had begun with the arrival of a fully present and committed listener had, in fact, allowed memory, and with it, narrative, to flow again. What is needed for healing is the creation of a testimonial community.
>
> (p. 264).

While President of the International Psychoanalytical Association, Horacio Etchegoyen made an important step in this direction: in the introduction to the Roster for 1996/7, he amended the list of presidents, reintroducing the name of Sándor Ferenczi. Certainly this act of reparation is laudable, but it is not sufficient to repair the damages or to initiate a process of transformation of the psychoanalytic community into a "testimonial community."

Testimony, noted Dori Laub (2014) in another work, "is a meeting place for the mutual witnessing and repair of trauma-induced fragmented memories and psychic disruption" (p. 195). Laub (1992) himself outlined a convergence between testimony and psychoanalysis, in that both are dialogic and reparative processes driven by an internal pressure to transmit and tell, which needs the presence of a listener. Ultimately, the disagreement between Ferenczi and Freud concerned the manner, the meaning, and the implication of listening.

After an initial period of his own over-involvement, Freud stepped back from participation, and adopted, or recommended, an attitude which he called "*Indifferenz*" – "neutrality" in Strachey's translation. If we place this recommendation in historical context, comparing it, for instance, to the conclusion of Freud's teacher in pediatrics, Baginsky, in 1909 that "to the really experienced connoisseur of the child the testimonies of the child before the court are nothing [*null und nichtig*], completely worthless and without meaning" (see Chapter 1), there is no doubt that "indifference" is less harmful: the child, or the traumatized patient, is at least allowed to speak and to have a voice. This itself was an extraordinary achievement. Yet Ferenczi discovered that it was not enough, because once the child/patient is allowed to have a voice, the drama, pain, and erasures are consigned to a listener who cannot, in turn, close the eyes. Without connectedness (Mucci, 2013), embodied empathy, and commitment the listening is only a "restrained coolness" and "professional hypocrisy," which is "not essentially different from that which in childhood had led to the illness," as Ferenczi says in the "Confusion of tongues" (1933, p. 159). The participating listener becomes a keeper of the traumatic pain and the testimony. The unbearable traumatic pain is transmitted from one person to the other. Differently from a repetition compulsion, by which erasures are perpetuated, the meaning of the transmission is reversed in mutual witnessing, and the process becomes potentially reparative. As Clara Mucci (2016) says, "by taking into ourselves the pain of the other we enable him/her to recover those parts that appear to have been erased." Isn't this the ultimate point of friction between Freud and Ferenczi?

Idealization or identification with the aggressor?

Reading and writing are also ways to bear witness. Reading *The Clinical Diary* can be a shocking experience; it was for me. The pages on Freud were especially shocking. At first I simply was unable to stand their disruptive power and stepped back to focus on other themes. Only now do I recognize that my scrupulous efforts to collect and to review all possible documents related to Jones's allegations of Ferenczi's insanity was a way to circumnavigate this disruptive question and to approach it from afar. Even though Ferenczi's *Clinical Diary* elicits increasing interest in the psychoanalytic community, what Ferenczi wrote about Freud remained insufficiently discussed and metabolized – for example, that Freud was determined "to be healthy" and not admit any "weaknesses or abnormalities"; Freud's remark that "Patients are a rabble . . . We cannot certainly help them"; and Ferenczi's conclusion that Freud was "the only one who does not have to be analyzed" (Dupont, 1985, pp. 62, 93, 188).[5]

According to Edgard Levenson (1992) the "devaluation of the patient's experience," so clearly expressed in these words, was inherited from the medical roots of psychoanalysis:

> Psychoanalysis, based on a nineteenth century medical model and having its roots in the hypnotic phenomena of submission and suggestion has always carried a thinly masked disdain for the "patient," defined etymologically as "the suffering one." . . . This long-standing and deeply imbedded tacit denigration of the patient qua patient had a number of profound implications . . . .
> (pp. 555–556)

Structurally connected to the disparagement of the patient is the idea that analysts have "superior mental health" (Fromm, 1947; Sullivan, 1940). Racker (1968) called this nodal point the "myth" that "analysis is an interaction between a sick person and a healthy one" (p. 132). Ferenczi was an aching flank in this myth, which, according to Racker, was the residue of the analyst's unresolved idealizing transference to his own analyst.

In this respect, the ease with which Jones's allegation was believed was fueled by a diffuse desire to preserve this very kind of idealizing transference. While working with Jones's allegations, I felt the need to contact the reviewers of Jones's who were still alive. In particular, Jacob Arlow (1958) and Robert Holt (1958), who had cast doubts on Fromm's criticism of Jones's allegation, asking them how they now considered their views of 40 years ago. Holt sent me the following comment on his review: ". . . at that time, I was quite credulous, still under the influence of my Freud-idolising friends and teachers, and ready to believe a large part of what I now recognise as hagiographic myth" (letter of April 8, 1996). Arlow admitted that he had long since been convinced that Jones's characterization of Ferenczi's mental state was "completely wrong" (letter of February 12, 1998). As regards Fromm's (1958) characterization of a "party line," he wrote:

> I would say that it was too broad a sweep, although the spirit was essentially correct. There was indeed a group of vehement partisans surrounding Freud who would brook no criticism or deviation. . . . As a matter of fact . . . I, too, was a target of that group. As a result, I came to appreciate how the attitude towards psychoanalytic 'heretics' was more than a simple matter of differences of theory that seemingly was indoctrinated in the teaching.

In his view this attitude was "an outcome of the nature of the psychoanalytic program, particularly the effects of the personal analysis." According to Arlow the essential point was that "an aura of omnipotence and omniscience surrounds the image of the training analyst," which "readily lends itself to confusion with an archaic ego ideal, or as the locus for projection of infantile illusions of grandeur." Since "beyond the training analyst, of course, was the image of Sigmund Freud," Arlow reaches a position similar to the one expressed by Holt. Ultimately, the suppression of a critical attitude was the result of a shared need to idealize and idolize Freud.

In his unsurpassed criticism of the psychoanalytic training system, Michael Balint (1948) pointed out its striking similarity with primitive initiation rites, whose general aim "is to force the candidate to identify himself with his initiator, to introject the initiator and his ideals, and to build up from these identifications a strong super-ego which will influence him all his life," along with a "surprising discovery." In contrast to a wish that candidates develop "a strong critical ego, capable of bearing considerable strains," this institutional behavior leads "to a weakening of these ego functions and to the formation and strengthening of a special kind of super-ego" (p. 167). Dogmatisms, division in factions, and cases of "abrupt conversions, changing a Saul into a Paul" (Balint, 1948) are all consequences of this unresolved transference. Luckily there still are "a certain number of people who arrive at becoming analysts despite and against everything," as further noted by Judith Dupont (2015, p. 75).

Epilogue

I also asked Robert Wallerstein and James Grotstein for their opinions since they had been especially active in fostering a re-integration of Ferenczi's line of thought. Wallerstein, who in the meantime had had to "totally revise" his perspective, simply said that he "had no reason then to disbelieve Jones's allegations about Ferenczi's mental status" (letter of June 29, 1998), while Grotstein wrote in his idiomatic style (letter of July 26, 1998):

> At century's end Ferenczi is rapidly reachiving the illustrious reputation, fame and acceptance that so long eluded him thanks to the apparent treachery of the psychoanalytic establishment. I have always regretted that Adler, Rank, and Jung were forcefully ostracized from the psychoanalytic movement, then Ferenczi. I suppose it is the need to protect the holy sepulcher of the innocent patient qua Christ, which sets up an atmosphere in which infidels must be located. Hitler, we must remember, was very good at uniting Germany by choosing the Jews as his scapegoat.

This comment moves the scene beyond the tendency to idealize and idolize. It takes us back to the "soul murder" (again a wording introduced by the "paranoiac Schreber"), whose humanness has been violated, and who, like the innocent "sacrificial lamb," must suffer the sins of others for their redemption and salvation (Grotstein, 1997). Grotstein found that the image of the crucified Christ played a key role in the transference/countertransference neurosis/psychosis of adult survivors of child abuse and trauma and, more generally, in one person's transfer of mental pain attached to a significant object in the past to another person in the present. A similar religious theme was active in Freud in the years when the foundation of the psychoanalytic building was laid. Psychoanalysis itself took shape as a container of this unresolved transference, which these two volumes of *The Cut* have been dedicated to detailing, articulating, deconstructing, and assimilating, as far as possible.

Freud's project aimed to dissolve this transference by replacing religion with science, in the tradition of the Enlightenment. This specific plan clearly failed. The outcome of these two volumes, beyond documenting that failure, proposes a reformulation of Freud's project with ethics instead of science, invoking Clara Mucci's view of testimony as an ethical necessity to speak and restore memory and truth in the individual and in society. Such a reformulation could transform the psychoanalytic community into a "testimonial community." Mucci (2016) illustrated this point by reading the heritage of Ferenczi through Elie Wiesel's answer to the question about the meaning of the sentence, "Am I my brother's keeper?" In an interview with Richard Heffner, Wiesel responded that the key element is *to be responsible*. In Mucci's understanding, psychoanalysis serves to be the witness of the patient's suffering and pain, the testimony of a truth that has been erased and that can be retrieved and reconstructed only in the presence and with the assistance of a benevolent other.

Notes

1 In the same issue was published Winnicott's paper, "Hate in the counter-transference," a Ferenczian echo if there ever was one.
2 When Trilling's review appeared, Virginia P. Robinson, who had an important position at the Pennsylvania School of Social Work at the time when Rank lectured at the faculty (from 1926 to 1937), immediately wrote to *The New York Times Book Review*, protesting against the reviewer's statements that Rank and Ferenczi "were involved with mental

pathology and issued in sordid tragedy" and that the two men "fell prey to extreme mental illness and they died insane." The letter was partly published on November 17, 1957, jointly with Trilling's recantation about Rank, which however "could not even begin to offset the damage done in his review" (Lieberman, 1985, p. 400). Rank continued to be depicted as insane in many psychoanalytic books till the 1980s, so that "considering the duration and extent of the attack on Rank, it stands out among examples of psychoanalytic character assassination" (Lieberman, 1985, p. xliii). Clara Thompson reacted to Hunt's article by sending a letter of protest to *The New York Times* on November 26, in which she wrote: "I was living in Budapest at the time of Ferenczi's last illness, and I saw him almost every day until his death, I can assure you that he never showed any behavior that could be called insane, aside from very occasional slight confusion, which is usually seen in desperately sick people."

3 As Fromm wrote to Clara Thompson on April 12, 1956: "It is only to a certain extent that theoretical creativeness is the result of talent. To quite a large extent it is a matter of character, of courage and of integrity, of being able to see things clearly and to penetrate the surface of public opinion and common sense" (Fromm Archives). Fromm (1965) praised "Groddeck's fierce sense of independence and his aversion to a bureaucratically-controlled science. Just as Groddeck was a rebel in the field of conventional medicine, he was also a rebel against any attempt to make psychoanalysis a movement controlled by an official bureaucracy" (p. 84). After the forced resignation of the Jewish members from the German Psychoanalytic Society, Fromm had become a member-at-large of the International Psychoanalytical Association. However, in 1953 he discovered that he had been excluded from the IPA (Roazen, 2001). On his role in the creation of the International Federation of Psychoanalytic Societies (IFPS) see Bonomi (2005) and Funk (2000).

4 The testimonies can be found in partial form in "Flight into sanity," in the *International Journal of Psychoanalysis* (Bonomi, 1999).

5 In another passage, titled *Doctor hating patients*, Ferenczi wrote: "Freud: 'rabble,' 'only good for making money out of, and for studying.' (Is true, but must be admitted to the patients)" (p. 118). Commenting on this passage, Peter Rudnytsky (1998) wrote: "From the debacle of his relationship with Freud, as well as his own setbacks as an analyst, Ferenczi learned two vital lessons. The first is the need for utter honesty with patients and a detestation of posturing of any sort. . . . The second lesson is that intellectual honesty is not enough, and can even be a species of brutality, if it is not leavened by love" (pp. 356–357).

Bibliographic references

Abraham, K. (1907a). On the significance of sexual trauma in childhood for the symptomatology of dementia praecox. In *Clinical Papers and Essays on Psycho-Analysis*. New York: Basic Books, 1955, pp. 13–20.
Abraham, K. (1907b). The experiencing of sexual traumas as a form of sexual activity. In *Selected Papers of Karl Abraham*. New York: Brunner/Mazel, 1979, pp. 47–63.
Abraham, K. (1912). Amenhotep IV: Psycho-analytical contribution towards the understanding of his personality and of the monotheistic cult of Aton. In *Clinical Papers and Essays on Psychoanalysis*. London: Hogarth Press, 1955, pp. 26–90.
Abraham, K. (1922). Manifestations of the female castration complex. *International Journal of Psycho-Analysis*, *3*: 1–29.
Abraham, N. (1962). Presentation de "Thalassa" (Presentation of "Thalassa"). In *L'Ecorce et le Noyau*, Paris:Aubier Flammarion, 1978, pp. 1–4.
Abraham, R. (1982). Freud's mother conflict and the formulation of the Oedipal father. *Psychoanalytic Review*, *69*: 441–453.
Ahbel-Rappe, K. (2006). "I no longer believe": Did Freud abandon the seduction theory? *Journal of the American Psychoanalytic Association*, *54*: 171–199.
Alexander, F. (1925). Review of Entwicklungsziele der Psychoanalyse. *International Journal of Psycho-Analysis*, *6*: 484–496.
Alexander, F. (1933). On Ferenczi's relaxation principle. *International Journal of Psycho-Analysis*, *14*: 183–192.
Alexander, F. (1950). Analysis of the therapeutic factors in psychoanalytic treatment. *Psychoanalytic Quarterly*, *19*: 482–500.
Alexander, F., & French, T. M. (1946). *Psychoanalytic Therapy: Principles and Application*. New York: The Ronald Press Company.
Anspaugh, K. (1995). Repression or suppression? Freud's interpretation of the dream of Irma's injection. *The Psychoanalytic Review*, *82*: 427–442.
Anzieu, D. (1975). L'auto-analyse de Freud et la découverte de la psychoanalyse. Paris: PUF.
Anzieu, D. (1986). *Freud's Self-Analysis*. New York: International Universities Press.
Appignanesi, L., & Forrester, J. (1992). *Freud's Women*. London: Virago Press.
Ariés, Ph. (1960). *L'enfant et la vie familiale sous l'ancien régime*. Paris: Pion (Centuries of Childhood: A Social History of Family Life. New York: Random House, 1962).
Arlow, J. A. (1958). Freud, friends, and feuds: 2. Truth or motivations? Toward a definition of psychoanalysis. *The Saturday Review*, June 14, 1958, pp. 14, 54.
Arlow, J. (1972), Some dilemmas in psychoanalytic education. *Journal of the American Psychoanalytic Association, 20*: 55[1-9]–[1-9]66.

Aron, L., & Harris, A. (1993). Sándor Ferenczi: Discovery and rediscovery. In L. Aron & A. Harris, *The Legacy of Sándor Ferenczi*. Hillsdale, NJ and London: The Analytic Press, pp. 1–35.

Aron, L., & Starr, K. (2015). Freud and Ferenczi: Wandering Jews in Palermo. In A. Harris & S. Kuchuck (eds.), *The Legacy of Sándor Ferenczi: From Ghost to Ancestor*. (Relational Perspectives Book Series). London: Routledge, 2015, pp. 150–167.

Baginsky, A. (1901). Über Suggestion bei Kindern. *Zeitschrift für Pädagogische Psychologie und Pathologie*, *3* (1): 96–103.

Baginsky, A. (1909). Die Impressionabilität der Kinder unter dem Einfluss des Milieus. *Beiträge zur Kinderforshung und Heilerziehung*, *27*: 5–21.

Baginsky, A. (1910). Die Kinderaussage vor Gericht. Vortrag gehalten in der Vereinigung der Richter in Berlin. Berlin: J. Guttentag, Verlagbuchhandlung.

Baldwin, J. M. (1899). *The Story of the Mind*. London: George Newnes.

Balint, M. (1948). On the psycho-analytic training system. *International Journal of Psycho-Analysis*, *29*: 163–173.

Balint, M. (1949). Sándor Ferenczi, Obit 1933. *International Journal of Psycho-Analysis*, *30*: 215–219.

Balint, M. (1950). Changing therapeutical aims and techniques in psycho-analysis. *International Journal of Psycho-Analysis*, *31*: 117–124.

Balint, M. (1955). Friendly expanses – horrid empty spaces. *International Journal of Psycho-Analysis*, *36*: 225–241.

Balint, M. (1958). Sandor Ferenczi's Last Years. *International Journal of Psycho-Analysis*, 39: 68.

Balint, M. (1960). Primary narcissism and primary love. *Psychoanalytic Quarterly*, *29*: 6–43.

Balint, M. (1968). *The Basic Fault: Therapeutic Aspects of Regression*. London: Tavistock.

Balint, M. (1969). Draft introduction. In J. Dupont (ed.), *The Clinical Diary of Sándor Ferenczi*. Cambridge, MA: Harvard University Press, 1988, pp. 219–220.

Baranger, M. (1993). The mind of the analyst: From listening to interpretation. *International Journal of Psycho-Analysis*, *74*: 15–24.

Baranger, M., & Baranger, W. (1961–1962). La situación analítica como campo dinamico [The analytic situation as a dynamic field]. In *Problemas del campo psicoanalítico* [Problems of the Psychoanalytic Field]. Buenos Aires: Kargieman, 1969, pp. 109–164.

Baskett, T. F. (2006). The history of pessaries for uterovaginal prolapse. In F. A. Scott (ed.), *Pessaries in Clinical Practice*. London: Springer.

Behrend, F. J. (1860). Über die Reizung der Geschlechtstheile, besonders über Onanie bei ganz kleinen Kindern, und die dagegen anzuwendenden Mittel. [On the stimulation of the sexual parts, especially on onanism in very small children, and the means to employ against it]. *Journal für Kinderkrankheiten*, *35*: 321–329.

Bérillon, E. (1889). Les applications de la suggestion à la pédiatrie et à l'éducation mentale des enfants vicieux ou dégénérés [The application of suggestion in pediatrics and the mental education of vicious or degenerate children]. In E. Bérillon (ed.), *L'hypnotisme expérimental et thérapeutique. Premier Congrès International. Comptes rendus*. Paris: Octave Doin, pp. 157–181.

Bérillon, E. (1892). Les faux témoignages suggérée chez les enfants [False testimony suggested in children]. *Revue de l'hypnotisme et de la psychologie physiologique*, *6*: 203–212.

Bérillon, E. (1898). *L'Hypnotisme et l'orthopédie mentale* [Hypnotism and Mental Orthopedics]. Paris: Rueff & Cie.

Berkhan, O. (1863–1864). Irrsein bei Kindern [Madness in children]. *Correspondenz-Blatt der deutschen Gesellschaft für Psychiatrie und Gerichtliche Psychologie*, *10* (5/6): 65–76; *11* (9/10): 129–137.

Berman, E. (2003). Ferenczi, rescue, and utopia. *American Imago*, *60*: 429–444.

Berman, E. (2004). Sándor, Gizella, Elma: A biographical journey. *International Journal of Psycho-Analysis*, *85*: 489–520.
Bernfeld, S. (1953). Freud's studies on cocaine, 1884–1887. *Journal of the American Psychoanalytic Association*, *1*: 581–613.
Bertin, C. (1982). Marie Bonaparte: A Life. New York: Harcourt Brace
Bettelheim, B. (1982). *Freud and Man's Soul*. New York: Vintage.
Billig, M. (2000). Freud's different versions of forgetting "Signorelli": Rhetoric and repression. *International Journal of Psycho-Analysis*, *81*: 483–498.
Billinsky, J. M. (1969). Jung and Freud (The end of a romance). *Andover Newton Quarterly*, *10*: 39–43.
Binet, A., & Féré, Ch. (1885). Hypnotisme et responsabilité [Hypnotism and responsability]. *La Revue Philosophique*, *19*: 263–279.
Blass, R. B., & Simon, B. (1994). The value of the historical perspective to contemporary psychoanalysis: Freud's "seduction hypothesis." *International Journal of Psycho-Analysis*, *75*: 677–693.
Blum, H. P. (1977). The prototype of preoedipal reconstruction. *Journal of the American Psychoanalytic Association*, *25*: 757–785.
Blum, H. P. (1996). The Irma dream, self-analysis, and self-supervision. *Journal of the American Psychoanalytic Association*, *44*: 511–532.
Boehlich, W. (ed.) (1990). *The Letters of Sigmund Freud to Eduard Silberstein 1871–1881*. Cambridge, MA: The Belknap Press of Harvard University Press.
Bollas, C. (2011). Introduction. In J. Sklar (ed.), *Landscapes of the Dark: History, Trauma, Psychoanalysis*. London: Karnac, 2011, pp. xv–xxiii.
Bonaparte, M. (1948a). Female mutilation among primitive peoples and their psychical parallels in civilization. In *Female Sexuality*. New York: International Universities Press, 1953, pp. 153–161.
Bonaparte, M. (1948b). Notes sur l'excision. *Revue française de psychanalyse*, *12*: 213–231. (Notes on excision. In *Female Sexuality*, New York: International Universities Press, 1953, pp. 191–208).
Bonaparte, M. (1951). *La sexualité de la Femme*. Paris: Presse Universitaires de la France. (*Female Sexuality*. New York: International Universities Press, 1953).
Bonaparte, M., Freud, A., & Kris, E. (eds.) (1950 [1954]). *Aus den Anfängen der Psychoanalyse. Briefe an Wilhelm Fliess*, Abhandlungen und Notizen aus den Jahren 1887–1902. (English translation: The Origins of Psychoanalysis: Sigmund Freud's Letters, Drafts and Notes to Wilhelm Fliess (1887–1902)). London: Imago, 1954.
Bonomi, C. (1994a). Freud, Jung, Ferenczi et la vision d'un petit pénis coupé [Freud, Jung, Ferenczi and the vision of a little cut-off penis]. *Le Coq-héron*, *134*: 69–84.
Bonomi, C. (1994a). Why have we ignored Freud the "paediatrician"? The relevance of Freud's paediatric training for the origins of psychoanalysis. In A. Haynal & E. Falzeder (eds.), *100 Years of Psychoanalysis: Contributions to the History of Psychoanalysis*. (Special Issue of *Cahiers Psychiatriques Genevois*). London: H. Karnac Books, pp. 55–99.
Bonomi, C. (1994b). "Sexuality and death" in Freud's discovery of sexual aetiology. *International Forum of Psychoanalysis*, *3*: 63–87.
Bonomi, C. (1996). Mute correspondence. *International Forum of Psychoanalysis*, *5*: 165–189. Reprinted in P. Mahony, C. Bonomi, & J. Stensson (eds.), *Behind the Scenes: Freud in Correspondence*. Oslo: Scandinavian University Press, 1997, pp. 155–201.
Bonomi, C. (1998). Jones's allegation of Ferenczi's mental deterioration: A reassessment. *International Forum of Psychoanalysis*, *7*: 201–206.

Bonomi, C. (1999). Flight into sanity: Jones's allegation of Ferenczi's insanity reconsidered. *International Journal of Psycho-Analysis*, *80*: 507–542.
Bonomi, C. (2005). International Federation of Psychoanalytic Societies (IFPS). In: Alain De Mijolla (Editor In Chief), *International Dictionary of Psychoanalysis, Volume 3*, Thomson Gale: Detroit, pp. 85–53.
Bonomi, C. (2006). Du sexe mutilé au culte du phallus. Contribution à l'histoire de la naissance de la psychanalyse. [From genital mutilation to the phallus cult. Contribution to the history of the birth of psychoanalysis]. Paper presented at the conference: Freud parcours secrets, XXI-ème colloque de la Société internationale d'histoire de la psychiatrie et de la psychanalyse, 2 décembre 2006, Paris.
Bonomi, C. (2007). *Sulla soglia della psicoanalisi. Freud e la follia del bambino* [On the Threshold of Psychoanalysis: Freud and the Insanity of the Child]. Torino: Bollati Boringhieri.
Bonomi, C. (2009). Infanzia, peccato e pazzia. Alle radici della rappresentazione psicologica del bambino [Childhood, sin and madness: The roots of the psychologic representation of the child]. *Rassegna di Psicologia*, *26*: 129–153.
Bonomi, C. (2010). Ferenczi and ego psychology. *Psychoanalytic Perspectives*, *7*: 104–130.
Bonomi, C. (2015). *The Cut and the Building of Psychoanalysis: Volume I: Sigmund Freud and Emma Eckstein*. (Relational Perspectives Book Series). London and New York: Routledge.
Borch-Jacobsen, M., & Shamsadani, S. (2012). *The Freud Files: An Inquiry into the History of Psychoanalysis*. Cambridge: Cambridge University Press.
Borgogno, F. (1999). *Psychoanalysis as a Journey*. London: Open Gate Press, 2007.
Borgogno, F. (2011). The Girl Who Committed Hara-Kiri and Other Clinical and Historical Essays. English translation, London: Karnac Books, 2013.
Bourdin, C. E. (1883). Les enfants menteurs [Children who lie]. *Annales médico-psychologiques*, *9*: 53–67, *10*: 374–386.
Bousset, W. (1896). *The Antichrist Legend: A Chapter in Christian and Jewish Folklore*. London: Hudchinson and Company.
Brabant, E., Falzeder, E., & Giampieri-Deutsch, P. (eds.) (1993). *The Correspondence of Sigmund Freud and Sandor Ferenczi, Volume 1, 1908–1914*. Cambridge, MA: Harvard University Press.
Braune, J. (2014). *Erich Fromm's Revolutionary Hope: Prophetic Messianism as a Critical Theory of the Future*. Rotterdam: Sense Publishers.
Brennan, B. W. (2015). The medium is the message. Turning tables with Elizabeth Severn. Paper presented at the XII International Sándor Ferenczi Conference Heritage of a Psychoanalytic Mind, May 7–10, 2015, Toronto, Canada.
Brenner, A. B. (1950). The Great Mother Goddess: Puberty initiation rites and the covenant of Abraham. *The Psychoanalytic Review*, *37*: 320–340.
Breuer, J. & Freud, S. (1893). On The Psychical Mechanism of Hysterical Phenomena: Preliminary Communication from Studies on Hysteria. In: S. Freud, *SE 2*: [1-9]–[1-9]7.
Breuer, J., & Freud, S. (1895). Studies on hysteria. In S. Freud, *SE 2*.
Brierley, M. (1958). Review of Sigmund Freud: Life and work: Vol. III. the last phase, 1919–1939. *International Journal of Psycho-Analysis*, *39*: 422–424.
Brierre de Boismont, A. (1858). Recherches sur l'aliénation mentale des enfants, et particulièrement des jeunes gens [Researches on the mental derangement of children and particularly of young people]. *Annales d'Hygiène publique et de Médicine Légale, Deuxième série*, *10*: 363–398.
Broedel, H. P. (2003). *The Malleus Maleficarum and the Construction of Witchcraft: Theology and Popular Belief*. Manchester and New York: Manchester University Press.
Bromley, A. (1957). Review of final contributions to the problems and methods of psychoanalysis: The selected papers of Sándor Ferenczi, M.D. Volume III. *Psychoanalytic Quarterly*, *26*: 112–114.

Broussais, F. S. V. (1828). *De l'irritation et de la folie* [On Irritation and Madness]. Paris: Delaunay.
Brown, N. O. (1966). *Love's Body*. New York: Random House.
Bryk, F. (1928). *Neger-eros. Ethnologische Studien über das Sexualleben bei Negern*. Berlin und Köln: A. Marcus & E. Weber. (*Dark Rapture: The Sex-Life of the African Negro*. New York: AMS Press, 1975).
Bryk, F. (1931). *Die Beschneidung bei Mann und Weib*. New Brandenburg: Gustav Feller Verlag. (*Circumcision in Man and Woman*, New York: American Ethnological Press, 1934).
Buriánek, V. (2015). Paradise lost and trauma mastered: New findings on little Sigmund. *International Forum of Psychoanalysis*, *24*: 22–28.
Burston, D. (2008). A very Freudian affair: Erich Fromm, Peter Swales and the future of psychoanalytic historiography. *Psychoanalysis and History*, *10*: 115–130.
Buxbaum, E. (1951). Freud's dream interpretation in the light of his letters to Fliess. *Bull. Menninger Clin.* *15*: 19[1-9]–[1-9]12.
Carus, F. A. (1808). *Psychologie Zweiter Theil: Special psychologie* [Psychology: Volume 2: Special Psychology]. Leipzig: Barth & Kummer.
Cassirer Bernfeld, S. (1951). Freud and archeology. *American Imago*, *8*: 107–128.
Charcot, J. M., & Richer, P. (1887). *Les demoniaques dans l'art*. Paris: A. Delahaye et E. Lescrosnier.
Colman, W. (1994). "The scenes themselves which lie at the bottom of the story": Julius, circumcision, and the castration complex. *The Psychoanalytic Review*, *81*: 603–625.
Compayré, G. (1893). *L'Évolution intellectuelle et morale de l'enfant*, published in English as *Development of the Child in Later Infancy (Part II of the Intellectual and Moral Development of the Child)*. New York: D. Appleton and Company, 1902.
Connolly, J. (1862). Recollections of the varieties of insanity, Part II Cases and consultations. *The Medical Times and Gazette*, *1*: 27–29, 130–132, 234–236, 372–374.
Crichton Browne, J. (1860). Psychical diseases of early life. *Journal of Mental Science*, *6*: 284–320.
Daly, C. D. (1950). The psycho-biological origins of circumcision. *International Journal of Psycho-Analysis*, *31*: 217–236.
Daly, M. (1978). *Gyn/Ecology: The Metaethics of Radical Feminism*. Boston: Beacon Press.
Deutsch, H. (1944–1945). *The Psychology of Women*, Volumes 1 and 2. New York: Grune & Stratton, Inc.
Devereux, G. (1953). Why Oedipus killed Laius: A note on the complementary Oedipus complex in Greek drama. *International Journal of Psycho-Analysis*, *34*: 132–141.
Doria-Medina, R. Jr. (1991). On Freud and Monotheism. *International Review of Psycho-Analysis*, *18*: 489–500.
Dorsey, D. (1996). Castration anxiety or feminine genital anxiety? *Journal of the American Psychoanalytic Association*, *44S*: 283–302.
Dupont, J. (ed.) (1985). *The Clinical Diary of Sándor Ferenczi*. Cambridge: Harvard University Press, 1988.
Dupont, J. (1989). La relation Freud-Ferenczi à la lumière de leur correspondance. *Revue internationale d'histoire de la psychanalyse2*: 181–200.
Dupont, J. (1994). Freud's analysis of Ferenczi as revealed by their correspondence. *International Journal of Psycho-Analysis*, *75*: 301–320.
Dupont, J. (2015). *Au fil du temps . . . Un itinéraire analytique*. Paris: Campagne Première.
Durand-Fardell, M. (1855). Étude sur le suicide chez les enfants [Study on suicide in children]. *Annales Médico-psychologiques*, *61*: 60–79.
Eastman, J. (2005). Freud, the Oedipus complex, and Greece or the silence of Athena. *Psychoanalytic Review*, *92*: 335–354.

Eckstein, E. (1900). Eine wichtige Erziehungsfrage [An important child-raising question]. *Die neue Zeit: Revue des geistigen und öffentlichen Lebens*, *18*: 666–669.

Eckstein, E. (1904). *Die Sexualfrage in der Erziehung des Kindes* [The Question of Sexuality in the Raising of Children]. Leipzig: Curt Wigand.

Eissler, K. R. (1952). Interview with Dr. Elizabeth Severn, December 20, 1952, in container 121. Sigmund Freud Collection, Manuscript Division, United States Library of Congress, Washington, DC.

Eissler, K. R. (1978). Creativity and adolescence: The effect of trauma in Freud's adolescence. *Psychoanalytic Study of the Child*, *33*: 461–517.

Ellenberger, H. F. (1964). The concept of "maladie créatrice." In M. S. Micale (ed.), *Essays of Henri Ellenberger in the History of Psychiatry*. Princeton, NJ: Princeton University Press, 1993, pp. 328–340.

Emminghaus, H. (1887). *Die Psychischen Störungen des Kindesalter* [The Psychic Disturbances of Childhood]. Tübingen: Verlag der H. Laupp'schen Buchhandlung.

Erikson, E. (1954). The dream specimen of psychoanalysis. *Journal of the American Psychoanalytic Association*, *2*: 5–55.

Esquirol, J. E. D. (1805). *Des passions considerées comme cause, symptomes et moyens curatifs de l'alienation mentale* [The Passions Considered as Causes, Symptoms and Means of Cure in Cases of Insanity]. Reprint. Venezia: Marsilio, 1982.

Esquirol, J. E. D. (1838). *Des maladies mentales considérées sous les rapports médical, hygiénique et médico-légal*, 2 vols. Paris: Bailliére. (Mental Maladies: A Treatise on Insanity. Philadelphia, PA: Lea and Blanchard, 1845).

Faimberg, H. (2007). A Plea for a Broader Concept of Nachträglichkeit. *Psychoanalytic Quarterly, 76*: 122[1-9]–[1-9]240

Falzeder, E. (1994). My grand-patient, my chief tormentor: A hitherto unnoticed case of Freud's and the consequences. In *Psychoanalytic Filiations: Mapping the Psychoanalytic Movement*. Karnac: London, 2015, pp. 19–48.

Falzeder, E. (1996). Dreaming of Freud: Ferenczi, Freud, and an analysis without end. *International Forum of Psychoanalysis*, *5*: 265–270.

Falzeder, E. (ed.) (2002). *The Complete Correspondence of Sigmund Freud and Karl Abraham 1907–1925*. London: Karnac.

Falzeder, E. (2007). The story of an ambivalent relationship: Sigmund Freud and Eugen Bleuler. In *Psychoanalytic Filiations: Mapping the Psychoanalytic Movement*. Karnac: London, 2015, pp. 177–196.

Falzeder, E. (2012a). Freud and Jung, Freudians and Jungians. In *Psychoanalytic Filiations: Mapping the Psychoanalytic Movement*. Karnac: London, 2015, pp. 221–241.

Falzeder, E. (2012b). "A fat wad of dirty pieces of papers": Freud on America, Freud in America, Freud and America. In *Psychoanalytic Filiations: Mapping the Psychoanalytic Movement*. Karnac: London, 2015, pp. 307–330.

Falzeder, E. (2015). *Psychoanalytic Filiations: Mapping the Psychoanalytic Movement*. Karnac: London, 2015.

Falzeder, E., & Brabant, E. (eds.) (2000). *The Correspondence of Sigmund Freud and Sándor Ferenczi, Volume 3, 1920–1933*. Cambridge, MA: Harvard University Press.

Falzeder, E., Brabant, E., & Giampieri-Deutsch, P. (eds.) (1996). *The Correspondence of Sigmund Freud and Sándor Ferenczi, Volume 2, 1914–1919*. Cambridge, MA: Harvard University Press.

Fausto-Sterling, A. (2000). *Sexing the Bodies*. New York: Basic Books.

Feldman, A. (1944). Freud's Moses and Monotheism and the three stages of the Israelitish religion. *The Psychoanalytic Review*, *31*: 361–418.

Ferenczi, S. (1912a). Transitory symptom-constructions during the analysis. In *First Contributions to Psychoanalysis*. London: Hogarth Press, 1952, pp. 193–212.
Ferenczi, S. (1912b). The symbolic representation of the pleasures and reality principles in the Oedipus myth. In *First Contributions to Psychoanalysis*. London: Hogarth Press, 1952, pp. 253–269.
Ferenczi, S. (1913a). A little Chanticleer. In *First Contributions to Psychoanalysis*. London: Hogarth Press, 1952, pp. 240–252.
Ferenczi, S. (1913c). Paresthesias of the genital region in impotence. In *Further Contributions to Psycho-Analysis*. London: Hogarth Press, 1950, p. 312.
Ferenczi, S. (1913d). Stages in the development of the sense of reality. In *First Contributions to Psychoanalysis*. London: Hogarth Press, 1952, pp. 213–239.
Ferenczi, S. (1913e). The symbolic representation of the pleasures and reality principles in the Oedipus myth. In *First Contributions to Psychoanalysis*. London: Hogarth Press, 1952, pp. 253–269.
Ferenczi, S. (1913b). On eye symbolism. In *First Contributions to Psychoanalysis*. London: Hogarth Press, 1952, pp. 270–276.
Ferenczi, S. (1915). The dream of the occlusive pessary. In *Further Contributions to the Theory and Technique of Psycho-Analysis*. London: Hogarth Press, 1950, pp. 304–311.
Ferenczi, S. (1916–1917). Two types of war neuroses. In *Further Contributions to the Theory and Technique of Psycho-Analysis*. London: Hogarth Press, 1950, pp. 124–141.
Ferenczi, S. (1917a). Disease or patho-neuroses. In *Further Contributions to the Theory and Technique of Psycho-Analysis*. London: Hogarth Press, 1950, pp. 78–87.
Ferenczi, S. (1917b). On the psychical consequences of "castration" in infancy. In *Further Contributions to the Theory and Technique of Psycho-Analysis*. London: Hogarth Press, 1950, pp. 244–249.
Ferenczi, S. (1919). The phenomena of hysterical materialization: Thoughts on the conception of hysterical conversion and symbolism. In *Further Contributions to the Theory and Technique of Psycho-Analysis*. London: Hogarth Press, 1950, pp. 89–104.
Ferenczi, S. (1920). The further development of an active therapy in psycho-analysis. In *Further Contributions to the Theory and Technique of Psycho-Analysis*. London: Hogarth Press, 1950, pp. 198–217.
Ferenczi, S. (1921). Psycho-analytical observations on tic. In *Further Contributions to the Theory and Technique of Psycho-Analysis*. London: Hogarth Press, 1950, pp. 142–174.
Ferenczi, S. (1922). Bridge symbolism and the Don Juan Legend. In *Further Contributions to the Theory and Technique of Psycho-Analysis*. London: Hogarth Press, 1950, pp. 356–357.
Ferenczi, S. (1923). The dream of the "clever baby." In *Further Contributions to the Theory and Technique of Psycho-Analysis*. London: Hogarth Press, 1950, pp. 349–350.
Ferenczi, S. (1924). *Thalassa: A Theory of Genitality*. London: Karnac Books, 1989.
Ferenczi, S. (1925). Contra-indications to the "active" psychoanalytic technique. In *Further Contributions to the Theory and Technique of Psycho-Analysis*. London: Hogarth Press, 1950, pp. 217–230.
Ferenczi, S. (1926). The problem of acceptance of unpleasant ideas: Advances in knowledge of the sense of reality. In *Further Contributions to the Theory and Technique of Psycho-Analysis*. London: Hogarth Press, 1950, pp. 366–379.
Ferenczi, S. (1929). The principle of relaxation and neocatharsis. In *Final Contributions to the Problems and Methods of Psycho-Analysis*. London: Hogarth Press, 1950, pp. 108–125.
Ferenczi, S. (1930–1932). Notes and fragments. In *Final Contributions to the Problems and Methods of Psycho-Analysis*. London: Hogarth Press, 1955, pp. 219–279.

Ferenczi, S. (1931). Child-analysis in the analysis of adults. In *Final Contributions to the Problems and Methods of Psycho-Analysis*. London: Hogarth, 1955, pp. 126–142.
Ferenczi, S. (1933). Confusion of tongues between adults and the child: The language of tenderness and of passion. In *Final Contributions to the Problems and Methods of Psycho-Analysis*. London: Hogarth, 1955, pp. 156–167.
Ferenczi, S. (1955). Final Contributions to the Problems and Methods of Psycho-Analysis. London: Hogarth.
Ferenczi, S., Rank, O. (1924). *The Development of psychoanalysis*. Madison, Connecticut: International Universities Press, 1986.
Fleischmann, L. (1878). Über Onanie und Masturbation bei Säugligen. [On onanism and masturbation in babies.] *Wiener medizinische Presse, 19*: 8–10, 46–49.
Fliess, W. (1906). *Der Ablauf des Lebens*. Grundlegung zur exakten Biologie. Leipzig and Vienna: Deuticke.
Fliess, W. (1925). *Von den Gesetzen des Lebens*. Frankfurt am Main: Campus Verlag, 1985.
Forest (de), I. (1942). The therapeutic technique of Sándor Ferenczi. *International Journal of Psycho-Analysis, 23*: 120–139.
Forest (de), I. (1954). *The Leaven of Love: A Development of the Psychoanalytic Theory and Technique of Sándor Ferenczi*. New York: Da Capo Press, 1984.
Fortune, C. (1993). The case "RN": Sandor Ferenczi's radical experiment in psychoanalysis. In L. Aron & A. Harris (eds.), *The Legacy of Sándor Ferenczi*. Hillsdale, NJ and London: The Analytic Press, 1933, pp. 101–120.
Fortune, C. (1994). A difficult ending: Ferenczi, "R.N.," and the experiment in mutual analysis. In A. Haynal & E. Falzeder (eds.), *100 Years of Psychoanalysis: Contributions to the History of Psychoanalysis*. (Special Issue of *Cahiers Psychiatriques Genevois*). London: H. Karnac Books, pp. 217–223.
Fortune, C. (ed.) (2002). *The Sándor Ferenczi-George Groddeck Correspondence 1921–1933*. London: Open Gate Press.
Frazer, J. G. (1890). *The Golden Bough: A Study in Comparative Religion*. London: Macmillan and Company.
Frazer, J. G. (1911). *The Dying God*. London: Macmillan and Co.
Fredericksen, B. F. (2008). Jomo Kenyatta, Marie Bonaparte and Bronislaw Malinowski on clitoridectomy and female sexuality. *History Workshop Journal, 65*: 23–48.
Freud, A. (1936). *The Ego and the Mechanisms of Defense*. New York: International Universities Press, Inc., 1946.
Freud, A. (1981). Insight: Its presence and absence as a factor in normal development. *Psychoanalytic Study of the Child, 36*: 241–249.
Freud, E. L. (ed.) (1960). *Letters of Sigmund Freud 1873–1939*. London: Hogarth.
Freud, S. (1886). Observation of a severe case of hemi-anaesthesia in a hysterical male. *SE, 1*: 23–31.
Freud, S. (1888). Hysteria. *SE, 1*: 37–59.
Freud, S. (1893a). On the psychical mechanism of hysterical phenomena. *SE, 3*: 25–39.
Freud, S. (1893b). Charcot. *SE, 3*: 7–23.
Freud, S. (1894a). The neuro-psychoses of defense. *SE, 3*: 43–61.
Freud, S. (1894b). Obsessions and phobias: Their psychical mechanism and their aetiology. *SE, 3*: 69–82.
Freud, S. (1895a). Project for a scientific psychology. *SE, 1*: 283–397.
Freud, S. (1895b). Draft K The Neuroses of Defence from Extracts from the Fliess Papers: (A Christmas Fairy Tale). *SE*, 1: 220-229.
Freud, S. (1896a). Heredity and the aetiology of the neuroses. *SE, 3*: 141–156.

Freud, S. (1896b). Further remarks on the neuro-psychoses of defence. *SE, 3*: 157–185.
Freud, S. (1896c). The aetiology of hysteria. *SE, 3*: 187–221.
Freud, S. (1898a). Sexuality in the aetiology of the neuroses. *SE, 3*: 259–285.
Freud, S. (1898b). The psychical mechanism of forgetfulness. *SE, 3*: 287–297.
Freud, S. (1899). Screen memories. *SE, 3*: 303–322.
Freud, S. (1900). The interpretation of dreams. *SE, 4–5*.
Freud, S. (1901). The psychopathology of everyday life. *SE, 6*.
Freud, S. (1905). Three essays on the theory of sexuality. *SE, 7*: 123–246.
Freud, S. (1906). My views on the part played by sexuality in the aetiology of the neuroses. *SE, 7*: 269–279.
Freud, S. (1907a). Delusions and dreams in Jensen's Gradiva. *SE, 9*: 3–95.
Freud, S. (1907b). Obsessive acts and religious practices. *SE, 9*: 115–128.
Freud, S. (1908). Character and anal erotism. *SE, 9*: 167–176.
Freud, S. (1909a). Analysis of a Phobia in a five-year-old boy. *SE, 10*: 1–150.
Freud, S. (1909b). Notes upon a case of obsessional neurosis. *SE, 10*: 151–318.
Freud, S. (1910a). Five lectures on psycho-analysis. *SE, 22*: 3–182.
Freud, S. (1910b). The future prospects of psycho-analytic therapy. *SE, 11*: 139–152.
Freud, S. (1910c). Leonardo da Vinci and a memory of his childhood. *SE, 11*: 57–138.
Freud, S. (1911). Psycho-analytic notes on an autobiographical account of a case of paranoia (dementia paranoides). *SE, 12*: 1–82.
Freud, S. (1912a). The dynamics of transference. *SE, 12*: 97–108.
Freud, S. (1912b). Recommendations to physicians practising psycho-analysis. *SE, 12*: 109–120.
Freud, S. (1913a). Totem and taboo. *SE, 15*: 1–240.
Freud, S. (1913b). The theme of the three caskets. *SE, 12*: 291–301.
Freud, S. (1913c). The disposition to obsessional neurosis, a contribution to the problem of the choice of neurosis. *SE, 12*: 311–326.
Freud, S. (1913d). Preface to Bourke's scatalogic rites of all nations. *SE, 12*: 333–338.
Freud, S. (1914a). On the history of the psycho-analytic movement. *SE, 14*: 1–66.
Freud, S. (1914b). The Moses of Michelangelo. *SE, 13*: 209–238.
Freud, S. (1914c). Remembering, repeating and working-through (Further recommendations on the technique of psycho-analysis II). *SE, 12*: 145–156.
Freud, S. (1915). Observations on transference-love (Further recommendations on the technique of psycho-analysis III). *SE, 12*: 157–171.
Freud, S. (1916–1917). Introductory lectures on psycho-analysis. *SE, 15*: 1–240; *16*: 243–463.
Freud, S. (1918a). From the history of an infantile neurosis. *SE, 17*: 1–124.
Freud, S. (1918b). The taboo of virginity. *SE, 11*: 193–208.
Freud, S. (1919a). "A child is being beaten": A contribution to the study of the origin of sexual perversions. *SE, 17*: 179–204.
Freud, S. (1919b). The "uncanny." *SE, 17*: 217–256.
Freud, S. (1919c). Preface to Reik's ritual: Psycho-analytic studies. *SE, 17*: 258–264.
Freud, S. (1919d). Lines of advance in psycho-analytic therapy. *SE, 17*: 157–168.
Freud, S. (1920). Beyond the pleasure principle. *SE, 18*: 3–64.
Freud, S. (1921). Group psychology and the analysis of the ego. *SE, 18*: 65–144.
Freud, S. (1923a). The ego and the id. *SE, 19*: 12–66.
Freud, S. (1923b). The infantile genital organization (an interpolation into the theory of sexuality). *SE, 19*: 139–146.
Freud, S. (1923c). A seventeenth-century demonological neurosis. *SE, 19*: 67–106.

Freud, S. (1924a). The dissolution of the Oedipus complex. *SE*, *19*: 171–180.
Freud, S. (1924b). The economic problem of masochism. *SE*, *19*: 155–170.
Freud, S. (1924c). The loss of reality in neurosis and psychosis. *SE*, *19*: 181–188.
Freud, S. (1924d). Neurosis and psychosis. *SE*, *19*: 147–154.
Freud, S. (1925a). An autobiographical study. *SE*, *20*: 7–70.
Freud, S. (1925b). Some psychical consequences of the anatomical distinction between the sexes. *SE*, *19*: 243–260.
Freud, S. (1925c). Some additional notes on dream-interpretation as a whole. *SE*, *19*: 123–138.
Freud, S. (1926a). Inhibitions, symptoms and anxiety. *SE*, *20*: 77–174.
Freud, S. (1926b). The question of lay analysis. *SE*, *20*: 181–258.
Freud, S. (1927a). Fetishism. *SE*, *21*: 147–158.
Freud, S. (1927b). The future of an illusion. *SE*, *21*: 5–56.
Freud, S. (1930a). Civilization and its discontents. *SE*, *21*: 57–145.
Freud, S. (1930b). The Goethe prize. *SE*, *21*: 205–214.
Freud, S. (1931). Female sexuality. *SE*, *21*: 223–243.
Freud, S. (1933a). New introductory lectures on psycho-analysis. *SE*, *22*: 1–182.
Freud, S. (1933b). Sándor Ferenczi. *International Journal of Psycho-Analysis*, *14*: 297–299.
Freud, S. (1936). A disturbance of memory on the Acropolis. *SE*, *22*: 237–248.
Freud, S. (1937a). Analysis terminable and interminable. *SE*, *23*: 209–254.
Freud, S. (1937b). Constructions in analysis. *SE*, *23*: 255–270.
Freud, S. (1938a). Splitting of the ego in the process of defence. *SE*, *23*: 271–278.
Freud, S. (1938b). An outline of psycho-analysis. *SE*, *30*: 139–208.
Freud, S. (1939). Moses and Monotheism: Three essays. *SE*, *23*: 1–138.
Freud, S. (1985). *A Phylogenetic Fantasy: An Overview of the Transference Neuroses*, edited by I. Grubrich-Simitis. Cambridge: Harvard University Press, 1987.
Freud, S. (2002). *"Notre coer tend vers le Sud." Correspondance de voyage, 1895–1923* [Our Heart Points to the South: Travel Letters, 1895–1923], edited by Christfried Tögel with assistance from Michael Molnar; foreword by Élisabeth Roudinesco, Paris: Fayard, 2005.
Fried, R. (2003). *Freud on the Acropolis: A Detective Story*. Helsinki: Therapeia Foundation.
Friedman, L. (1978). Trends in the psychoanalytic theory of treatment. *Psychoanalytic Quarterly*, *47*: 524–567.
Friedman, P. (1960). Review of *Jewish Symbols in the Greco-Roman Period* by Erwin R. Goodenough, (Bollingen Series XXXVII), Volumes 1–6. New York: Published for the Bollingen Foundation Inc. by Pantheon Books, Inc., 1953, 1954, 1956. *Psychoanalytic Quarterly*, *29*: 254–263.
Friedreich, J. B. (1839). *Handbuch der allgemeine Pathologie der psychischen Krankheiten*, Band I. Erlangen: J.J. Palm & E. Enke.
Fromm, E. (1947). *Man for Himself*. New York: Holt, Rhinehart and Winston.
Fromm, E. (1958). Freud, friends, and feuds: 1. Scientism or fanaticism? [Psychoanalysis: Science or party line?]. *The Saturday Review*, June 14, 1958, pp. 11–13, 55–56.
Fromm, E. (1959). *Sigmund Freud's Mission: An Analysis of His Personality and Influence*. New York: Harper & Row, 1972.
Fromm, E. (1965). Review of the *Wild Analyst: The Life and Work of Georg Groddeck* by Karl M. Grossman and Sylvia Grossman. New York: George Braziller, 1965. *Contemporary Psychoanalysis*, 2: 83–84.
Fromm, E. (2000 [1935]). The social determinants of psychoanalytic therapy. *International Forum of Psychoanalysis*, *9*: 149–165.
Funk, R. (2000). Erich Fromm's role in the foundation of the IFPS: Evidence from the Erich Fromm Archives in Tübingen. *International Forum of Psychoanalysis*, *9*: 187–197.

Gamwell, L., & Wells, R. (eds.) (1989). *Sigmund Freud and Art: His Personal Collection of Antiquities.* London: State University of New York and Freud Museum.

Gattel, F. (1898). *Über die sexuellen Ursachen der Neurasthenie und Angstneurose.* Berlin: A. Hirschwald.

Geller, J. (2007). *On Freud's Jewish Body. Mitigating Circumcisions.* New York: Fordahm University Press.

Gero, G. (1961). *Review of Asexualization: A Follow-Up Study of 244 Cases by Johan Bremer.* Oslo, Norway: Oslo University Press, 1958, p. 366. Psychoanalytic Quarterly, 30: 587–589.

Ghent, E. (1990). Masochism, submission, surrender: Masochism as a perversion of surrender. *Contemporary Psychoanalysis, 26*: 108–136.

Gicklhorn, R. (1969). The Freiberg period of the Freud family. *Journal of the History of Medicine, 29*: 37–43.

Gilman, S. L. (1993). *The Case of Sigmund Freud: Medicine and Identity at the Fin De Siècle.* Baltimore and London: The Johns Hopkins University Press.

Ginsburg, L. M. (1999). Long-term manifestations of "death-watch" imagery and related Jewish rituals for a significant family member during the early Childhoods of Sigmund Freud and Abram Kardiner. *Canadian Journal of Psychoanalysis, 7*: 63–78.

Ginzburg, C. (1989) Clues: Roots of an Evidential Paradigm in Clues, *Myths, and the Historical Method,* Baltimore: John Hopkins University Press, pp. 9[1-9]–[1-9]25..

Glover, E. (1924). "Active therapy" and psycho-analysis: A critical review. *International Journal of Psycho-Analysis, 5*: 26[1-9]–[1-9]11.

Good, M. I. (1994). The reconstruction of early childhood trauma: Fantasy, reality, and verification. *Journal of the American Psychoanalytic Association, 42*: 79–101.

Good, M. I. (1995). Karl Abraham, Sigmund Freud, and the fate of the seduction theory. *Journal of the American Psychoanalytic Association, 43*: 1137–1167.

Goodenough, E. R. (1953–1968). *Jewish Symbols in the Greco-Roman Period.* (Bollingen Series XXXVII). New York: Pantheon Books.

Gould, S. J. (1977). *Ontogeny and Phylogeny.* Cambridge, MA: Harvard University Press.

Griesinger, W. (1861). *Die Pathologie und Therapie der Psychischen Krankheiten, 2.* Aufl. Stuttgart: Adolph Krabbe.

Grigg, K. A. (1973). "All roads lead to Rome": The role of the nursemaid in Freud's dreams. *Journal of the American Psychoanalytic Association, 21*: 108–126.

Grinstein, A. (1980). *Sigmund Freud's Dreams.* New York: International Universities Press.

Grotstein, J. S. (1979). Who is the dreamer who dreams the dream and who is the dreamer who understands it: A psychoanalytic inquiry into the ultimate nature of being. *Contemporary Psychoanalysis, 15*: 110–169.

Grotstein, J. S. (1990). Nothingness, Meaninglessness, Chaos, and the "Black Hole" I—The Importance of Nothingness, Meaninglessness, and Chaos in Psychoanalysis. II—The Black Hole. *Contemporary Psychoanalysis, 26*: 25[1-9]–[1-9]90; 37[1-9]–[1-9]07.Grotstein, J. S. (1995). Projective identification reappraised: Projective identification, introjective identification, the transference/countertransference neurosis/psychosis, and their consummate expression in the Crucifixion, the Pietà, and "therapeutic exorcism," Part II, The countertransference complex. *Contemporary Psychoanalysis, 31*: 479.

Grotstein, J. S. (1997). Why Oedipus and not Christ? A psychoanalytic inquiry into innocence, human sacrifice, and the sacred – Part I: Innocence, spirituality, and human sacrifice. Part II: The Numinous and Spiritual Dimension as a Metapsychological Perspective. *American Journal of Psychoanalysis, 57*: 193–218; 317–335.

Grotstein, J. S. (1998). The numinous and immanent nature of the psychoanalytic subject. *Journal of Analytical Psychology, 43*: 41–68.

Grotstein, J. S. (2000). *Who Is the Dreamer Who Dreams the Dream? A Study of Psychic Presences*. (Relational Perspectives Book Series). Hillsdale, NJ: Analytic Press.
Guasto, G. (2015). *La passione della cura. Aforismario psicoanalitico*. Brescia: Arpa Edizioni.
Haeckel, E. (1866). *Generelle Morphologie der Organismen* [General Morphology of Organisms]. Berlin: Reimer.
Hamilton, E. (1930). *The Greek Way*. New York and London: W. W. Norton & Company.
Hamilton, E. (1942). *Mythology*. New York: Little, Brown & Company.
Hannah, B. (1976). *Jung: His Life and Work: A Biographical Memoir*. New York: Putnam.
Harris, A. & Kuchuck, S. (editors) (2015). *The Legacy of Sándor Ferenczi. From Ghosts to Ancestors*, (Relational Perspectives Book Series) London: Routledge.
Harrison, I. B. (1988). Further implications of a dream of Freud's: A subjective influence on his theory formation. *International Review of Psycho-Analysis*, 15: 365–372.
Haynal, A. (1988). *The Technique at Issue*. London: Karnac Books.
Haynal, A. (1992). Introduction. In E. Brabant, F. Falzeder, & P. Giampieri-Deutsch (eds.), *The Correspondence of Sigmund Freud and Sándor Ferenczi, Volume I, 1908–1914*. Cambridge, MA and London: The Belknap Press of Harvard University Press, 1992, pp. xvii–xxxv.
Haynal, A. (2002). *Disappearing and Reviving: Sándor Ferenczi in the History of Psychoanalysis*. London and New York: Karnac Books.
Haynal, A. E. (2005). In the shadow of a controversy: Freud and Ferenczi 1925–33. *International Journal of Psycho-Analysis*, 86: 457–466.
Hirschmüller, A. (2005). Introduction. In *Sigmund Freud, Minna Bernays, Correspondence 1882–1938*. (French edition prefaced by Élisabeth Roudinesco). Paris: Éditions du Seuil, 2015, pp. 23–50.
Hirschmüller, A. (2007). Freud and Minna Bernays: Evidence for a sexual relationship between Sigmund Freud and Minna Bernays? *American Imago*, 64: 125–129.
Hirst, A. (undated manuscript). Analysed and Reeducated by Freud Himself. Sigmund Freud's papers, Supplemental File, 1765–1998, Box 61. Library of Congress, Manuscript division.
Hochsinger, C. (1938). *Die Geschichte des ersten Öffentlichen Kinder-Kranken-Institutes in Wien während seines 150 jährigen Bestandes 1788–1938*. Vienna: Verlag des Kinder-Kranken-Institutes.
Holmes, K. R. (1983). Freud, evolution, and the tragedy of man. *Journal of the American Psychoanalytic Association*, 31: 187–210.
Holt, R. (1958). Review of Sigmund Freud: Life and work: Vol. III. The last phase, 1919–1939. *Contemporary Psychoanalysis*, 3: 145–148.
Ideler, K. W. (1852). Über den Wahnsinn der Kinder. *Annalen der Charité*, 10: 311–334.
Jimenez Avello, J. (2013). *L'île des rêves de Sándor Ferenczi*. Paris: Campagne Première.
Johnsdotter, S. (2012). Projected cultural histories of the cutting of female genitalia: A poor reflection as in a mirror. *History and Anthropology*, 23: 91–114.
Jones, E. (1933). Sándor Ferenczi, 1873–1933. *International Journal of Psycho-Analysis*, 14: 463–466.
Jones, E. (1953). *Sigmund Freud Life and Work, Volume I: The Young Freud: 1856–1900*. London: Hogarth.
Jones, E. (1955). *Sigmund Freud Life and Work, Volume II: Years of Maturity: 1901–1919*. London: Hogarth.
Jones, E. (1956). The Leaven of Love. A Development of the Psychoanalytic Theory and Technique of Sandor Ferenczi. *International Journal of Psycho-Analysis*, 37: 488.
Jones, E. (1957). *Sigmund Freud Life and Work, Volume III: The Last Phase: 1919–1939*. London: Hogarth.
Jones, E. (1958). Sándor Ferenczi's last years. *International Journal of Psycho-Analysis*, 39: 68–68.

Jung, C. G. (1912). *Wandlungen und Symbole der Libido*. Beiträge zur Entwicklungsgesischte des Denkens. Vienna: Deuticke.

Jung, C. G. (1917). *The Psychology of the Unconscious Processes, Being a Survey of the Modern Theory of Analytical Psychology: Collected Papers on Analytical Psychology*. London: Ballieère, Tindall & Cox.

Jung, C. G. (1961a). *Memories, Dreams, Reflections*, edited by A. Jaffé. London: Flamingo, 1983.

Jung, C. G. (1961b). Symbols and the interpretations of dreams. In *Collected Works*, Volume 18. Princeton, NJ: Princeton University Press, 1977.

Kerr, J. (1994). *A Most Dangerous Method: The Story of Jung, Freud, & Sabina Spielrein*. London: Sinclair-Stevenson.

Kevles, D. J. (1986). *In the Name of Eugenetics: Genetics and the Uses of Human Heredity*. Berkeley and Los Angeles: University of California Press.

Kindt, H. (1971). Vorstufe der Entwicklung zur Kinderpsychiatrie im 19° Jahrhundert. Zur Wertung von Hermann Emminghaus und seiner "Psychischen Störungen des Kindesalter" (1887). *Freiburger Forschungen zur Medizingeschichte, N.F./1*.

Klerk, A. de (2008). Die Bedeutung der Kastrationsangst und der Beschneidung in Freuds Werk und Leben. [The significance of castration anxiety and circumcision in Freud's work and life.] In: G. Schlesinger-Kipp, & R-P. Warsitz (eds), *"Die neuen Leiden der Seele". Das (Un-)behagen in der Kultur*. Deutsche Psychoanalytische Verein. Frankfurt/Main: Vertrieb Geber & Reusch; pp. 279–304.

Knight, M. (2001). Curing cut or ritual mutilation? Some remarks on the practice of female and male circumcision in Graeco-Roman Egypt. *Isis, 92*: 317–338.

Königliche Museen zu Berlin (1886). *Führer durch die Königlichen Museen*. Berlin: W. Sperman.

Krafft-Ebing, R. von (1900). *Psychopathia Sexualis with Especial Reference to the Antipathic Sexual Instinct: A Medico-Forensic Study*, translation of twelfth German edition. New York: Rebman Company.

Kuhn, P. (2000). The Cultivated Italian (or) who Reminded Freud How to Remember Signorelli?. *Psychoanalysis and History, 2*: 11[1-9]–[1-9]22

Kupfersmid, J. (1993). Freud's rationale for abandoning the seduction theory. *Psychoanalytic Psychology, 10*: 27[1-9]–[1-9]90.

Lacan, J. (1954–1955). The Seminar of Jacques Lacan. Book II. The Ego in Freud's Theory and in the Technique of Psychoanalysis 1954–1955. Cambridge: CUP, 1988

Lacan, J. (1966). *Écrits*. Paris: Seuil.

Lacan, J. (1973). The Freudian unconscious and ours. In J.-A. Miller (ed.), *The Seminar of Jacques Lacan, Book XI, the Four Fundamental Concepts of Psychoanalysis*. New York and London: W. W. Norton & Company, 1981, pp. 17–28.

Ladame, P. (1887). L'hypnotisme et la pédagogie [Hypnotism and pedagogy], II. *Revue de l'Hypnotisme Expérimentale et Thérapeutique, 2*: 359–370; 361–362.

Laplanche, J. (1992). Interpretation between determinism and hermeneutics: A restatement of the problem. *International Journal of Psycho-Analysis, 73*: 429–445.

Laub, D. (1992). Bearing witnesses, or the vicissitudes of listening. In S. Felman & D. Laub (eds.), *Testimony: Crises of Witnessing in Literature, Psychoanalysis, and History*. New York and London: Routledge, pp. 57–74.

Laub, D. (2005). From speechless to narrative: The cases of Holocaust historians and of psychiatrically hospitalized survivors. *Literature and Medicine, 24*: 253–265.

Laub, D. (2014). Listening to my mother's testimony. *Contemporary Psychoanalysis, 51*: 195–215.

Lax, R. F. (1994). Aspects of primary and secondary genital feelings and anxieties in girls during the preoedipal and early oedipal phases. *Psychoanalytic Quarterly*, *63*: 271–296.
Leach, E. (1986). The Big Fish in the biblical wilderness. *International Review of Psycho-Analysis*, *13*: 129–141.
Lebovici, S. (1976). Review of Janet, Freud et La Psychologie Clinique [Janet, Freud and clinical psychology] by Claude M. Prévost. Paris: Petite Bibliothèque Payot, 1973. *Psychoanalytic Quarterly*, *45*: 133–136.
Levenson, E. A. (1992). Mistakes, errors, and oversights. *Contemporary Psychoanalysis*, *28*: 555–571.
Levy, L. (1998). Trois lettres sur la maladie de Sándor Ferenczi. *Le Coq-Héron*, *149*: 23–27.
Liébeault, A-A. (1883). *Étude sur Zoomagnetisme*. Paris and Nancy: G. Masson.
Lieberman, E. J. (1985). *Acts of Will: The Life and Work of Otto Rank*. Amherst, MA: University of Massachusetts Press, 1993.
Lieberman, E. J., & Kramer, R. (eds.) (2012). *The Letters of Sigmund Freud and Otto Rank: Inside Psychoanalysis*. Baltimore: Johns Hopkins University Press.
Lippman, R. L. (2009). Freud's Botanical Monograph screen memory revisited. *The Psychoanalytic Review*, *96*: 579–595.
Lipton, S. D. (1977). The advantages of Freud's technique as shown in his analysis of the Rat Man. *International Journal of Psycho-Analysis*, *58*: 255–273.
Little, M. (1957). Review of the selected papers of Sandor Ferenczi, M.D. Vol. III: Final contributions to the problems and methods of psycho-analysis. *International Journal of Psycho-Analysis*, *38*: 121–123.
Lombroso, C. (1876) *L'uomo delinquente*. Torino: Fratelli Bocca Editori, 5° edizione, 1896. (*Criminal Man*, Durham NC: Duke Univerity Press, 2006)
Lothane, Z. (2007a). The Sigmund Freud/Minna Bernays romance: Fact or fiction? *American Imago*, *64*: 129–133.
Lothane, Z. (2007b). Sigmund Freud and Minna Bernays: Primal curiosity, primal scenes, primal fantasies – and prevarication. *Psychonalytic Psychology*, *24*: 487–495.
Löwenfeld, L. (1899). Sexualleben und Nervenleiden: Die nervösen Störungen sexuellen Ursprungs. Wiesbaden: J. F. Bergmann.
Lucian of Samosata. *De Dea Syria*, www.sacred-texts.com/cla/luc/tsg/tsg07.htm
Ludwig, E. (1957). *Doctor Freud: An Analysis and a Writing*. New York: Hellman, Williams & Company.
Lugrin, Y. (2012). *Impardonnable Ferenczi*. Paris: Campagne Première.
Luke, D. (1994). Introduction. In J. W. Goethe (ed.), *Faust Part II*. Oxford: Oxford University Press.
Lupton, M. J., & Lupton, J. R. (1990). Annotated bibliography of Claude Dagmar Daly (1884–1950). *American Imago*, *47*: 81–89.
Luzes, P. (1990). Fact and fantasy in brother-sister incest. *International Review of Psycho-Analysis*, *17*: 97–113.
Lynn, D. J. (1997). Sigmund Freud's psychoanalysis of Albert Hirst. *Bulletin of the History of Medicine*, *71*: 69–93.
McGrath, W. J. M. (1986). *Freud's Discovery of Psychoanalysis: The Politics of Hysteria*. Ithaca, NY: Cornell University Press.
McGuire, W. (ed.) (1974). *The Freud/Jung Letters: The Correspondence between Sigmund Freud and C. G. Jung*. London: Routledge and The Hogarth Press.
Maciejewski, F. (2002). *Psychoanalytisches Archiv und jüdisches Gedächtnis. Freud, Beschneidung und Monotheismus*. Vienna: Passagen Verlag.
Maciejewski, F. (2006). Freud, his wife, and his "wife." *American Imago*, *63*: 497–506.

Maciejewski, F. (2008). Minna Bernays as "Mrs. Freud": What sort of relationship did Sigmund Freud have with his sister-in-law? *American Imago, 65*: 5–21.

Mackay, C. S. (ed.) (2006). *The Hammer of Witches: A Complete Translation of the Malleus Maleficarum*. Cambridge, UK: Cambridge University Press.

Mahony, P. (1982). *Freud as a Writer*. New York: International Universities Press.

Mahony, P. (1992). Freud as family therapist. In T. Gelfand & J. Kerr (eds.), *Freud and the History of Psychoanalysis*. Hillsdale, NJ: Analytic Press, pp. 307–318.

Mahony, P. (2002). Freud's writing: His (w)rite of passage and its reverberations. *Journal of the American Psychoanalytic Association, 50*: 885–907.

Mahony, P., Bonomi, C., & Stensson, J. (eds.) (1997). *Behind the Scenes: Freud in Correspondence*. Oslo: Scandinavian University Press.

Makari, G. (2008). *Revolution in Mind: The Creation of Psychoanalysis*. New York, NY: Harper Collins.

Manheimer, M. (1899). *Les Troubles Mentaux de l'Enfance. Précis de psychiatrie infantile avec les applications pédagogiques et médico-légales* [Childhood Mental Disorders: Manual of Infantile Psychiatry with Pedagogical and Medico-Legal Applications]. Paris: Societé d'Editions Scientifiques.

Marcel, M. (2005). *Freud's Traumatic Memory: Reclaiming Seduction Theory and Revisiting Oedipus*. Pittsburgh: Duquesne University Press.

Masson, J. M. (1983). Freud, biologist of the mind: Beyond the psychoanalytic legend: By Frank J. Sulloway: New York: Basic books, 1979. *Journal of the American Psychoanalytic Association, 31*: 739–747.

Masson, J. M. (1984). *The Assault on Truth: Freud's Suppression of the Seduction Theory*. New York: Farrar, Straus & Giroux.

Masson. J. M. (ed.) (1985). *The Complete Letters of Sigmund Freud to Wilhelm Fliess 1887–1904*. Cambridge, MA: Harvard University Press.

Masson, J. M. (1986). *A Dark Science: Women, Sexuality and Psychiatry in the Nineteenth Century*. New York: Farrar, Straus & Giroux.

Masson, J. M. and Masson, T. C. (1978). Buried Memories on the Acropolis: Freud's Response to Mysticism and Anti-Semitism. *International Journal of Psycho-Analysis, 59*: 19[1-9]–[1-9]08.

Maudsley, H. (1867). *The Physiology and Pathology of the Mind*. London: Macmillan.Mautner, B. (1991). Freud's Irma dream: a psychoanalytic interpretation. *International Journal of Psychoanalysis, 72*: 275–286.

May, U. (2007). Freud's patient calendars: 17 analysts in analysis with Freud (1910–1920). *Psychoanalysis and History, 9*: 153–200.

Mazlish, B. (1968). Freud and Nietzsche. *Psychoanalytic Review, 55*: 360–375.

Menninger, K. A. (1935). A psychoanalytic study of the significance of self-mutilations. *Psychoanalytic Quarterly, 4*: 408–466.

Mészáros, J. (2008). *Ferenczi and beyond: Exile of the Budapest School and Solidarity in the Psychoanalytic Movement during the Nazi Years*. London: Karnak Books, 2014.

Mészáros, J. (2015). Ferenczi in our contemporary world. In A. Harris & S. Kuchuck (eds.), *The Legacy of Sándor Ferenczi*. London and New York: Routledge.

Moll, A. (1898). *Untersuchungen über die Libido sexualis*. Berlin: H. Kornfeld.

Molnar, M. (ed.) (1992). *The Diary of Sigmund Freud 1929–1939: A Record of the Final Decade*. London: Hogarth.

Molnar, M. (1994). Reading the look. In S. L. Gilman, J. Birmele, J. Geller, & V. D. Greenberg (eds.), *Reading Freud's Reading*. New York and London: New York University Press, 1994, pp. 77–90.

Moore, A. (2009). Relocating Marie Bonaparte's clitoris. *Australian Feminist Studies*, *24*: 149–165.
Moreau de Tours, P. (1882). *De l'homicide commis par les enfants*. Paris: Asselin.
Moreau de Tours, P. (1888). *La folie chez les enfants*. Paris: J.-B. Baillière.
Morehouse, L. R. (2012). Dismemberment and devotion: Anatomical votive dedication in Italian popular religion. *Classics Honors Projects, Paper 17*, http://digitalcommons.macalester.edu/classics_honors/17
Morel, B. A. (1857). *Traité des dégénérescences physiques, intellectuelles et morales de l'espèce humaine*. Paris: J.-B. Baillière.
Morel, B. A. (1860). *Traité des maladies mentales*. Paris: Victor Masson.
Morris, R. T. (1892). Is evolution trying to do away with the clitoris? *Transactions of the American Association of Obstetricians and Gynecologists*, *5*: 288–302.
Motet, A. (1887). Les faux témoignages des enfants devant la justice. *Annales d'hygiène publique et de la médicine légale*, *17*: 481–496, published in English as "False testimony given by children before courts of justice," in J. Masson (1986), pp. 90–105.
Mucci, C. (2013). *Beyond Individual and Collective Trauma: Intergenerational Transmission, Psychoanalytic Treatment, and the Dynamics of Forgiveness*. London: Karnac Books.
Mucci, C. (2015). Psychoanalysis and/as the future of testimony. Paper read at the International Psychoanalytic Association Congress held in Boston, July 2015.
Mucci, C. (2016). Psicoanalisi come nuovo umanesimo: testimonianza, connectedess, memoria e perdono per una "persistenza dell'umano." (Psychoanalysis for a new humanism: Testimony, connectedness, memory and forgiveness as the "persistence of the human"). Paper read at the annual meeting of the Associazione culturale Sandor Ferenczi, December 2016.
Naso, O. P. (1893). *The Metamorphoses of Ovid*, translated from Latin by H. T. Riley. London: George Bell & Sons.
Naumburg, M. (No Date). Margaret Naumburg papers. Ms. Coll. 294 University of Pennsylvania: Kislak Center for Special Collections, Rare Books and Manuscripts.
Neumann, H. (1859). *Lehrbuch der Psychiatrie*. Erlangen: Verlag von Ferdinand Enke.
Niederland, W. G. (1951). Three notes on the Schreber case. *Psychoanalytic Quarterly*, *20*: 579–591.
Niederland, W. G. (1959a). Schreber: Father and son. *Psychoanalytic Quarterly*, *28*: 151–169.
Niederland, W. G. (1959b). The "miracled-up" world of Schreber's childhood. *Psychoanalytic Study of the Child*, *14*: 383–413.
Niederland, W. G. (1968). Schreber and Flechsig—A Further Contribution to the "Kernel of Truth" in Schreber's Delusional System. *Journal of the American Psychoanalytic Association*, *16*: 740-748
Niederland, W. G. (1969). Freud's "déjà vu" on the acropolis. *American Imago*, *26*: 373–378.
Niederland, W. G. (1984). *The Schreber Case: Psychoanalytic Profile of a Paranoid Personality*. Hillsdale, NJ: The Analytic Press.
Nietzsche, F. (1895). *The Anti – Christ*. London: Penguin Books, 1990.
Nissim Momigliano, L. (1987). A spell in Vienna – but was Freud a Freudian? An investigation into Freud's technique between 1920 and 1938, based on the published testimony of former analysands. *International Review of Psychoanalysis*, *14*: 373–389.
Nunberg, H. (1947). Circumcision and problems of bisexuality. *International Journal of Psycho-Analysis*, *28*: 145–179.
Owens, M. E. (2004). Forgetting Signorelli: Monstrous visions of the resurrection of the dead. *American Imago*, *61*: 7–33.

Paskauskas, R. A. (ed.) (1993). *The Complete Correspondence of Sigmund Freud and Ernest Jones 1908–1939*. Cambridge, MA: The Belknap Press of Harvard University Press.
Patai, R. (1978). *The Hebrew Goddess: Third Enlarged Edition*. Detroit, MI: Wayne State University, 1990.
Percy, W. A. (1996). *Pederasty and Pedagogy in Archaic Greece*. Urbana: University of Illinois Press.
Peterfreund, E. (1978). Some critical comments on psychoanalytic conceptualizations of infancy. *International Journal of Psycho-Analysis*, *59*: 427–441.
Pines, M. (1989). On history and psychoanalysis. *Psychoanalytic Psychology*, *6*: 121–135.
Ploss, H., & Bartel, M. (1885). *Das Weib in der Natur- und Völkerkunde*, 5° edition, Leipzig: Th. Grieben's Verlag, 1897. First English translation on the 11th (1927) edition, *Woman: An Historical Gynaecological and Anthropological Compendium*, Volume 1. London: William Heinemann, 1935.
Prager, D. (1960). An Unusual Fantasy of the Manner in which Babies Become Boys or Girls. *Psychoanalytic Quarterly*, *29*: 4[1-9]–[1-9]5.
Preyer, W. (1882). *Die Seele des Kindes: Beobachtungen über die geistige Entwicklung des Menschen in den ersten Lebensjahren*. Leipzig: Grieben [The Mind of the Child, the Senses, and the Will. New York: Appleton, 1888].
Prichard, J. C. (1835). *A Treatise on Insanity and Other Disorders Affecting the Mind*. London: Sherwood, Gilbert, and Piper.
Purcell, W. J. (1999). The agon with fate. *Psychoanalysis and Contemporary Thought*, *22*: 343–363.
Rachman, A. W. (1989). Confusion of tongues: The Ferenczian metaphor for childhood seduction and emotional trauma. *Journal of the American Academy of Psychoanalysis*, *17*: 181–205.
Rachman, A. W. (1997). *Sándor Ferenczi: The Psychotherapist of Tenderness and Passion*. Northvale, NJ: Jason Aronson.
Rachman, A. W. (2003). *Psychotherapy of Difficult Cases: Flexibility and Responsiveness in Contemporary Clinical Practice*. Madison, CT: Psychosocial Press.
Rachman, A. W. (2015). Elizabeth Severn: Sándor Ferenczi's analysand and collaborator in the study and treatment of trauma. In A. Harris & S. Kuchuck (eds.), *The Legacy of Sándor Ferenczi: From Ghosts to Ancestors*. (Relational Perspectives Book Series). London and New York: Routledge, pp. 111–126.
Rachman, A. W., & Kett, S. A. (2015). *Analysis of the Incest Trauma: Retrieval, Recovery, Renewal*. London: Karnak.
Racker, H. (1968). *Transference and Countertransference*. New York: International Universities Press.
Rado, S. (1925). The economic principle in psychoanalytic technique. *Int. J. Psycho-Anal.*, 6:3[1-9]–[1-9]4.
Rand, N., & Torok, M. (1995). *Questions à Freud. Du devenir de la psychanalyse*. Paris: Les Belles Lettres.
Rank, O. (1912). *Das Inzest-Motiv in Dichtung und Sage*. Grundzüge einer Psychologie des dichterischen Schaffens. Leipzig und Wien: Franz Deuticke, 1912.
Rank, O. (1913). Die Nacktheit in Sage und Dichtung. *Imago*, *2*: 267–301, 409–446.
Rank, O. (1924a). *The Trauma of Birth*. New York: Harper & Row, 1973.
Rank, O. (1924b). *Der Mythus von der Geburt des Helden*. Vienna: Internationaler Psychoanalytischer, Verlag. [*Myth of the Birth of the Hero*, Nervous and Mental Disease Monograph Series, No. 18, Washington, DC].
Rank, O. (1926a). The genesis of the guilt-feeling. In *Otto Rank. A Psychology of Difference: The American Lectures: Selected, Edited, and Introduced by Robert Kramer*. Princeton, NJ: Princeton University Press, pp. 131–139.

Rank, O. (1926b). The genesis of the object relation. In: *Otto Rank. A Psychology of Difference. The American Lectures. Selected, edited, and introduced by Robert Kramer.* Princeton (NJ): Princeton University Press, pp. 140-150.

Rank, O. (1926c). Foundation of a genetic psychology. In O. Rank, *A Psychology of Difference. The American Lectures. Selected, edited, and introduced by Robert Kramer.* Princeton (NJ): Princeton University Press, pp. 9[1-9]–[1-9]06.

Rank, O. (1932). *Art and Artist: Creative Urge and Personality Development.* New York and London: W. W. Norton & Company. Reprinted as a Norton Paperback, 1989.

Reik, T. (1931). *Ritual: Psychoanalytic Studies.* New York: Norton.

Rice, E. (1990). *Freud and Moses: The Long Journey Home.* New York: SUNY Press.

Rickman, J. (1950). Claude Dangar Daly, Lt.-Col. (Ret.), 1884–1950. *International Journal of Psycho-Analysis*, *31*: 290–291.

Rieger, C. (1896). Über die Behandlung "Nervenkranker." *Schmidt's Jahrbücher der Medicin*, *251*: 19[1-9]–[1-9]98, 27[1-9]–[1-9]76.

Rieger, C. (1900). *Die Castration in rechtlicher, socialer und vitaler Hinsicht.* [Castration in Legal, Social and Vital Perspectives.] Jena: Gustav Fischer.

Roazen, P. (1975). *Freud and His Followers.* New York: Da Capo Press, 1992.

Roazen, P. (1995). *How Freud Worked: First-Hand Accounts of Patients.* Northvale, NJ: Jason Aronson.

Roazen, P. (2001). The exclusion of Erich Fromm from the IPA. *Contemporary Psychoanalysis*, *37*: 5–42.

Roazen, P. (2002). The problem of seduction. In *The Trauma of Freud: Controversies in Psychoanalysis.* New Brunswick, USA and London: Transaction Publishers, pp. 1–14.

Robertson Smith, W. (1889–1890). *Lectures on the Religion of the Semites.* London: Adam and Charles Black, 1894.

Róheim, G. (1932). Psycho-analysis of primitive cultural types. *International Journal of Psycho-Analysis*, *13*: 1–221.

Róheim, G. (1940). The dragon and the hero. *American Imago*, *1B*: 40–69.

Róheim, G. (1943). The origin and function of culture. In *Nervous and Mental Disease Monographs No. 69.* New York: Johnson Reprint Corp., 1968.

Romanes, G. J. (1888). *Mental Evolution in Man: Origin of Human Faculty*, Kegan Paul, Trench & Co., London.

Roscher, W. R. (ed.) (1884–1890). *Griechischen und Römischen Mytologie. Erster Band.* Leipzig: Druck und Verlag von B.G. Teubner.

Rose, A. C. (2011). Between psychology and pedagogy: "Moral orthopedics" and case studies of children in *Fin-De-Siècle* French medicine. *History of Psychology*, *14*: 26–52.

Rosenberg, S. (1978). *Why Freud Fainted.* Indianapolis: Bobbs-Merrill.

Rosenzweig, S. (1992). *Freud, Jung and Hall the King-Maker: The Historic Expedition to America* (1909), with G. Stanley Hall as Host and William James the Historic as Guest. Seattle: Hogrefe and Huber.

Roudinesco, E. (2010). *Mais pourquoi tant de haine?* Paris: Éditions du Seuil.

Roudinesco, E. (2014). *Sigmund Freud en son temps et dans le nôtre.* Paris: Éditions du Seuil. [*Sigmund Freud in His Time and Ours.* Boston: Harvard Universitz Press, 2016].

Roudinesco, E. (2015). Pour l'amour de Minna. In *Sigmund Freud, Minna Bernays, Correspondence 1882–1938*, preface by Élisabeth Roudinesco. Paris: Éditions du Seuil, pp. 7–20.

Rudnytsky, P. L. (1987). *Freud and Oedipus.* New York: Columbia University Press.

Rudnytsky, P. L. (1998). The analyst's murder of the patient. *American Imago*, *55*: 349–359.

Rudnytsky, P. L. (2002). *Reading Psychoanalysis: Freud, Rank, Ferenczi, Groddeck.* Ithaca, NY: Cornell University Press.

Rudnytsky, P. L. (2011). *Rescuing Psychoanalysis from Freud and Other Essays in Re-Vision*. London: Karnac.

Rudnytsky, P. L. (2012). The etiology of psychoanalysis: Freud's abuser, sibling incest, and the affair with Minna Bernays. Paper presented at the Discussion Group of the Committee on Research and Special Training (CORST) at the National Meeting of the American Psychoanalytic Association in New York City, January 2012 – Unpublished.

Rudnytsky, P. L. (2015). The other side of the story: Severn on Ferenczi and mutual analysis. In A. Harris & S. Kuchuck (eds.), *The Legacy of Sándor Ferenczi: From Ghosts to Ancestors*. (Relational Perspectives Book Series). London: Routledge, pp. 134–149.

Rush, B. (1812). *Medical Inquiries and Observations upon the Diseases of the Mind*. Philadelphia: Kimber & Richardson.

Sabourin, P. (2011). *Sándor Ferenczi, un pionner de la clinique*. Paris: Campagne Première.

Sajner, J. (1968). Sigmund Freuds Beziehungen zu seinem Geburtsort Freiberg (Príbor) und zu Mähren [Sigmund Freud's relation to his birthplace in Freiberg/Příbor, and to Moravia]. *Clio Medica, Acta Academiae Internationalis*, *3*: 167–180.

Sajner, J. (1981). Drei dokumentarische Beiträge zur Sigmund-Freud-Biographik aus Bohmen und Mahren. *Jahrbuch Psychoanalysis*, *13*: 143–152.

Schimek, J. G. (1974). The parapraxis specimen of psychoanalysis. *Psychoanalysis and Contemporary Science*, *3*: 210–230.

Schimek, J. G. (1975). The interpretations of the past: Childhood trauma, psychical reality, and historical truth. *Journal of the American Psychoanalytic Association*, *23*: 845–865.

Schimek, J. G. (1987). Fact and fantasy in the seduction theory: A historical review. *Journal of the American Psychoanalytic Association*, *35*: 937–964.

Schopenhauer, A. (1816). *The World as Will and Representation*. http://en.wikisource.org/wiki/The_World_as_Will_and_Representation

Schorske, C. E. (1974). Politics and patricide in Freud's interpretation of dreams. *Annual of Psychoanalysis*, *2*: 40–60.

Schröter, M., & Hermanns, L. M. (1992). Felix Gattel (1870–1904): Freud's first pupil. *International Review of Psycho-Analysis*, *19*: 91–104; 19[1-9]–[1-9]07

Schröter, M., & Tögel, C. (2007). The Leipzig episode in Freud's life (1859): A new narrative on the basis of recently discovered documents. *Psychoanalytic Quarterly*, *76*: 193–215.

Schur, M. (1963). Marie Bonaparte – 1882–1962. *Psychoanalytic Quarterly*, *32*: 98–100.

Schur, M. (1966). Some additional "day residues" of the specimen dream of psychoanalysis. Reprinted in M. Kanzer & J. Glenn (eds.), *Freud and His Self-Analysis*. New York: Jason Aronson, 1979, pp. 87–116.

Schur, M. (1969). The background of Freud's "disturbance" on the Acropolis. Reprinted in M. Kanzer & J. Glenn (eds.), *Freud and His Self-Analysis*. New York: Jason Aronson, 1979, pp. 117–134.

Schur, M. (1972). *Freud: Living and Dying*. New York: International Universities Press.

Severn, E. (1913). Psycho-Therapy: Its Doctrine and Practice. London: Rider.

Severn, E. (1917). *The Psychology of Behaviour: A Practical Study of Human Personality and Conduct with Special Reference to Method of Development*. New York: Dodd, Mead.

Severn, E. (1933). *The Discovery of the Self: A Study in Psychological Cure*. Philadelphia: McKay.

Shengold, L. (1972). A parapraxis of Freud's in relation to Karl Abraham. *American Imago*, *29*: 123–159.

Shengold, L. (1993). Fliess, Karl Abraham, and Freud. In *"The Boy Will Come to Nothing!": Freud's Ego Ideal and Freud as Ego Ideal*. New Haven, CT: Yale University Press.

Sklar, J. (2011). *Landscapes of the Dark*. London: Karnac Books.

Slipp, S. (1993). *The Freudian Mystique: Freud, Women, and Feminism*. New York: New York University Press.
Smith, N. A. (1998). "Orpha reviving": Towards an honorable recognition of Elisabeth Severn. *International Forum of Psychoanalysis*, 7: 241–246.
Solomon, M. (1973). Freud's father on the Acropolis. *American Imago*, 30: 142–156.
Spitz, R. A. (1952). Authority and masturbation: Some remarks on a bibliographic investigation. *Psychoanalytic Quarterly*, 21: 490–527.
Steiner, R. (1994). In Vienna Veritas . . . . *International Journal of Psycho-Analysis*, 75: 511–573.
Stern, M. M. (1968). Fear of death and neurosis. *Journal of the American Psychoanalytic Association*, 16: 3–31.
Stolorow, R. D., & Atwood, G. E. (1978). A defensive-restitutive function of Freud's theory of psychosexual development. *Psychoanalytic Review*, 65: 217–238.
Stouten, H. (2012). "Professor geht es gut!" Der Briefwechsel zwischen Max Schur und Marie Bonaparte. *Luzifer-Amor*, 49: 114–131.
Strachey, J. (1931). The function of the precipitating factor in the aetiology of the neuroses: A historical note. *International Journal of Psycho-Analysis*, 12: 326–330.
Strachey, J. (1934). The nature of the therapeutic action of psycho-analysis. . *Int. J. Psycho-Anal.*, 15:12[1-9]–[1-9]59.
Sullivan, H. (1940). *Conceptions of Modern Psychiatry*. New York: W. W. Norton & Company.
Sulloway, F. J. (1979). *Freud, Biologist of the Mind: Beyond the Psychoanalytic Legend*. New York: Basic Books.
Swales, P. (1982). Freud, Minna Bernays and the conquest of Rome. *New American Review*, Spring/Summer, pp. 1–22.
Swales, P. (1987). Freud, Martha Bernays and the language of flowers: Masturbation, cocaine and the inflation of fantasy. Privately published paper.
Swales, P. (1992). What Jung didn't say. *Harvest: Journal for Jungian Studies*, 38: 30–43.
Swales, P. (2003). Freud, death and sexual pleasure: On the psychical mechanism of Dr. Sigm: Freud. *Arc de Cercle*, 1: 4–74.
Swan, J. (1974). Mater and nannie: Freud's two mothers and the discovery of the Oedipus complex. *American Imago*, 31: 1–64.
Szekacs-Weisz, J., & Keve, T. (eds.) (2012a). *Ferenczi and His World: Rekindling the Spirit of the Budapest School*. London: Karnac.
Szekacs-Weisz, J., & Keve, T. (eds.) (2012b). *Ferenczi for Our Time*. London: Karnac.
Thompson, C. (1943). "The therapeutic technique of Sándor Ferenczi": A comment. *International Journal of Psycho-Analysis*, 24: 64–66.
Thompson, C. (1988). Sándor Ferenczi, 1873–1933. *Contemporary Psychoanalysis*, 24: 182–195.
Thompson, N. (2003). Marie Bonaparte's theory of female sexuality: Fantasy and biology. *American Imago*, 60: 343–378.
Tractenberg, M. (1989). Circumcision, crucifixion and anti-semitism: The antithetical character of ideologies and their symbols which contain crossed lines. *International Review of Psycho-Analysis*, 16: 459–471.
Trumbull, H. C. (1885). *Blood Covenant: A Primitive Rite and Its Bearing on the Scripture* (2nd ed.). Philadelphia: John D. Wattles, 1893.
Tuckey, Ch. L. (1890). *Psycho-Therapeutics; or Treatment by Hypnotism and Suggestion* (2nd ed., revised and enlarged). London: Baillière, Tindall, and Cox.
Velikovsky, I. (1941). The dreams Freud dreamed. *Psychoanalytic Review*, 28: 487–511.
Vermorel, H., & Vermorel, M. (1993). *Sigmund Freud et Romain Rolland: Correspondance 1923–1936*. Paris: Presses Universitaires de France.

Vida, J. E. (1991). Sandor Ferenczi on female sexuality. *Journal of the American Academy of Psychoanalysis*, *19*: 271–281.

Vida, J. E. (1999). Considering androgyny: Another dimension of Ferenczi's disagreement with Freud. *International Forum of Psychoanalysis*, *8*: 257–262.

Vischer, R. (1879). *Luca Signorelli und die italienische Renaissance*. Leizig: Vein und Company.

Vitz, P. (1988). *Sigmund Freud's Christian Unconscious*. New York: Guilford Press.

Voisin, A. (1887). Observations d'onanisme guéries par la suggestion hypnotique. *Revue de l'Hypnotisme Expérimentale et Thérapeutique*, *2*: 151–153.

Waelder, R. (1951). The structure of paranoid ideas: A critical survey of various theories. *International Journal of Psycho-Analysis*, *32*: 167–177.

Weiss, J., & Sampson, H. (1986). *The Psychoanalytic Process*. New York: Guilford.

West, Ch. (1854). *Lectures on the Diseases of Infancy and Childhood* (3rd ed., enlarged). London: Longman, Brown, Green, and Longmans.

West, Ch. (1860). On the mental peculiarities and mental disorders of childhood. *Medical Times & Gazette*, February 11, 1860, pp. 133–137.

Wimpfheimer, M. J., & Schafer, R. (1977). Psychoanalytic methodology in Helene Deutsch's the psychology of women. *Psychoanalytic Quarterly*, *46*: 287–318.

Winnicott, D. W. (1949). Hate in the counter-transference. *International Journal of Psycho-Analysis*, *30*: 69–74.

Winnicott, D. W. (1964). Memories, dreams, reflections. *International Journal of Psycho-Analysis*, *45*: 450–455.

Wolstein, B. (1997). The first direct analysis of transference and countertransference. *Psychoanalytic Inquiry*, *17*: 505–521.

Young-Bruehl, E. (1988). *Anna Freud: A Biography*. New York: Summit Books.

Zepf, S., & Zepf, F. D. (2011). "You are requested to close an eye": Freud's seduction theory and theory of the Oedipus complex revisited. *Psychoanalytic Review*, *98*: 287–323.

Zilboorg, G. (1962). *Psychoanalysis and Religion*. New York: Farrar, Straus & Cudahy.

Index

Abraham, K. 64, 138, 149, 155, 165; female castration 180
Abraham, N. 173–4
Adonis: Freud's identification with 128, 149; Great Pan 111; legend 103–5; personification of the Penis 16, 103, 109–10, 116, 121, 146; *see also* Aphrodite; Astarte; Great Lord Penis
Androgyne: Plato's myth 101, 186
Anzieu, D.: Freud's identification with a bleeding woman 137; Freud's scar fantasy 95; Herr Zucker 90–1; Minna and incest taboo 117, 122, 128–9
Aphrodite 101–10, 121, 149–50, 164, 290; *see* Astarte
Arlow, J.A.: criticism of the psychoanalytic training system 242; on Ferenczi 236–7, 242
Arpad (little Chanticleer or little Rooster-Man) 170–1, 175, 177
Astarte: Ayesha 128; primeval sexual cult 102; repression of the cult 103, 109–10; ritual self-castration of the priests 102, 134
autotomy (self-cut): animal 210; autoplastic adaptation 198; formal structure of both sacrifice and trauma 199

Baginsky, A.: children's testimony before the court 42, 240; Freud's studies in Berlin 20, 31–3, 42, 107
Balint, M.: flying and floating 136, 173, 176; Freud's preference for obsessionality 109; Jones's allegations 236, 237; psychoanalytic training system 242; rehabilitation of Ferenczi 232, 239; Thalassa 172
Behrend, F. J. 4, 19
Beira, M. 18–19, 137

Berman, E.: Gizella and Elma 152; rescue fantasies 44
biotrauma 14, 16, 62, 84, 181
bisexuality: androgeny 150; circumcision 101, 134, 197; repression (Fliess) 51, 61, 220, 225
Bollas, C. 2
Bonaparte, Marie: analysis with Freud 189; coitus as battle between two males 187; criticism of excision as cure of masturbation 11, 190; Freud on excision 177, 189–91; Freud's letters to Fliess 191–2, 222; genital mutilations in Europe and among primitive tribes 190; psychoanalytic ethnological expedition 186–7; Schur 188, 194; surgical interventions 188; vilified by feminists 191
Borgogno, F. 19
Brennan, B. W. 206, 210
brith milah 10, 54, 126, 160–1, 179
Brown, I. B. 179
Brown, N. O. 172–3
Bryk, F. 189–90, 194

Cassirer Bernfeld, S. 93, 97–8
castration: carried for eugenic reasons 181; erasure from psychoanalytic discourse 12, 84; performed on women and girls 4, 11–14, 226; in primeval times 57, 177
castration complex 7, 96, 125, 169, 199; barrier against incest 59, 121; biological castration of the female 191; circumcision trauma in disguise 96; confusion between the loss of an illusory phallus and real injury of the genitals 179–81, 193; father's prohibition against incest 59; female castration complex 14, 180; Freud's disparity between

268 *Index*

males and females 179, 183; Freud's theory that girl accept castration or don't fear castration 15, 18, 183, 186–7; overestimation 198; paradigmatic punishment 122; severest trauma 65, 213; ubiquity 181
circumcision: cure of masturbation in children 4, 14; equivalent of castration 193; female circumcision controversy 186; mimetic reproduction of the cut of the umbilical cord 182, 193; psycho-biological origins 186; puberty rites 178, 185; relic 177
clitoris: ablation of c. as model for Freud's castration theory 227–8; amputation 17–18, 179–80, 186–7, 190; archaic relic of the woman's penis 62; challenge to gender separation 62; Ferenczi's phylogenetic theory 184; Freud's extinction theory 62; length and size 61–2, 186; primitive rites 178, 189–90; short bridge 131; vestige of a phylogenetic past 61, 189; *see also* Bonaparte; Bryk; Daly; Deutsch; Fleischmann; Ploss and Bartel; Róheim.
creation myths 101–2, 112, 174

Daly, C. D. 186
death instinct 60, 83–4, 131, 163, 165, 173–4, 198
Deutsch, H.: teleological theory of the clitoris 62
Devereux, G.: cut of ombelical cord as model for circumcision 193; Oedipus legend 81, 85
Dimitrijevic, A. 19
Dorsey, D.: loss of an illusory phallus and fear of injuring the genitals 193
dreams: (Freud) bad treatment 87, 93–4, 110, 134; botanical monograph 105, 110; break-fast-ship 126–7, 143, 160–1; (Ferenczi) climbing a mountain alone 155; Count Thun 117; cut-off penis on a saucer 157–8, 160, 162, 171, 176, 208, 228; dangerous coitus 158–9, 162; dead customs official 144; dead mother 77; (Jones) dead mother still alive 165; dishonesty 227; (Eckstein) gigantic snakes 51, 61, 62, 206, 135, 220, 225; Hella 52, 78, 105–6, 118, 219, 221; Hollthurn, 80, 117, 217; (Jung) house with two skulls in the cellar 142–3; (Severn) I attend my own funeral 204; Irma's injection, 1–2, 7, 10–11, 37–8, 44, 74, 76, 79, 86, 91, 100, 130, 156, 221–2, 225–6; occlusive pessary 168–70, 174, 202; open air closet 117–18; Rome dreams 87–8; Secerno, 220; self-dissection of the pelvis, 2, 17, 87, 98, 113, 127–35, 137, 143–4, 155, 166, 169, 173–4, 198–9, 203, 205, 218, 222, 227; three fates 121–2, 148–9; traveling up the stairs 78–9
Dupont, J.: 15, 19, 242; analysis with Freud 166–7

Eastman, J.: Freud's somatization of his feelings of aggression toward his mother 79–80
Eckstein, Emma.: analysis (first) 38–9, 46–52, 74–6, 88, 91–2; analysis (second) 5–7, 147; bleeder 46; candy 38, 91–2; circumcision scene 1, 10–11, 50–1, 178, 192, 221; corner-stone 8, 76, 86, 92–125; cutter 46; destruction of her clitoris 131, 135, 227–8; erasure of her actual castration 11, 13, 84; fantasy/hallucination to have a penis 10, 76, 227; Ferenczi 9; Freud's countertransference 16, 126; loss of her "Phallus" 84; masochistic phantasies 6; needle scene 75–6, 86; operation on the nose 38, 157, 160; publications on masturbation 3–4, 220; replacement with Schreber 7–8; scenes with the father 52
Eissler, K. R.: Freud's fantasy that women are "dangerous monsters" 224, 230; interviews with Hirst 54, Jung 149, Severn 221
Erikson, E.: Freud's Irma dream 38, 86, 100, 225
Etruscan necropolis (objects and grave): 98, 126–9; 131, 133, 136–7, 143–4, 147, 160–1, 214–15

Falzeder, E. 19, 60, 149, 169, 211
Ferenczi, S.: active technique 195, 197; analysis with Freud; analysis with Severn 202–4; castration hysteria 151, 158, 169, 203; circumcision 171, 174, 185, 197; compulsive desire to help suffering women 150, 203; criticism of Freud's castration theory of femininity 14–15, 179; crown-prince fantasy 155, 164; deconstruction of Freud's phallocentric system 65, 198–9; fantasies on Freud's affair with Minna 153, 159–60; fragmentation of mental life 41, 65, 67, 100, 199, 202, 204, 207, 212, 214;

fulcrum of psychotherapy 197; hatred of women 167, 201, 203; identification with Freud 157, 160, 174, 203; incorporation of Freud's split 2, 17, 159–61, 174; insensitivity 200; intellectualization of psychoanalysis 196–7; intergenerational implications of infantile amnesia 65; introspection 169, 175, 239; male and female 184–5; mutual analysis 201–2; nasal symptoms and surgery 157; ostracizazion from the psychoanalytic movement 231–9; reception of Freud's three sisters motif s-caskets motif 153; repeat-repair 197, 208; vacillations between mother (Gizella) and sister (Elma) 150–3; *see also* Arpad; autotomy; autoplastic adaptation; dreams; gap in the psyche; identification with the aggressor; incarnation; narcissistic split of the self; Palermo incident; penis; repetition-compulsion; shock; Thalassa; trauma; wise baby

Ferenczi and Rank's heresy 233

Ferenczi's family: Baruk and Rosa Ferenczi 19; Elma Palos (Laurvik) 151–5, 158–9, 164–5, 169; Gisela Ferenczi 158–9; Gizella Altschul (Palos, Ferenczi) 151–2, 155, 159, 167, 169; Lajos Ferenczi 151; Magda Palos 151; Saroltà Altschul 159–60, 167; Sophie Ferenczi (Erdös) 235

Fleischmann, L. 3–4, 33

Forest, I. de 232, 234–5, 237–8

formulation of the Oedipus complex 83; Ferenczi's reformulation 66–7, 208

Fortune, C. 202, 206

Frazer, J. G. 101, 104

Freud and incest taboo 15, 17, 105–6, 121, 129, 164–5; affair with Anzieu 144; affair with Ferenczi 153, 160, 162; affair with Jung 144–6; affair with Minna 116–19, 122–3; dissociation of feelings of impotence and rage against his mother 15, 79–80; fainting spells 136, 155–6; fantasy of being buried alive 125, 136–7, 173; funeral fantasy 126–9, 136, 143–4, 149, 155, 173, 205; libidinal fixation to phallic women 225; "mute sister" 159; punishments for his incestuous wishes 95–6; sexual initiation 94; socialization of the human beast and fear of castration as a barrier against incest 58–9, 121; *Stumm-Tod* (mute-death) symbolism 148, 162, 165; urinary incontinence 85, 155

Freud, S.: accounts of the collapse of his seduction theory 55–6; Acropolis incident 143–4, 214–21; archeology 97, 125–6, 146; dynamic model of intrapsychic conflict 213; identification with Emma Eckstein 92, 94–5; pediatric studies 13–14, 31–3; totem and taboo 109, 162–3, 177, 179, 209; understanding of "instincts" 60; *see also* biotrauma; castration complex; death drive; dreams; Eckstein; Etruscan necropolis; gap in the psyche; ocenic feeling; penis; perversion; primal fantasies; repetition-compulsion; Saurian code; self-castration; shock; Signorelli slip; trimethylamin; trauma

Freud's controversy with Ferenczi: belief/diesbelief 217; *Indifferenz* (neutrality) 200, 211; meaning of hallucinations 216–17; posthumous assimilation of Ferenczi's views 213–14; synthetic nature of the ego 212–13, 223, 228; technical measures to fill the gaps 223, 228–9, 241

Freud's devaluation of women 223–5; blind spot 80, 181–2; disparity between males and females with respect to actual circumcision and castration 179; psycho-biological theory of the excision of the clitoris 190–1; repudiation of femininity 9

Freud's family: Alexander 50–1, 77, 117, 126, 129, 147, 160–1, 215, 221; Amalia 2, 77, 97, 136; Anna (daughter) 41, 97, 154, 163–4, 192–3, 234, 237–9; Anna (sister) 53, 105, 110; Emanuel 110; Ernst 132; Hella 105; Jacob 50–1, 98, 113–14, 132, 161, 215–16; Jean Martin 132; John 90, 110, 224; Julius 97, 215; Martha 119, 136, 145, 149, 160, 224–5, 230; Minna 117–23, 129, 135, 137, 144–5, 149, 153, 159–60, 162; Oliver 132; Pauline 53, 90, 110, 224; Philipp 97

Fried, R. 18, 54, 78–9, 161, 176; Freud's Acropolis incident 214–19, 229; Freud's "Saurian age" 224–5, 230; Freud's sexual initiation 94

Fromm, E.: exclusion from IPA 244; on Ferenczi 166, 195; on Freud 234; on Groddeck 197, 244; reaction to Jones's allegations 234–9

Funk, R. 18, 244

gap in the psyche 2–3, 40, 208; amputation of Emma Eckstein's clitoris 227–8; in collective memory 13, 142; "constructions" in analysis 209, 228;

and the death drive 84; filled by Erikson with the image of "The Circumcision of Christ" 86; filled by Ferenczi with dreams 160–1; filled by Freud with the transcendental Phallus 18; filled with miracles 10; in Freud's Acropolis incident 220, 227; hallucinations 217; Irma dream 2, 10, 75; Schopenhauer's theory of madness 24; Signorelli's slip 121, 124, 227; and the Thalassa myth 222
Good, M. I. 64, 70
Gould, S.J. in Ferenczi 172; recapitulationism in Freud 60
Grigg, K. A. 90–1, 94
Grinstein, A. 91, 121, 131, 133, 136
Groddeck, G. 152, 167, 171, 197, 234, 244
Grotstein, J. S.: "black hole" 100; dreams and intersubjectivity 77; innocence 70; ostracism of Ferenczi 242–3; religious reveries in sexually abused persons 87; transfer of mental pain 92

Haeckel, E.: recapitulation 59, 70, 133, 172
Harris, A. 18–19
Haynal, A. 19, 152, 202, 213, 215, 232
Hirschmüller, A. 13, 20, 118, 123
Hirst, A. 5–6, 8, 19–20, 54

Ideler, K. W. 25–6, 35
identification with the aggressor 41, 109, 157, 171; in the Oedipus legend 82, 85; in the psychoanalytic training 241
incarnation 104, 170, 202, 208–9; reincarnation 111, 128–9, 137, 193, 196
infibulation 187, 191

Janet, P. 213, 228
Jimenez Avello, J. 19
Jones, E.: allegation about Ferenczi's insanity 231–8; Freud's "terrifying thought" of dying before his mother 136; reverberation of Freud's *Stumm-Tod* [mute-death] symbolism 162, 165; switch from the seduction theory to the discovery of the Oedipus complex 105
Jung, C.G. 20, 132, 142–9, 160, 162, 166; Freud's fear to lose his "authority" 145, 155–6, 201; ritual of self-castration 146; *see also* dreams

Krafft-Ebing, R. von, 43, 45, 53

Lacan, J. 37–8, 120, 123, 137, 226
Laub, D.: testimony and psychoanalysis 240

Levenson, E. A. 241
Levy, L. 236–8
Lippman, R.L. 110
Löwenfeld, L. 45, 53
Lugrin, Y. 19

McGrath, W. J. M. 105, 132
Maciejewski, F. 95–6, 98, 118, 137
Mahony, P.: Freud's analysis of his daughter Anna 164–5
Makari, G. 58
Marcel, M. 44, 53, 85
Masson, J. M. 12, 19, 27, 31, 36, 217, 229
Menninger, K. A. 199, 205, 210
Mészáros, J. 19, 20
milah: transcript of amy 1, 2, 221
Mucci, C. 18; psychoanalytic community as a "testimonial community 240–3

narcissistic split of the self 199, 228; wound 171
Niederland, W. G. 7, 10–11, 100, 215
Nietzsche, F. 116, 118, 120, 122–3
Nunberg, H. 87, 101, 134, 193

oceanic feeling 136, 173, 176, 221
original sin 28–9, 34, 70, 177, 209
Orpha 205, 207, 210

paedophilia erotica 43, 53
Palermo incident 7–9, 164, 167
Pan: death of Pan 11; Signorell's Pan 106–9; Signorelli's slip 120–1
Parousia: *Nachträglichkeit* 39
penis: Great Lord Penis 10, 76, 102–3, 109, 121, 134, 227; flying penis (bird) as soul symbol 210; identity of mutilated-penis and dead-child 175; identity of Penis, Fish, and Child 174; identity of Penis, Fish, and Christ 172–3; memorial of a great catastrophe 65, 172, 198; symbol of the total person 16, 82, 199; symbol of the umbilical cord 193
perversion 26, 35, 43, 49, 53, 93; atavism and animal vestige 58, 61, 102; hysteria as repudiated perversion 60; inborn disposition 29, 59, 63–4, 66; result of a post-traumatic split 66, 70, 171; theory of the "perverse father" 48–50, 52, 60, 113–14
Ploss, H. & Bartel, M. 62, 179
primal fantasies 56–7

Rachman, A. 19, 201–2
Rank, O.: "analytic situation" 208; campaign against the castration complex 198; curse on female genitals 181; Freud's blind spot 80, 181–2; Isaac and Oedipus 193; Melusine 230; mother as first "bad" object in the child's life 182; ostracization 233, 236–8, 244; puberty rites 178; remembering and repetition 68, 196; rejection of determinism 182–3; social dimension of analytic therapy 196
repetition-compulsion 43, 49–50, 53–4, 60, 68, 75, 81, 83–4, 90, 131, 133, 148, 164, 172–4, 198
rescue fantasies 38, 44, 101
reunion fantasy: 101, 112, 136, 174, 207; intrauterine life 173; restoration of a pretraumatic state 172; *see also* creation myths
Roazen, P. 55, 69, 211, 223, 234, 244
Róheim, G. 135, 186–7, 189, 191, 194
Roudinesco, E. 118, 123, 149, 189
Rudnytsky, P. L. 19, 80, 85, 123, 160, 202–3, 211, 244

Sabourin, P. 19, 171, 173
Saurian code: Ichthyosaura 223–5, 230, Melusine 224–5, 230; Propionsäure 225
Schopenhauer, A.: madness as an illness of memory 24
Schreber's delusional system 7–11; *Grundsprache* 99–102; soul murder 243
Schur, M.: Acropolis incident 220; Emma Eckstein's circumcision scene and Freud's abandonment of his seduction theory 13, 50, 192; Freud's death anxiety 53, 155; Freud's Irma dream 11; Freud's letters to Fliess 192, 194; Freud's obsessive symptoms 48, 165, 221; personal physician of Bonaparte and Freud 188
secret committee 163, 165, 235, 238
self-castration: in Ferenczi's dreams 157–8, 168–9; in Ferenczi's theory 198; in Freud's dreams 129–34; in Jung's theory 146–7; ritual of the worshippers of the Great Mother Goddess 102, 134, 138, 146
self-mutilation 199, 205
Severn, E. 17, 195, 201–11; analysis by Ferenczi 201, 204, 206; analysis of Ferenczi 202–4; Ferenczi's "evil genius" 201, 217; Orpha 205, 207; psycho-surgical ovariotomy against her will 206, 210; reunion fantasy 207; witness of Ferenczi's last months 235

Sklar, J. 19
shock 3, 16, 18, 37–8, 55, 63, 65–6, 68–9, 100, 158–9, 195, 203–7, 216, 219, 226, 234, 241
Signorelli L.: beautiful Terribilità 114; Last Things 106; Preaching and Deeds of the Antichrist 115–16, 119; Resurrection of the Flesh 112–13, Triumph of Pan 107–9
Signorelli slip 17, 87, 100, 119–24, 214, 227, 230
Spitz, R. A. 11, 20, 28
Strachey J.: superego as fulcrum of psychotherapy 196; theory of precipitating factor 63
Swales, P. 90, 117, 122–4, 137
Szekacs-Weisz, J. & Keve, T. 19

Telecky, D. 5–6
Terribilità 114, 122
Tertullian: Christ as "our Ichthys" 134; *ministri poenarum* 114
Thalassa 12, 16–17, 65, 82, 136, 141, 171–6, 178, 184, 198, 212, 222
Thompson, C.: Ferenczi's fear of Freud 172, 195; reaction to Jones's allegation 244; rehabilitation of Ferenczi 232; witness of Ferenczi's illness 234–5
Tractenberg, M. 87
trauma (psychic): autoplastic and alloplastic reaction 67, 198; birth trauma 181–4; erasure 44, 84; foreign body 73–5, 212–13; fragmentation 65, 214; gap in the psyche 3, 208, 209; insensitivity 66, 200, 211; intergenerational transmission 50, 65, 172, 174; intrapsychic attack 67, 182; misrecognition 65; narcissistic wound 171; precipitating factor 63; psychical deadness 66, 199; psychic reaction that failed to take place 3, 19, 66–7; retranscription 39; spilt between intellect and affect 66, 131; unformulated 1, 9, 84; *see also* autonomy; rescue fantasies
traumatolytic 174
traumatophilia 6, 47–8, 64, 69, 77, 90
trimethylamin 10, 38, 54, 91, 98, 126, 135, 160, 165, 222, 225
Trumbull, H. C.: "blood-transfer is soul-transfer" 92

Vida, J. E. 18, 151
Vischer, R. 107, 109, 111, 114, 116, 122

wise baby 2, 170, 239

Printed in the United States
By Bookmasters